D0071688

ABU

OUR MAN IN TOKYO

OUR MAN IN TOKYO

An American Ambassador

and the Countdown

to Pearl Harbor

STEVE KEMPER

MARINER BOOKS

New York   Boston

FIRST EDITION

Designed by Chloe Foster

Library of Congress Cataloging-in-Publication Data

Names: Kemper, Steve, author.
Title: Our man in Tokyo : an American ambassador and the countdown to Pearl Harbor / Steve Kemper.
Description: New York : Mariner Books, [2022] | Includes bibliographical references and index.
Identifiers: LCCN 2022026045 (print) | LCCN 2022026046 (ebook) | ISBN 9780358064749 (hardback) | ISBN 9780063268173 (other) | ISBN 9780358066705 (ebook)
Subjects: LCSH: Grew, Joseph C. (Joseph Clark), 1880-1965. | United States—Foreign relations—Japan. | Japan—Foreign relations—United States. | United States—Foreign relations—1933-1945. | Japan—Foreign relations—1912-1945.
Classification: LCC E748.G835 K46 2022 (print) | LCC E748.G835 (ebook) | DDC 327.7305209/043—dc23/eng/20220608
LC record available at https://lccn.loc.gov/2022026045
LC ebook record available at https://lccn.loc.gov/2022026046

ISBN 978-0-358-06474-9

22 23 24 25 26 LSC 10 9 8 7 6 5 4 3 2 1

For Jude—still here, still dancing

When will they speak, or stir? They wait for you
To recollect that, while it lived, the past
Was a rushed present, fretful and unsure.

—Richard Wilbur, "This Pleasing Anxious Being"

Contents

List of Characters

Japanese
(with family names first, in the traditional Japanese form)

ABE NOBUYUKI. General and prime minister.

ARAKI SADAO. General, war minister, and education minister.

ARITA HACHIRO. Vice foreign minister and foreign minister.

HARA YOSHIMICHI. President of the Privy Council.

HARADA KUMAO. Baron and private secretary to Prince Saionji Kinmochi, the genro.

HATA SHUNROKU. General and war minister.

HAYASHI SENJURO. General, war minister, and prime minister.

HIRANUMA KIICHIRO. Baron, prime minister, and home affairs minister.

EMPEROR HIROHITO. 1926–1989.

HIROTA KOKI. Foreign minister and prime minister.

ITAGAKI SEISHIRO. General and war minister.

KABAYAMA AISUKE. Count, businessman, privy counselor, Grew's best Japanese friend.

KIDO KOICHI. Marquis, minister of education, home affairs minister, and lord keeper of the privy seal.

KONOYE FUMIMARO. Prince and prime minister.

KURUSU SABURO. Diplomat and special assistant to Ambassador Nomura.

MAKINO NOBUAKI. Count and lord keeper of the privy seal.

MASAKI JINSABURO. General, inspector general of military training, and extremist plotter.

MATSUOKA YOSUKE. Japan's delegate to the League of Nations in 1933 and later foreign minister.

NAGANO OSAMI. Admiral, navy minister, and navy chief of staff.

NOMURA KICHISABURO. Admiral, foreign minister, and ambassador to the United States.

OHASHI CHUICHI. Vice foreign minister under Matsuoka.

OIKAWA KOSHIRO. Navy minister.

OKADA KEISUKE. Prime minister.

OSHIMA HIROSHI. General, Japan's military attaché in Berlin, later ambassador to Germany.

SAIONJI KINMOCHI. Prince, politician, the genro.

SAITO MAKOTO. Viscount, prime minister, and lord keeper of the privy seal.

SHIRATORI TOSHIO. Ambassador to Italy, then special advisor to Matsuoka.

SUETSUGU NOBUMASA. Admiral and home affairs minister.

SUGIYAMA HAJIME. General, war minister, and army chief of staff.

TOGO SHIGENORI. Foreign minister.

TOJO HIDEKI. General, war minister, and prime minister.

TOYODA TEIJIRO. Admiral and foreign minister.

UCHIDA KOSAI. Foreign minister.

UGAKI KAZUSHIGE. General and foreign minister.

YAMAMOTO ISOROKU. Admiral, vice navy minister, then commander of Japan's Combined Fleet; chief strategist of the attack on Pearl Harbor.

YONAI MITSUMASA. Admiral, navy minister, and prime minister.

Others of Note

BALLANTINE, JOSEPH W. Head of Japan Desk, Far Eastern Division, Department of State.

CHIANG KAI-SHEK. Military and political leader of the Republic of China.

CRAIGIE, SIR ROBERT. Great Britain's ambassador to Japan.

DOOMAN, EUGENE H. Counselor, US embassy in Tokyo.

HORNBECK, STANLEY K. Special advisor on the Far East to Secretary of State Hull.

HULL, CORDELL. US secretary of state.

OTT, GENERAL EUGEN. Germany's military attaché in Tokyo, later ambassador to Japan.

RIBBENTROP, JOACHIM VON. German foreign minister.

STIMSON, HENRY. Secretary of state under President Hoover; secretary of war under President Roosevelt.

WELLES, SUMNER. Under secretary of state under Hull.

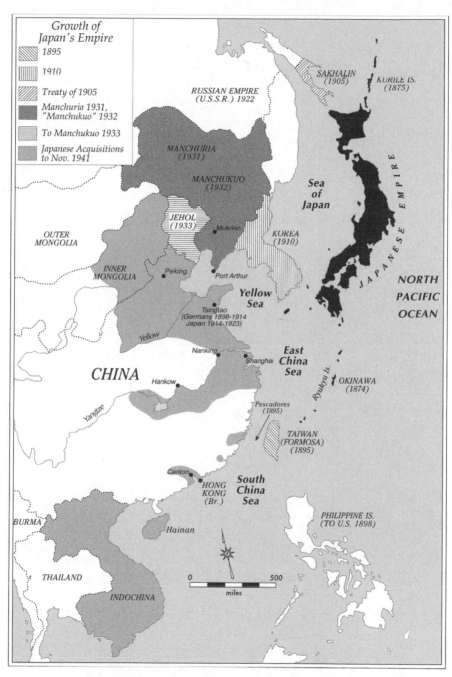

Growth of Japan's Empire

▨	1895
▥	1910
▨	Treaty of 1905
■	Manchuria 1931, "Manchukuo" 1932
☰	To Manchukuo 1933
▤	Japanese Acquisitions to Nov. 1941

RUSSIAN EMPIRE
(U.S.S.R.) 1922

SAKHALIN
(1905)

KURILE IS.
(1875)

MANCHURIA
(1931)

MANCHUKUO
(1932)

Sea
of
Japan

JAPANESE EMPIRE

OUTER
MONGOLIA

JEHOL
(1933)

Mukden

KOREA
(1910)

NORTH
PACIFIC
OCEAN

INNER
MONGOLIA

Peking

Port Arthur

Yellow
Sea

Tsingtao
(Germany 1898-1914
Japan 1914-1923)

Yellow

Nanking

Shanghai

East
China
Sea

OKINAWA
(1874)

CHINA

Hankow

Ryukyu Is.

Yangtze

Pescadores
(1895)

TAIWAN
(FORMOSA)
(1895)

Canton

HONG
KONG
(Br.)

South
China
Sea

PHILIPPINE IS.
(TO U.S. 1898)

BURMA

Hainan

THAILAND

INDOCHINA

0   500
miles

THE GROWTH OF JAPAN'S EMPIRE, 1895-1941

(Map by Dick Gilbreath, University of Kentucky Cartography Lab)

OUR MAN IN TOKYO

PROLOGUE

THE AMBASSADOR WOKE, stirred by some faint shift. The clock said 1:00 A.M. Half-asleep, he glanced out the porthole at the dark waters of Tokyo Bay, with Yokohama silhouetted beyond—so familiar after a week's confinement aboard the anchored *Asama Maru*. A piece of driftwood slipped by, moving a bit too fast, then another moving faster.

He snapped alert: the *Asama Maru* was underway. After six and a half months of internment in the Tokyo embassy and a week aboard ship, the ambassador and his fellow Americans were finally headed home. The passengers included journalists, missionaries, and businesspeople, as well as diplomats, plus the few women and children who hadn't been evacuated in the tense months before the surprise attack on Pearl Harbor. Some of the nondiplomats had been imprisoned, beaten, or waterboarded as suspected spies. One imprisoned reporter had lost his feet to frostbite and gangrene. A handful of passengers had told the ambassador that if negotiations for their release failed, they would kill themselves rather than return to land. But now Japan was disappearing in their wake.

It was June 25, 1942, ten years and nineteen days after Joseph Clark Grew first set foot in Japan as ambassador. Grew was a legend in the State Department. By the time he boarded the *Asama Maru* he had been in the Foreign Service for nearly forty years in fourteen posts, among them Cairo, Mexico City, Saint Petersburg, Vienna, and Berlin, where he closed the US embassy during World War I. After that he served on the peace commission to Versailles. Following a stint in Washington, DC, he became ambassador to Denmark, then Switzerland, before returning to Washington as second-in-command at the State Department. In 1927 he was named ambassador to Turkey, a tricky post. That was where he got word in early 1932 that President Herbert Hoover wanted him as ambassador to the most difficult mission in the world at the time: Japan.

Most ambassadors remain nameless to the American public, but Grew became so well known that whenever he was home on leave people stopped him on the street. His words and photo appeared constantly in newspapers and newsreels. He was handsome and athletic, over six feet tall, with an emphatic moustache, swept-back salt-and-pepper hair, and bristling eyebrows above keen eyes. *Time* put him on its cover in 1934. In 1940 *Life* ran a long feature in which writer John Hersey, later famous for his book *Hiroshima*, called Grew "unquestionably the most important US Ambassador" and Tokyo the "most important Embassy ever given a US career diplomat."

Grew spent ten years trying to preserve peace amidst assassinations, nationalist fanaticism, and plots to overthrow the government as Japan's rabid press stoked war fever and the swaggering Japanese military provoked international crises. After each fresh typhoon, Grew tried to find some way to rebuild diplomatic relations. Now, sailing home, he comforted himself with the knowledge that he had never stopped trying to halt, or at least slow down, the momentum toward war. Mere hours before bombs hit Pearl Harbor he had driven to the home of the Japanese foreign minister at midnight with a last-minute appeal from President Roosevelt to Emperor Hirohito. "I worked for peace up to the end," Grew wrote.

During his six months of internment he reviewed the past decade, especially the last year. He reexamined his diary and the dispatches to and from the State Department. He reread his correspondence with Roosevelt, whom he had known since their days at Groton and Harvard. He had sometimes guessed wrong, misread situations, made mistakes, but he had always been willing to correct misperceptions or flawed assumptions. Had he missed something that might have altered events?

As always he did his thinking through his fingertips, tapping away on his Corona typewriter. What came out was a thick document that recounted Japan's rash belligerence and the replacement of civilian government with unrestrained military ambition. He noted, once again, the synchronized buildup of a massive war machine with a propaganda campaign that demonized Western nations while exhorting all Japanese to sacrifice everything, including their lives, for the glory of their divine emperor. He summarized meetings with Japan's foreign ministers and prime ministers, the constant attempts to find terms agreeable to both nations. He described how Japan's militarist leaders had sabotaged every prospect for peace.

But the Japanese weren't the sole cause of the frustration marbling this document. He also catalogued what he considered missteps by the White House and the State Department, lost opportunities to avert or delay tragedy. The State Department had often ignored his reports and rejected his recommendations, especially his urgent plea in the fall of 1941 for President Roosevelt to accept the invitation of Japan's prime minister, Prince Konoye Fumimaro, to meet somewhere in the Pacific for a last-ditch attempt to prevent war. Grew cited telegrams sent to Roosevelt and Secretary of State Cordell Hull warning that the American government was gravely misreading the mood in Japan.

"Japan may go all-out in a do-or-die effort, actually risking national hara-kiri," he cabled on November 3, five weeks before Pearl Harbor. "Armed conflict with the United States," he added, "might come with dangerous and dramatic suddenness." The next day he wrote in his diary, "That important telegram is on the record for all time."

Even as his misgivings about US policy grew, he faithfully conveyed that policy to the Japanese government. But after Pearl Harbor he felt compelled to leave a frank record of his views. When he finished writing, he followed his usual practice with important dispatches, asking close subordinates in the embassy to critique it. All endorsed his analysis.

He thought of it as his final report from Tokyo and intended to deliver it to President Roosevelt and Secretary Hull as soon as he reached America. Somewhere in the Atlantic he added a thirteen-page cover letter to Roosevelt summarizing his view that the United States government had failed to do everything possible to delay war, partly because it had disregarded his reports about the true situation in Japan. "There are some things," he wrote to Roosevelt, "that can be sensed by the man on the spot which cannot be sensed by those at a distance."

On August 25, two months and eighteen thousand miles after the detainees left Japan, the Statue of Liberty rose into view, lit by the morning sun. Behind it soared the skyline of New York City. Someone on board began singing "America the Beautiful." Fifteen hundred voices joined in, many through tears.

Grew was the first passenger to debark, waving and smiling, dapper in a well-cut gray flannel suit. He talked to a scrum of reporters and spoke into a microphone for a newsreel in the accent of patrician Boston, with the staccato rhythms of the 1930s and 1940s. "To be actually standing on the soil of our beloved country again," he said, "gives us a sense of happiness far too deep and keen to describe in words." Then he and his personal secretary, Robert Fearey (Groton, Harvard), ducked into a black limousine that took them straight to the station, where they boarded a train to Washington, DC.

The next morning they drove from Grew's Washington home, down Rock Creek Parkway to the State Department in the Old Executive Office Building. The ambassador carried his confidential report. A dozen reporters and cameramen awaited him in the hallway. He offered quick replies to their questions before entering the outer office of the secretary of state, where he was promptly shown in to see Secretary Hull. Fearey waited in the anteroom.

"About twenty-five minutes later," recalled Fearey, "the Secretary's raised and clearly irate Tennessee accent penetrated the oaken door." Hull was notorious for his volatile temper and colorful tirades. "I could not make out what he was saying," continued Fearey, "but it was obvious that the meeting was not going well. Soon the door opened and Grew emerged looking somewhat shaken, with Hull nowhere in sight."

Grew suggested an early lunch at the exclusive Metropolitan Club, where he was a member, two blocks away. Once seated there, Grew described how he had presented the gist of the report, then asked for an explanation about what bothered him most—the government's rejection of Prime Minister Konoye's proposal for a peace summit with Roosevelt. Hull hadn't received any of this well.

"If you thought so strongly," Hull said to Grew, "why didn't you board a plane and come to tell us?"

Grew answered that he had sent a blizzard of urgent telegrams on the subject and often wondered if anyone even read them. He didn't respond to the absurd idea of abandoning his post during a crisis for a long trip to Washington and back.

As Hull skimmed the report, his face grew progressively more "hardened and flushed." He abruptly flung the pages back across the desk. "Mr. Ambassador," he thundered, "either you promise to destroy this report and every copy you may possess or we will publish it and leave it to the American people to decide who was right and who was wrong."

Stunned, Grew said that destroying the report would violate his conscience and perhaps the historical record. Publishing it while the country was at war, however, might damage the public's trust in the administration, an offense against Grew's deep sense of patriotism. Hull told him to return with a decision tomorrow at ten o'clock. He didn't show the ambassador to the door.

The next morning Grew and Fearey drove back to the State Department. Grew disappeared behind the big oak door. This time Fearey didn't hear Hull's raised voice. After thirty minutes the two men walked out, smiling and exchanging cordial goodbyes. Grew again suggested lunch at the Metropolitan. Fearey asked what had happened. Nothing much, said Grew, then added that neither he nor Hull had even mentioned the report, a statement difficult to believe after the previous day's fireworks. He offered nothing more. Fearey was too junior to pry.

Years later Grew gave his papers to his beloved alma mater, Harvard. His archive comprises many thousands of pages that include his diary (kept since 1911, including 6,000 pages during his Tokyo years alone), letters, speeches, dispatches, synopses of important conversations, and news clippings. His final report, with all the supporting addenda attached, had grown to 276 pages. It is labeled "Dispatch No. 6018," with the dateline "Tokyo, February 19, 1942."

But the original document is missing. A typed note inserted by Grew into the bowdlerized version explains, "Upon submission of the despatch in its final form, pages 13 to 146 inclusive are eliminated." Grew evidently complied with Hull's command to destroy all copies of the final report, but his typed insert makes clear he did so under protest. He also decided that his cover letter to Roosevelt was technically separate from the report and therefore outside Hull's order. The letter survives in the archive. At the top of it, handwritten in Grew's scribble, is the notation "not sent." At the point in the letter where he mentions the final report, he penciled in the margin, "destroyed at Mr. Hull's request." Grew obeyed his superior's order but refused to clean up the crime scene.

No copies of the original report have ever turned up. Fearey, who had read it, searched for years. Yet Grew documented so much of his experience and thinking in other places—his diary, his letters, thousands of dispatches to the State Department, his memoirs *Ten Years in Japan* and *Turbulent Era*—that the final report survives like a palimpsest. So does its enticing, wrenching question: What if?

Grew knew the question was unanswerable. This book is about how he came to ask it—about the experiences of the man on the spot during ten years of intrigues, provocations, and failed negotiations that preceded December 7, 1941. Grew is a lens into a decade of world-shaking history.

THE MISSION BEGINS

ON MAY 15, 1932, as Joseph Grew was traveling across the United States toward his new post, nine young Japanese naval officers in full uniform visited the Yasukuni Shrine in Tokyo to honor the nation's war dead. Armed with revolvers and daggers, they took two taxis to the official residence of Prime Minister Inukai Tsuyoshi. They burst in to find the diminutive seventy-six-year-old premier with his wife and pregnant daughter-in-law. A week earlier Inukai had dared to give an anti-militarist speech, an insult to the glorious destiny of the Japanese empire and its divine monarch.

Inukai lit a cigarette and tried to reason with the officers. "If we could talk," he said, "you would understand."

They shot him in the neck and stomach. Then they turned themselves in, serene in the conviction that they had done their patriotic duty. The assassins had coconspirators in the navy, the army, and right-wing patriotic societies bent on killing capitalists and politicians affiliated with what they considered the plunderbund exploiting Japan. Also slated for assassination were several palace advisors accused of influencing Emperor Hirohito toward the West and away from Japan's ancient traditions. The plotters hoped to sow chaos and terror that would embolden the army to impose martial law. Grew was on the kill list, too, and not for the last time, but wouldn't arrive in Japan for three weeks.

The next day at the Chicago train station Grew saw a headline: JAPANESE PREMIER SLAIN—SERIOUS REVOLT—PALACE IN PERIL. Inukai was the second prime minister assassinated in eighteen months. Grew knew the premier's death was the most recent stain on a history of bloody turmoil.

In September 1931 a bomb blew up some tracks on a railroad owned by Japan in Manchuria. Japan's Kwantung Army, stationed nearby, blamed the explosion on Chinese terrorists and invaded the province to protect Japanese interests. In fact the army had planted the bomb as an excuse to occupy Manchuria, a territory bigger than Texas, New Mexico, and Oklahoma combined. The army did so without consulting the Japanese government, though with the tacit consent of the army general staff and the war minister. The Japanese press quickly uncovered the ruse, but most preferred the army's lie and printed it with nationalistic fanfare. Newspaper sales boomed, and the Japanese press, almost without exception, made the fateful choice of profits and jingoism over truth. The Japanese people wouldn't learn the facts about Manchuria and many other military actions until after World War II.

The army had usurped the government's power, but Japan's civilian leaders felt boxed in by the fait accompli of the invasion and the public's enthusiasm. Politicians huffed and clucked but didn't dare punish the responsible officers. Neither did the army, which renamed the occupied territory Manchukuo and installed a puppet government on the pretext of protecting Manchukuo's new "autonomy" from the Chinese majority in this Chinese province. The army coveted Manchuria's natural resources, especially its coal, which Japan needed for the massive military buildup envisioned by its military leaders. The army and its supporters also wanted Manchuria as a colony to relieve Japan's overflowing population of 65 million.

The invasion violated international treaties signed by Japan after World War I. The United States, Britain, and other countries objected. Japan called them hypocrites for condemning what Western imperialists had always done. American secretary of state Henry Stimson declared that the US government would never recognize the legitimacy of a territory seized by force, and the Japanese press retaliated with furious anti-Americanism.

In February and March of 1932 more violence erupted in Tokyo. An ultranationalist society called the League of Blood (or Blood Brotherhood) murdered a former finance minister and the director general of a Japanese zaibatsu (business conglomerate) because the two men opposed the military's expansionist ambitions. Then on May 15 Prime Minister Inukai was murdered.

As the boat carrying Grew; his wife, Alice; and their youngest daughter, twenty year old Elsie, docked at Yokohama on June 6, 1932, basic elements of Japan's parliamentary democracy were eroding—civilian control of government, a justice system willing to punish sedition and political assassination, respect for international agreements and territorial sovereignty.

En route to Tokyo, Grew had written in his diary that of all his fourteen posts, Japan "promises to be the most adventurous of all." Over the next decade that promise was one of the few Japan kept.

The prospect of adventure had drawn Grew to the Foreign Service. Born in 1880, he was the third and youngest son of Edward Sturgis Grew and Annie Crawford Clark. The Grews had been Bostonians since before the Revolution. Edward made his fortune in wool. The family lived on Beacon Hill. They spent some weekends at their estate in Hyde Park outside Boston and summers at another home in Manchester-by-the-Sea on the North Shore. Young Grew's life was privileged but not always soft. At age twelve he was sent off to Groton, where he got a rigorous education and was instilled with the principle of service. During his teen years he spent most vacations outdoors, camping, canoeing, sailing, fishing, and hunting for elk and caribou, from Maine to Wyoming to Canada.

Male Grews were predestined for Harvard, followed by sober money-making careers in Boston business or banking. Grew's older brothers, Randolph and Henry, conformed to the mold. (Grew also had a younger sister, Eleanor.) Grew eagerly followed his brothers to Harvard, where he played football, ran track, and rowed, with enthusiasm but without distinction. He was an editor of the *Crimson* and a member of the Fly Club. He later wrote that these activities were the highlights of his college career, "with lecture rooms a poor fourth!"

After graduating in 1902 he balked at the foreordained next step. "Banking held no more allure for this particular young man than walking a treadmill," he wrote. His head was filled with Kipling and Stevenson, not ledgers. His alarmed father agreed to fund a year of dillydallying abroad, but only if Grew trod the proper Boston path upon returning to America.

The usual tourist spots didn't interest Grew. He spent fifteen months roughing it across the East, climbing mountains and hunting big game in Kashmir, Baltistan, India, Malaya, Singapore, Tasmania, New Zealand, China, and Japan. He got malaria in the forests of the Malay Peninsula and had to be carried out in a hammock. The fever returned savagely in Bombay. The United States consul general came to check on the ill American and took charge of his care for a month. The man's selfless dedication to serving his country in a faraway place influenced Grew's path.

Near the end of his trip Grew hunted China's famed Amoy tiger. Guides tracked one to a small cave. Grew belly-crawled through a tight tunnel, dragging his rifle behind him. When the guides pushed long bamboo torches through crevices to light the cave, Grew saw the tiger lying four feet from his head. He inched the rifle up to his hip and fired. The blast blew out the torches. The tiger roared and leaped around the dark cave. Grew fired twice more, blindly. The dead tiger measured ten feet, six inches from nose to tail.

In December 1903 Grew's father met him at Boston's train station. Grew delivered bad news. His travels had not only extinguished all interest in banking, but he now wanted to join the Diplomatic Service (forerunner of the Foreign Service)—State Department, not State Street. His father was appalled. The occupation was neither serious nor situated in Boston. They reached a desperate compromise. If his father could find him a position, Grew would enter a field that was at least minimally respectable and could be practiced in town: publishing.

While waiting, Grew did two things that would change his life. First, he took a touch-typing course. He was a natural left-hander, throwing and golfing as a southpaw, but his father had forced him to learn penmanship laboriously with his right hand. Typing freed him. He became a maestro of the Corona, composing everything directly on it for nearly sixty years. Second, he went to a dance where he met his future wife: Alice de Vermandois Perry, the twenty-year-old daughter of Boston Brahmins Thomas Sergeant Perry, a Harvard scholar, and Lilla Cabot Perry, an artist who had spent ten summers in Giverny, France, occasionally painting with her friend and neighbor Claude Monet. Alice was also the great-great-great-granddaughter of Benjamin Franklin and the great-grandniece of Commodore Matthew Perry, who "opened" Japan to the West in 1853. Alice had just returned from three years in Japan, where her father had been teaching literature. She spoke some Japanese, which later became useful. Japan had captivated Grew. Alice's connection seemed like kismet. She was lovely and poised, as well as sharp-minded and quick-tongued, formidable at bridge and poker. She also turned out to be remarkably adaptable to a roving life. They made a striking couple.

Since a position in publishing hadn't materialized, Grew went to live with a family in France to perfect his French, then the international language of diplomacy. There, he got a wire from one of his former professors. The US vice consul in Cairo was looking for a private secretary at six hundred dollars per year. Grew wired back that he needed two weeks to think about it—that is, to rush home and seek his father's consent. Then he took an agitated walk, "wrestling with a stubborn New England conscience which assured me that to stray from the ancestral fold of State Street was to be damned to all eternity." After four hours of pacing, he chose damnation. He wired back, "Accept unconditionally."

The position in Egypt was paid for by the vice consul and wasn't part of the Diplomatic Service. Congress hadn't yet funded career positions for diplomatic officers, so the service was filled with political appointees—cronies from college or business, or cronies' indolent sons, wealthy amateurs interested in soirees, not diplomacy. The service had a deservedly poor reputation among the general public. Grew believed wholeheartedly in the concept of "foreign service" and its importance to the nation, but in 1906 the service was still a club for the connected rich. Grew needed a political sponsor, and after two years in Egypt he still hadn't found one. Meanwhile he had married Alice in October 1905 and required an occupation.

Enter Alford Cooley, family friend and part of President Theodore Roosevelt's "Tennis Cabinet." Cooley often mentioned Grew to the president, but Roosevelt scorned diplomats as effete exemplars of corruption. No young man of substance would aspire to join them. One day Cooley told Roosevelt about the Amoy tiger. That changed everything. Here was a young man who embraced the strenuous life. The next day, March 1, 1906, Grew was appointed third secretary to the embassy in Mexico City.

Four years later, in 1910, he published a book about his youthful adventures called *Sport and Travel in the Far East*, with an introductory note by Roosevelt.

Congress eventually funded a professional class of diplomatic officers, but the spoils system would live on, to Grew's consternation. He championed these reforms and became known as one of the fathers of the modern Foreign Service. He sometimes joked to new diplomatic officers that they had entered the service merely by passing an exam. "I," he told them, "had to shoot a tiger."

On June 7, the day after reaching Tokyo, Grew was introduced to imperial Japan. A minion of the grand master of ceremonies at the palace called to say the emperor would accept the new ambassador's credentials on June 14. At precisely 10:20 that morning, five imperial coaches pulled by imperial horses and escorted by imperial cavalry passed through the embassy gates. The plumes on the coachmen's hats drooped under hard rain. Grew wore full ambassadorial regalia: dark swallowtail coat, starched white shirt with wingtip collar, white bow tie, striped pants, white gloves, top hat. He was comfortable in the getup and looked good in it.

The coaches left at precisely 10:35 A.M. They clattered across the pebbled Imperial Plaza and over the double-arched stone bridge spanning the palace's moat, dug in the fifteenth century. Branches of ancient pines brushed the moat's quiet green water. The coaches passed through massive wooden doors ornamented with a golden sixteen-petaled chrysanthemum, symbol of the imperial family. To a bugler's fanfare, they entered the palace grounds, 280 acres in the center of Tokyo. The grand master of ceremonies greeted Grew with a bow, then led him and the others to a reception hall decorated with exquisite screens.

At 11:00 A.M. sharp Grew was summoned to the emperor's presence. Following protocol, Grew bowed as he entered the room, bowed again halfway through his approach to Hirohito, and bowed a third time upon reaching him. The emperor, as always, was elevated above the floor. Grew read his speech, which was translated for Hirohito, then presented his credentials. Hirohito, in a high singsong voice, speechified back, his words translated for Grew. Still following protocol, the emperor "asked two or three of the usual formal questions," wrote Grew, "which I did my best to answer intelligently in spite of hearing only one word in four," partly because he was deaf in one ear from childhood scarlet fever, but also because the translator was forbidden from raising his voice in the emperor's presence. Protocol next directed Grew to present his staff. They entered one by one, triple-bowing forward to the emperor, triple-bowing backward to exit.

Grew had ample time to study Hirohito. He wore the resplendent formal uniform of the Japanese military. Braided gold epaulets encrusted his shoulders. Ornamental gold cords dangled. Two columns of gold buttons ran the jacket's length. Gold embroidery swirled down each arm. Colorful sashes belted and crossed him. A row of ribboned medals spangled his upper left chest. Below them four oversize medals effloresced like golden fireworks. Around his neck hung a collar of circular medallions made of gold and green enamel, evoking the blossoms and leaves of chrysanthemums. Suspended from this collar, encircled by more golden blossoms and green leaves, was the Supreme Order of the Chrysanthemum, a four-pointed spray of white enamel sunbeams flaring from a red garnet—the rising sun of Japan.

The uniform outshone the man. Hirohito's thin moustache and soft features made him look younger than his thirty-one years, an impression reinforced by rimless glasses. Grew noticed that he had "a sort of tick [sic], he is never still and his face and body are continually jerking." He looked more like a geek who spent his free time studying marine mollusks—which he did—than like a divinity.

For Grew the labyrinthine task of understanding Japan's culture, politics, and psychology began with the emperor. The Japanese believed the first emperor had been sent from the heavens by the Sun Goddess herself. This divine connection, according to the story, stretched unbroken for twenty-six hundred years. The story itself, however, had been invented less than a century earlier. Nevertheless, the Japanese embraced it as foundational truth. Not only was their ruler the Son of Heaven, but the whole Nippon race sprang from his line, starting with the first emperor. Every Japanese citizen contained a fragment of divinity, linking all of them by blood to their celestial ruler, the patriarch of his obedient children. Absolute loyalty to the emperor was expected of all citizens unto death. Ultranationalists extended the idea of Japan's heavenly origins even further, asserting that Japan had a special destiny to free Asia's lesser peoples from the dominion of the imperialist white race, and bring them under the guidance of the emperor.

Tributes to the emperor took many forms. Newspaper stories about the imperial family had to appear at the top of the front page. Every school displayed the emperor's photograph, which received frequent bows. Citizens riding streetcars bowed as they passed the palace. Soldiers bowed toward the palace when leaving for war, and bowed again if they returned. No one was permitted to look down upon the emperor. At public events or private dinners and conferences, he was elevated above all others. Few of his subjects had ever heard his voice. On the rare occasions when he left the palace grounds, the streets on the route were closed and cleaned. Anything that might offend the imperial gaze was removed. Bumps or potholes that might jolt the imperial person were smoothed. All buildings along the route were ordered to draw curtains and lower blinds above the first story so no one could view the emperor from above. Crowds gathered in hopes of glimpsing the crimson motorcycles escorting the emperor's crimson Rolls-Royce limousine—only royalty could have crimson vehicles. Police commanded onlookers to remove their overcoats as a sign of respect, even in freezing temperatures. When the emperor held formal occasions outdoors in winter, Grew learned to wear several layers of thermal insulation beneath his swallowtails.

Worship of the emperor had profound consequences on Japanese politics. Japan's feudal shogunate government had ended in 1868 with the restoration of Emperor Mutuhito and constitutional monarchy. This structure was modified in 1889 by the Meiji Constitution, which created Asia's first parliamentary government. The new constitution also enshrined the emperor as Japan's spiritual leader, head of state, and commander in chief. Yet as a god he was above politics and infallible. To ensure this infallibility, he wasn't allowed to make any decisions, nor could he be held responsible for decisions made by others. He had all power yet no power, all responsibility yet no responsibility.

This wasn't Eastern mysticism, it was confusion. The root problem was the constitution. It put the cabinet and the Diet (the parliamentary assembly) in charge of civil government, with the military separate under the emperor. The intention was to minimize the military's clout in politics, a sensible aim undermined by dangerous constitutional flaws.

The most powerful person in civil government was the prime minister. He wasn't elected by the people or appointed by the majority political party but chosen by the genro, a group of retired elder statesmen and palace advisors whose recommendation to the emperor was invariably approved. The prime minister then picked a cabinet—except for the ministers of war and the navy, who were appointed by the army and navy respectively. This gave the military disproportionate political leverage. If they disliked the genro's choice of prime minister or the prime minister's proposed cabinet—say, a foreign minister friendly to Western nations—the army or navy could refuse to appoint a war or navy minister and cause the cabinet to fail. Similarly, if the prime minister adopted policies the military disliked—budget cutbacks or resistance to territorial ambitions—the minister of war or the navy could resign and bring down the cabinet. Japanese cabinets fell like cherry blossoms. During his ten years in Japan, Grew dealt with twelve prime ministers and seventeen foreign ministers.

In effect, the prime minister served at the pleasure of the military. Instead of minimizing the military's clout, the constitution put it beyond civilian control. Further, the military pledged loyalty to the emperor, not to the constitution. From this a dangerous logic unfolded. Since the military devoted itself to carrying out the emperor's will, any action it took was motivated by loyalty to the divine ruler and therefore was patriotic by definition.

Three other centers of power influenced the nation's politics. First, there were the palace courtiers, most importantly the lord keeper of the privy seal, chief political advisor to the emperor. The second extra-governmental influence was the genro. By the time Grew got to Japan, the genro had dwindled to one man, eighty-two-year-old Prince Saionji Kinmochi. Hirohito would never consider appointing a new prime minister without seeking Saionji's advice and approval, and the prince's influence throughout government was substantial.

The final locus of political influence was a wild card—the Japanese people. Japanese society was rigidly hierarchical. Centuries of tradition had trained the public to obey their leaders. The public had little power, but when their anger and fears were directed, they became a potent force. Like Hitler and Goebbels in Germany, the Japanese ultranationalists understood this and fed the public an unending stream of fake news and propaganda designed to incite fear, resentment, and hatred.

All these groups tussled for position. Japan differed from Germany and Italy in that there were clusters of power but no central control, tiers of authority but no one in charge. For a diplomat looking for the levers of power and influence, the Japanese political system was a maze.

SETTLING IN

IN GREW'S FIRST weeks, protocol required that he make formal calls, in full regalia, on six of the seven ambassadors in Tokyo. He could skip the seventh because the United States government hadn't yet recognized the Union of Soviet Socialist Republics, formed in 1922. Next he had to receive at his embassy all thirty-two of the ambassadors, ministers, and chargés d'affaires stationed in Tokyo. Then he had to reciprocate their courtesy by calling on all of them. That added up to sixty-four appointments and visits. The imperial princes, who numbered fifteen, also expected calls.

"A thoroughly cruel infliction," wrote Grew. "Thus does an ambassador get into harness—by the sweat of his brow." At the end of June, as temperatures rose, he was still slogging around town to fulfill diplomatic obligations. Protocol could be tedious and irksome, but it mattered. It signified tradition and respect, and it was the first step toward friendships that might be useful later.

The United States was Japan's primary trade partner, accounting for 40 percent of Japan's exports and 30 percent of its imports. Tokyo was crowded with American businesses, trade associations, and cultural groups, as well as US–Japanese consortiums. All of them wanted the new ambassador's ear or his presence. In his first three weeks, in between diplomatic calls and embassy appointments, Grew also gave nine speeches, for the American Association, the American Merchants Association, the Oriental Culture College, the American School, and the Kojunsha Club, among other organizations.

Grew's most important early speech was at a welcoming dinner on June 21 at the America-Japan Society. This prominent group had been founded in 1917 in reaction against the anti-Japanese movement in California. The society promoted friendship between the countries and hosted speakers who drew large audiences from both nations. The US ambassador was the honorary president, and the welcoming dinner typically confined itself to speeches larded with platitudes delivered to dignitaries in tuxedoes, gowns, and kimonos.

But these were not typical times. Viscount Ishii Kikujiro, former ambassador to the United States, rose to address the audience of 250, including Prime Minister Saito Makoto. Speaking in English, he noted "the criminal propaganda deliberately attempting to create suspicion and fear" between their two countries. Neither country wanted war, of course, but if the United States prevented Japan from expanding, "then indeed a grave situation would be created." The western Pacific was Japan's sphere of operation, he said, and the United States could avoid trouble by not interfering there. The crowd looked stunned. But the Western nations needn't worry about their investments in China, he continued, because Japan would always honor the "open door"—a policy established at the turn of the century by the United States, European powers, and Japan to ensure equal trade opportunities in China and, with less emphasis, support for China's sovereignty.

The audience acted shocked, but not Grew. "While the tone of it was distinctly inflammatory," he wrote, "we could hardly take exception to the substance" because "after all he told the truth."

Grew's reaction exposed a crack between his views and the State Department's. Japan's invasion of Manchuria certainly violated international law, but unlike Stimson and others in the State Department, such as Stanley K. Hornbeck, chief of the Division of Far Eastern Affairs, Grew recognized Japan's legitimate concerns. Japan was exasperated by China's constant violation of Japanese rights in Manchuria. The warlord chaos throughout China also worried Japan. In Grew's view, Western scolding about Manchuria was self-righteous posturing that damaged relations now and lessened America's influence down the road. Japan was the dominant power in East Asia, economically and militarily, so Grew didn't agree with Stimson and Hornbeck that Japan was unreasonable to expect some deference in the Eastern Hemisphere, just as the United States did on the other side of the Pacific. Grew also sympathized with Japan's anxieties about its future. Overpopulated, with few natural resources, Japan would shrivel into irrelevance unless it found ways to sustain its economic expansion. But the worldwide depression had caused countries to slap tariffs on Japanese goods and put high export fees on raw materials crucial to Japan's growth.

So when Grew stood to give his speech, he ignored Viscount Ishii's provocations. He flattered the Japanese for their ancient culture and dished up the usual tropes about cooperation and friendship. He meant them. His main job, he said, was "to interpret each country to the other." But nice words wouldn't suffice. Serious problems existed and needed to be solved, he continued, preferably "during the next few months." After that remark it was probably superfluous to add, "I am an optimist both by nature and conviction and I firmly believe in the ability and the intelligence of man to overcome and master the difficulties which are now besetting the world."

That captured his temperament and diplomatic creed. He had faith that rational, well-intentioned people would choose compromise over conflict. He believed in nurturing personal relationships to build trust. He was certain that nations linked by business, cultural exchange, and mutual political benefit would be guided in their dealings by logic and enlightened self-interest. He needed to believe in these things, because they were the fundamentals of diplomacy. Without them diplomacy failed.

"The staff decidedly needs jacking up in the matter of office hours," wrote Grew within days of arriving. They were "simply going through the routine motions and obeying instructions when received but with no initiative at all, so far as I can see." The code filing system and general security also were "sloppy beyond belief," and he ordered immediate fixes. "Very likely our telegrams are all read," he noted, "but we don't need to hand them around on a platter." A stickler for grammar, precision, and organization, he made clear that from now on reports and dispatches would be better written and cleansed of typos and misspellings.

His management style matched his personality: warm, hyper-attentive, collaborative. He also wanted to infuse the staff with his own energy for the mission. He encouraged them to drop in whenever they had suggestions or useful information. Gathering intelligence was one of an embassy's most vital tasks, so he asked the staff to be his eyes and ears as they circulated among Tokyo's diplomatic, political, commercial, and military sectors. He wanted to hear gossip and rumors picked up at clubs or dinners, news carelessly spilled at sake-fueled geisha parties. Any tidbit might shine a light or clarify a picture. Two weeks later he noted, "I have the staff pretty well stirred up now, and they are on tip-toe to bring me information, comments, suggestions for telegrams, etc., so that a continual stream of people, either outside or inside of the Embassy, continually come and go."

He also encouraged the correspondents from the *New York Times*, *New York Herald Tribune*, *Chicago Tribune*, United Press, Associated Press, and other newspapers and news services to drop by to exchange information. Hugh Byas of the *Times* and Wilfrid Fleisher of the *Herald Tribune* and the *Japan Advertiser* became frequent visitors. By the end of 1933 Grew had the reputation of being the best-informed member of Tokyo's diplomatic corps. Ambassadors and ministers sought him out to ask what he knew about various matters, and Grew pumped them in return.

That summer rumors drifted into the embassy about radicals planning to kill the emperor or move him to the ancient capital of Kyoto. The Italian ambassador told Grew, "Anything can happen at any time." A member of the Metropolitan Police Board blurted to Grew's military attaché, "When something serious will occur it is very hard to say. It may happen at any time. The young Army officers are out of hand. . . . The whole place is full of malcontents." Six Japanese policemen guarded the embassy against possible attack and doubtless reported everyone who went in or out. Grew quickly understood that "the military are distinctly running the Government and that no step can be taken without their approval."

He put all these concerns into dispatches to the State Department, but rumors couldn't impede his enjoyment of Japan, starting with the embassy itself. The walled compound, built in 1930, occupied two acres on a terraced hill in central Tokyo. The walls enclosed four buildings of vaguely Moorish design, featuring bright white stucco with black doors and ironwork trim. The chancery offices sat on the lower terrace, flanked by two buildings with apartments for junior officers. The ambassador's residence perched at the top of the hill and overlooked the city. In clear weather Mount Fuji was visible.

The L-shaped residence was perfectly designed for entertaining while simultaneously cultivating sources of information in groups large or intimate. On one wing, a loggia led to a ballroom or reception hall. The other wing housed a petite salon, a dining room that seated fifty, and a grand salon whose tall windows overlooked a sunken garden with a circular fountain. Beyond these a wide lawn made a lovely site for outdoor receptions. Grew especially liked the cozy library, with its walnut paneling, fireplace, abundant bookshelves, and deep cupboards, "where at last I shall have space enough to file and store, separate and catalogue to my heart's content." Upstairs: seven bedrooms and four bathrooms. His commute down the hill to the chancery took him through a Japanese rock garden into a grove, past a marble swimming pool and a reflecting pool, and finally through flower gardens and lawns to whatever the new day brought.

Grew and Alice ran a newspaper ad inviting all Americans in Tokyo to the residence for a July 4 celebration. Foreigners typically weren't included when an embassy celebrated a national holiday, but the Grews invited everyone from every diplomatic mission, plus the Japanese Foreign Office. Three hundred fifty people showed up, including Premier Saito. The Grews served champagne, punch, and a buffet. Some guests wandered the terraced lawns, others danced in the ballroom to a small orchestra. Afterward a dozen guests sat down to a late supper on the terrace beneath Japanese lanterns and moonlight.

The State Department covered a small portion of this expense, but not for a drop of alcohol. Prohibition wasn't repealed until the end of 1933, and besides, the department was cheap. Ambassadors were expected to entertain but were given minimal funding. That tended to limit the ambassadorial pool to the wealthy. Grew's salary was $17,500 per year, a good wage during the Depression, and his housing was free. But his expenses were high because he considered entertaining a key part of the job. He trawled social networks for influence and intelligence, and alcohol was a social lubricant. Besides, there was his own delight in crisp Riesling and mellow whisky.

Grew's comfortable inheritance allowed him to afford embassy gatherings, and he didn't stint. Before leaving Istanbul for Japan he ordered liquor sent to Tokyo, starting with fourteen dozen bottles of Italian wine from a dealer in Rome (he later asked to be reimbursed for four broken bottles). From a London liquor shop he ordered six 12-bottle cases of blended Scotch whisky (and later asked to be reimbursed for one missing bottle). From Fortnum & Mason in London he ordered ten dozen bottles of rum, ten dozen bottles of sherry, four dozen bottles of port, two dozen bottles of fifteen-year-old brandy, and six bottles of green Chartreuse. He put in similar orders several times a year. He also shipped his large collection of French and German wines.

The serious entertaining couldn't begin until fall, when "informative contacts" and "useful Japanese" returned to Tokyo from seasides and mountains after escaping the torrid span from mid-July to mid-September.

3

TEMBLORS

THE SUMMER WEATHER stunned the Grews. The rainy season started in mid-June, followed by slamming heat and humidity. The combination was the worst they had ever experienced, topping Egypt, Mexico, and Turkey. It rained at some point every day. By 7:00 A.M. the temperature was already in the upper eighties. Mold grew everywhere. Grew and Alice began each day with a cooling swim in the embassy pool. "We take cold shower baths and change our clothes several times a day," he wrote.

He felt his first earthquake on June 16. Tremors were common. Two weeks later he was already a bit blasé, noting that he had forgotten to mention that the previous week's quake had broken a glass lantern by the reflecting pool.

The city outside the embassy's walls excited him. He loved the attention to aesthetic detail in gardens and Shinto shrines, laid out to delight strollers—shaded paths that curled through palettes of flowers and skirted ponds decorated with goldfish and water lilies. At tiny shelters, priests in white robes offered tea. A night of Kabuki and Noh theater was fascinating but strange. The music's frenzied discordance gave him, a connoisseur of classical music, a headache.

By late July, Grew, Alice, and Elsie couldn't stand Tokyo's heat any longer. They rented a Japanese-style house in the mountain resort of Karuizawa, three and a half hours north by train. The days there were pleasant, the nights cool. The wooded mountains offered serenity and spectacular views. In the distance, volcanic Mount Asama occasionally puffed, lightly showering Karuizawa with ash. Karuizawa became their summer retreat for the rest of their time in Japan. Grew swam in a cold stream-fed pool, played tennis, hiked, picnicked, and indulged his passion for golf. He played every day, rain or shine, with other vacationing diplomats and Japanese, anywhere from eighteen to forty-five holes per day. His enthusiasm for golf outran his skill. Despite playing at least twice a week year-round, he rarely broke one hundred for eighteen holes.

Grew's athletic life in Karuizawa energized him. "One feels like a giant up here, full of pep all day," he wrote to his daughter Anita. He was fifty-one years old.

Political tensions forced Grew's return to Tokyo. The Japanese press had exploded with attacks against Secretary of State Stimson because of a speech on August 8 about aggression in the Far East. On August 13 Grew sent Stimson a dire memo. "The Japanese Army is making extraordinary preparations for war," he wrote. Airplanes, ships, and tanks were being churned out day and night, made possible partly by the government's huge purchases of American machine tools. "The people of the cities are being urged to buy and man anti-aircraft equipment; anti-aircraft practice goes on daily in Tokyo."

Grew's memo included a section on "Psychological Preparations," in which he reported rafts of articles intended to "incite war fever." He quoted one in particular written by the war minister himself, General Araki Sadao. "The Imperial Principle of the Japanese nation," wrote Araki, ". . . must be propagated over the seven seas and extended over the five continents. Anything that may hinder its progress must be done away with even by the use of force. . . . The countries of Eastern Asia are made objects of oppression by the white peoples. This is an undeniable fact and Imperial Japan should no longer let their impudence go unpunished."

The military was preparing the public for war. Subscription drives asked everyone, including schoolchildren, to raise funds to buy planes, tanks, armored cars, and anti-aircraft equipment. Grew reported that the murder of Premier Inukai had neutered the civilian government and handed power to the military, whose only remaining opponents were the palace advisors. This small group was under threat of assassination or forced removal. "On the other hand, when we look for indications of a peace-seeking or concil-iatory nature," wrote Grew, "we find nothing tangible."

Militarists and nationalists were the strongest forces in Japan, but they weren't unopposed. Many moderates (sometimes called liberals, a misnomer anywhere except in Japan) favored good relations with Western countries and were dismayed by right-wing threats to Japan's peace and prosperity. The moderates' predecessors had shaped modern Japan by pushing the country from primitive feudal isolation to world power in less than fifty years, one of the most astonishing transformations in history. They had ac-complished this by importing Western technologies and ideas and applying them in business, industry, education, government, and the military. Many of these moderates went to colleges in Britain or the United States and later sent their sons there too. Promising army officers went to Germany for extra training. The navy sent exceptional officers to the US Naval Academy or Britain's Royal Naval College. In 1921 Hirohito visited Europe, the first crown prince ever to leave Japan. He became an Anglophile who ate a full English breakfast almost every morning.

Business interests tied Japan closely to the West as well, especially to the United States and Britain. Western music, movies, food, and fash-ion became wildly popular in Japan. American-style bars and dance halls were common. American-style restaurants served waffles. Theaters offered Hollywood movies and popcorn. Frank Lloyd Wright's byzantine Imperial Hotel opened in 1923 and became a hub for Western-Japanese interactions (and for the Japanese police surveilling them). The houses of wealthy Jap-anese often included a "Western room" with couches and chairs instead of mats and low tables. Japanese businessmen wore tailored Western suits or complemented their kimonos with fedoras and straw boaters. Many shuffled in their wingtips, which they bought several sizes too big for easy off-on when entering Japanese homes or restaurants. Women in kimonos and wooden clogs strolled the retail Ginza district alongside fashionistas in tight skirts and cloches atop bobbed hair. At news stalls in ancient lanes, Japanese lanterns cast shadows on posters of American movie stars.

Japanese nationalists, meanwhile, viewed these Western influences, in-cluding parliamentary government, as corruptions of the imperial way.

They also nursed long resentments over Western slights, often with good reason. Japan had entered World War I on the side of the Allies and afterward was invited to the table at Versailles as a world power. In the covenant for the new League of Nations, Japan wanted to guarantee immigration rights by including clauses about racial and religious equality. Those hopes were torpedoed, partly through the machinations of US president Woodrow Wilson. Then in 1924 the United States passed the National Origins Act, more bluntly called the Exclusion Act, which prohibited Asian immigration. Some Western states in America also prohibited Japanese residents from becoming citizens or owning land, laws upheld in the early 1920s by the US Supreme Court. Japan had strict immigration laws of its own against other nationalities, but the American laws against them stung.

After World War I, Japan tried to claim what it considered its rightful spoils in Siberia, Sakhalin, and China. When the Western imperialist powers objected, Japanese nationalists smelled hypocrisy and racism. They complained that the "have" nations wanted to shut out the "have-nots." Then came the worldwide depression. Japanese exports suffered from tariffs. The silk industry collapsed, and the country's farmers and factory workers endured desperate hardship. The divide between rich and poor widened. As in Germany, Italy, and other European countries, economic hardship led to political paralysis at the top of society and boiling anger everywhere else.

This was fertile ground for ultranationalism and xenophobia, and for appeals to a glorious past. In Japan, as in Germany, membership in patriotic societies skyrocketed, and these groups forged links with criminals and like-minded factions within the military and the police. Their anger needed targets. In Japan the easy scapegoats were Western powers and their elite moderate friends. Assassinations followed. Fear pushed some moderates into silence, leaving a widening space to the right wing.

That concerned the genro, Prince Saionji, and his private secretary, Baron Harada Kumao. Harada was Saionji's worker bee. Because of the genro's standing, Harada could buzz into every sector of Japanese power and gather information. High military officers, government officials, and palace advisors spoke to him eagerly in hopes of influencing the genro or learning his response to some development. Harada's direct line to Saionji gave him influence as well, and he didn't hesitate to tell military leaders or cabinet ministers how they should proceed.

In August he spoke with Prince Chichibu Yasuhito, the younger brother of Hirohito, at the Imperial Palace. Chichibu had attended Oxford. His wife, Princess Chichibu Setsuko, was born in England and graduated from Sidwell Friends School in Washington, DC, while her father was ambassador to the United States. This worldly couple was popular among foreigners in Tokyo, including the Grews. Chichibu and Harada were worried about the unpredictable zeal among young military officers and the effects of letting insubordinate officers escape justice.

"The trouble lies in the fact that these groups of men have the idea that what they think will be good for the nation," said Chichibu.

"In the final analysis, it is against the law," said Harada, "and if it does not comply with the Army regulations all must be punished whether the motive is just or not. Otherwise the trust we have in laws cannot be maintained."

Grew was unaware of such conversations, but he spoke often to moderates, such as Harada, Chichibu, and Count Kabayama Aisuke (businessman, politician, graduate of Amherst College). They assured Grew that, despite appearances, Prime Minister Saito was reining in the army and that moderates were reclaiming power. Grew didn't buy it. He telegrammed Stimson that moderates in Japan "carry little or no weight" and that nothing could stop the government's program in Manchuria except outside force. He was dismayed that sensible Japanese could disregard facts and logic by vehemently arguing that 27 million Chinese in Manchuria had joyously rejected China and embraced the puppet government forced upon them.

"After a careful study of the situation," he wrote, "I can find no approach by which the present Japanese intransigence might be overcome or modified." His optimism in June that relations between America and Japan could be repaired in a few months had vanished. He now grasped the complexity and unpredictability of his task. Still, whatever was coming, he felt confident that diplomacy could manage it.

Meanwhile, he caught the evening train to Karuizawa.

A RASH OF ESPIONAGE

FOR SEVERAL DAYS in early September 1932, the skies above Osaka buzzed with aircraft practicing defensive maneuvers against imaginary fighter planes. On the ground, soldiers drilled citizens in tactical responses to incendiary bombs, a terrifying threat in a nation of flimsy wooden homes with paper walls.

These frenetic activities put an officer in the Kempeitai, Japan's military police, on high alert. His vigilance had been amplified by a popular new movie, *Bombing Squadron of the Pacific*, the panicky Japanese title given to an American film called *Hell Divers*, starring Wallace Beery and Clark Gable. The movie focused on cocky dive bombers from an American aircraft carrier off Panama and featured dramatic footage supplied by the US Navy of thrilling takeoffs, landings, and aerial sequences performed by Curtiss F8C-4 Helldiver planes.

So when the Kempeitai officer saw someone from a foreign company taking photographs of buildings in downtown Osaka, he detected suspicious reconnaissance. He ordered the photographer to stop and filed an apprehensive report. The press blew the story up into what became known as the National City Bank affair. "The matter would be ludicrous if it were not serious," wrote Grew.

The bank's headquarters in New York had asked its branches throughout the Far East to send photos of emerging business areas that were good candidates for new branches or business loans—standard market research. The Kempeitai officer and the press, however, smelled espionage. Newspapers shouted that the photographs had been taken to show American planes what to bomb. Calls rose for Japanese bank officials to resign from the American bank or be branded as traitors. Gangs from patriotic societies visited the bank to intimidate employees into quitting.

The initial rumor set off a rash of others. The press reported that the United States was building air bases in the Aleutians (false), that three American aircraft carriers were lurking off the Kuril Islands north of Japan (false), that the US fleet was in the Pacific (true—thousands of miles away in California). Paranoia went viral. The Kempeitai in Kagoshima began investigating four fishy Americans, including one suspiciously named Stimson, who they claimed had climbed a mountain and taken photographs "for a certain purpose."

Grew believed the military had engineered the uproar to intensify anti-American feelings. A bit wearily he sent his military attaché to Kempeitai headquarters to ask for a statement absolving the bank of this nonsense. The officers laughed. The bank's president appealed to the vice minister of foreign affairs, who seemed sympathetic until asked to announce an official exoneration. After some silence the vice minister said, "Well, how can we prove to our satisfaction that the action of the bank was not open to suspicion?"

The *Los Angeles Times* covered the story under the headline AMERICA AGAIN FLAYED IN TOKYO. The article quoted the Japanese paper *Kokumin*—the mouthpiece of military ultranationalists—blaming the United States for the entire incident. "Unless the United States abandons her selfish and tyrannical attitude," lectured *Kokumin*, "it is impossible that Japanese feeling should resume tranquility."

Japanese press coverage died down after about a week, and Grew decided to drop the issue instead of pursuing a formal apology. If he got one, the whole debacle would roar back to life and the Foreign Office would be accused of bowing to Western demands. It was a matter of saving face. A short-term win about a trivial matter wasn't worth the long-term damage to his relationship with the Foreign Office.

Grew already understood the importance of face in Japanese relations. Elaborate manners and the intricate equivocations of the Japanese language were expressions of the necessity to maintain face, a combination of dignity and social respect. Criticisms and disagreements were best approached aslant, to leave room for face-saving compromise. Sharp disapproval often triggered aggression, not self-analysis. Face was fused to honor. To lose one was to lose the other. The only way to preserve both under direct confrontation was to attack. "Saving face," Grew told Stimson prophetically, "is the most dangerous factor in the whole situation. If the military clique finds that its program is being impeded and is likely to fail, whether from internal or external influences, it is quite capable of plunging the country into any kind of disaster rather than give in to the saner and more moderate elements in the country and acknowledging the defeat of their plans."

The vitriolic press and impending crises didn't reduce Grew's regular diplomatic duties. He threw himself into the teas, dances, and golf outings that helped him build the intricate relationships essential to his job. His days and evenings were packed with callers and activities, often ceremonial. Obligatory luncheons and dinners were a constant. "If we don't earn our salary in any other respects," he wrote, "we certainly do it by eating our way through the winter." And drinking. He once remarked that diplomacy was "hell on the head but double hell on the liver." Invitations would keep them busy seven nights a week if he and Alice hadn't agreed long before to take two nights off every week.

On those evenings Grew usually read history or murder mysteries, or did double-crostics, or listened to classical music with Alice, or answered letters. His correspondence for 1932 included thank-yous to a man who sent him Japanese stamps, to someone asking for his autograph, and to seven Japanese clubs for offering him honorary memberships. (The Japanese never allowed him to pay for golf or caddies or theater tickets.) No one was ignored: "Thank you very much indeed," he wrote, "for sending us that delicious celery."

October 14 was a typical ambassadorial day. First a speech at a conference for English teachers. Then the Argentine chargé d'affaires called at the embassy at 10:00 A.M., followed at 11:00 by an Anglican bishop who had come to Japan as a missionary in the early 1900s. At noon Grew received the president of the Corn Products Refining Society, and at 12:30 he had "the usual chat" with journalist Wilfrid Fleisher to trade information.

That evening Grew and Alice gave a going-away dinner for Debuchi Katsuji, who was returning to Washington, DC, as ambassador. Half of the twenty-two guests were Japanese, a typical ratio for the Grews. The *Japanese Advertiser* published the guest lists of diplomatic dinners, and Grew noted with perplexed amusement that most of his colleagues never invited any Japanese.

In his view, the near perfection of Japanese hospitality—the food, wines, flowers, service—often "was ruined by the blinding glare of unshaded electric lights." He was charming and gregarious, but when the customary seating put him between two Japanese women, he struggled. "As usual I had terribly uphill work in dinner talk because the Japanese women, with few exceptions, won't help to keep the ball of conversation rolling; it dies after each remark, and even when they make an observation it is whispered and I have to get my ear down into their plates to hear." Because of his partial deafness Alice sometimes had to help him get his own volume right, especially in public speeches. A finger to her ear meant too soft, to her mouth meant too loud.

Most of the time he admired the precision and beauty of Japanese social events. At the emperor's birthday lunch seven or eight hundred high officials and diplomats in formal gold-laced uniforms or dress suits were served dozens of dishes. The emperor, elevated on a dais at the front of the room, ate alone at a red-lacquered table. His waiter placed each dish gently on the table's edge and slowly pushed it into the imperial view. After lunch Grew rushed to the embassy to change into his swallowtails for a speech at the fiftieth anniversary celebration of a Japanese Methodist school.

A few days later came the biggest event of the autumn social season, the imperial chrysanthemum garden party in the palace's Shinjuku Gyoen Garden. Nine thousand invited guests sat at tea tables outdoors, "all in perfectly ordered formation so as not to interfere with the magnificent vista from the Emperor's seat." Despite the cold, no one wore overcoats out of respect for the imperial presence. Afterward, half-frozen, Grew and Alice hurried home to drink hot rum punch in front of a fire. They went to bed wondering who would win that day's American presidential election and what it would mean for their future.

• • •

Grew had abandoned many aspects of starchy conservative Boston, but not its allegiance to the Republican Party. Five of the six presidents he had served were Republicans. Because of the Depression almost everyone expected Hoover to get crushed in 1932 by Franklin Delano Roosevelt, and that was what happened.

Grew and Roosevelt knew each other from Groton and Harvard, where Roosevelt had been two years behind. At Harvard they were connected through the Fly Club and the *Crimson*. They called each other Joe and Frank but weren't close. Now Frank was Joe's impending boss—unless Frank replaced him with a fellow Democrat. Grew hoped to stay. The job was unfinished and too complex to award to a wealthy amateur. The new president was a question mark. Grew confided to his diary, "I have very little knowledge of Frank Roosevelt's potential capabilities . . . or whether he has both the wisdom and the courage to formulate sound policies and see them through regardless of the desires of the party hacks."

Grew took indirect steps to keep his job. "Dear Frank," he wrote to Roosevelt a few days after the election, congratulating him and wishing his administration success. "Harvard, Groton, and The Fly are tremendously proud—and they have good right to be." On December 5, following tradition, he sent Roosevelt an official letter offering to resign. But he added that the president could count on his "wholehearted support and cooperation in the great work which lies ahead." Grew wouldn't learn his fate under the new administration until March.

Throughout the autumn and early winter, rumors of violent plots constantly circulated. The targets were moderate leaders, including Prime Minister Saito and palace advisors. The atmosphere felt tense. In mid-November when Grew went to the train station to see Debuchi off to Washington, a squad of police rushed the Japanese ambassador aboard at the last minute to foil potential assassins. As Grew began to leave the station, two pairs of waiting police fell in before and behind him and escorted him to his car. "Probably our servants have instructions to telephone our movement to the police," he wrote.

Yet he also saw glimmers of change. In November the police arrested a number of young men belonging to a patriotic group called the Society of Heavenly Action and accused them of plotting assassinations. Those arrested included Toyama Hidezo, who had been linked to the assassination of the prime minister on May 15, which the authorities had shown little interest in investigating. More striking, the police had raided the home of Toyama's father, Toyama Mitsuru, the notorious godfather of Japan's ultranationalists. Previously considered untouchable, the "Shadow Shogun" was infamous for his links to violent crimes and political assassinations in Korea, Manchuria, and Japan. Despite this, and partly because of it, he was admired throughout the nation as a superpatriot. The previous June, the *Japan Times* had published a special section in honor of him. It included an appreciation by his close friend, Prime Minister Inukai, written a few weeks before he was murdered.

Grew wrote to Stimson that these police actions suggested the authorities had decided to stand up to the patriotic societies and their military supporters. This didn't mean the moderates had regained power. "But it does mean that the chauvinistic military hotheads and the so-called patriotic societies, who were directly or indirectly responsible for the former political terrorism, are less firmly intrenched, and are giving way, it is hoped, to a more constructive statesmanship."

Japan's new representative to the League of Nations was Matsuoka Yosuke. He made prudent people nervous. Yoshida Shigeru, Japan's ambassador to Italy, was among those who worried that Matsuoka would blow things up in Geneva instead of trying to resolve them. Yoshida casually advised Matsuoka to take an experienced diplomat with him. But Matsuoka craved the spotlight and furiously refused. "Before you leave," said Yoshida, offering some backup advice, "you had better go to the insane asylum and take a cold bath." A few years later Matsuoka would become the most exasperating and destructive foreign minister of Grew's tenure in Japan.

The main purpose of the league's assembly in Geneva was to find a compromise between Japan and China over Manchuria. At the opening session in December, Matsuoka gave a long speech. Japan was a loyal supporter of the league, he said, and always abided by its principles. But when the oppressed people of Manchuria rose up in revolt, Japan's leaders "could not stop the sympathy of the Japanese people" for the new independent government of Manchukuo. Japan's actions, said Matsuoka, should be supported by the league as advancing peace and human welfare.

A week after Matsuoka extolled Japan's devotion to peace in Manchuria, a reporter named Edward Hunter called on Grew. Hunter had just returned from Manchuria and wanted to tell Grew what he had learned about "the alleged Fushun massacre," as Grew called it. Fushun was a coal-mining city. In late November China had accused Japanese soldiers there of massacring two thousand seven hundred nearby villagers. Japan's Foreign Office denounced this as a fabrication and demanded an apology. Papers in the United States reported the allegation and the denial.

Unlike other reporters, Hunter went to Fushun to investigate. Villagers told him that Chinese guerrillas had attacked a Japanese garrison near Fushun and killed several soldiers. While pursuing the rebels, the avenging soldiers stopped in several villages along the way to massacre any available Chinese on the charge of complicity. The villagers told Hunter that about three thousand men, women, and children had been lined up along a ditch, machine-gunned, and bayoneted. To destroy the evidence, the soldiers burned the bodies and the villages.

"Inclined to be sensational," wrote Grew of Hunter after listening to his account. Grew's reluctance to believe this sickening story was understandable. Every decent instinct recoiled from the slaughter of thousands of unarmed civilians along a ditch. But Hunter's sensational account of indiscriminate massacre was the truth or close to it. Within a few years Grew would no longer dismiss such stories because they poured in from all over China. Terrorism and atrocities against civilians became standard tactics for the Japanese military. So did constant denials and excuses from the Japanese military and Foreign Office.

On December 20 Grew and Alice went to the Christmas concert of the Tokyo Madrigal Club. During intermission he talked with the British ambassador, Sir Francis Lindley, who updated him about the negotiations in Geneva over Manchuria, including the instructions given to the American representative. Grew was embarrassed that he had to learn from a foreigner about his own State Department's strategies on a matter so crucial to his mission. He was often peeved at the department for leaving him out of the loop and in the dark. He sometimes blamed it on the department's cheapness, trying to save money on telegrams, which he considered penny-wise but diplomatically foolish.

During his first five months in Japan, Grew had not heard a word of feedback from the department about his actions, speeches, and reports concerning the situation in Japan. When he left for Tokyo his instructions from Hoover and Stimson had been to get Japan out of Manchuria. But he quickly realized that Japan would not leave except by force. He reported as much to Stimson, who sent no guidance in response. After asking for instructions for five months, Grew finally wrote Stimson to suggest a policy—no retreat from the principles of the peace treaties, but also no bluster that would inflame anti-Americanism. Stimson finally replied that he agreed completely.

Looking for a bright side, as he always tried to do, Grew thought the department's silence might indicate its trust in him. But he couldn't do the job correctly without feedback about the information sent by the embassy. What was useful to the department? What wasn't? Were there blank spaces or obscurities that the embassy could try to illuminate? Since the department rarely offered a clue, Grew and his staff had to guess what Washington was thinking. These frustrations with the department's unresponsiveness would persist for the next ten years.

For six months Grew had worked hard to develop relationships with the Japanese in the upper echelons of politics, business, and the palace, where all important decisions in Japan were made. He invited dignitaries to the embassy for intimate dinners and official functions. They sensed his goodwill and reciprocated. In late December Baron Harada gave a small geisha dinner for the Grews and the Nevilles (Edwin Neville was the embassy's counselor, second-in-charge), as well as half a dozen Japanese.

It was the Grews' first geisha dinner. Everyone sat on the floor. The Japanese men wore kimonos. Each guest was assigned a geisha, who served delicious dishes and enchanting smiles. Harada slid along the floor to each guest, made brief conversation, then asked for the guest's cup of hot sake.

He toasted the guest's health and drank from their cup, then washed it, refilled it, and handed it back so the guest could toast him in return. The guests, too, could slide around and conduct their own toasty visits. Grew, always a gallant charmer, caused a small flutter when he glided over to one of the prettiest geishas and invited her to trade toasts. Around them, Noh dancers and singers entertained until the diners reached such a glorious state of health that they took over the singing.

"It was a great evening and we had a lot of fun," wrote Grew, "even though my legs were so stiff when we got up after about three hours on the floor that for a few minutes I couldn't move at all."

Neville, who had been in Japan since 1916, told Grew "he had never seen the Japanese unbend in this way when entertaining foreigners. They sort of took us into the family circle." It was a testament to how well Grew's campaign of sincere friendliness was working.

A YEAR OF SMALL FIRES

SOON AFTER THE invasion of Manchuria, Japan began telegraphing its intention to expand into the Chinese province of Hebei (Jehol) by claiming it was part of Manchuria. China vehemently disagreed and made clear that it wouldn't tolerate another bite out of its territory. On the night of January 1, 1933, in a port city in Hebei called Shanhaiguan, the Kwantung Army replayed the old Manchurian con. They apparently threw a grenade at the doors of their own headquarters, fired off some rifle rounds, then blamed it all on Chinese agitators.

The Japanese forces didn't seem caught by surprise. Within two days trainloads of infantry and artillery arrived, as well as warships, airplanes, and armored trains. On January 3 the Japanese military bombarded the walled city and its civilians without cease from 10:00 A.M. to 1:00 A.M. the next day, destroying large sections and causing fires that razed houses. Then the tanks went in. The Japanese army occupied the city. Since the operation had ostensibly been conducted in self-defense, the Kwantung Army hadn't bothered to seek permission from the Japanese government.

China protested to the League of Nations, reporting the bombing of civilians and subsequent atrocities by the occupying soldiers. The Japanese government claimed that the Chinese had started the violence and denied the accusations of terrorism. As with Fushun, Grew wanted to believe Japan's version of the story. "In choosing between the two," he wrote to a correspondent who had sent him news clips about the terror campaign, "I personally would generally prefer to give more credence to the Japanese reports of developments than to those which come from China, and I base this opinion entirely on personal observation and experience."

On the first day of the incident, the genro, Prince Saionji, asked Baron Harada to have the grand chamberlain tell the army chief of staff that the emperor was anxious about Hebei. "Since it is presumptuous to trouble the Emperor directly," added Saionji, "I want you to confer first with the lord keeper of the privy seal."

And so Harada began one of his typical yet astonishing tours through the labyrinthine Japanese hierarchy. Each leader passed the problem of the Hebei occupation on to the next. Harada talked to the lord keeper, the foreign minister, and the prime minister, each of whom was deeply concerned that the army might decide to go beyond the Great Wall toward Beijing, which would anger the Western powers. Then Harada spoke with General Araki. The brusque war minister wasn't worried at all and dismissed concerns about international reactions. "No matter what Japan does at present," he said, "we will not be spoken well of and it is of no use for us to try to behave ourselves."

"We are not concerned with behaving ourselves," retorted Harada. "It is very disadvantageous to have the powers think of us as the cause of unjustified wars."

Next Harada asked the navy minister to do what he could to control the army, which wasn't much. Then it was back to the palace to see the lord keeper and the grand chamberlain. "The Emperor is very anxious over it," said the grand chamberlain.

Harada's circular journey had lasted twelve days and yielded nothing except fretting and buck passing—no plan, no solution beyond passivity. Everyone agreed that the army was likely to do something alarming and that someone should try to stop it, but no one wanted to take any responsibility and no one was willing to tell the army to stand down.

Takahashi Korekiyo did his part. The blunt-spoken seventy-eight-year-old finance minister was not easily intimidated. With a round face framed by a white beard, he looked like a Japanese version of Ernest Hemingway. At thirteen he had sailed to California, where he was tricked into indentured servitude. He escaped after a year and returned to Japan, where he worked his way from obscurity to become head of the Bank of Japan, minister of finance, minister of agriculture and commerce, and prime minister.

Now in his second stint as finance minister, he was trying to pull Japan out of the Depression with deficit spending and controlled budgets. He had joined Saito's cabinet, he said, to stop the nation's drift toward fascism and "to restore the Government to the true course of constitutional parliamentarism." His financial and political goals put him in the crosshairs of ultranationalists. His name always appeared on their assassination lists.

Throughout the fall of 1932 Takahashi butted heads with War Minister Araki over the army's proposed budget, which called for a massive military buildup. Takahashi said the outrageous increase would benefit neither peaceful goals nor the Japanese people and would endanger the nation's financial structure. Takahashi asked Araki to think like a statesman, not a soldier, but that would have been a strain. Araki believed that Japan's imperial destiny required a massive army. Like all Japanese military men, he worried about war with the nation's perennial enemy, Russia. This fear intensified when Soviet communists committed the blasphemy of overthrowing an imperial ruler, which suggested how they would treat a divine emperor.

Takahashi suggested a different solution to the Russian threat. Instead of bankrupting Japan, why not work out a peace agreement with the Soviets? He pressed Foreign Minister Uchida Kosai at every opportunity, who always said the army opposed it. Takahashi called the army's blockage "disgusting." Araki tried to blame the delay on public opinion, which riled Takahashi. "There is no such thing as public opinion at present," he said. "If you say anything unfavorable to the Army, then the Kempei"—the military police—"rattle their swords or point a gun and threaten you. . . . The situation of the Kempei following statesmen around as if they were spies is very disgusting."

The Kempeitai had almost unlimited powers of arrest and were as feared in Japan as the Gestapo soon would be in Germany. Araki, red-faced with anger, protested that the military police were not suppressing speech. This was a blatant falsehood, but not a single cabinet member supported Takahashi. Nevertheless, the finance minister wasn't finished with Araki. Takahashi wanted to talk about Hebei, though he, too, had succumbed to the self-justifying euphemisms often used by the army. What would Japan do, he asked, if "the disturbances extend south of [the Great Wall] by force of circumstances"?

Even sensible Harada, uneasy about the Kwantung Army's volatility, fell into rationalizations about their potential insubordination. "We must avoid the pitfalls which may appear if our forces should accidentally spread to the Peking, Tientsin area," wrote Harada, "and if the Chinese make a pretend issue of it and cause intervention by the Powers."

At the League of Nations in Geneva, the powers were discussing the Lytton Report, which demolished Japan's rationalizations about the invasion of Manchuria and recommended Manchuria's return to China. Matsuoka, Japan's envoy, said that Japan would neither withdraw from the independent nation of Manchukuo nor accept any censure. If the powers refused these terms, Japan might withdraw from the league.

In Tokyo, opinions about withdrawal were mixed. Prime Minister Saito told Harada that exiting the league would damage Japan's standing in the world. The navy opposed withdrawal, too, as did most of the cabinet, the palace advisors, and Saionji and Harada. On the other side was the army and its ally, the jingoistic press. The papers were howling at the accusation that Manchukuo had been created by the Japanese army and not by a spontaneous uprising of freedom-loving Manchurians. If the league insulted Japan, withdrawal must follow.

Grew noticed signs of physical stress among Japan's leaders. "The Emperor seemed very nervous and twitched more than usual," he wrote after attending a small luncheon at the palace on February 11. Saito, the prime minister, "looked terribly old and worn."

On February 15 the League of Nation's Committee of Nineteen unanimously approved the Lytton Report. The committee scheduled a vote by the full membership the following week. "This brought about a very unpleasant atmosphere," wrote Harada. Foreign Minister Uchida had already joined Araki in calling for withdrawal from the league. Now the navy suddenly reversed itself and agreed. Prime Minister Saito visited Saionji for advice. The genro said it was too late, nothing could be done. This was the fatalistic paralysis by which moderates abdicated responsibility throughout the 1930s. On February 20, despite opposition by Saito and Takahashi, the Japanese cabinet voted to withdraw from the league if it endorsed the Lytton Report. Grew telegraphed this news to Stimson that same day and added that the assault on Hebei was expected momentarily. It began the next day.

On February 24 in Geneva, before the vote on the Lytton Report, Matsuoka stood at the rostrum and told the members that Japan would not compromise. "Manchuria belongs to us by right," he shouted, forgetting to pretend that Manchukuo was an independent state. "Japan has been and will always be the mainstay of peace, order, and progress in the Far East," he thundered as Japanese troops slammed their way through Hebei. He urged the delegates to reject the report and accept the new reality. The vote was 42–1, the sole nay cast loudly by Matsuoka. Afterward he stood and dramatically marched the Japanese delegation out of the hall. "We are not coming back," he said.

Grew admitted in his diary that he had misjudged Japan's commitment to the league. He now saw that withdrawal followed logically from everything that had transpired. "Their policy is to face the world with one *fait accompli* after another," he wrote. "The military are still supreme and form a dictatorship of terrorism." Prince Saionji's opinions mattered little to the militarists and were anathema to the extremists. Hence the moderates "give in to the violent elements, always hoping in vain that later they will get control and that in the meantime it is best for the country to avoid further affairs like that of May 15," when Prime Minister Inukai was assassinated. Grew worried that if the army marched on Beijing, it might spark another world war. "The outlook could hardly be blacker than it is."

He also confided many doubts to his diary about the "peace machinery" that had failed to prevent Japan's belligerence. He agreed in theory with the league's recommendations about Manchuria, "but the trouble is that they are ineffective in practice because they don't fit the facts and at least at present are unworkable." The facts were that in Manchuria, China had been violating its treaty agreements with Japan for years. Rapacious warlords, political fragmentation, and domestic conflicts roiled China, but when Japan appealed to the league and Western powers through the peace machinery, nothing was done. Japan was left alone to deal with China's chaos.

Japan's solution—invasion—was insupportable. But the peace machinery had failed to prevent it by failing to support Japan. Then the league and the United States worsened matters by holding to absolute principle and offering Japan no option except withdrawal from Manchuria. That rigid stance gave Japan an excuse to exit the league and throw off other treaty obligations as well, on the grounds that Japan needed to look out for itself because the Western powers wouldn't help.

Grew didn't want to reward Japanese aggression, but he was willing to acknowledge Japan's claims in Manchuria if that would keep the country in the diplomatic conversation.

The Manchuria incident exposed subtle but consequential differences between Grew's approach to diplomacy and the State Department's. The discrepancies stemmed from the tension between fact and theory, practicality and principle. Grew's intimate perspective from the front lines sometimes conflicted with the distant view from Washington. Stress fractures were inevitable.

KEEPING HIS SHIRT ON

ROOSEVELT REPLIED TO Grew's letter of congratulation with a letter of his own that began "Dear old Joe." But by the time the new president was inaugurated on March 4, Grew still hadn't heard whether he was in or out. On March 23 he was informed by the new secretary of state, Cordell Hull, whom Grew didn't know, that Roosevelt wanted him to continue as ambassador. "It makes us very happy to know definitely that we are to carry on," wrote Grew.

Hull wasn't a member of the Ivy League, Republican wing of the Foreign Service. He was born in a log cabin in the Tennessee hills and began his education in a one-room school. He graduated from National Normal University in Lebanon, Ohio, then earned a law degree after one year at Cumberland University in Lebanon, Tennessee. He set up practice in nearby Celina, population 223. He won a seat in the Tennessee House of Representatives at age twenty-two. After a stint as a judge he was elected to Congress in 1907 and served as a representative and senator. Until Roosevelt tapped him for the State Department, he was best known for championing free trade. His expertise in international commerce was thin preparation for a world about to explode with belligerent totalitarianism.

He was sixty-two years old and tall, with white hair, a tightly set mouth, and cast-iron principles. Unlike his quicksilver president, Hull plodded his way toward decisions and delivered them bluntly. Hardworking and conscientious, he was a man of convictions, not imagination. He often got lost in rambling homilies about ideals or trade that could leave listeners bored or baffled. He spoke with a high voice and a lisp, a combination particularly noticeable during his periodic diatribes. Roosevelt once remarked, "If Cordell says 'Oh Chwist' again, I am going to scream with laughter."

Roosevelt sometimes bypassed or disregarded Hull, as he did all his cabinet members, but the two had enough mutual respect to work together for nearly twelve years. Roosevelt often acted as his own secretary of state, but during much of the 1930s he focused mainly on Europe and the growing problem of Hitler. With a few exceptions, he largely entrusted Japan to Hull, and to Hull's Far Eastern advisors.

Grew and Hull started from different places in their approach to Japan. "I shall do my utmost to keep a detached and balanced point of view," wrote Grew in his diary upon being appointed. "An ambassador who starts prejudiced against the country to which he is accredited might just as well pack up and go home, because his bias is bound to make itself felt sooner or later and render impossible the creation of a basis of mutual confidence upon which alone he can accomplish constructive work." Grew aspired to be open-minded, gathering facts and information before forming a hypothesis. He also allowed new facts to alter obsolete assumptions. His approach was fluid, flexible, inductive, and pragmatic. But in time Grew would learn that these qualities, when viewed through the prism of inflexible principle, could be misinterpreted as appeasement.

Hull, by contrast, was deductive. He began with fixed principles and convictions that he stamped onto reality. "As I entered the State Department," he wrote, "I had two points on the Far East firmly in mind. One was the definite interest the United States had in maintaining the independence of China and in preventing Japan from gaining overlordship of the entire Far East. The other was an equally definite conviction that Japan had no intention whatever of abiding by treaties but would regulate her conduct by the opportunities of the moment. Japan's diplomatic record was that of a highway robber." From the beginning he was "convinced," he wrote, "that Japan was merely marking time until she could consolidate her gains in Manchuria and then advance farther."

That turned out to be right, as self-fulfilling prophecies often are. In coming years Hull would negotiate earnestly and tirelessly with Japan, but his foreordained certainty that the Japanese were incapable of anything except treachery narrowed the chances for a different outcome. In 1933 Grew didn't yet grasp Hull's fundamental distrust of Japan, or the impact of the advisors who stoked it, including his chief advisor on the Far East, Stanley Hornbeck.

At the end of April, after weeks of rain and gray, the sun shone on the emperor's thirty-second birthday. The cherry trees were blooming, turning Tokyo into a dazzling tribute to spring and royal beginnings. Grew was invited to the imperial luncheon following Hirohito's inspection of the troops at the Yoyogi parade grounds. The emperor arrived in a magnificent carriage pulled by horses, then mounted his white Arabian stallion, the only white horse allowed at the event. For more than an hour his troops streamed past him: cavalry, lancers, goose-stepping infantry, heavy artillery pulled by tractors as fighter planes zoomed in formation overhead. Then the emperor dismounted, climbed back into his imperial coach, and left the field. The luncheon guests followed, past rows of police, to a sumptuous banquet at the palace.

At another luncheon, Count Kabayama assured Grew that his patience and personality had begun to soften even the hard-line militarists, such as Araki. Kabayama admitted that the army's hotheaded young officers were still troublesome but insisted that the moderates were poised to regain influence over foreign policy. The prospect of that, wrote Grew, "is, so far as I can see, not a whit more propitious than it has been all along."

The evidence supported him. In late April thousands of cheering people welcomed Matsuoka home to celebrate Japan's defiance of the Western bullies in Geneva. "The whole country is treating him as a national hero," noted Grew. In the press, anti-American screeds and spy paranoia had kicked up again. American companies had been stopped from gathering standard commercial information. The press also concocted fake news about an American plan to attack Japan by air. A new medical tower at Saint Luke's Hospital, built with American money, was condemned by a Tokyo paper as a spy lookout.

Grew wrote to Hull that most anti-American incidents and rumors of attack stemmed from military propaganda intended to divert public attention from the immense expenditures in Manchuria. The "spy mania" was a nuisance for businesses, but none of the anti-American agitation seemed dangerous yet. Most of it was too absurd to merit a response, which would only feed the frenzy and lower the embassy's prestige. "One of the principal jobs of the American Ambassador," Grew once said, "was to practice keeping his shirt on."

Three weeks later he sent Hull a confidential five-page letter describing the strength of the Japanese military and the Japanese people. He warned against underestimating either. In the United States, Japan was often shrugged off as too small to be a threat. Grew dispelled that illusion. Japan was larger than Germany, France, Italy, or Spain. Add Manchuria, and Japan had more land mass than all those countries combined. Grew called Japan's military the most powerful fighting machine on the globe. "The machine probably could not stand a protracted, severe war," he added, "as industrial supplies would become exhausted, but for a quick, hard push I do not believe that the machine has its equal in the world."

But his most urgent message was that Japan's military machine wasn't its greatest strength. "The thing which makes the Japanese nation actually so powerful and potentially so menacing," he wrote, "is the national morale and esprit de corps . . . the force of a nation bound together with great moral determination, fired by national ambition, and peopled by a race with unbounded capacity for courageous self-sacrifice is not easy to overestimate."

The letter caused a stir in the State Department. Hull passed it on to Roosevelt with a note stating, "The accompanying letter from Minister [sic] Joseph Grew at Tokyo is so exceedingly interesting that I feel sure you will desire to read it." Stanley Hornbeck wrote to Hull that Grew's letter was "one of the most important documents that has come in for a long time."

Hornbeck's opinion was important to Hull and therefore to Grew. After earning a doctorate from the University of Wisconsin, Hornbeck spent four years teaching at colleges in China. He thereafter focused his intense intellectual energy on the Far East, with a special interest in China. He joined the State Department in 1928 to run the Division of Far Eastern Affairs without ever having worked in a diplomatic mission. Now fifty years old, he had a reputation for intelligence, pugnacity, and sarcasm. He was brusque to the point of rudeness. A fervent bureaucrat, he papered the department with memos, all expressed with absolute certainty in orotund syntax. Like many overconfident people, he was thin-skinned. Admired by some, detested by others, he was acknowledged by everyone as the major force in Far Eastern policy.

Hornbeck's personality contrasted sharply with Grew's. In 1933 Hornbeck's antipathy toward Japan hadn't fully hardened, nor had he started undermining Grew at the State Department. Grew still considered him a possible ally. Hornbeck could influence policy, so Grew needed to influence Hornbeck.

In a buttery letter on May 8, Grew flattered him while also trying to educate him about his preferred methods of diplomacy. Grew made clear, in amiable language, that his job was not to be a messenger boy "making cut-and-dried representations to the Foreign Office." Effective diplomacy, he wrote, "must be done quietly, gradually and in many different unofficial ways." This required patience and informal personal approaches, he told the impatient, impersonal, by-the-book Hornbeck. Results couldn't be guaranteed, "but the important thing anyway is to prevent the boat from rocking."

LOVERS AND PATRIOTS

IN THE SPRING of 1933 Tokyo was riveted by an outbreak of suicides, mostly young women. "Hardly a week goes by," wrote Grew, "without published reports of several such youths throwing themselves into the crater of the volcano on Oshima island, a popular Sunday excursion." The impulse spread like a contagion, creating a market for gawkers. Tour operators began running trips to the overlook favored by the suicides. A few sightseers, overwhelmed by emotion and the sight of bodies at the bottom of the crater, leaped. By the end of the year more than five hundred youths had jumped into the volcano. The craze didn't end until 1936, when the authorities made one-way tickets to the island illegal.

Not all the news that spring was bad. At the end of May, Japan and China signed a truce that stopped the fighting in Hebei and in the five northern provinces collectively called North China. China gave up its claims to Manchuria and Hebei. To Chiang Kai-shek, China's military and political leader, peace with indignity was the pragmatic choice. He needed his resources to fight Chinese communists, which he still considered a bigger threat than Japan.

Grew noted a few signs that relations between the United States and Japan were improving. An anti-American spokesperson for the Foreign Office was pushed out, which Grew read as a shift toward restraint. On June 1 he and Alice traveled to Kurihama, where Commodore Matthew Perry had waded ashore from his "black ships" in 1853 to pry open the closed doors of feudal Japan. In the eighty years since, Japan had vaulted out of isolation and into dominance of modern Asia. Most Japanese considered this progress, but some ultranationalists marked Perry's arrival as the first day of Japan's decline from noble tradition. The descendants of those leaders who had greeted Perry now welcomed his descendants in turn, including Alice Perry Grew and her husband. Hundreds of schoolchildren waved American and Japanese flags, shouting "Banzai!" Dignitaries delivered speeches. Photographers snapped and reporters jotted notes, then they attached their materials to homing pigeons that flew to news agencies in Tokyo for the evening editions.

The benevolence stretched into the next day with the arrival of Admiral Montgomery M. Taylor, commander of the United States Asiatic Fleet, on the flagship USS *Houston*. This kicked off a week of luncheons, dinners, and dances hosted by Grew and Japanese naval officers for Taylor and his officers. Expressions of amity abounded. Meanwhile, businesses in Tokyo and Yokohama were entertaining the *Houston*'s seven hundred freshly paid sailors. As they left the ship for their shore leave, touts on the pier handed out cards advertising bars, dance halls, and enticements in the "pleasure quarter" of Yoshiwara. Yokohama threw a picnic for more than two hundred sailors in a local park. Forty-three chalk-faced geishas in kimonos strolled and tittered among the seamen. Other Japanese women poured cold keg beer from bottomless pitchers. International relations advanced toward détente.

That's also the way Grew was seeing things at the moment. In late June the Kojunsha Club held a luncheon to honor him for doing so much in the past year to mend the bond between Japan and the United States. In his speech Grew's theme was that most of the ill feeling between the two countries sprang from sensational fake news. Controversies and distortions sold newspapers. He was pleased that the members of the Kojunsha Club recognized "the clearing weather on the horizon between our two countries" rather than the "cloudbursts and calamities" hyped by the press. When people were fed nothing but conspiracies and fabricated perils, he continued, they started mistaking falsehoods for reality. "The modern world can function properly only if the public generally is correctly informed," he said. Then people could make decisions based on accurate facts instead of inflamed emotions or sensationalized misinformation.

• • •

Personal relations also made Grew happy that summer. His youngest daughter, Elsie, twenty-one, got engaged to Cecil Lyon, a lowly third secretary at the embassy. Lyon had been smitten first by Grew. Every Foreign Service officer, Lyon later wrote, hoped to join Grew's staff and aspired to emulate him. Lyon effused that the ambassador was handsome, charming, and athletic, a Bostonian of wealth and culture "without any of the stuffiness which that might imply."

Then he fell for Elsie and vice versa. After just a month in Japan, Lyon worked up the nerve to ask Grew's permission to marry her. Grew, taken aback, said it seemed a bit quick. "Can you blame me?" said Lyon. "To which, of course," wrote Grew in his diary, "there was nothing more to be said."

Well, maybe a bit more, according to Lyon.

"And what is your situation?" asked Grew.

"Sir," said Lyon, drawing himself to full height, "I'm a Foreign Service officer, class 8, unclassified C."

"What on earth does that mean?" asked Grew. "What do you earn? What are your prospects?"

"Twenty-five hundred a year."

Grew groaned and said he would have to talk to Alice. But Alice liked Lyon, and so did Grew despite his fatherly concerns. They approved the engagement.

The Grews' four daughters were born in Giverny, Saint Petersburg, Berlin, and Vienna. The oldest, Edith, died of scarlet fever in Venice at seventeen. The other three married career Foreign Service officers, all Harvard graduates. "To have given three daughters to the service must, I should think, constitute a record," wrote Grew. *Fortune* magazine called the Grews "the royal family of the Foreign Service." Grew sent each daughter five hundred dollars per month to help with expenses, as his mother had done for him early in his career. His frequent and affectionate letters to them made clear that he understood completely why anyone would be enchanted by any of them.

• • •

"Easy days, these," wrote Grew in mid-July. Hardly any telegrams came in or out, and nothing much was happening, "except for the recent flurry caused by the discovery of another alleged plot to assassinate Saito, Makino, etc." Grew brushed it off—another fringe group foiled.

Baron Harada, with more information, was more concerned. A patriotic society called the Shimpeitai (Heavenly Soldiers or God-Sent Soldiers) had decided to kill the people behind the recent improvements in foreign relations. The minister of justice and the chief of the Metropolitan Police told Harada they had thwarted the plot just hours before its execution. It had been serious and well financed. The entire cabinet was to be murdered, along with officials from the palace, the Diet, and business. In addition to sixty gang members arrested in Tokyo, the police had seized another hundred conspirators. The plotters intended to follow the usual blueprint—assassinate, incite riots, demand martial law. "And then," wrote Harada, "to make a world of their choosing." The police stationed guards around the residences of cabinet members, as well as the American and British embassies.

Grew was equally blasé after a scare on July 18 at the official residence of Prime Minister Saito, where Inukai had been killed the previous year. Grew and Alice had been invited for dinner. They walked through a cordon of policemen whose numbers had been doubled because of the recent plot. When the Grews reached the door, an alarm went off inside. The police rushed in, revolvers cocked, swords drawn. This time it was a false alarm. One of the guards had pushed the wrong button.

"There is naturally a tense atmosphere about that mansion, considering the constant threat of assassination," wrote Grew. "Viscountess Saito looked terribly depressed throughout the evening."

Tokyo's smothering humidity had descended. To elude the heat, they began dining on the roof of the Imperial Hotel and watching Hollywood movies there. In late July the Grews left for Karuizawa again. The previous summer Grew had returned to Tokyo six times to tend to crises, but this time he stayed until September 5 without a hitch. He kept in touch with the embassy by phone and mail but mostly relaxed in their rented home deep in the woods. His days began with a swim in a pool fed by a cold brook, followed by golf, often thirty-six holes a day.

"It's a fine care-free life for a change," he wrote to his brother Harry. In six weeks he added only three pages to his diary. At the end of his vacation he noted, "Conditions in Japan have been moderately quiet all summer . . . There have been no great developments."

Baron Harada's summer wasn't as relaxing. The trial of the naval officers who had assassinated Prime Minister Inukai in May 1932 began in late July. So did the trials of their coconspirators: about a dozen cadets from the army and the navy, as well as civilians from the ultranationalist League of Blood. The minister of justice told Harada he intended to prosecute thirty-five civilians for attempted murder.

The press gave the trials saturation coverage. Evidence about the plotters' homicidal terrorism horrified the public at first. The accused were allowed to orate for days about the purity and nobility of their motives. They spun wild conspiracies about Western-influenced corruption, arguing that nothing short of a blood purge could save the nation. At a naval review of ships in Yokohama, Harada heard the accused's fabrications repeated as facts by high navy officers who had read them in the papers. When Harada corrected the lies about Prince Saionji and others, the officers were surprised. But few Japanese benefited from fact-checked news.

The fictions and conspiracies spouted by the accused flooded the newspapers and radio. Facts were slowly overwhelmed, then logic, then law. Day after day the accused and their lawyers shouted indignantly about "national betrayal" that justified "patriotic crimes." The press began elevating these murderers and terrorists into noble reformers motivated by profound love of Japan. How could such virtue deserve punishment? Hundreds of thousands of people signed petitions, often in blood, urging leniency. Women cut off their hair in grieving solidarity. Nine schoolboys wrote to Minister of War Araki extolling the patriotic sacrifice of the nine assassins and asking him to please accept their small reciprocal sacrifice in the accompanying wooden box: nine amputated fingers.

Support for the assassins wasn't limited to the fringes of political thought. Thirty-two thousand members of the Order of the Golden Kite, Japan's highest military decoration, signed a petition expressing admiration. The Osaka Bar Association asked the court to consider absolving the killers on grounds of self-defense. Nevertheless, the navy's prosecutor pushed for severe sentences. In his closing argument he stated that violations of Japan's laws and constitution shouldn't be tolerated under the aegis of patriotism. "You cannot say," he told the court, "that because the motive was sincere, an act is not illegal if the results violate the law."

Saionji and Harada considered this rational and just, but they were in the shrinking minority. Araki opined in the Diet that if the motive was sincere patriotism, the act didn't matter. A press campaign had already begun to undercut the navy prosecutor, who previously had been hailed for his courage.

The Ministry of Justice asked that the army cadets who had played minor roles be sentenced to eight years. This indicated the government's intention to punish the assassins severely. But on September 20 the military court decided that four years (some of which had already been served) was enough. Harada commented that "the intelligent public" found the sentence ridiculously light, and he worried that the navy would be pressured into equal leniency. But the military, the press, and the public were outraged for the opposite reason—heroes were being punished for their patriotism.

Araki then had a brainstorm that reflected the topsy-turvy thinking that turned murderous traitors into heroes. He wanted the emperor to issue a blanket pardon not only to everyone charged in the May 15 incident but to anyone charged with plotting assassinations. The pardoned criminals, he said, "will become inspired by the Emperor's grace and, with all Japanese nationals cooperating under a new atmosphere, will start entirely new. By carrying this out the general restlessness will be eradicated."

Harada, alarmed, took the next train to deliver this news to Saionji at his home in coastal Okitsu, a hundred miles southeast. "Why, that would be comparable to revolution," said Saionji.

Araki's idea seemed preposterous, but in the end the general didn't need the emperor's approval. Most of the plotters walked free or served minimal sentences that were soon suspended. Instead of death, the killers received sentences of three to fifteen years, which they didn't fully serve. Another dangerous precedent had been set. Terror, treason, and assassination, if done sincerely in the name of the emperor, were acts of patriotism.

BISON AND NAZIS

ELSIE'S WEDDING TO Cecil Lyon was the Grews' major social event in the autumn of 1933. Four hundred guests attended the reception at the Grews' residence, among them the prime minister, foreign minister, and war minister. From the palace came the lord keeper and the grand chamberlain, among others. The principal members of the diplomatic corps were there, along with a big crowd of Elsie's Japanese and Western friends. Prince and Princess Chichibu, representing the royal family, sat on the terrace on a raised platform.

The empress sent Elsie a gorgeous gold lacquer jewelry box ornamented with an imperial chrysanthemum. It was displayed on its own table on a high stand. A nearby painting by Alice's mother had been removed because nothing could be above the imperial gift. Presents from other royals sat on slightly lower stands. On tables below these were crowded the offerings of ordinary mortals.

Several episodes enlivened the early winter of 1933. A group of thirty young farmers who called themselves the Saitama Young Men's Patriotic Storm Troops had been plotting to assassinate a minister and a political leader scheduled to speak in their small town on November 14. Afterward, to widen their revolt, they planned to travel to Tokyo and kill the prime minister, the lord keeper, and Prince Saionji. For their finale they would commit hara-kiri on the plaza facing the imperial palace. The hitch was money. To fund transportation to Tokyo and the necessary arsenal—they could muster only one pistol and a few swords—they first had to rob a bank. The police got wind of this ingenious scheme and arrested the principals on November 13.

The second event, in early December, was announced by posters hung throughout Tokyo: Buffalo Week. William Randolph Hearst, the American newspaper magnate whose publications often warned against the "yellow peril" of Asian immigration, shipped three adult bison to a publisher in Tokyo as a gift. Several thousand people swarmed the dock and the transport trucks in hopes of glimpsing the fabled American beasts. Bicyclists raced with the trucks through Tokyo, past other posters signed by the Kenkokukai (Association of the Founding of the Nation) calling for war with the Soviet Union. At the zoo, a huge crowd witnessed the uncrating. Then came ceremonies and speeches.

"I found that the bison were rather easily irritated," said the Japanese captain of the ship that had carried these icons of wild America. "They would shake their great heads and make the cages rock and look as if they were going to break loose at any moment."

On Saturday, November 16, the Soviet ambassador to Japan, Konstantin Yurenev, phoned Grew to set up a time for an inaugural diplomatic call. That was how Grew learned that the United States had recognized the Soviet Union. Once again, to his intense irritation and embarrassment, the State Department had decided to save a few dollars by sending important news via circular telegram, which went first to Shanghai or Beijing instead of directly to Tokyo.

On the following Monday the two ambassadors exchanged visits. First they toasted each other with sherry in Grew's study. Within the same hour, Grew went to the Soviet embassy for caviar sandwiches and cherry brandy. Yurenev was delighted by the official recognition but pessimistic about avoiding war with Japan. Grew was more optimistic. He thought the possibility of an alliance between the United States, the Soviet Union, and China would restrain the Japanese militarists.

Over the next four years Yurenev would become popular in the foreign community for throwing huge parties with flowing vodka and mounds of caviar—the real stuff in one room for the ambassadors and ministers, pressed caviar for minor officials and reporters in another. "Marvelous fresh caviar, bowls and bowls of it," wrote Grew about one such party. "Recognition fully justified."

To rationalize their exorbitant requests for money, the army and navy continued to cry wolf about imminent attacks. Finance Minister Takahashi continued to balk. Takahashi's concerns went beyond bankrupting the nation. At a cabinet meeting on December 5 he accused the army and navy of trying to generate support for their budget requests by spreading propaganda about imminent wars with Russia and the United States. "The pro-war atmosphere of Japan is creating a very bad feeling in diplomacy, and this appears in trade relations," said Takahashi. "For these reasons the military must use prudence in their speech and actions. There will be no such crisis in 1935 and 1936."

"That is not true," said War Minister Araki angrily. "There will be a crisis."

Politicians and the public, especially farmers, also were getting weary of the military's budgetary gluttony and had begun speaking out. "The voice of resentment against the Army from all circles has become very strong," noted Harada. "Until today the public reserved its opinions, in fear of the military, but we greatly fear that the military may become now an object of common hatred because it has carried things to extremes, not knowing when to stop." All this criticism, he added, had put the military into "a neurotic state."

The army and navy issued a joint statement on December 10. Their budget requests were not excessive, they said, nor were they using propaganda to frighten the public about imminent wars. They denied that shunting hundreds of millions into defense would affect spending that benefited ordinary Japanese. Considering the precarious international situation, said the statement, the amounts requested were actually the minimum necessary. The statement didn't mention that this situation had been created, at least in Asia, by the Japanese military. They separated their critics into two groups—communists, of course, despite their marginal presence in Japanese politics, and a shadowy faction trying to "disturb the harmonious unity of the public mind, the most essential basis of national defense." They added ominously, "And the military authorities cannot overlook it. . . . It is outrageous to make such statements against the Army and Navy."

Harada's comment on the statement was succinct: "This is certainly a ridiculous thing to do."

At 7:00 A.M. on December 23 Alice woke Grew. "It's the siren," she said. The blast persisted for a full minute, announcing the birth of an imperial child. Everyone in Tokyo held their breath for the next ten seconds. When the siren blasted again, Grew and Alice clapped and shouted. Two sirens meant that the empress, after giving birth to four daughters, had delivered a crown prince. For Grew it represented another step toward political equilibrium. His informants had told him that the army had been getting nervous about the absence of an imperial heir, and another daughter would have put the emperor in jeopardy of a coup. The birth of a crown prince also meant that Prince Chichibu, Hirohito's brother and next in line to the throne, was no longer forbidden from having children.

On the day of the birth, Harada visited the palace to drink champagne with the lord keeper and the grand chamberlain. The entire country was delirious with happiness. Festivities went on for a week, culminating with the naming celebration on December 29. Between sundown and midnight, half a million people paraded across the Imperial Plaza, cheering and carrying white paper lanterns decorated with the red orb of the rising sun. They paused at the double-arched bridge leading to the palace and bowed or kneeled with their foreheads to the earth. Then they stood and shouted "Banzai!" three times to honor the emperor, empress, and crown prince. Across the moat, in the palace, lanterns waggled to thank the crowd.

This joy pleased Harada for political reasons as well as personal ones. "The fact that the feeling of the people had been stabilized (by the birth of the Crown Prince) was especially noteworthy," he wrote. "I felt that this was highly auspicious." So did the rightists. They began pressuring the emperor to use the birth of the imperial heir as a reason to grant amnesty to prisoners, especially the jailed plotters. Hirohito warned Prime Minister Saito about this and said, "Care must be taken to prevent the sanctity of law from being impaired by sentiment."

But Saito crumbled under pressure from the extremists. He told the em‐
peror, "The Government considers that under the present circumstances
some sort of amnesty must be granted." Saito advised preserving the rule
of law by excluding burglars and murderers from the pardon, but he felt
it necessary to include the treasonous plotters who had attempted coups
against the government, including those from the May 15 incident and the
League of Blood incident. In early February 1934 the cabinet adopted and
announced Saito's amnesty plan.

In addition to the imperial birth, the end of December marked another
arrival: the new German ambassador to Japan, appointed by Hitler. Herbert
von Dirksen was a tall, hatchet-faced anti-Semite with a weak handshake
and a disconcertingly high voice. He immediately sent an underling to the
Japan Advertiser, Japan's main English-language newspaper, to complain
about its coverage of Hitler. He warned that unless the paper changed its
attitude, Berlin would be notified. "Horrible threat!" commented Grew.

Dirksen's wife was equally tactful. She told a reporter for the *Advertiser*
that she expected to understand the Japanese quickly "because we Ger‐
mans are unusually sensitive to foreign psychology." She showed similar
finesse in her congratulations on the birth of the crown prince. "So soon
upon my arrival at my post," she told the newspaper, "I consider it a per‐
sonal honor to me."

Nazi arrogance in Japan would soon take on a darker tone. Hitler had
been busy since becoming the chancellor early in the year. In February the
Reichstag Fire Decree abolished individual rights and legal due process,
allowing the authorities to arrest and imprison anyone without cause. In
March the Enabling Act gave Hitler the power to decree laws. By April,
Jewish shops were being boycotted nationwide, and in May the trade
unions were dissolved. In July all political parties except the Nazis were
banned. Germany withdrew from the League of Nations in October after
the other world powers refused Hitler's demand for full military rearma‐
ment. Book banning, press censorship, and uniformed thuggery all got
robustly underway.

In his diary Grew noted that Hitler knew nothing about foreign affairs
and showed no interest in learning about them. He had alienated all of

Germany's former allies, and he viewed every problem through myopic nationalism. Foreign criticism, noted Grew, "confused and enraged him." Like the leaders of Japan, "he demands that Nazi Germany be left alone to work out its own destiny. He has not yet learned the extent to which that destiny, on the lines on which he is working it out, makes it increasingly difficult for him to be left alone."

A DECEPTIVE CALM

IN EARLY JANUARY 1934 the Japanese press was aflutter over an article by Admiral Suetsugu Nobumasa. In it, he accused the United States of surveying the Aleutian Islands in preparation for building air bases there, and with constructing air bases along the Chinese coast. Neither was true. He noted that Charles and Anne Morrow Lindbergh had recently made an emergency landing in Russia's Kuril Islands, just five hundred miles off Japan, allegedly because of bad weather. "It may be imagination, of course," wrote Suetsugu, who clearly had a surplus, "but it is equally possible that they reconnoitered in that part of the country." Such leapfrogging logic led Suetsugu to conclude that Japan might soon be attacked by planes based in China, Alaska, and Russia: "They would surround Japan by air raids in three directions."

He presented rumors and conspiracy theories as facts, then used this fake news to fabricate threats against Japan. Sensible people read the essay as paranoia verging on hysteria, but the jingoistic press depicted it as military wisdom.

In other military news that month, War Minister Araki was hospitalized with severe pneumonia and resigned on January 21. The army replaced him with General Hayashi Senjuro. Taciturn, with a shaved head and a handlebar moustache, Hayashi had earned his reputation for toughness in the field. Some of Grew's informants thought his appointment signaled another step toward war. Others said the old soldier disapproved of the army meddling in politics or inflaming the public and was likely to temper the military's impact on foreign relations.

That was what started to happen. Unlike Araki, Hayashi kept his mouth shut, which in itself eased tensions between Japan and the United States. A few Japanese politicians sensed the public's displeasure with the military's greed and rediscovered some courage. When the Diet opened, cabinet members traditionally appeared before the assembly to answer questions. This time, shockingly, Diet representatives dared to challenge the military. They heckled the ministers of war and the navy for interfering in politics and causing international tension.

Grew saw the militarists' stranglehold loosening. Uchida and Araki were gone, replaced by the more moderate Hayashima and the new foreign minister, Hirota Koki, who seemed less willing to kowtow to the services. A career diplomat, Hirota allied himself with Takahashi against the military's warmongering budgets and its contempt for foreign relations, which he planned to mend. He had calmed the anti-American press, and he exchanged goodwill messages with Hull.

"Stanley Hornbeck's hair must be getting whiter and whiter," wrote Grew. It had become apparent to Grew that Hornbeck opposed any offer of concession to Japan or even friendly cooperation. In April, Count Kabayama had asked Grew his opinion about sending an exhibit of fine Japanese art to America, sponsored by each country's America-Japan Society. Grew thought the gesture could be useful for political relations. "I did not consult the Department," he wrote in his diary, "being afraid that Stanley Hornbeck might disapprove, and I think that would have been unfortunate."

Grew noted that the Japanese government was encouraging these "goodwill missions" to the United States, especially by old Harvard acquaintances of Roosevelt. Hirota and others, wrote Grew, had "probably been told that the Department of State is hard boiled in its Far Eastern policy; they complain that Stanley Hornbeck is anti-Japanese and very pro-Chinese and won't talk shop with such Japanese as see him, and also that the Far Eastern Division is predominately staffed by experts on China with only one or two experts on Japan. Therefore, they assume that the only way to get results is by direct appeal to the President over the head of the Department."

Grew saw the pendulum in Japan swinging back toward sanity. "The tumult and shouting, the hysteria and fanaticism are dying down and the nation is awakening, with a throbbing financial hang-over, to the realization that Japan has more enemies than friends, and that friendship must be cultivated if Japan is to avoid disaster," he wrote in a dispatch to Hull. "Isolation may be a proud pose, but cooperation is the surer path to peace and prosperity."

But he ended the letter by noting two factors that could derange this fragile equilibrium. First, Japan's peculiar constitution put the military beyond control of the civilian government. Second: "Due to the character of the Japanese people, at once excitable and easily led, this country will remain an unstable quantity in international relations until time has worked more fundamental changes."

If Stanley Hornbeck noticed any positive signs in Japan, he disregarded them. Instead, his hair whitening at the prospect of new proposals from Hirota, Hornbeck sent Hull a thirty-eight-page memo on April 14 entitled "The Problem of Japanese-American Relations." In a cover note he modestly advised, "I feel that the memorandum should be read in its entirety."

He warned that Japan's goal was domination of the Far East, including territorial expansion. The only obstacles to Japan's plans were the economic and military muscles of the United States and Britain. American policy, Hornbeck advised, should be to "stand pat"—say little, concede nothing. Japan wanted to rewrite old agreements about trade and other matters in Asia. Instead, Hornbeck recommended "continuous, patient, thoughtful and skillful day-to-day diplomatic action." This repeated Grew's earlier advice to him and Stimson. The crucial difference was the assumption underlying the approach. Grew felt that diplomatic firmness could alter Japanese policies and actions. Hornbeck believed nothing could do that.

Three days after Hornbeck sent his memo, the spokesperson for the Foreign Office, Amo Ejii, casually dropped a diplomatic bomb. He announced that Hirota had informed Japan's minister in China that Japan intended to take charge of all important matters in the Far East, including protecting China from exploitation by other countries—that is, by countries other than Japan. The Japanese government had been increasingly upset by financial, technical, and military aid being sent to Chiang Kai-shek by Germany, Britain, and the United States. It now meant to stop such aid.

This declaration of a Monroe Doctrine for Asia, dubbed the Amo Statement, caused an uproar. China, Russia, and the Western powers objected vociferously. Hirota immediately walked the statement back, claiming that it wasn't authorized and had been mistranslated. But over the next few days the Foreign Office's vague explanations and revisions kept the pot boiling. The West needed to understand, said one revision, that Japan had a "special position" and a "mission" in China and East Asia. "We oppose, therefore, any attempt on the part of China to avail herself of the influence of any other country in order to resist Japan." Specifically this meant Japan opposed any assistance that could help China defend itself against the only aggressor in the Far East—Japan. Providing China with military equipment or expertise, continued the statement, threatened the peace in East Asia. Japan intended to preserve that peace, if necessary by force.

The furor passed. Grew saw a bright side, clarity after a storm. Whether Hirota had authorized the statement or Amo had bungled the translation was immaterial, "for the statement accurately expresses the policy which Japan would like to pursue." Japan had exposed its true ambitions. Hirota assured Grew that the Japanese government would respect the open door as well as China's territorial integrity. He added that these were also the emperor's beliefs, and that he, Hirota, would fulfill them despite threats on his life. Grew had heard the rumors about assassination. The militarists were attacking Hirota in the press for retreating from the original statement by Amo, losing face for Japan on the world stage. Yet Grew also was certain that Hirota supported the idea of Japanese hegemony over East Asia.

"It is precisely here that we find a deep-rooted antithesis," wrote Grew to a correspondent. The Amo Statement illustrated the "incompatibility between the desire of Hirota to win friends for Japan and the fundamental ambitions of the nation." Grew understood the antithesis, and he believed Hirota genuinely wanted to find a synthesis.

Seven thousand miles away, Hull and Hornbeck had a less nuanced take on the debacle. They saw simple deceit, not the stresses and complexities of antithesis. The Amo Statement, wrote Hull, "simply meant that, after pretending for a brief period to harbor peaceful intentions, Japan was in fact . . . merely settling back into her fixed notorious course of armaments, treaty breaking, and aggression." (His memoirs describe the seven years of diplomacy between 1934 and 1941 as an unbroken stretch of Japanese treachery.)

For Hornbeck the Amo Statement seemed to mark a turning point in his opinion of Grew. When Grew sent Hull his final analysis of the Amo affair, Hornbeck jotted sarcastic criticisms in the margins implying that Grew's thinking and information were flawed. Grew knew of Hornbeck's animus against Japan, but he didn't yet realize that he was included in it. At the time of the Amo Statement, Grew still hoped to win Hornbeck as an ally. Like all successful diplomats, his antennae were sensitive, and he probably intuited Hornbeck's resistance. Maybe that's why Grew began sending Hornbeck his diary in May 1934, as a means of winning him over. Grew believed his diary might someday be valuable to historians, but in the meantime, sending carbon copies of it was a practical way to share his experiences and his thinking in real time with his daughters, his brothers, and a few close friends to whom he regularly sent it.

Hornbeck didn't fit into any of these categories. Grew still began his letters to him, "Dear Mr. Hornbeck." But Grew probably hoped that a firsthand, unofficial account of the situation in Japan would temper Hornbeck's views. The diary contained political analysis and accounts of serious incidents, as well as chitchat about social events and daily life. Like Grew, the diary was open and conversational, never angry or salacious or undiplomatic, but in unfriendly hands it could cause mischief. Hornbeck eagerly accepted Grew's offer because it gave him a window into Grew's thinking—a useful view for an opponent. Hornbeck ignored anything in Grew's diary that didn't match his own assumptions and he stockpiled what conflicted with them.

Grew almost immediately had second thoughts about sharing the diary with Hornbeck. He confided to his son-in-law J. Pierrepont Moffat that he wasn't sure Hornbeck was "the type of person to whom it is advisable to send so personal a document as the diary." His instincts were correct, but he went against them in hopes of reaping a benefit for Japanese-American relations. His plan backfired.

A CABINET FALLS

IN THE SPRING of 1934 Grew and Tokyo were diverted by the American Revue Troupe, a traveling show organized by vaudeville impresario A. B. Marcus. It advertised itself as a "Saturnalia of wanton rhythm, fastest of all dancing shows, a maelstrom of lithesome sprites in divertissements of exotic and daring conception culminating in the terpsichorean piece de resistance, a garden of girlhood, lavish with a myriad of delectable rosebuds bursting into full bloom." Translation: forty-five showgirls in scanty costumes sang and danced to jazz and popular music, interspersed with comic skits. Grew described it as "probably the best foreign show of its kind ever staged in Japan," though he was glad that some of the comedians' vulgar remarks went over the heads of the Japanese. He saw it three times in five weeks.

The show packed Tokyo's biggest theater for six weeks, with two shows daily. Another six weeks were booked elsewhere in Japan, but Marcus had gotten the wrong visas and needed an extension from the Home Ministry. He was denied and told to get his troupe out of Japan on the first liner after its April 15 performance. Marcus appealed to the embassy for help, but it wasn't really an embassy matter. The expulsion was legal, and besides, it might be awkward to throw the might of the United States government behind a Saturnalia of wanton rhythm. Grew decided an intermediary would be best, so one night at the Tokyo Club he asked an influential Japanese to speak to Foreign Minister Hirota about extending the visa.

The Tokyo Club was an exclusive social organization based on the stodgy British model, with heavy leather furniture, carved ceilings, massive

Victorian chandeliers, and signs commanding SILENCE PLEASE. Its aura of awesome sanctuary was so forbidding that even the police and Kempeitai didn't dare enter. It also offered a good library and a selection of foreign newspapers and was one of the only places in Tokyo where foreigners could mingle privately with Japanese politicians and influential citizens. Grew sometimes dropped by or met people there because he could pick up intelligence from high-placed informants, or do some off-the-record lobbying for American objectives.

Grew's contact reported back that Hirota had done his best to help the troupe, but the home minister wouldn't budge. Several patriotic societies had protested that Japanese citizens shouldn't be allowed to waste time and money on frivolous foreign entertainments. Newspapers in the United States covered the deportation and quoted Ambassador Saito Hiroshi saying that the show was too nude for Japanese audiences—despite six weeks of sold-out performances.

A month after the Amo Statement, on the morning of May 16, the Japanese ambassador to America (also named Saito, but unrelated to Premier Saito) asked Hull for a secret meeting at Hull's apartment in the Carlton Hotel. "He had the air of being about to communicate a secret of tremendous import," noted Hull. Saito handed Hull a three-page document that the ambassador described as unofficial and off the record. "These are entirely my private thoughts," began the statement, but it was difficult to believe the proposals weren't Hirota's.

The statement noted that the United States suspected Japan of territorial ambitions in Asia and war plans against America, while Japan suspected the United States of "constantly [trying] to obstruct Japan from working out her national aim, which is nothing but the establishment of peace and order in the Far East." Both countries just needed to trust each other, said the statement. So why not make a joint declaration that divvied up the Pacific? The United States could have the eastern half, Japan the western half. Equal, fair, and reasonable. "All war talk will immediately be silenced," said the document, "the psychology of men will undergo a change and whatever question may arise between our two countries will become capable of easy solution."

The proposal infuriated Hull. It was the Asian Monroe Doctrine all over again, only worse, and it reinforced Hull's fundamental opinions about the Japanese as untrustworthy and shifty. Saito and Hirota were suggesting that Japan and the United States make a side deal that would require both countries to betray every principle embedded in many multilateral treaties, not to mention the nations that had signed them. The document justified selfishness under the rationale of peace, and it exposed Japan's naked objective: free rein in the Far East. Agreeing to the proposal, wrote Hull, "would have been a sort of underwriting of Japan's ambitions in China. It would have made us a kind of silent partner in Japan's aggressions." He rejected it.

No one from the State Department bothered to tell Grew about Saito's secret offer for a month. Hull finally sent a short memo on June 15 that said details would follow by the biweekly diplomatic pouch. Those finally arrived sometime in late June or early July in a long dispatch written by William Phillips, the under secretary of state and also an old friend of Grew's. Coincidentally, just before Grew finally heard about Saito's proposal, he had sent a letter to Phillips via pouch. Grew and others in the embassy had noticed that when Hull and Phillips were asked in press conferences about a current issue they didn't want to discuss, they often pleaded ignorance and claimed they hadn't heard anything from Tokyo. Grew understood the tactic.

"At the same time," he added, "we wonder here if it is necessary to give the Embassy, quite so often, a public reputation for being asleep at the switch." The tactic demoralized the hardworking staff, said Grew, who were in fact "pumping cabled information into the Department." He sent two pages of examples: quotations from Hull and Phillips blaming the embassy, followed by dispatches sent on exactly the subjects under question.

When Phillips's belated note about Saito arrived three days later, Grew was probably still smarting from the department's scapegoating of the embassy. His diary is silent about Saito's proposal and Hull's failure to communicate it. Perhaps the slight was just too galling for words.

• • •

By late June the Saito cabinet was shaky, partly because of scheming by Baron Hiranuma Kiichero, an ultranationalist who controlled the Justice Ministry and now was angling for prime minister. Hiranuma had been a force in Japanese politics for decades. He believed Japan had been led astray from its traditional spirit and values by harmful Western ideas, such as democracy, individualism, and communism. To combat these evils and return Japan to its ancient roots, he started the Kokuhonsha (National Foundation Society), a group of chauvinistic extremists whose membership grew to nearly one hundred thousand and included many prominent Japanese from business and the military. General Araki, former minister of war, was an enthusiastic member.

Prince Saionji considered Hiranuma a fascist and opposed everything about him. Baron Harada had heard a rumor that Hiranuma wanted to be named home minister, which would give him control of the secret police. The possibility of Hiranuma as home minister or prime minister alarmed Saionji. He told Harada to warn the lord keeper so the emperor would be aware of Hiranuma's machinations.

In late June word circulated that the Ministry of Justice was about to arrest some ministers in a financial scandal. Saito would have to resign. Who would replace him? At a diplomatic dinner on July 2, Grew predicted someone improbable: Admiral Okada Keisuke. The other diplomats laughed. Two days later he told some foreign correspondents, "Watch Admiral Okada." That afternoon the palace announced that the Saito cabinet had resigned and the emperor had named a new prime minister: Okada. The press and the diplomatic corps "now regard me as an oracle," wrote Grew. He had gotten the information from Count Kabayama, "which was as good as getting it from [lord keeper] Makino himself."

Harada recorded how it happened. When Saito told the lord keeper that he was resigning, the intricate gears of the selection process started turning. The grand chamberlain was required to send an imperial messenger to the genro, summoning him to Tokyo to advise the emperor on a new premier. Forty Japanese reporters had gathered near Saionji's house in a town near Mount Fuji. "There was quite a commotion," wrote Harada. The next morning Saionji and Harada took the 7:05 train to Tokyo and arrived at 9:40. They went directly to the palace. The lord keeper, the grand chamberlain, the president of the Privy Council, and four previous prime ministers awaited them. After some small talk, Saionji said, "The Emperor's wishes are that the spirit of the Constitution must be respected in every sense, and that affairs of state, whether foreign or domestic, should not be conducted unreasonably." He asked them to recommend someone who could manage that.

Saito, newly resigned, suggested Admiral Okada. Finance Minister Taka-hashi agreed. So did the others, including Saionji. The genro took this rec-ommendation to the emperor. "If it is Okada," said Hirohito, "it will ease my mind very much." And so it was done. At 2:00 P.M. Okada was sum-moned by the emperor and given the imperial command to form a cabinet.

Okada was as surprised as anyone by his selection. He had no political experience or ambitions and no influential friends. In fact these were his most appealing qualities at such a touchy moment. The selection of Okada angered the ultranationalists. Nor were they happy when Okada retained Hirota as foreign minister and Hayashi as war minister, key posts again denied to the far-rightists. Count Kabayama told Grew that the United States government itself couldn't have chosen a cabinet more sympathetic to good relations. He called it a victory for moderates. Grew agreed.

His spirits were excellent that evening at a dinner dance for about thirty people on the embassy's terrace. The guests included Japanese friends and diplomats from Italy, Spain, Poland, Brazil, Chile, Romania, Norway, and Uruguay. Around midnight, to cool off from dancing, most guests swam in the lighted pool. "After the swim," wrote Grew, "as my ordinary evening mess jacket was by then wringing wet from dancing, I donned Japanese costume and found that even the Beautiful Blue Danube could success-fully be negotiated in kimono, hakama, and sandals." The party ran past 2:00 A.M.

A week later he and Alice left Tokyo for the woods of Karuizawa. Grew drove his new "little Ford runabout," purchased because Japan's roads were often too narrow for his Cadillac, especially outside Tokyo. After being chauffeured everywhere, he was out of practice at the helm. He also had to adjust to driving in the left lane with the steering wheel on the right and the shifter to his left. He called the trip a success—only two visits into the roadside ditch, "with no harm done save for a few bruises on Alice's knee." The journey took five hours and ended with a "joyous reunion." Their daughters Lilla and Elsie and three grandchildren were waiting for them. "I will now pause to take breath," he wrote, "for what I hope may be an uninterrupted six weeks—well knowing that I shall have no such luck. It's a grand and glorious feeling anyway."

A SWASHBUCKLING TEMPER

THE SUMMER STAYED relatively quiet. Minor issues pulled Grew back to Tokyo just three times. He greeted the Harvard baseball team, touring Japan for exhibition games. Baseball was immensely popular in Japan. Boys played it everywhere, from side streets to vacant lots. Games between organized teams were highly attended, and American big leaguers were celebrities.

Harvard's first opponent was the Imperial University. A band played the national anthems of America and Japan, and then "Fair Harvard"—"accurately," commented Grew, "but alas at a fox trot pace which ruined its dignity." The opening pitch was heaved by Japan's minister of education, dressed in a black morning coat, starched collar, and cuffs. Though he had been practicing for a week, his throw almost sailed over Grew's head, but the ambassador snagged it with a southpaw mitt while wearing a crisp white suit and two-toned wingtips. Harvard's boisterous cheering section, mostly Japanese alumnae, waved school flags and sang school songs. Grew noted that the Japanese never yelled at the umpires. Harvard won 4–2.

On September 19, 1934, Grew and Alice left Tokyo for twenty-four days to visit Elsie and Cecil Lyon at the young couple's new post in Beijing. They sailed from Kobe. The crowd on the dock threw hundreds of rolls of multicolored paper streamers onto the ship, holding one end as friends and relatives on board held the other, until the liner pulled away and the tie was broken as everyone shouted "Banzai!"

That night their ship caught the edge of a typhoon that knocked them around, but they were lucky. Typhoons and earthquakes often battered Japan, but the Muroto typhoon was the most devastating in Japan's recorded history. It killed three thousand people and destroyed huge expanses of housing, factories, and rice farms, leaving two hundred thousand people homeless and shaking Japan's rickety economy.

The young new finance minister, Fujii Sanenobu, told Prime Minister Okada that the military budget had to be reduced to shift money toward recovery and aid to farmers. The nation couldn't fund the recovery and also meet the military's request for a massive budget hike without piling the national debt dangerously high. Fujii's priorities outraged the military, but he held firm. At best, he said, the military budget should stay flat while the government prioritized aid.

The debate seethed for the rest of the year. A marathon cabinet meeting was called on November 22 to settle it. When the meeting finally adjourned, Prime Minister Okada called Harada. Okada sounded elated and asked the baron to come over immediately so he could take a report to Prince Saionji. It was 3:30 A.M. The army and navy had ultimately gotten an increase of 40 million yen each—exactly what they had demanded at the start. Okada and the military ministers had hammered Fujii until he broke, overwhelmed with emotion and fatigue. The victims of Muroto were sidelined. Three days later Fujii was hospitalized, drained by the mental and physical fatigue of trying to stand up to the military.

Okada asked Takahashi, who had recommended Fujii as his successor, to return as finance minister. By then it was too late for the scrappy budget hawk to alter anything. The Diet chastised the cabinet for caving in to the military's demands but ultimately approved the increases. Once again the military had bulldozed opposition with help from the civilian government, and once again nearly half of the nation's budget would be shoveled to feed the military's voracious appetite. But money alone couldn't sate the Japanese army and navy. To achieve their dreams of empire, they also needed oil—lots and lots of oil.

British, American, Dutch, and Japanese oil companies had built extensive facilities in Japan to refine and store imported crude. From Japan's perspective, that was the problem. More than 90 percent of its oil had to be imported, most of it from the United States. This posed a terrifying threat to Japan's economy and military. If access to imported oil was cut off, Japan would be reduced to a third-rate power. To control its destiny, it needed to control the flow of oil.

In 1934 the oil issue took two forms. The Japanese government proposed a law giving it strict jurisdiction over the oil business in Japan. For instance, the law would require all oil companies to maintain a six-month supply in storage tanks, which the government could commandeer. Second, Japan established a national monopoly in Manchukuo—owned by Japanese investors—that had the sole right to sell and distribute oil in the territory formerly known as Manchuria. Essentially, Standard Oil and other Western companies with refineries and investments in Manchukuo would be put out of business.

The United States, Britain, and the Netherlands objected. Japan shrugged them off. Grew abandoned his usual patience. He saw the broken promises about free trade in Manchukuo as a power play that should be stopped before such tactics could spread throughout Japan's foreign policy. On August 20 he sent a long telegram to Hull. Grew hesitated to suggest anything that might damage relations with Japan, he wrote, but some issues couldn't be fixed by diplomatic protests alone. If Japan and Manchukuo got away with the oil monopoly, the open door policy would be rendered hollow, and other monopolies would follow, probably in China as well. He recommended a shot across Japan's bow: the threat of a joint embargo by the United States and Britain on crude oil. Even a hint of this possibility, such as announcing a review of all American oil exports, probably would be enough to frighten off the Japanese monopolists. Two weeks later the department told Grew the United States would not support the threat of an embargo.

Grew still believed that better information from Japan could change minds in Washington. A week after the department rejected the idea of an embargo, he sent a telegram summarizing the latest head-spinning statements about Manchukuo from the Japanese government. Foreign Minister Hirota contended that Japan couldn't respond to objections by the United States and Britain because it didn't have the right to interfere with the "autonomous" nation of Manchukuo. Manchukuo, on its part, contended that its promises about honoring the open door were nullified because the United States and Britain had refused to recognize its independence.

These evasions pushed the British government to lodge a formal protest about Manchukuo's monopoly and Japan's absurd denial of responsibility for the policies of its puppet state. When Grew reported this, Hull asked if he would recommend a similar formal objection. Yes, said Grew. But he added that diplomatic protests not backed by practical consequences "tend to lower American prestige in the eyes of the Japanese. They believe that American protests on almost any issue can safely be disregarded."

From late summer into winter, much of Grew's time and attention had been claimed by oil. The entire embassy staff, he wrote, had been "steeped in it." On December 21 a diplomatic pouch arrived with a bundle of memoranda about all the cross-conversations between the State Department and the other players in the oil controversy—the governments of Britain, China, the Netherlands, and the Japanese embassy, as well as internal departmental memos. The material dated back to August. Grew hadn't seen any of it.

"Why is the department so parsimonious in sending information?" he wrote to his daughter Lilla. "As I have remarked before, one can't play good baseball unless one can constantly see the pitcher."

Baseball was still on the ambassador's mind. Babe Ruth had barnstormed through Japan in November with a team of stars including Lou Gehrig and Lefty O'Doul. *Time* magazine reported that one hundred thousand Japanese had swarmed the Ginza to throw confetti at Ruth and shout, "Banzai Babe!" The team played seventeen games in twelve cities against Japan's new professional team, the Tokyo Giants, who took the field in sandals. Japanese fans waited in line overnight for tickets. All the games sold out immediately, with crowds up to fifty-five thousand. Most games were double-digit blowouts. "They're nice little ball players," said Ruth after the tour, "but they can't hit the old onion." Ruth hit .408 with thirteen homers.

Grew took in several games and played golf with Ruth and O'Doul, who gave him a set of left-handed clubs. Ruth advised Grew not to swing so hard, amusing guidance from the Sultan of Swat with his corkscrew swivel.

Afterward Grew and O'Doul had a beer while Ruth downed a "boiler-maker's highball," a blue-collar concoction unfamiliar to patrician Grew: "a big slug of whiskey followed immediately by a whole glass of beer." Like the Japanese, Grew found Ruth enormously entertaining, though a bit rough around the edges. "He is a great deal more effective ambassador than I could ever be," he wrote.

One member of the American baseball team had been added late. Moe Berg was a journeyman catcher who didn't get much playing time in Japan or anywhere else. His main responsibility seemed to be shooting film of the players with a camera provided by Movietone News, a newsreel company.

On November 29, while the rest of the team was playing an exhibition, Berg put on a kimono, bought some flowers, and went to Saint Luke's Hospital in Tokyo. He told reception he wanted to visit Elsie Grew Lyon, who had just given birth to her first child. Once past reception he threw away the flowers, and instead of visiting Elsie he rode to the hospital's roof-top piazza on the seventh floor. From there he climbed a spiral staircase to the bell tower—the same tower that paranoid Japanese had accused the hospital of erecting to permit American espionage. The tower was one of the highest vantages in the city and offered panoramic views in all directions. Berg pulled his camera from under his kimono and filmed Mount Fuji. He also shot Tokyo's shipyards, industrial plants, and military bases.

Berg was a mediocre catcher but a pretty good spy. Paranoia does sometimes link up with reality.

Rumors of assassination plots abounded that fall. In October the police investigated rightists planning to kill the lord keeper and other moderates for supporting "weak-kneed diplomacy." In November five army cadets and two officers were arrested for plotting a coup d'état, to be sparked by the assassinations of the lord keeper, Prince Saionji, Finance Minister Takahashi, and Premier Okada. The jingoistic press worked with the military to keep the public inflamed about the dangers threatening Japan.

One of these dangers concerned the treaty ratios of naval tonnage among the United States, Britain, and Japan, which were scheduled to be renegotiated soon. The current ratio was 10-10-7—that is, for every ten tons of naval vessels built by the United States and Britain, Japan could build seven tons. The ratio had been agreed to by all three nations on the theory that America and Britain, unlike Japan, needed ships in two oceans. Hirota told the Diet that in the upcoming negotiations, nothing was acceptable except parity. The navy minister agreed, as did most Japanese. They called the current ratio unfair, especially since the situation in the Far East had changed since the last renegotiation. The United States and Britain replied that if the situation had changed, the cause was Japan's aggression. The two Western powers had no intention of agreeing to parity. The naval treaty was designed to prohibit exactly what Japan was planning—a massive naval buildup that jeopardized peace.

The naval talks got underway in December. Japan's lead negotiator was Admiral Yamamoto Isoroku. Yamamoto had studied at Harvard and spent time as a naval attaché in Washington, DC. He spoke perfect English, and he respected America's spirit and vast resources. In coming years he would oppose war with the United States right up to the moment when Japan called on his military genius to mastermind the unthinkable. To no one's surprise, the Japanese refused to budge from their demand for parity. On December 29 Ambassador Saito notified Secretary Hull that Japan would withdraw from the treaty when it expired in 1936.

By the end of 1934 Grew was even more certain that diplomacy alone couldn't stop Japan's growing military ambitions or dent its intransigence about oil and other matters. On December 27 he sent Hull a seventeen-page memo about the situation in Japan. He wrote that the United States had two choices in the Far East. The first, as some American isolationists proposed, was a full diplomatic withdrawal. The benefit: no risk of war with Japan. The price: the nullification of treaties, the closure of the open door, and the abandonment of American rights, principles, and investments in the Far East.

The other choice was "to insist, and to continue to insist, not aggressively yet not the less firmly, on the maintenance of our legitimate rights and interests in this part of the world." Roosevelt and Hull had clearly chosen this latter course, and Grew agreed with it. But this was a razor's edge strategy, and it required expert diplomacy to succeed. Yet even masterful diplomacy would fail if the Japanese refused to take American warnings seriously. At the moment, Grew wrote, "there is a general tendency to characterize our diplomatic representations as bluff and to believe that they can safely be disregarded without fear of implementation." This tendency was encouraged by the comments of American pacifists and isolationists, who were always given prominent play in Japan's press. Most Japanese believed that this group represented the dominant feeling in the United States.

"It is difficult for those who do not live in Japan to appraise the present temper of the country," he wrote. If Americans visited they would hear and read everywhere that Japan's imperial destiny was to rule the Far East from Vladivostok and China to Southeast Asia and the Philippines. To depend upon treaties to restrain Japan, he continued, "would be reprehensibly somnolent." Sane leaders did exist in Japan, but the hope that moderates might wrest the country back from the militarists was misplaced. The country's moderates were impotent, and they showed no signs of reclaiming political influence.

Grew advised building up the US Navy to maintain superiority to Japan's. He believed that if America flexed some naval muscle to back up its rights and diplomacy, the Japanese military would back down. "There is a swashbuckling temper in the country," noted Grew, fostered by military propaganda. He warned that Japan's armed services were "perfectly capable of overriding the restraining control of the Government and of committing what might well amount to national hara-kiri in a mistaken conception of patriotism."

Grew would issue this same warning repeatedly, in almost identical language, right up to December 1941. But the State Department believed, until it was too late, that the Japanese military was bluffing. Grew likewise repeatedly warned the Japanese government that the United States could quickly throw off its lambskin and turn into a lion. But the Japanese, too, refused to believe him, and based their war plans on the false impression that America was too soft to fight.

PHOBIAS

THE DELIVERY TRUCK barreled out of a side street onto the main road without slowing down. Grew's Japanese chauffeur slammed on the brakes and swerved but clipped the speeding truck, which smashed into a honey cart whose fragrant contents splattered both vehicles. No one was injured. Grew felt lucky to escape with just a dented fender.

Driving in Tokyo was an adventure. "When an automobile collision is avoided by a hair's breadth," wrote Grew, "the chauffeurs never scowl at each other as they do in every other country; they grin." Drivers grinned often. "The most elementary traffic rules are constantly violated," noted Grew. Vehicles passed on the inside or made sudden turns across all lanes without signaling. Taxis stopped abruptly wherever they spotted a potential fare. Taxis were a nightmare in general because most cabbies employed an assistant whose main job was to lean on the horn, usually a blatting Klaxon.

Drivers also contended with swarms of motorcycles, often with side-cars, that darted through Tokyo's narrow, twisting streets. Bicyclists posed another major hazard, though the danger was far greater for the bikers, despite the constant chinging of their warning bells. Japanese pedestri-ans were as unpredictable as Japanese drivers, a recipe for serious injury. Oblivious walkers stepped into the street without looking. Many of them clopped along on blocky wooden geta and stood little chance of dodg-ing a speeding car. Amidst all of it, rickshaw men jogged and shouted, peddlers pushed handcarts, and farmers hunched atop oxcarts, sometimes protected by raincoats made of straw.

Face played a role even in traffic. No Japanese taxi driver would ask for directions, "although he knows he is lost and you know he is lost," wrote Grew. "He prefers to cruise around helplessly for hours . . . simply for the sake of preserving the appearance of knowledge, thereby saving face." Getting lost was inevitable. Streets didn't have names. Addresses were assigned according to the building date within the block, so number 1 could be next to number 40, with number 2 nowhere nearby. To confuse things further, buildings on the same block often had the same address. Because of face, noted Grew, a Japanese driver "will never, if he can help it, give way. He will smile genially as he goes by just in front of you, but go by he will if it is humanly possible and even if it means your jamming on your own brakes to avoid a collision."

One embassy officer lived on a narrow street where he once found two trucks stopped nose to nose. The standoff was ongoing. Both drivers were asleep, neither willing to lose face by backing up.

In early January 1935 Grew commended his staff for working hard to report and analyze the tensions in the Far East from an American standpoint. Next he wanted them to be equally thorough in trying to understand the Japanese perspective. The exercise was typical of his open-mindedness and willingness to look for new avenues of diplomacy. "However much we may disagree with Japanese policy and actions," he wrote in his diary, "we should not overlook the fact that Japan deserves a good deal of sympathy in her economic predicament."

Grew sent the embassy's long analysis to Hull on February 6. Western nations wanted to stop Japan from reaching commercial dominance in the Fast East, he wrote, yet they also imposed tariffs and other restrictions to block Japanese imports, thwarting Japan's need to expand trade. Japan believed that dominating Asian commerce was the only way to ensure the nation's economic progress and survival. "It therefore behooves us," he wrote, "to examine this expansionist urge in Japan as the reasonable and logical operation of well-nigh irrepressible forces based on the underlying principle of self-preservation . . . the driving impulse of the whole nation."

If that was true, wrote Grew, then the United States should protect its interests in the Far East by strengthening its own military, while also offering Japan economic "safety valves" for its expansionist energies and survival fears. If Western nations insisted on preserving the status quo while ignoring Japan's explosive internal pressures, Grew warned, the result would likely be war. The memo was Grew's strongest attempt yet to dent the hardening views of Hull and Hornbeck.

Empathizing with Japan's perspective was a useful diplomatic exercise but was hard to sustain amidst Japan's disregard for any perspective but its own. Oil, for instance, remained the lubricant that caused friction. Despite all objections from the West, Japan sped ahead with plans for the oil-control law and the oil monopoly in Manchukuo.

Paranoia still thrived. On the Japanese colony of Formosa (Taiwan), police arrested an American and his two travel companions, a German and a Russian—suspicious allies suggestive of an international operation. Worse, the American had graduated from the United States Naval Academy. The men claimed to be sailing a ketch around the Far East in search of lost treasure and tropical women. The Japanese police on Formosa saw through that ruse repeatedly, detaining the sailors three separate times. Grew let the Japanese authorities know that he was looking into the arrests. Despite strenuous investigations, the police released the men each time for lack of evidence but slapped them with small fines to save face.

Spy phobia also flared up elsewhere that spring. An elderly Australian woman landed in jail for her suspicious habit of walking the beach at Kagoshima. An American actress was charged with espionage after photographing a clothesline hung with drying pickles. The secret police on the isolated northern island of Hokkaido regularly raided a community of Trappist monks who farmed and made cheese: obvious subterfuges for collecting military secrets.

The pinnacle of 1935's spy phobia was the arrest and interrogation of an American tourist and mortician named Mark A. Pierce. A former state lawmaker in California, Pierce had worked against anti-Japanese bills and often helped the Japanese consul solve problems for Japanese citizens. His Japanese friends in California had inspired him to visit their ancestral country.

As his ocean liner approached Kobe, Pierce snapped photos of the coast. A Japanese detective on board seized him for espionage. Over the next several days the American sank deeper into criminality. When the police asked where he had been standing when he took his photos, Pierce said, "The port side." Clear evidence of naval training. When the police learned he was a former member of the California legislature, they brought in the Home Ministry's special Thought Police to ferret out why a high state official with naval training was taking surveillance photos of Japan's fortified coast.

The police searched his belongings and found a small notebook written in secret code: GM, GE, AT&T, and other enigmatic cryptographs followed by numbers. Pierce explained that he used the notebook to track his stocks, but the police detected an ingenious system for recording military information. Then they pounced on a lapel pin promoting Rotary International—evidence of Pierce's connection to the communist Internationale. They also found a button embossed with runic symbols linking him to a worldwide secret society—the Masonic Shriners. Pierce appeared to be an agent in contact with Japan's enemies across the globe. The investigators discovered another incriminating item in his luggage—a police shield. Pierce tried to clarify that he wasn't a policeman, just a former police commissioner in California.

So, said his interrogators, you are a naval officer, a government official, an international agent, and you once directed a police force in a major American state with a large Japanese population. Furthermore, how did he explain this document identifying him as a high-ranking naval officer, a commodore? Yes, I'm a commodore, said Pierce, at the San Pedro Yacht Club. So he *was* a commodore, said the police, as well as a government official, an international agent, and a police commander. And on top of all that, they said, we found another official document in your luggage identifying you as a colonel. Well, yes, said Pierce, a *Kentucky* Colonel—let me explain.

The police grilled Pierce for ten days, asking the same questions over and over until he hardly knew what he had said. "Their examination of suspects," wrote Grew, "takes the form of intensive questioning day after day from early in the morning until late at night." Grew told the American consul in Kobe to let the police know the US government was monitoring the case and to assist Pierce however possible. After ten days Pierce was released for lack of evidence but charged a tiny fine so the police could save face.

Pierce told his story to the *Japan Advertiser*, flinging lots of egg on lots of faces while declaring that he couldn't wait to get out of this infuriating country. American papers picked up the story. The Japanese Tourist Bureau was dismayed. The palace and the Foreign Office were embarrassed. "Thus a useful friend of Japan in America has quite unnecessarily been converted into a permanent and probably active antagonist," wrote Grew.

Japanese paranoia stemmed partly from xenophobia rooted in racism. This combination wasn't peculiar to Japan, as the Nazis were demonstrating in Germany. In the United States, the 1924 Exclusion Act remained in force, prohibiting all immigration from Asia. Some Western states didn't think the Exclusion Act went far enough, because it hadn't gotten rid of the Japanese who had immigrated before the United States slammed the door. Xenophobes argued that these immigrants were now breeding more Japanese, who were recognized, outrageously, as American citizens under the Fourteenth Amendment.

Farmers in California and Arizona were especially hostile. Even before the Exclusion Act, these states had passed Alien Land Laws severely restricting the property rights of Japanese. Then in 1934 a group of farmers in Arizona's Salt River Valley began agitating to kick Japanese farmers out, alleging that they had flooded into the region and were depriving farmland from deserving whites who were already hurting from the Depression. They also demanded that white landowners stop leasing acreage to Japanese farmers. The white farmers and their supporters held rallies and parades, blaring their message of exclusion.

In the fall of that year, night riders began a campaign of terrorism. They dynamited irrigation canals used by Japanese farmers and threw dynamite bombs at their homes and barns. The leaders of the Japanese community tried to point out that only 700 Japanese lived in the valley and most had been there for more than twenty years. Three hundred fifty of them were American citizens, and only 125 worked in agriculture, mostly for American farmers. Facts made no impression on the white farmers' racist resentments. Some local officials exploited the bigotry for political gain.

The Japanese government protested all this. Hull didn't want a few farmers to cause an international incident and pushed the governor of Arizona to fix the problem. The governor blamed the terrorism on communist agitators. Dynamite bombs continued to explode on Japanese farms through the fall of 1934. The local and state police maintained a perfect record—not a single arrest. In early February 1935 the Arizona legislature began considering a bill that would forbid Japanese immigrants from owning or leasing land. If they managed to grow anything, it could be confiscated. Any white farmer who leased to a Japanese would be abetting a crime. (Japan had similar laws against foreigners owning farmland.)

American leaders and newspapers quickly condemned the proposed law as shameful, but farmers in Arizona remained enthusiastic. Japanese papers covered the controversy as well. One fascist group, wearing uniforms featuring skulls and waving a big skull flag, protested several times at the US embassy in Tokyo. Patriotic societies began pressuring Hirota to stand up for Japan's honor. He and Japan's representatives in Washington asked the American government to do something. Arizona politicians got word that if the bill passed, millions of dollars in New Deal money might go elsewhere. Nevertheless, on March 19 the Arizona senate passed the bill. On March 21 the state house of representatives, inspired more by fears of evaporating federal aid than by racial tolerance, let the bill die. The incident left a bad taste all around.

While this was working itself out, Grew's private secretary received a letter from a young American of Japanese descent who had traveled through Tokyo on his way home after working for six months in the Far East. The letter described his experiences upon returning to the United States. In San Francisco immigration officials refused to let him back into the country despite his US passport. He showed them his American birth certificate, but they waved it aside. "Finally, after much heckling and discussion," he wrote, "they let me land after my making an affadavit to the effect that I was myself and that the passport and birth certificate were bona fide. They checked with my parents later."

Then came customs. The agents tore apart his luggage and held him for five hours. Finally released into America, he found a weird new atmosphere. In Tokyo he had been "pretty sore at the junk the Japanese press had [written] about the U.S.," he wrote, "but they were bouquets compared with the arrant nonsense and deliberate lies in the American press" about the Japanese. One story warned that alleged Japanese fishing boats were actually torpedo craft in disguise. Another story reported "thousands of Japanese troops drilling in the middle of the desert in summer." Feverish articles claimed that five hundred thousand armed Japanese soldiers were embedded in America, waiting for the war signal. Every American of Japanese descent, wrote the young man drily, had evidently been trained and equipped by Japanese army officers, "so that we will swell the ranks of the enemy and seize this country as ours." These conspiracy theories and fake news stories weren't limited to Hearst's "yellow peril" papers and tabloids, such as the *New York Daily News*. Respectable papers were running these xenophobic delusions as well.

The letter disturbed Grew. He passed it along to Hornbeck with the comment that the young man was "thoroughly American in his outlook and reactions, in short in everything but his appearance." Perhaps Grew was still thinking about his reactions to an event at the America-Japan Society two months earlier, held for several hundred "American-born Japanese" working in Tokyo. Grew seemed both pleased and surprised to realize they were "absolutely American in their attitude, manners and point of view and few of them even spoke Japanese." He was also surprised when one of them thanked the Japanese for treating them well, as if they were foreigners. "There was no question of their loyalty to the United States," noted Grew, adding that they "were homesick for 'home.'" The quotation marks were eloquent.

A PURGE, AN ORGAN, ANOTHER ASSASSINATION

GREW MAINTAINED HIS usual round of diplomatic duties that spring. Another imperial duck hunt, another imperial luncheon where the emperor dined alone above his seven hundred guests. The Grews gave and attended the usual fetes, including a dinner at the Italian embassy, flawed only by the wines. "I like Italian wines in their place," wrote Grew, "and we always have them at our own table for small informal luncheons, but a whole dinner of them, with Asti Spumante instead of champagne, is a bit too nationalistic."

In May he and Alice hosted a dinner for three hundred guests to welcome a group of women from the American Garden Club. In June Grew welcomed Mr. and Mrs. America—two life-size dolls sent on a goodwill mission to Japan by Mayor Fiorello La Guardia of New York City, in cahoots with the Japan Tourism Bureau. "A publicity stunt, pure and simple," wrote Grew. He participated because Prime Minister Okada and the mayor of Tokyo also were receiving the dolls, so declining would be offensive. He was also happy to promote travel by Americans to Japan, anything to increase mutual understanding. Besides, the silliness amused him. As Mrs. America entered the embassy residence, her arm fell off. But once this break with protocol was repaired, photographers clicked as Grew and Alice shook the dolls' hands without further incident.

Off duty, the Grews often diverted themselves with new American movies, a bit of home. They preferred private showings at the Tokyo headquarters of the film companies, before the Japanese censors made their prudish cuts—no kissing allowed. Radio broadcasts of music from Europe cheered them, though sometimes the sound faded or crackled with so much static, they turned it off. They entertained several diverting guests: Noël Coward, Douglas Fairbanks, Gene Tunney. At the poker table they continued to empty opponents' pockets. Grew played golf as often as possible, as much to relieve stress as for pleasure. "Those hours on the links," he wrote, "twice a week or so, are absolutely necessary if one is to keep one's balance and one's nerves in control. They are the best antidote I know to avoid getting swamped in the pessimism, discouragement and the big and petty irritations which tend increasingly to beset us."

After three years without a break, he had asked the State Department for a furlough. He and Alice both needed it. Grew's characteristic energy and high spirits were flagging, mostly because of nagging respiratory complaints caused by Tokyo's bad air and damp. Alice contracted conjunctivitis, followed by severe bronchitis that kept her in bed for a few weeks that spring. "The time has come for a change," wrote Grew in April, "and I hanker for July 19 when we now hope to sail by the *President Hoover*. The weather is vile too; rain almost daily."

Count Kabayama told Grew that the volatile situation in North China would soon calm down, because Prime Minister Okada and War Minister Hayashi were determined to control the military there. The strongest political influences at the moment were moderates, he said, including the old guard of Prince Saionji, Lord Keeper Makino Nobuaki, and the emperor himself.

Harada's diary contradicted Kabayama's rosy view. Hirota, Okada, Hayashi, Saionji, and the emperor were all worried that the army might do something stupid in North China. But Okada also blamed the tension on China for refusing to recognize the puppet government of the stolen territory of Manchukuo. Harada questioned that line of thought. How would Japan react if Russia took Hokkaido, Japan's northernmost island, then insisted that Japan recognize it as a foreign territory? The demand was absurd.

Okada was deeply concerned that extremists were trying to topple three moderate ministers—Hayashi, Hirota, and Takahashi—and therefore his cabinet, for blocking the ultranationalists' glorious imperial plans in China. One major obstacle was General Masaki Jinsaburo, inspector general of military training. This made him the third-most powerful man in the army, behind the war minister and the chief of the army general staff. Masaki was a close ally of General Araki, the fire-breathing former war minister, and was esteemed by ultra-rightist young officers. Masaki and his young followers believed that the army answered only to the emperor and was beyond the authority of civil government. This attitude was incompatible with civilian oversight or peace. It also was out of step with the goals of Okada, Hayashi, and Hirota, as well as the emperor.

To regain control over the army's hotheads, Hayashi decided to divide and conquer. He ordered transfers to break up pockets of radical young officers, placing them on reserve or assigning them to minor posts. Masaki frustrated Hayashi by blocking the transfers. To reform the army, Masaki had to be forced out, but only the emperor had the power to remove the army's top three officers. That left Hayashi with one last risky move—so risky, it could bring down the cabinet. Hayashi outlined his plan to Prime Minister Okada. Okada approved the ploy for ousting Masaki, whom he called "the evil root of all this mess." (Harada labeled Masaki "this gangrenous sore of the Army.")

Hayashi next requested an audience with Hirohito. As Hayashi made his case, the emperor nodded vigorously. He granted Hayashi an imperial sanction to appoint a new inspector general. Masaki didn't dare defy a direct imperial authorization and was forced to resign. He was replaced by a moderate, General Watanabe Jotaro, who instantly joined the right wing's assassination list. For the moment, a few people, including the emperor, had found the courage to defy the army's radical wing.

As this was unfolding, a right-wing member of the House of Peers, the upper house of the Diet, stood and asked that the academic tomes of Japan's most distinguished constitutional scholar, Professor Minobe Tatsukichi, be banned as insulting to the emperor. At first Minobe ridiculed the criticism, but the extremists in the patriotic societies and the military, including Masaki, turned the issue into a conflagration that they hoped would singe if not incinerate Okada's cabinet.

Minobe's offense was his "emperor organ theory," first proposed in 1912 without controversy. The theory explained the Japanese constitution by using the familiar metaphor of the body politic. The nation was the body. The emperor, as the nation's head, was the body's principal organ, neither separate from the state nor superior to it. Minobe also wrote that the Diet, another essential national organ, needed to control the constitutional power given to the emperor over the military. Minobe's sudden critics accused him of lowering the emperor from the clouds into the body politic, implying that he was imperfect and fallible rather than divine. The extremists also were incensed by Minobe's suggestion that the Diet could limit the imperial emperor's absolute military power.

At first most Japanese ignored all this as academic bickering. Prime Minister Okada commented that he had tried to read the books but couldn't understand them. But the extremists, with Masaki in the forefront, wouldn't let the issue die. They wanted Minobe arrested and his books forbidden. The other side stayed silent, afraid to draw fire from the right. Many members of the House of Peers were Minobe's former students. Not one of them defended him. Nor did anyone in the cabinet or any major newspaper.

Ultranationalist indignation gradually took over the press. Public opinion shifted against the professor. Furious extremists in the army were demanding that Hayashi issue a statement condemning Minobe, but the war minister stayed silent, perhaps because his plan to oust Masaki would soon cause enough uproar. Okada asked Minobe to resign from the House of Peers. When he refused, Okada banned some of his books. That wasn't enough for the frothing rightists. The minister of justice told Baron Harada on June 4 that he had been willing to drop the charges if Minobe resigned, but Minobe was being stubborn, so extremist pressure might force him to indict based on Minobe's "defilement of the dignity of the Imperial Household." Okada agreed that charges now seemed necessary. Saionji told Harada that if the rightists succeeded in crushing Minobe, other victims would surely follow.

On July 18, the day before he left on furlough, Grew visited Hirota and asked if the foreign minister had any message for Roosevelt and Hull.

Remind them, said Hirota, that good relations with the United States remained the cornerstone of his policy. After two difficult years Hirota felt those relations were now "distinctly good," and he saw no big problems ahead. Grew left for home certain that things were moving in the right direction. After forgoing a break for three years, he had asked for and received extra time off. He would be away for five months.

About a month after he sailed, a Japanese lieutenant colonel named Aizawa Sabura walked into the War Office building, past two old door-keepers smoking cigarettes near their charcoal brazier. They couldn't imagine any reason to stop an officer in uniform. Inside, Aizawa asked directions to the office of Lieutenant General Nagata Tetsuzan, chief of the Military Affairs Bureau.

Aizawa found Nagata sitting at a table listening to a report about extremist army officers. Aizawa drew his sword. As Nagata stood and turned, Aizawa lunged, piercing Nagata's back. When Nagata slumped over the table, Aizawa slashed him in the head and neck, killing him.

Nagata had been dedicated to restoring discipline in the army and suppressing rebellious officers. War Minister Hayashi had put him in charge of the recent transfers of fanatical officers as part of the Masaki purge. Aizawa, a member of the Masaki/Araki faction, had been ordered to leave his regiment for a training school in Formosa. The message was clear: exile. The murder was Aizawa's revenge for himself, the ultranationalists, and Masaki, who may have inflamed him into killing Nagata.

The assassination horrified the public and part of the military. As a distraction, Masaki, Araki, and their followers began a loud campaign against the war minister, using outrage about the emperor organ theory as accelerant. In late August, three weeks after Nagata's assassination, Hayashi heard that a thousand young officers were plotting mayhem. He told Prime Minister Okada that to deflate the possibility of a serious insurrection he needed to resign. He did so on September 4.

The ultranationalists had punished the reformers by killing Nagata and chasing out Hayashi. Next they turned to larger prey—the cabinet itself. The chief of the Metropolitan Police confirmed to Harada that Masaki, Araki, and Hiranuma were plotting to overthrow the cabinet. Some factions in the army were paying reservists to travel from rural areas to

Tokyo, then filling them with food, sake, and angry propaganda against the government. It was all part of a plot by the rightists, noted Harada, "to chase out the Genro, the senior statesmen, and others close to the Emperor by means of the Emperor Organ theory, and to take over themselves, with Hiranuma as their leader."

The moderate faction that had seemed to be strengthening before Grew left was now besieged and endangered. Lord Keeper Makino told Harada to ask Saionji to start thinking about a new cabinet. Makino also wondered if Hiranuma should be promoted from vice president to president of the Privy Council to quiet the ultranationalists. "I am absolutely against the promotion of Hiranuma," said Saionji. "In any case, we must make that sort of a man powerless as soon as possible for the good of the world."

Meanwhile the Kwantung Army in North China once again started causing alarm. Hirota was still attempting to open relations with China, but the prospect of negotiations threatened the Kwantung Army's plans for Chinese submission. Hirota heard that some factions were scheming to set up an autonomous government in North China along the lines of Manchukuo. Nevertheless, in mid-December Hirota told Harada that relations with China had greatly improved despite the huffing of the army. "It is rather a nuisance to have our foreign policy criticized," said Hirota, "since we know that the Army is merely bluffing and has no intention of acting violently." That proved to be a spectacular misjudgment.

Four days later, on December 16, the Grews landed in Yokohama and were welcomed back by a crowd of embassy staff and press. Five months away had reinvigorated Grew. In Washington he had had three long conversations with Roosevelt, who greeted him affectionately and radiated "complete optimism, cheerfulness, and energy." Roosevelt hadn't written often, he told Grew, because he had no complaints. He impressed Grew with his detailed understanding of the Tokyo mission. Grew met Hull for the first time and had useful sessions with Hornbeck and others from the department.

He also relaxed. In Yankee Stadium he watched Joe Louis pummel Max Baer. He unwound in New England for weeks, staying with friends and relatives in Boston, the North Shore of Massachusetts, Newport, Rhode

Island, and the Perry family compound in Hancock, New Hampshire. Alice's health worried him. She was still worn out from Japan and had lost control of her right hand and leg. Grew told a friend at the State Department that if she didn't improve with rest, he might have to resign.

The Grews had arranged their trip to be with their daughter Anita when she gave birth to their newest grandchild in Paris, where Anita's husband was secretary to the ambassador. Grew took the opportunity to order twelve cases of champagne shipped to Tokyo. He also tried another treatment from an ear specialist, as he had many times before. "Of course this deafness is a great handicap to me in my profession," he wrote to the doctor, "and I shall be eternally grateful if you can succeed in improving my hearing in even a small degree."

He took his first airplane flight, Paris to London—one hundred miles per hour, exhilarating. In England he stayed with his cousin Jane and her husband, J. P. Morgan Jr. Grew recorded that he and Morgan talked about everything, including politics, but they probably avoided certain subjects. Morgan's bank, through partner Thomas Lamont, had helped finance the rise of Mussolini and had made excuses when another client, Japan, invaded Manchuria. Morgan hated Roosevelt, whose push to investigate "banksters" had caused Morgan to be hauled in front of a Senate committee in 1933.

The Grews reached Italy in November, a month after Mussolini invaded Ethiopia, a further demonstration of the League of Nations' impotence. The US ambassador there told Grew that speaking English in the street had become hazardous. In Venice the Grews visited their daughter Edith's grave. As they chatted on the train to Genoa, a passenger glared at them for talking in English.

They went through the Suez Canal and across the Indian Ocean to the South China Sea. Singapore, Manila, Hong Kong. For Grew the journey revived memories of his youthful rambles. They reunited with daughter Elsie; her husband, Cecil; and granddaughter Alice in Shanghai (Cecil was posted to Beijing). In a hotel ballroom, Grew enjoyed "a few good waltzes with Elsie." Four days later, on December 16, they docked at Yokohama. "A grand voyage, ended all too soon," wrote Grew that day. "But we are glad enough to be home again. And now—on with the dance once more."

• • •

Grew jumped back in with gusto, making calls and receiving streams of visitors. In an upbeat speech at the America-Japan Society he told his audience that he had found the United States filled with optimism and energy, like President Roosevelt, who was deeply familiar with Japanese issues. He was confident of finding a way to keep Japanese-American relations on "an even keel with a mutual and common sense comprehension and appreciation of both sides of the picture."

He was less cheery in a dispatch at the end of 1935 that summarized Japan's side of the picture. He described an "intensification of the urge toward nationalism" and "the growing belief that Western civilization has nothing further to offer Japan." As examples he cited the fanatical outburst about the emperor organ theory and the recent creation of an official government news agency, Domei, to control all incoming foreign news "so that only the approved nationalistic point of view shall be presented." A continuing irritant was oil and the government's threat to seize foreign supplies of it. In North China the army appeared to be obeying the emperor's command to stay north of the Great Wall, for the moment.

The day after he returned to Japan, Grew placed a large liquor order— fifteen cases of scotch, gin, sherry, and port. He seemed to be anticipating the need for a stiff drink in 1936. Once again he was prescient.

In late December thirty young army officers met at a restaurant in Tokyo to launch a plot that would end in multiple murders and shake the Japanese government.

INSURRECTION

IN FEBRUARY 1936 the papers were feasting on the trial of Aizawa Saburo, who had hacked General Nagata to death in his office the previous
year. Aizawa's defense took the usual line: he was a patriot whose sword
struck blows for the glory of his emperor and against the sinister politicians, palace advisors, greedy capitalists, and military officers corrupting
the spirit of Japan. His lawyer warned that if his client was punished,
other angry young Aizawas would rise up and follow his example, because
such military patriots answered to no authority except the emperor. Never
mind that the emperor had appointed or approved all of Aizawa's targets:
Nagata, the palace advisors, the cabinet, the military leaders. Aizawa and
officers like him defied the authority they claimed to honor.

The army was determined to make an example of him and regain control over the young officers in the Araki/Masaki faction. But the trial was
interrupted by the worst explosion of ultranationalist violence since Grew's
arrival in Japan.

It had been a bitter winter. On February 4 the most severe blizzard in fifty
years dropped nearly a foot of snow on Tokyo. Temperatures plummeted.
Snow mounds turned to ice, further narrowing Tokyo's streets. The electricity snapped off, leaving the city in the dark. On some nights residents
heard the muffled steps of troops marching by, training in the cold before
their transfer to Manchukuo. Gunfire near dawn was common because
of the drill grounds all around the city.

On February 25 dark clouds sagged over Tokyo, threatening more snow. The Grews were hosting a dinner that evening to honor the new lord keeper of the privy seal, Viscount Saito, the former prime minister. The guest list of thirty-six covered the Grews' customary mix—several Americans, sixteen Japanese, and people from the missions of Italy, Spain, Romania, and the Netherlands. To entertain Saito after dinner Grew selected *Naughty Marietta*, a movie musical with Jeanette MacDonald and Nelson Eddy. The seventy-seven-year-old count tended to nod off after dinner, so Grew put him in a comfortable armchair. One night Grew had watched him fall asleep and drop his cigar. But Saito had never seen a talkie and was enthralled. He and his wife even stayed for the light supper afterward and didn't leave until 11:30 P.M. When Grew saw them out, snow had started falling.

It was still snowing when the Grews' phone rang early the next morning with urgent news. The ambassador and his staff began collecting fragments of information to telegraph to the State Department. "The military took partial possession of the Government and city early this morning," said the first dispatch at 10:00 A.M., "and it is reported have assassinated several prominent men." Grew telegraphed that the revolt appeared to be meticulously planned.

It was. A coordinated assault led by ultranationalist officers from the Araki/Masaki faction had begun around 5:00 A.M. Higher-ups in the army such as Masaki not only knew about the plot but incited it. The extremist officers and their troops had been issued orders for transfer to Manchukuo as part of the purge. When the officers roused their men in the snowy dark of February 26, the soldiers didn't yet know that this time their maneuvers weren't an exercise but a revolt. The soldiers, trained for absolute loyalty, obeyed their commanders. The falling snow was taken as an omen. In one of Japan's most famous stories, forty-seven samurai *ronin* had avenged a dishonored master by cutting off the offender's head and then committing mass hara-kiri, all during a snowstorm.

Assassination squads made simultaneous attacks before dawn. At 5:30 A.M. Lord Keeper Saito's wife heard a commotion and opened their bedroom door to find the hallway filled with soldiers. She tried to protect her husband and was shot in the arm. As Saito rose from bed, soldiers opened up with machine guns, perforating him with more than three dozen bullets. The murderers burned incense next to the body.

Another squad broke down the gate at the home of Takahashi, the eighty-two-year-old finance minister hated for his opposition to swollen military budgets. The soldiers shot him several times, then hacked him to death with swords. They lit candles next to his body. General Watanabe, on the kill list because he had replaced Masaki as inspector general of military education, was machine-gunned in his home in front of his wife and daughter. His murderers burned incense next to his body. Grand Chamberlain Suzuki's wife shouted at the killers who had invaded her home, but their gunfire hit her husband in the head, chest, and groin. As he lay in his blood, the assassins burned incense and left him to die. The papers reported his death, but Suzuki survived.

Another group of assassins barged into the official residence of Prime Minister Okada, where Inukai had been murdered four years earlier. Okada's brother-in-law, a retired colonel, heard the ruckus and went to protect the prime minister, who was guarded by two policemen. They hid Okada in a bathroom and went back out. Rebel soldiers gunned them down. An officer held a framed photo of Okada next to the dead colonel's face and misidentified the corpse as the prime minister, shouting "Banzai!" Later that day the papers reported Okada's death. He escaped the house two days later disguised as a mourning servant who was following the prime minister's coffin—his own coffin, filled with his brother-in-law's body—past the soldiers and out of the house. He shocked the emperor by turning up at the palace.

Two squads were assigned to kill people outside of Tokyo. The squad assigned to kill Saionji evidently decided they couldn't murder the old genro and never left Tokyo. The other squad went to Yugawara, the hot springs town where former lord keeper Makino was resting in an inn. His police guard shot a couple of soldiers and was shot in turn. The assassins set fire to the inn to flush Makino out. Meanwhile a nurse and Makino's granddaughter were hustling the old man out the back door and up a steep hill. The rebels spotted them and fired, but the women draped their kimonos over Makino, and the soldiers evidently couldn't bring themselves to shoot.

Before Grew got out of bed that morning, almost fifteen hundred mutineers had taken over the War Office, the army general staff office, the new unfinished Diet building, the Metropolitan Police headquarters, and a hotel. The rebels turned tablecloths into banners with slogans such as LOYALTY TO THE EMPEROR AND DEATH TO HIS ENEMIES. Grew and his staff could observe it all from his hilltop residence. Across the street from the rebels, the regular army hurriedly placed barricades and barbed wire around the Imperial Palace. Lines of soldiers stood with fixed bayonets. The surviving members of the cabinet took refuge in the palace, fairly certain the rebels wouldn't cross the imperial moat. Soldiers on both sides built sandbag breastworks, slowly covered by snow until they resembled children's winter forts.

It was a peculiarly Japanese coup d'état. After the initial assassinations no more shots were fired, nor did the rebels attempt to take any more territory. Life in the city carried on. Streetcars ran, stores and offices opened, children walked to school. Commuters entering Tokyo wondered why some roads were blocked, and why crowds of soldiers were milling about.

The rebels issued a manifesto condemning the "Elder Statesmen, financial magnates, government officials, and political parties" for leading Japan and the emperor into error. "Therefore it is our duty to take proper steps to safeguard our fatherland by killing those responsible." The rebels had done their patriotic duty. Now they wanted to talk about a new direction for Japan. They demanded the release of the assassin Aizawa and the formation of a new cabinet with Araki, Masaki, or Hiranuma as prime minister. The authorities ignored the demands but seemed stymied about how to proceed. They were uncertain whether loyal troops would fire on their rebel brothers.

On the coup's second day, tension mounted and the city began to tighten down. Several times a day sirens announced extra editions from Tokyo's five main newspapers, hawked by newsboys who shouted and shook bells. But the government had imposed a blackout on most stories, so trustworthy information was scarce.

"I have just returned from a harrowing experience," wrote Grew that day. He had paid a sympathy call at the Saito home. The murdered lord keeper lay on the floor, covered with a sheet. Grew knelt and burned some incense. Viscountess Saito appeared and knelt beside him, her wounded arm in a sling.

At 1:00 P.M. Grew sent an update to Hull. No forceful measures were anticipated against the rebels, he wrote, because the authorities didn't want civilian casualties or destruction of downtown Tokyo, and they especially didn't want to endanger the emperor. Nor did they want to turn the rebels into martyrs. More troops poured into the city, and tanks were positioned near the occupied area. Tokyo Bay filled with cruisers and destroyers capable of shelling the rebel quarter. The next morning, February 28, an army officer called at the embassy to advise all personnel to evacuate because the compound was in the firing zone. Grew declined, certain the embassy's basement would keep everyone safe if necessary.

Emperor Hirohito was angry. He bluntly called the incident a mutiny by "rebels." The grand chamberlain cautioned him: "It would be regrettable if the word 'rebel' should cause ill feelings among the troops."

"Any soldier who moves Imperial troops without my order is not my soldier," retorted Hirohito, "no matter what excuse he may have." He commanded the war minister to restore order immediately. The generals used their best weapon, a command issued in the emperor's name: disperse by eight o'clock tomorrow morning or prepare to die. A few rebels surrendered, but most stayed put. People could hear them singing for much of the afternoon and night, possibly because they were draining the liquor in the occupied Sanno Hotel. Americans holed up in the embassy heard tanks racketing through the streets all night long.

The predawn hours of February 29 were windy and bitter cold. The dark sky again filled with falling whiteness, but this time it was thousands of leaflets dropped by planes into the rebel zone. The leaflets addressed the enlisted men. You have been misled and will be forgiven, said the message, but now you must obey the emperor's command to return to your barracks. "Otherwise you will be branded as traitors, and your fathers, brothers, mothers, and sisters will be weeping." Loudspeakers and the radio station aimed the same message at the rebel lines. In Japan the supreme loyalties were to the emperor and to family honor. This appeal was the generals' last attempt to avoid bloodshed. Announcements told the public to stay away from the occupied zone. "You will hear the sound of gunfire today," they warned, "but remain calm."

The first hours of daylight were taut with the expectation of violence. Overnight, Japanese troops had built up the barricades around the American embassy and were posted in machine-gun nests, with gas masks strapped to their faces. Airplanes crisscrossed the skies. The streets were empty. But then, watching from his hill, Grew saw a trickle of soldiers begin crossing the barricades with their rifles held before them. The stream widened and flowed for several hours. Trucks hauled the rebel soldiers away. By 1:00 P.M. almost all of the insurgents had surrendered. At 2:00 P.M. the homemade flag over the prime minister's residence came down. Only the rebel officers remained inside.

For the next one hundred minutes the generals made no move to blast them out. Everyone understood why. The officers were being given the opportunity to redress their dishonor by committing hara-kiri. Only one officer chose that way out. (Another did so later.) The others surrendered, expecting a trial like Aizawa's, where they could pontificate about the purity of their motives and agenda. The coup ended without another shot. The government announced that normal life would resume at 4:10 P.M.

Of the nearly 1,500 officers, soldiers, and civilians involved, only 124 were charged. Of those, 77 were found guilty. Most were let go or received minor sentences. Masaki, clearly complicit, was indicted, but powerful allies derailed a conviction. The surviving ringleaders—19 officers and several civilians—didn't get their wish for a grandstanding public trial. The army did everything in secret. The leaders were sentenced to death, put against a prison wall, and shot. So was Aizawa. When the news broke, public approval was nearly unanimous.

Grew hoped for a revulsion against the military. For a fleeting moment it seemed possible that the insurrection might shock Japan into abandoning violent ultranationalism. That wasn't what happened.

A LULL

AFTER THE INSURRECTION everyone in Japan wanted to recover equilibrium. Diplomatic traditions resumed. A telegram arrived from the State Department ordering one of the third secretaries to report to the godforsaken post of Baghdad. He took his distress to Counselor Neville, who was having a bad morning of his own, having survived salt in his orange juice and pepper in his coffee. He shouted that the third secretary should check the date and use his head. Pranks were protocol on April 1.

Grew took comfort in his usual diversions. "Golf followed by poker makes the perfect day," he wrote on March 8, "and I might add that the ideal climax is reached when one can spend the evening reading such a vivid detective story as 'Headed for a Hearse.'" His new reading also included Sinclair Lewis's 1935 novel *It Can't Happen Here*, about a fascistic demagogue who gets elected president on a platform of fear, resentment, nationalism, and a promise to make America great again. "A rather horrible story which makes one stop to think," wrote Grew.

He also kept up with everything written about Japan, often commenting on books and articles in his diary. In April 1936 he was intrigued by a piece in *Foreign Affairs* magazine by Barbara Wertheim (whose married name would soon be Tuchman), recently returned from a year in Japan. He nodded at most of Wertheim's observations: the more other nations disapproved of Japan, she wrote, the more self-righteous it became. This self-righteousness fed a belief among Japanese that other nations purposefully misunderstood them and were "insincere" in their dealings. Japan was always the victim, wrote Wertheim, never the victimizer.

These attitudes and even the vocabulary were familiar to Grew. He also agreed with Wertheim that the effect, or perhaps the purpose, of this cluster of self-justifications was the peculiar Japanese ability to deny facts and reality, including that it had invaded and occupied Manchuria. Wertheim's comments on this trait so completely matched Grew's own experience that he transcribed them into this diary:

> In real bewilderment the foreigner asks himself what purpose the Japanese believe could be served by such obvious pretense. The only answer is that to the Japanese it is not a pretense. . . . A fact as such means little to a Japanese; should he be forced to face certain unacceptable facts, he will cut them dead, just as we might cut an unwelcome acquaintance on the street.
>
> Responsible for this attitude is the conception of "face." Everyone has heard of the importance of face to the Oriental, but unless one has lived in the Orient one cannot realize just how vital a part it plays, how it enters into every word, thought, and act of existence. The appearance put upon an act, and not the act itself, gives or causes loss of face.

The rebellion unnerved the Japanese government, military, and public. Killing for patriotic reasons might be tolerable, even praiseworthy, but wholesale murder and revolution threatened Japan's core. Officials knew something had to change, or at least appear to, to restore control and the public's trust. In Japan that usually meant appointing a new cabinet. The emperor asked Saionji to recommend a prime minister to replace Okada. The ultranationalists were still pushing for Araki or Hiranuma, which suggested that the revolt hadn't abashed them. Saionji couldn't stomach either man. He considered the situation so dire that he decided it was time to bring forward his protégé, Prince Konoye Fumimaro.

Everyone knew Konoye. He had accompanied Saionji to the peace conference in Versailles and had served in the House of Peers. Forty-four years old, slender and tall for a Japanese at nearly six feet, he came from one of Japan's most noble families. Great things were expected of him, and the premiership was considered inevitable. But the weight of expectations often seemed to buckle Konoye. He sometimes disappeared from view for weeks with nervous ailments, especially at moments of crisis, like now.

When Saionji told him that Japan needed him to become premier, Konoye tried to beg off, but Saionji insisted. Konoye received an imperial summons, and Hirohito ordered him to form a new cabinet. After leaving the emperor, Konoye saw Baron Harada and Marquis Kido Koichi, former secretary to the lord keeper. "I am in trouble," said Konoye. "Please let me meet Prince Saionji again." Konoye begged Saionji to get him out of the imperial command. The genro, dismayed and embarrassed, returned to the emperor and withdrew Konoye's name. "Never before have I been placed in such an awkward position as this," said Saionji.

The second choice was the foreign minister, Hirota, a moderate who intended to continue his efforts to improve foreign relations. On March 9 the emperor gave Hirota three directives: abide by the constitution; be peaceful in international relations; be frugal and measured in domestic policies. But the military had already established that the emperor's directives must sometimes be disobeyed for his own glory.

In April Hirota chose Arita Hachiro, another moderate, as his foreign minister. Grew was pleased. "With Hirota and Arita in charge of policy," wrote Grew, "I do not look for any running amuck." The question was whether the military would allow them to control foreign policy.

The generals were briefly chastened by the February 26 insurrection. It forced them to see that extremist young officers threatened the army's internal order. The mild tactics previously used to restrain the hotheads, such as transfers and lenience for insubordination, had encouraged a revolt instead of prevented one. The generals also understood that reforms were necessary to restore the public's confidence in the army. Without the people's fervent support, the army couldn't hope to sustain its massive budgets and imperial ambitions.

The moment was evanescent. Because the army handled the rebellion peacefully and punished the ringleaders swiftly, and because the public was terrified of another military revolt, the army's prestige among the public was ultimately burnished instead of tarnished. Its control over government tightened. In his memoirs Admiral Okada, the former prime minister, wrote that the February 26 incident may have been Japan's best opportunity to wrest the government back from the military. "But the fear of seeing bloodshed again was stronger than confronting the Army," he wrote. "As a result, the military's clout became even stronger."

The fear of more bloodshed was legitimate. The Kempeitai detected new plots almost immediately among young officers in both the army and navy. "Even very highly placed persons," wrote Grew, "think that further revolts in the Army are not only possible but probable."

In this atmosphere the Grews were reluctant to resume normal diplomatic dinners out of respect for the anxiety felt by the Japanese. Grew noted that most of the diplomatic corps had no such compunction, nor did they change their habit of excluding Japanese from their dinners. Attending these soirees was part of Grew's job, and they were a source of news and gossip. He also relished human idiosyncrasy, and his fellow diplomats offered a rich trove. For instance, the French counsel who emphasized his distant relation to Napoleon "by wearing his hair low across his forehead and standing with one hand inside his lapel." Or the Italian ambassador, formerly glum, now transformed by Italy's mighty victory over Ethiopia into a swaggering mini-Duce, conqueror of all before him. At an embassy dinner he energetically embosomed the wife of the Romanian chargé d'affaires. Grew commented that Italy evidently wasn't satisfied with Ethiopia but must now have Romania.

Instead of large formal dinners, the Grews held smaller affairs with a few diplomats and Japanese friends. On April 3 the guest list consisted of ten Westerners and nine Japanese, including Prince Konoye. The Japanese appreciated the Grews' sensitivity to the country's fraught moment. "We are gratified that the Japanese seem to loosen up and enjoy themselves informally at our Embassy as they do at no other," wrote Grew. "Even the Japanese ladies, whom Alice got working at a jig-saw puzzle after dinner, thawed out as if they really felt at home." Two nights later the Grews were invited with several Japanese to a small dinner at Konoye's house. Afterward they conversed, perhaps about Konoye's son, a member of the golf team at Princeton, while a well-known Japanese artist painted for their entertainment. Prominent Japanese often invited the Grews into their homes, an atypical gesture toward Westerners that reflected mutual friendship.

But the mood in Japan remained tense and solemn, as if the nation was holding its breath. Grew noticed that his Japanese friends "seem to have lost all of their usual gaiety and humor; they are visibly depressed and thoughtful." Grew felt it himself. At a Danish luncheon he flirted with a Viennese woman, murmuring to her in German, "Cozy Vienna, city of my dreams" a line from a popular song—then wrote, "Why am I writing such rot? There seems to be nothing else to fill up the diary with these days—and yet how well I know that this is merely the calm before the storm; periods of restfulness never last long in Tokyo."

The stress was personal as well as political. Alice couldn't seem to recover her health. Laryngitis, exhaustion, bronchial maladies, vertigo. By early May, Grew was alarmed enough to write Under Secretary of State William Phillips and ask for another short leave. He hadn't expected a furlough in 1936, he wrote, but if Alice's health worsened into a physical breakdown, he would have to resign and take her home. The department didn't want to lose him in Tokyo and granted his request. Shortly afterward he was thrilled by an invitation to be a marshal of dignitaries at Harvard's tercentenary celebration in September. The Grews made plans to leave Japan in late August.

At the end of April Grew wrote a long memo to Hull describing Japan's "two schools of thought" about finding raw materials and new economic markets. The "continental" school, led by the army, wanted to expand Japan's reach from Manchuria to the west and north, into the continent of Asia—China, Mongolia, Russian Siberia. The "blue water" school, led by the navy, envisioned expansion to the south—the Dutch East Indies, Southeast Asia, and the Philippines. Both schools purported to have peaceful intentions motivated by a desire to continue Japan's economic growth. Grew didn't know which school would win but was certain Japan would expand somewhere. In a confidential memo entitled "The Importance of Naval Preparedness in Connection with Future Developments in the Far East," he warned that "the present lull" in Japanese expansionism was temporary. "Nothing is with certainty predictable in the Far East except that the inherent urge toward Japanese expansion is uncontrollable and will continue," he wrote. Sooner or later, he added, American interests would be "injured by the juggernaut."

Meanwhile, storm clouds rolled in from several directions. Japanese and Soviet troops clashed on the border between Russia and Manchukuo. In North China, Japanese and Koreans smuggled oil, gas, kerosene, and other goods blatantly and rampantly. If a Chinese customs official arrested a Japanese for smuggling, the Japanese authorities demanded an apology. The smuggling was so vast in scale, it was disrupting foreign trade and robbing China of critical revenues. The ambassadors to China from the United States and Britain finally protested to the Japanese government. Arita claimed to be concerned but added that he couldn't do anything now because he would appear to be caving in to foreign pressure and thus lose face. The circular rationalization was maddening.

The source of this storm cloud was the Kwantung Army, which protected the smugglers. Despite the momentary quiet, the army was unpredictable. War Minister Terauchi Hisaichi told Foreign Minister Arita he was determined to bring the Kwantung Army under central control and to stop its "political scheming in North China" so the Foreign Office could handle foreign policy there. "However," Arita told Baron Harada, "it seems to me that the War Minister has not yet grasped the real situation." Arita had recently returned from China and had witnessed the Kwantung Army's machinations. "At present the Foreign Minister cannot touch the matter at all," said Arita to Harada. "In short," he continued, "whether small or large, the Army is handling all negotiations with foreign nations in North China."

Harada heard similar worries about the Kwantung Army from Yuasa Kurahei, who had replaced the murdered Saito as lord keeper of the privy seal. Yuasa knew that Hirota expected Terauchi to purge the army's extremists in Japan and clean up the Kwantung Army. "I think the Prime Minister is somewhat too optimsitic," said Yuasa. He agreed with General Araki's comment that trying to alter the army's conduct in North China was like telling someone not to get involved with a woman after he had impregnated her. The simile was apt. The consequence would be born the following year.

A PACT

THE EXECUTIONS OF Aizawa and the rebel leaders in July 1936 agitated the rightists. Baron Harada often checked with the police and the Kempeitai about rumors of new plots. They said the young hotheads were buzzing but nothing tangible was afoot. Harada also heard alarming information about Prince Konoye. The prince had told several people that Prince Saionji and the elder statesmen were old and out of touch, obstacles to progress. When his shocked listeners reported this remark to Harada, they ascribed Konoye's views to his recent meetings with ultranationalists. His bright future and Saionji's sponsorship attracted people who wanted to influence him, and he was easily swayed. A few days later Saionji spoke to Harada about his wayward protégé.

"Somehow Konoye seems to defend Masaki and Araki," said the genro. "I don't know whether he is saying such things out of fear, or whether he thinks that he will be in a better position if he says such things in view of the present situation." Since Konoye was destined to be prime minister, Saionji wondered if there was a way to bring him back onto the proper path.

Harada also reported to Saionji that the Japanese ministers of war, the navy, and foreign affairs had presented China with three demands for better relations that he feared would instead guarantee conflict. First, China must help stifle communist movements by allowing Japan to build air bases and wireless stations in North China. Second, China must give "special rights" to Japan, which probably referred to trade, military presence, and access to raw materials. Third, China must eradicate anti-Japanese feeling. The old statesman was dumbfounded. "What are they planning to do with China anyway?" he said. "We really have a group of stupid men."

During the main event of Harvard's three-day tercentenary celebration, seventeen thousand scholars, dignitaries, and officials sat in Harvard Yard getting pelted by rain. Top hats covered some heads, mortarboards others. Many wore morning coats, others academic robes. The rain ran over Grew's top hat and down his neck, but Noah's flood couldn't have dampened his pride and enthusiasm about this event to honor his alma mater.

As a marshal of dignitaries he was settling into his front-row seat when someone bellowed, "Hello, Joe!" It was President Roosevelt, wearing a topper. At a luncheon Grew was chatting with Admiral William Harrison Standley, chief of US Naval Operations, when he noticed a Japanese stranger hovering at their elbows while pretending to study the middle distance. Grew and Standley exchanged a look and moved off. "After carefully watching my step for four years in Japan and never speaking without looking around," wrote Grew, "it seemed ironical to have to do the same in Memorial Hall." The man would no doubt report the conversation to Tokyo, which suited Grew. Standley had been telling him that Roosevelt intended to greatly strengthen the navy and the reserves, a message Grew wanted Tokyo to receive.

He spent the next six weeks rotating between the North Shore, Boston, Hancock, New York, and Washington. The break from Japan was serving its purpose. "Alice seems better than I have seen her for years," wrote Grew. In Washington he met several times with Hull. Grew found him "exceedingly vague." Whenever Grew tried to steer the conversation toward America's Far East policy, Hull meandered off into disquisitions about trade.

By contrast he had "a bully talk" with Roosevelt. Grew made two requests. First, because the exchange rate had dropped and the cost of living in Japan had risen, the embassy's Japanese employees could no longer support their families on their "penurious salaries." Despite Grew's repeated requests, their pay hadn't risen in five years. He had spent more than two thousand dollars from his own pocket to keep them alive and out of debt, but he was about to lose many of them to better jobs if the government failed to budget the embassy another twelve hundred dollars for raises. Roosevelt said he would do his best.

Grew's second request was personal. He was fifty-six. Retirement had become a possibility. Roosevelt was running for a second term. It would be helpful to know, said Grew, whether Roosevelt wanted him to stay in Japan if he won reelection. Roosevelt immediately said yes. Grew offered to serve there for as long as Roosevelt needed him, because it was the most important post he could imagine, but on one condition: that he and Alice could take an annual leave to recuperate physically and psychologically, if the situation allowed his absence. (For five of the next six years, it wouldn't.) Roosevelt agreed.

On Election Day, November 3, the Grews were on a train bound for Los Angeles. They joined others in a club car to hear the returns on the radio. "By 9 o'clock in the evening," wrote Grew, "it was clear that Roosevelt had won by the greatest landslide in American history, Landon carrying only two states." They would be staying in Japan.

"After a vacation like that," wrote Grew on November 27, the day he and Alice arrived in Tokyo, "one feels ready for anything." He listed a few of the issues before him: the mysterious pact between Japan and Germany; the failing negotiations between Japan and China; more skirmishes on the Siberian-Manchurian border; a fresh outbreak between Chinese troops and Japanese-supported Mongols in Inner Mongolia; a 40 percent increase in the already massive military budget. "Just one damn thing after another," he wrote, not unhappily.

Two days before Grew's return, Japan and Germany had signed the Anti-Comintern Pact, ostensibly directed at international communism. The agreement had been designed by Hitler's close advisor and ambassador-at-large, Joachim von Ribbentrop, and by Japan's military attaché in Berlin, General Oshima Hiroshi, who admired Hitler and hated the Soviet Union. Both nations claimed that the agreement was aimed solely at stopping the spread of communism through peaceful means. They swore it contained no secret military provisions or targeted countries.

They were lying. The public document didn't mention military commitments, but the agreement between Japan and Germany included secret military protocols aimed at the Soviet Union. Oshima, Ribbentrop, and Hitler had pushed for the protocols, which committed both nations to a military alliance against the USSR. But Prime Minister Hirota and Foreign Minister Arita were wary. They didn't want to provoke the Soviets or damage Japan's improving relations with Britain and America. They refused to tie Japan to Germany with an offensive alliance, but they did agree to a secret defensive alliance that could be triggered only by an unprovoked attack from the Soviet Union.

Harada heard about the agreement from Arita several days before it became public. He took the news to Saionji. "Eventually it will only result in Germany exploiting us," said the genro, "and we stand to gain nothing."

Nazis immediately began to establish themselves in Japan. Hitler Youth groups sprouted in German schools in Tokyo and Yokohama. Nazis infiltrated Japan's ministries and police forces, advising them on everything from surveillance to the names of Germans who should be banned from teaching or conducting business in Japan, starting with socialists and Jews. The German embassy itself wasn't immune. The chief of the embassy's trade department was dismissed in April 1937 because his wife was Jewish. Even Germany's ambassador to Japan, Herbert von Dirksen, became a target of harassment and surveillance. Still, the Nazis in Japan disapproved of Aryans mingling too freely with Japanese. A German who worked for the Nazi Party wasn't allowed to give his child a Japanese first name. Few Japanese knew that the original version of Hitler's *Mein Kampf* referred to the Japanese as imitators devolving into the state of savages, passages omitted in the Japanese edition.

Grew heard that the Kwantung Army was scheming again, this time to expand Japanese control west toward Inner Mongolia. The army had provided money, armaments, and military advisors to build a large militia of Mongols to strike Chinese forces. After a few exploratory clashes, this ragtag militia attacked in Mongolia's Suiyuan Province in mid-November 1936. The Chinese forces not only repulsed the Japanese puppets, they chased the invaders back to their headquarters and captured it. The campaign marked the first time the Chinese army had defeated the Japanese. The news electrified China and mortified the Kwantung Army. Face needed to be saved.

In Tokyo the skirmish raised the alarming possibility of a rogue retaliatory invasion by the Kwantung troops. War Minister Terauchi, backed by Hirota and Arita, ordered the Kwantung Army to stand down. Arita worried that hotheads within the war ministry and on the army general staff would support their counterparts in Manchukuo. "The Premier and I are determined to check them at the risk of losing our present posts," Arita told Harada. "However," he added, "I believe that it is impossible to check them."

KOKUTAI

ON JANUARY 23, 1937, Prime Minister Hirota summoned Baron Harada to his office to convey an important message. His cabinet was resigning en bloc that afternoon. The genro's counsel would be necessary to choose the next premier. Saionji was eighty-seven and had been bedridden for ten days at his coastal home in Okitsu. Harada called the grand chamberlain and explained that the genro couldn't possibly answer the imperial summons. He asked for permission from the emperor to send the lord keeper to Saionji instead. Minutes later the grand chamberlain called back. The emperor had granted the request.

By 10:00 A.M. the lord keeper was on the train to Okitsu. Harada ushered him to the genro's bedside at 2:40 P.M. They spoke for forty minutes, comparing notes on possible candidates. They agreed upon someone who seemed acceptable, or at least tolerable, and whom the genro could endorse in good conscience to the emperor. The lord keeper left on the 4:41 P.M. train and arrived in Tokyo at 7:45 P.M. He hustled to the palace and presented the emperor with their recommendation: sixty-eight-year-old General Ugaki Kazushige, most recently the governor-general of Korea.

Meanwhile, word of the new cabinet leaked from the palace. Several hundred reporters and photographers descended on Ugaki's home in Tokyo. They unloaded trucks and trampled the garden, setting up tents adorned with the flags of their newspapers. They hung lanterns and lit charcoal braziers for tea and heat against the winter night's chill. Tables held inkpots, brushes, and rice paper, the tools of Japanese journalism.

Caged pigeons cooed, waiting to fly dispatches and photo negatives back to headquarters. Less urgent news would travel by motorcycle.

At the palace the emperor waited for Ugaki to answer the imperial summons. Shortly after midnight as Ugaki's car glided alongside the palace moat, an officer of the Kempeitai emerged from the shadows and motioned the car to the side. Ugaki was puzzled, then puzzled again to see the commander of the Kempeitai walking toward him. The commander told Ugaki the army wanted to advise him that he was not in good health and should go home. The threat astonished the general, but his emperor had summoned him and he told his driver to proceed through the palace gates. At 12:30 A.M. Hirohito gave him the imperial mandate to form a new cabinet.

That should have been that, but the army intervened to correct what it considered an imperial error. Ugaki had made enemies during his long military career. One faction had never forgiven him for following orders to reduce the size of the army as war minister in the 1920s. More recently he had angered young army officers by turning moderate. As governor-general of Korea he had worked with the zaibatsu to develop industry, which meant that capitalists and financiers approved of him, another black mark. He was popular with the political parties and with the public, and he opposed the growing military faction enamored with the Nazis. These very qualities had recommended him to Saionji but made him dangerous to the plans of the army's extremists. They pressured the army's Big Three, who once again allowed the tail to wag the dog. The leaders decided to kill Ugaki's cabinet in the crib.

Their strategy was simple. The constitution empowered the army's Big Three to appoint the war minister, so they simply refused to send Ugaki a name, preventing him from forming a cabinet. For four days Ugaki looked for a compromise. The army's maneuver angered the imperial court, politicians, business leaders, and the public. The army defied them all, deferring to the extremist young officers over the emperor's mandate. On the afternoon of January 29, Ugaki returned to the palace to apologize to the emperor for his failure. In a statement to the press he bitterly criticized the army for interfering in politics. The army banned Japan's newspapers from publishing the general's remarks.

The Kwantung Army had engineered Ugaki's failure because they wanted the candidate they had been grooming: Prince Konoye. His supporters had urged him to pursue the position before Ugaki was chosen, but he had declined for reasons of health. Yet he also said he would accept an imperial mandate "even at the risk of his life." Encouraged, his supporters began lobbying for his selection. That frightened Konoye. Every time he saw Harada over the coming days he said, "Please arrange it so that I will not be selected. I do not want it." He sent his private secretary to Saionji with the same message.

Meanwhile the selection process began again. The lord keeper took the train to see Saionji and returned with a name for the emperor. Another imperial summons went out, to General Hayashi, former war minister in the Hirota cabinet. This time the army allowed the imperial mandate to stand. Blocking Hayashi would have redoubled the resentment over Ugaki and jeopardized the army's public support. Besides, unlike Ugaki, Hayashi was a political cipher. Saionji and the army both saw him as a benign placeholder. That was also the way Hayashi saw himself. He told Harada, "My desire is to get things quiet as soon as possible and then give way to an experienced man."

Saionji's recommendation of Hayashi indicated desperation, not enthusiasm. The genro mourned that the country he had helped to build was moving swiftly away from him and his principles. "A military man," he said to Harada, "cannot really understand such things as the welfare of a nation or the welfare of a people. . . . They advocate national unity, but their national unity is not unity at all. It just means submission to them." Saionji seemed "greatly grieved over this," noted Harada.

After the flare-up over Ugaki, Grew appreciated the lull in military scheming that arrived with Hayashi. The new prime minister filled his cabinet with moderates. The army continued to disperse radicals via transfers, which momentarily lowered the voices of most extremist officers. A few members of the Diet dared to criticize the army and the government. All these developments pleased Grew. It seemed as if Count Kabayama's optimistic predictions about the return of moderates were coming true.

But Grew, like Saionji, knew better. The military had not relaxed its grip. Grew considered the calm after Hayashi's appointment an interlude before the next wave of Japanese expansion. "One feels a little like living on a volcano here, never knowing when an explosion is going to occur," he wrote, "and I am quite sure that the day of possible explosions is by no means past."

Japan's volatility stemmed partly from its internal disagreements about how to define itself against the behemoths that had influenced it most: China and the West, especially the United States. China had shaped Japan's language and traditional culture; Japan's modern facade derived from the West. In the years of foment between the world wars, Japan was searching for a vision of itself as unique among nations.

In March 1937 the Ministry of Education settled the matter with a book called *Kokutai no hongi* (*Cardinal Principles of the National Entity of Japan*, or *Fundamentals of Our National Polity*). Translations of the title varied because the word *kokutai* was so capacious and prismatic. *Kokutai* encompassed all of Japanese culture, history, values, traditions, and polity. It expressed Japan's essence as well as its elemental principles and eternal identity.

Kokutai no hongi nailed down that essence and those principles by condensing what most Japanese already believed in their bones. The text squeezed the national spirit into a tight mold. Anything that didn't fit was pruned. The book was quickly adopted as national scripture and infused into every teacher, student, and citizen as a philosophy of state.

This catechism explained that "extreme conceptions" found in the West, such as liberalism and socialism, were rooted in the poison of individualism, which had led the West into "social confusion and crisis." Fortunately, its authors claimed, the West was beginning to understand the dangers of individualism, as evinced by the heartening rise of totalitarianism, fascism, and Nazism, which correctly subsumed the individual into the state. Individualism was inimical to *kokutai*, whose source was Japan's divine emperor. "Hence, offering our lives for the sake of the emperor does not mean so-called self-sacrifice but the casting aside of our little selves to live under his august grace." In a true state of *kokutai*, the book asserted, absolute loyalty to the emperor ensured access to the fountainhead of the divine. This made the Japanese a blessed and superior race.

This version of *kokutai* was tailor-made to justify state control of everything in the name of loyalty to the emperor. Politics, the press, business, all needed to submit to *kokutai*. Properly understood, *kokutai* made Japan's labor unrest unpatriotic, made Japan's crushing rural poverty trivially individualistic, made criticisms of the emperor's military treasonous. *Kokutai* could guide thought itself into proper channels—the final frontier of totalitarianism—if necessary with help from the Home Ministry's Thought Police.

A section of *Kokutai no hongo* entitled "Martial Spirit" explained that Japan's warrior spirit differed from other nations' because it existed "for the sake of peace" and was therefore sacred. If that sounded contradictory, the next sentence tried to clarify: "Our martial spirit does not have for its objective the killing of men but the giving of life to men." Still confused? The passage barreled on, belching fog: "War, in this sense, is not by any means intended for the destruction, overpowering, or subjugation of others; and it should be for bringing about great harmony, that is, peace, doing the work of creation by following the Way." War was a vital expression of *kokutai* and of Japan's divine mission to impose peace and superior civilization by force.

As Hayashi's new cabinet was installed, diplomatic life proceeded as usual, though the Grews cut back on social engagements because they had been feeling poorly. Alice was exhausted by a constant high temperature and hobbled by a swollen knee. Grew battled a stubborn sinus infection, then caught the flu, then got conjunctivitus. They said goodbye to Soviet ambassador Yurenev and his caviar soirees when he was transferred to Berlin. (Later in 1937 Yurenev was arrested in Stalin's Great Purge. He was executed the following year, part of an estimated one million.)

April often brought an influx of Americans expecting to be entertained. The Grews enjoyed visitors from home, if they didn't arrive in a bunch. April's highlight was Helen Keller, the world-renowned author and activist, who was deaf, blind, and mute. "Japan is turning itself inside out for her," wrote Grew. Everyone wanted to meet her, including the emperor and the prime minister. From mid-April until her departure in early July she visited thirty-nine cities and gave ninety-seven lectures, attracting great crowds.

She amazed Grew with her ability to converse rapidly via hand taps interpreted by her companion, Polly Thomson. Keller engaged with her physical surroundings through her highly developed sense of touch, and she delighted in "seeing" the embassy's Japanese jades and vases. At an audience with Prince and Princess Takamatsu, the princess "was clearly a little embarrassed when Miss Keller felt her all over from head and face to kimono and obi so that she could visualize her." In a tactful letter Grew suggested that Keller refrain from perceiving the emperor and empress in this way since it could cause serious misunderstanding.

In May, Grew also welcomed Eugene Dooman as the embassy's new counselor and second-in-charge. Grew knew Dooman by reputation and had requested him for Tokyo. The new counselor wrote and spoke Japanese perfectly. A decade younger than the ambassador, Dooman was a BIJ (born in Japan), the son of missionaries. He had lived in Japan for his first thirteen years, attending elite schools with Americans and Japanese. After graduating from Hartford's Trinity College in 1912, he entered the Foreign Service and asked to be assigned to Japan. He spent most of the next twenty-one years there. He also resumed his childhood friendships with Japanese who were moving into influential positions in business and government. In 1933 he was posted back to Washington to run the Japan desk in Far Eastern Affairs. His chief was Hornbeck.

"And it was for me a very unpleasant experience," said Dooman later, "because I did not feel I could deal with Dr. Hornbeck as a person with a completely objective mind. I discovered that he had two supreme passions. One was a feeling of affection and sympathy for China. And the second was a pathological hatred of Japan and the Japanese."

In Tokyo, Dooman and Grew immediately meshed. Both loved classical music, Latin phrases, Japanese food, and golf. Both squawked about dispatches marred by grammatical errors. More important, they loved Japan and were dismayed by its slide into belligerent totalitarianism. Dooman promptly became Grew's most indispensable officer. The ambassador valued and relied on Dooman's deep knowledge of the country. For the next four years they worked hard to give the State Department the most thorough possible understanding of the situation there.

• • •

Prime Minister Hayashi tired of his role as placeholder, or perhaps radical factions in the army grew impatient to insert their man. On May 3, just three months after taking office, Hayashi sent a messenger to Prince Konoye saying he wanted to resign, with Konoye as his replacement. Konoye declined, citing his health. Word about this circulated at the palace. About a week later the lord keeper harangued Konoye for two and a half hours about accepting the position. "My health will not possibly allow it," Konoye finally told him. "I won't do it."

This ferment and dithering went on throughout May. Hayashi was determined to quit. On May 29 he sent another messenger to Konoye saying that he was resigning and asking Konoye to step in. Konoye again refused. Hayashi called Baron Harada. Since Konoye wouldn't serve, he said, he intended to recommend the army's second choice to the emperor, War Minister Sugiyama Hajime. The genro instantly squashed the idea. "It is undesirable to have the Minister of War become Premier," said Saionji. "Isn't it possible to force Konoye to accept it?" Saionji considered his protégé perhaps the last hope to check the nation's momentum toward military totalitarianism.

Harada called Marquis Kido and told him to start working on Konoye to accept the premiership. He also called the lord keeper, who didn't think Konoye would consent. Nevertheless, the lord keeper agreed to come to Saionji the next morning to receive the genro's recommendation and convey it to the emperor. By the time Harada called Konoye, Kido had pressured him into agreement, but he was fretful and hoping for a way out. "You are putting me on the spot," Konoye complained. "Unless you have an alternate it will be distressing to me." Harada called Saionji with this news. The genro was emphatic. "No matter what is said, Konoye is the best choice. Under the circumstances, this is regrettable. However, it is unavoidable." The next day, May 31, Konoye received the imperial summons and the mandate to form a cabinet.

Prince Konoye and his cabinet were installed on June 4. The public cheered. Konoye was immensely popular, a source of hope because of his youth (forty-five) and his noble lineage. Grew was pleased that Hirota returned to his post as foreign minister.

Other signs were less promising. Harada noted that the Kempeitai had

become troublesome, holding rallies during which their leaders made ve-
hement speeches that encouraged members to accost citizens on any pretext. He also heard rumors that military extremists were already agitating
against the new government. The army was hounding Konoye with requests. The emperor complained to the grand chamberlain, "The Army
has been insistently saying: 'Konoye, Konoye,' and wanting him for Premier. Finally, when Konoye became Premier, they seem to make all sorts
of difficult demands. Just what is their reason?" One of those demands was
a pardon for Masaki, on trial for his part in the February 26 insurrection.
Konoye was considering it to avert an outbreak by the hotheads.

Harada advised the chief secretary of the cabinet to restrict access to the
fragile, pliable prime minister. "I have known Prince Konoye for a long
time," explained Harada. "As he is of weak character, it is well known that
he is easily influenced. So please see that he doesn't meet certain groups or
hear certain propaganda."

Konoye needed supervision to stop him from listening to the wrong
people and making foolish errors. That soon proved impossible.

QUAGMIRE

ON JULY 7, 1937, Japanese troops on night maneuvers ventured too close to a Chinese garrison guarding the Marco Polo (Lugouqiao) Bridge spanning the Yongding River near Beijing. Rifle fire clattered. Each side blamed the other for shooting first. Local military authorities arranged a truce two days later and the incident seemed closed, but sporadic exchanges of gunfire kept the situation unsettled. To maintain face, both sides made huffy demands, immediately rejected.

Over the next few days the situation escalated swiftly. Chiang Kai-shek sent six divisions to North China, vowing to fight. Japan had again violated Chinese sovereignty, and Chiang feared that submitting to Japan once more would unseat him as China's leader. Meanwhile Japan argued that North China was "a special almost independent region" where the government of China had no jurisdiction.

Konoye at first rejected War Minister Sugiyama's request to send more troops but soon reversed his stance. He reasoned that if he dismissed the minister's guidance, Sugiyama would have to resign to save face and the cabinet would fall. "Thus Premier Konoye made a pathetic decision," said the lord keeper. Sugiyama planned to send a large force to smash the Chinese quickly. Harada went to see Konoye and found him in bed with indigestion. His cabinet and the military had been pulling him in different directions. The army was urging the newspapers to promote war with China and was suppressing any news about peace agreements. Neither

Konoye, the Foreign Office, nor the navy knew what was really going on. Konoye couldn't even get reports from his war minister.

The army's unpredictability and Konoye's abdication to it alarmed sensible Japanese. Almost everyone wanted a quick settlement. The ministers of finance, foreign affairs, and the navy feared that a major conflict would severely damage the nation's economy, the public's trust, and international relationships. Prince Saionji warned that the army's meddling in China might cause "an unimaginable crisis." Even the war minister and the chief of the army general staff assured the emperor on the night of July 14 that despite the dispatch of reinforcements, they planned to settle the incident locally without widening the conflict. But Harada noted that "a certain stubborn part of the Army is still clamoring boisterously."

The army also was frustrating Foreign Minister Hirota. He was still optimistic about finding a local solution, but the army was so obstructive and internally chaotic that he now communicated with its leadership only through the navy minister. The army's expansionists had a similar disregard for Hirota. They criticized him to Konoye, sowing doubt. Chiang was compounding the tension. Like most Japanese, he hoped for an agreement that would save face, but to save face he also urged all Chinese to resist Japanese aggression in North China. That played into the hands of the Japanese expansionists and caused anti-Chinese frenzy in the Japanese press.

Even the leaders who preferred peace, such as Hirota, made the arrogant miscalculation that Chiang eventually would submit to Japan's demands, as he had before, rather than challenge the mighty Imperial Army. They further believed that if Chiang did dare challenge Japan, his army would quickly be crushed. Japan's civil and military leaders barreled toward their familiar, destructive mistake: abdicating control to an extremist army faction determined to steer the nation away from peace and toward their violent dreams of empire. This time the consequence wasn't a few assassinations or a quick victory over a weak province but tragedy on a massive scale.

At the end of July, swayed by the young military expansionists, Konoye began changing his tone about China. In the Diet he suggested that this might be the moment for Japan to embrace its imperial destiny. Japan, he said, "seeks an awakening of the Chinese people to the consciousness of their role." That is, to accommodating Japan's plans for China.

Hirota told Japan's official news agency, Domei, that the China matter had moved out of the Foreign Office's hands and into the army's. The Foreign Office hoped hostilities wouldn't expand to the walled city of Beijing, where Western nations had citizens, soldiers, and property. Japan demanded that China remove all troops from there. Hirota assured Grew that even if China provoked conflict by ignoring this reasonable ultimatum to abandon a major Chinese city, American lives and property in Beijing would be protected. He made the same statements to the Diet, adding that Japan had no territorial ambitions in China. The members cheered wildly and then unanimously passed a special $30 million war appropriation. Grew noted an uptick in military bustle throughout Tokyo. "Facts are elusive," he wrote, "but it is evident that a crisis is approaching."

Japan mobilized forty thousand men for immediate departure to China. It sent several thousand more troops into Shanghai and parked thirty warships offshore. In response, China also sent more troops into Shanghai. The ambassadors from Western nations in Tokyo and Nanjing insisted—Britain's ambassador loudly, Grew behind the scenes—that combat in Shanghai must be avoided to protect its three million residents and the International Settlement filled with foreigners, including three thousand Americans.

On August 13 the two armies in Shanghai exchanged fire. Each side blamed the other. The bombings intensified, the majority by Japanese planes. Japan's expansionists cheered. To them, the battle of Shanghai smashed open the door to a glorious imperial future. In addition to residential areas, the bombs hit an American missionary compound and an American oil tank. On August 21 a Chinese anti-aircraft shell missed its target and hit the USS *Augusta*, killing one American and injuring eighteen. A Chinese plane also bombed an American commercial liner in Shanghai harbor, killing one, quickly followed by an apology from Chinese officials. In these early days of the Second Sino-Japanese War, the Japanese also apologized for bombing American citizens and property. But apologies entailed loss of face, so they soon stopped except in the most egregious cases.

The Japanese asked the American and British embassies for specific locations of properties owned by their citizens near Shanghai and elsewhere so Japanese fighter pilots could avoid them. Japanese officials advised foreigners to mark these properties with large national flags, either on poles or painted on rooftops. Frequent night bombings meant that the markings needed to be well lit after dark. Whenever tensions with Britain or the United States worsened, these displays seemed to function as targets rather than safeguards. The Japanese air campaign spread to Nanjing and Hangzhou (Hangchow). Panic spread throughout China, and refugees fled the bombings.

Japan's irresponsible belligerence and slippery diplomacy alarmed Grew. He spoke often and urgently to Foreign Minister Hirota. They liked and respected each other and preferred to meet alone, without translators, since Hirota's English was excellent. (Grew was fluent in French and German, with smatterings of Spanish, Danish, Russian, Hindustani, Arabic, and Malay, but he never learned Japanese.) Their warm relationship had grown beyond the usual formalities imposed by diplomacy and Japanese culture. Hirota had recently been to the embassy for a small luncheon where he enjoyed the cocktails so much—ice-cold gimlets—that he asked for the recipe. Both men valued this congeniality and the space it opened for frank discussions. But the Japanese military's actions in China made frankness increasingly difficult for Hirota.

For two weeks Grew and other ambassadors had been urging the foreign minister not to ignite an international incident by indiscriminately bombing civilians and foreigners. Specifically they asked Japan to avoid hitting Shanghai's International Settlement, Nanjing's diplomatic quarter, Beijing's foreign neighborhoods, Qingdao's (Tsingtao's) many Western businesses, and certain railroads and motorways filled with fleeing foreigners. In every case the requests were violated by war-happy Japanese pilots.

Grew felt the situation slipping downhill. On September 1 at 5:00 P.M. he met Hirota at his official residence and deployed every diplomatic tactic. He appealed to personal friendship, history, and higher ideals. He also issued warnings. All of their mutual hard work to improve US–Japanese relations could be demolished, he said, if errant bombs killed Americans and inflamed the American public. Japanese pilots had repeatedly killed civilians and damaged foreign property far removed from any fighting. Japan was making enemies around the world, a foreign minister's nightmare. Grew asked Hirota to stand up for diplomacy and humanitarianism instead of military goals.

In response Hirota said Japan's military forces aimed to attack only military establishments but "sometimes the bombs failed to reach their precise objectives and accidents happened." That blasé self-justifying response left little room for diplomacy. Hirota was becoming another mouthpiece for the military. He insisted to Grew that Japan only wanted peace. It could be so simple. Japan was asking Chiang to accept just three conditions: first, establish good relations with Manchukuo; second, withdraw all troops from North China to create a buffer zone; and third, develop good relations with Japan.

The last two conditions were absurd. China would not abandon its five northern provinces. When added to the thefts of Manchuria and Hebei and the ongoing bombing of Chinese cities, the demand for good relations became a dark joke to anyone except empire-minded Japanese.

"If Chiang Kai-shek will accept my conditions," Hirota told Grew that afternoon, "I can stop this war immediately." The conversation ended on that non sequitur.

A few days after meeting with Grew, Hirota told the Diet that China had "failed to manifest a grain of sincerity" and had ignored Japan's "true motive," peace in Asia. Despite Japan's efforts toward harmony, the nation now must "compel China to mend her ways" and "act in unison with the high aim and aspirations of Japan!" Other rousing speeches by the prime minister, war minister, and navy minister inspired the Diet to give the military another supplement for China, this time a whopping two billion yen. It wasn't for forging peace.

Japanese air raids escalated. More troops poured onto the mainland (600,000 by the end of the year, more than 1 million by 1939). On September 12 an American mission hospital at Huizhou was destroyed. On September 19 the Japanese military declared its intention to annihilate the Nationalist capital of Nanjing, starting two days later at noon, and warned all foreign diplomats and citizens to evacuate. The United States, Britain, Germany, and France all protested that the bombing would violate international law.

"This is no time for pussyfooting," wrote Grew on September 20. That day at 6:00 P.M. he went to see Hirota again to try to prevent the assault on Nanjing. Hirota listened "gravely and silently," without rebuttal. "He appeared to me to receive my observations rather sadly," wrote Grew. When Grew finished, Hirota offered what little he could. The government had ordered pilots not to bomb foreign and civilian areas in Nanjing.

Japan responded to the international protests by delaying the bombing of Nanjing for one day. On September 22 fifty planes pounded the city for ninety minutes. Other air squadrons hit Guangzhou (Canton) six times in twenty-four hours. High explosive bombs flattened some districts, and incendiary bombs burned down matchstick neighborhoods. Grew immediately filed a protest with Hirota and asked Japan to pay for damages to American property. Japan rejected the claim, blaming China for forcing it to bomb Chinese cities.

The Japanese public enthusiastically followed its leaders toward the nation's glorious destiny. War fever gripped almost everyone. The accelerating conflict required multiple thousands of military draftees, who were celebrated with boisterous departures.

"The first thing a family did when a son was conscripted," wrote reporter Phyllis Argall,

> was to buy up all the sake (rice brew) they could and invite the whole neighborhood to make a night of it. Friends, relatives, patriotic societies, neighborhood associations, sent huge wreaths of paper flowers or Japanese flags, in honor of the occasion. Many also sent banners, large or small, silk or cotton, undecorated or fringed with heavy gold, as individual means permitted, on which the conscript's name was inscribed. Wreaths and banners were hung outside the house, to tell the world that a popular son was going to war in his Emperor's service. The night before the conscript was to join up, the party met, and sake flowed until the early hours, when a fleet of trucks and taxis, already bargained for, conveyed the whole shouting, singing, hilarious group to the railroad station to give him a fitting farewell.

Edward Crocker, second secretary at the American embassy, wrote to his mother, "Now, as I write, truck-load after truck-load of recruits and soldiers are passing by under my window cheering and screaming 'Banzai, Banzai!' as they roar on." Crocker's wife, Lispenard, wrote of this nonstop commotion, "It is rather like the roar of the sea if you are not too near it. Ned says he either has to keep his windows shut at the Embassy and smother, or be deafened by the cheers. It seems as though every man, woman, and child walks about with a little paper flag and waves it as each truck load passes."

These drunken, careening truckloads caused so many fatal accidents that the authorities soon banned them. The parades continued on foot. The railway stations were crowded with soldiers and their families and well-wishers. They sang patriotic songs until departure time, then waved flags and shouted "Banzai!" as the trains took their loved ones to war.

A note of stoic sadness sometimes tempered these send-offs. "Frequently also an old woman and a young one, perhaps with a baby in her arms," wrote Argall, "would detach themselves . . . and walk to the end of the platform, so that they would be able to see the very last of the train as it vanished in the distance. These women did not sing and laugh. Nor did they cry, for Japanese women do not cry in public, especially when their son or husband is going to serve the Emperor. They just stood there, bleak, alone, with a look of resignation, bitter or composed, on their faces."

On street corners in the main business districts of Tokyo, especially the Ginza, clusters of young girls asked passing women to stop for a moment and put a stitch into the thin white cotton sashes they held. The sashes were given to departing soldiers. The Japanese believed that if one thousand women each took one stitch in a sash, it would protect a soldier from death. No woman refused the sashes, which entailed many stops on each block.

The Japanese press stoked the public's enthusiasm for the war, posting "daily reports of an unbroken series of victories," noted Grew wryly. Shattered Chinese planes rained down like burning confetti while Japanese planes returned to base unscathed. It was fake news but the only news allowed. The military, the Foreign Office, and the Home Ministry had been controlling the press for years, but after Marco Polo Bridge the restraints tightened. Bad news was forbidden, especially about military or diplomatic issues. All information was censored for public consumption, usually by the reporters themselves, typically boosters of the military or intimidated by it. Reporters who wrote stories that the Home Ministry considered "contrary to the interests of the state" were visited by the police.

Newspapers and magazines that entered Japan from abroad had to pass through the censor's scissors. A woman told Grew about getting a packet of newspapers from Shanghai that looked neat and orderly, but when she opened it, every news story had been cut out, leaving only the advertisements. Foreign news and foreign coverage of Japan reached the Japanese public only through the state news agency, Domei, which filtered out undesirable information—for instance, reportage about Japanese setbacks or atrocities. On the other hand, Domei waved through any foreign stories that reinforced Japanese propaganda. Whenever American congressmen or organizations bashed Roosevelt for straying from isolationism, they were heard loudly in Japan, but American outrage about Japanese actions didn't reach the Japanese people unless it could be used to inflame them. Consequently most Japanese were ignorant about the true shape of the conflict in China and the Western reactions to it, and were certain that the American public consisted mostly of timid isolationists who would never let Roosevelt enter a conflict. Deprived of facts and knowledge by their government and their media, most Japanese lived in an echo chamber rarely penetrated by truth.

Grew had several sources of foreign and domestic news. He and his staff gathered information from contacts throughout the Japanese government and military. He met frequently with foreign correspondents. News and newspapers also came in via State Department dispatches and the diplomatic pouch. The discrepancies between what Grew knew and what the Japanese press reported were mind-boggling. He became increasingly frustrated that even influential cosmopolitan Japanese refused to believe the news reports he showed them about Japanese atrocities and intentional bombings of civilians, hospitals, and missionary compounds. Their government had warned them against fake news planted by the enemies of Japan. Stories were true only if they reflected and reinforced the glorious narrative fed them by the government.

BOMBING, REGRETS, BOMBING, REGRETS

FOLLOWING HIS USUAL practice, Grew sat in his study at the residence, pounding out a draft dispatch to the Department of State on his Corona, his head wreathed in smoke, sometimes from a pipe, sometimes a cigarette. His longtime secretary, Marion Arnold, typed a clean version on carbon paper and sent copies to key embassy staff for comments and amendments. When their suggestions came back, Grew "applied the ambassadorial pencil" and then Arnold typed a final draft.

On August 27, 1937, Grew's subject was an analysis of the situation in Japan followed by policy suggestions. The dispatch advised the department to continue its policy of working behind the scenes to protect American lives and property while staying impartial and not openly criticizing Japan, which could ruin the good relations reestablished over the past five years. Grew argued that poisoning future relations would bring few benefits beyond a claim to the high ground.

Grew must have suspected the message would roil Hull because he spent pages defending it in his diary. Somehow America must retain both its principles and Japan's friendship, he wrote. This required "Real Politik," which he defined as relations based on facts rather than ideals or sentiment. Hull's "high-minded, far-seeing, statesmanlike pronouncements" against Japan's aggression were praiseworthy and necessary for the record, but would have absolutely no effect on Japan's actions. "In other words," he wrote, "the righteous indignation theme can now do no further good and should be soft-pedalled."

Hull, and no doubt Hornbeck, didn't receive this well. What Grew considered realpolitik Hull saw as abandonment of fundamental principles and mollycoddling of Japan. Hull reminded Grew that Japan had dismissed the rights of noncombatants and other nations, and had shown scant interest in preserving friendly international relations. The United States would remain strictly neutral, but the government wouldn't be guided or hindered by what might displease either Japan or China. "There appears to be a fairly wide divergence of views," wrote Grew when Hull's reprimand arrived, "and we are for the first time given an insight into the depth of feeling at home."

Grew sent Hull a long official reply and also a confidential letter. In both he took pains to say that their views were "close if not identical." But he didn't retreat from his view that refraining from public indignation would better serve American interests in the long run. That didn't mean tiptoeing around the Japanese or sacrificing principle, he told Hull. He was advocating an approach, not a softening in policy. He pointed out that both the United States and Britain had strongly censured Japan over China, but Britain had done so repeatedly in public, an assault on Japanese face. Now the Japanese press was filled with anti-British vitriol and appreciation for America's neutrality. He argued that the United States had preserved Japan's goodwill and the possibility of future influence without sacrificing any principle.

Three days later President Roosevelt gave a speech in Chicago. An embassy staffer handed Grew a telegraphed summary. He read it and said, "There goes everything I have tried to accomplish in my entire mission in Japan."

It became known as the "quarantine speech." Roosevelt didn't mention Japan, Germany, or Italy by name, but he didn't need to. He decried nations that spent 50 percent of their budgets on armaments instead of people. He condemned nations that broke global treaties and invaded other countries, spreading "international anarchy and instability." He described civilians "being ruthlessly murdered with bombs from the air." These belligerent nations were few, he said, but were jeopardizing the 90 percent who wanted peace. This "epidemic of world lawlessness" must be stopped by the peaceful 90 percent, who should quarantine the contagion. "There is no escape through mere isolation or neutrality," he said.

"The reaction against the quarantine idea," noted Hull, "was quick and violent." Including his own. The State Department had written the Chicago speech as part of Hull's careful campaign to slowly melt American isolationism while avoiding provocative public statements—much like Grew's advice about how to handle Japan. Then Roosevelt inserted his revisions about a quarantine and an end to isolationism. Hull estimated the speech set back his campaign for international cooperation by six months. It inflamed the isolationists, who raged that Roosevelt was a dictator determined to entangle America in another foreign war. These strong protests, wrote Hull, were "dulcet to the ears of Hitler, Mussolini, and the Japanese war lords."

The speech landed like a bomb in the Tokyo embassy. The staff and their spouses were so angry and disheartened that Grew called a meeting to remind them that they represented the American government and must not criticize that government outside embassy walls. But he shared their dismay. "This was the day that I felt my carefully built castle tumbling about my ears," he wrote, "and we all wandered about the chancery, depressed, gloomy and with not a smile in sight."

A few days later he unloaded his exasperation into his diary. The quarantine speech reverted to a policy of self-righteous words about broken treaties. That approach had failed to deter aggression in Manchuria, Abyssinia, and Spain. It would keep failing, he wrote, "*unless we are willing to fight*," underlining the words with hard jabs at his keyboard. He abhorred Japan's invasion of China and the bombing of noncombatants. Japan's claim of self-defense was "not worthy of kindergarten mentality." But Roosevelt's speech had blown up any chance of good American influence on Japan. "Having been working to build up that influence during the past five years," wrote Grew, "is there any wonder that I feel like the architect who sees his edifice demolished overnight?"

The subject nagged at him. He wrote to his cousin Rita Crosby, "The mere preaching of idealism and the hurling of moral thunderbolts are unwise." He added, "I have been telling Washington precisely what I think and I daresay that some of my recommendations have not been found very palatable. At any rate, we in the Embassy are unanimous in our views and estimates and I shall be quite content to let history judge of their soundness."

On the night of November 15, Konoye called Baron Harada, who had just reached Kyoto on the evening train, and asked him to return to Tokyo as soon as possible.

"Is it a matter of extreme concern?" asked Harada.

"It is a matter of anxiety," said Konoye. He asked Harada to see Marquis Kido first upon his return. Konoye's fits of nerves always worried Harada. He took the late-night train back to Tokyo and arrived in the morning. Kido told him, "Konoye has started saying: 'I must resign immediately,' and I am very distressed." Harada asked what had brought this on. Kido explained that Konoye felt disrespected by War Minister Sugiyama and the army. The premier had recently complained to the emperor, "I have heard nothing about the operations of the Army and such. There is nothing for me to do but just watch them do as they please." The emperor, worried, had concluded that the army was making all decisions and that Konoye was pitiable.

Now Konoye wanted to resign and had asked Kido to tell Harada so it could be approved by Prince Saionji. Konoye's weakness angered Kido. Resigning would tarnish the emperor and damage the public's confidence. It also would panic the economy and harm Japan's prestige abroad. In short, Kido told Harada, resignation was unthinkable. Harada agreed. So did Saionji. "I really thought Konoye had a great deal of vision," said Saionji when Harada brought this news, "but it looks as if he doesn't have any judgment."

"Konoye has a great deal of vision," said Harada. "However, if he uses it once and is beaten, he withdraws. He is very cowardly and perhaps that makes it appear as if he doesn't have any vision."

They agreed that Harada and Kido must force him to continue.

Despite Grew's fears that the quarantine speech had crippled US influence in Japan, his personal standing there remained strong thanks to the relationships he had cultivated in Japan's highest echelons. Hull never understood the value of that or how to use it. By necessity Hull's perspective was horizontal across world affairs, while Grew's was deeply vertical into Japan. Hull and Hornbeck increasingly believed that Grew was too close to the Japanese to see them clearly, but in fact he saw things they missed, and he understood nuances lost on people far away and unfamiliar with Japanese politics and thinking. Hull and Hornbeck sometimes ignored or dismissed diplomatic opportunities that Grew detected.

A striking example arose that same day in mid-November as Konoye tried to resign. Grew was summoned to the residence of Foreign Minister Hirota at 9:30 A.M. Hirota wanted to discuss the possibility of using the United States to mediate informal, private peace talks with China to end the war. If the United States wanted to help, it could urge Chiang to negotiate, preferably before Nanjing fell, when the terms would be harsher. Hirota also pledged that Japan wouldn't seize any territory beyond Nanjing.

Grew saw promise in Hirota's proposal and floated the idea of American mediation in several exchanges with Hull. The secretary of state maintained that any peace negotiations must follow the framework laid out in the Nine Power Treaty of 1922, which had established China's sovereignty and territorial integrity while also guaranteeing equal commercial opportunity under the open door. Grew considered Hull's bureaucratic stance inflexible and unimaginative, a way of strangling the idea of mediation before it could be explored. "It would be deplorable," wrote Grew in his diary, "if we were to insist upon a peace by collective action to a point where any prospect of peace outside of the machinery of the Nine Power Treaty would be rendered impossible." Yet that was what Hull required, and then the opportunity slammed shut as events in China overtook any possibility for peace.

Chiang had rejected Japan's terms of settlement for months, hoping for intercession by the Western powers. Meanwhile Japan continued to bomb Nanjing, Hangzhou, and other Chinese cities, pushing Chiang's forces back at every turn. On December 3 Chiang finally tried to agree to Japan's terms, but he had waited too long. Japanese troops were almost at the gates of his capital, Nanjing. Young Japanese army officers were clamoring for harsh measures to crush China. The press insisted that the war must continue because China's desire for peace lacked "sincerity."

The assaults in China intensified. Konoye chose this charged moment for another shrinking fit. "I can no longer bear it," he burst out while talking to Harada. He wanted to resign as soon as Nanjing fell. Harada, aghast at this irresponsibility, told him resignation at this turning point was impossible. "It will mean that you are betraying the trust of the people," he said.

That evening the newspapers announced that Konoye had appointed a new home minister, Admiral Suetsugu Nobumasa. An ultranationalist, Suetsugu had once accused the United States of building air bases in China and the Aleutians to attack Japan. Lately he had been among those demanding amnesty for all seditious conspirators. He advocated the expulsion of the white race from China, which he considered Japan's domain, and he favored war with Britain to hasten the process. Harada realized that Konoye had purposefully kept the appointment secret from him that afternoon to avoid his disapproval. For the same reason, Konoye hadn't consulted the foreign minister, navy minister, lord keeper, or Saionji. The prime minister was ignoring moderates and appointing extremists.

Shortly after taking office, Suetsugu promoted Tomita Kenji from head of the Home Ministry's Peace Preservation Bureau to chief of the Police Affairs Bureau. Tomita, wrote Harada, "was a person with the most extreme Fascist tendencies in the whole Home Ministry." Even the emperor was alarmed. He sent for Suetsugu and asked why he had elevated Tomita. When this imperial misgiving became public knowledge, the ultranationalists were incensed. They attacked the lord keeper for slandering Tomita to the emperor. The extremists, wrote Harada, "have started to say: 'Clear the Court of corrupt elements.'" The uproar agitated Konoye. He took to his bed for several days with a cold.

In late October a Japanese plane fired on British and American citizens in Shanghai. For months, Grew had sent protests to Foreign Minister Hirota about Japanese bombings and strafings of civilian targets in China, and now he complained again. The Foreign Office promised to investigate. The next day Hirota sent a note calling the Shanghai bombing accidental. The pilots would be punished and remedies would be implemented. Yet the pilots seemed drawn to American church missions, perhaps because they were marked with huge American flags. The pilots destroyed mission compounds, hospitals, and a girls' school. They were out of control.

At the end of November, describing the Japanese response to another protest about the bombing of yet another mission, Grew wrote, "Of course, as usual, they plead low visibility and error, express profound regret and offer to consider indemnification. Bombing, regrets, bombing, regrets, further bombing."

THE *PANAY* INCIDENT

"THIS WAS A black day indeed." It was December 13, 1937. Early that morning Grew had dressed to play golf, then stopped at the chancery to read the overnight telegrams. The news was ominous. The Japanese were shelling Chinese troops fleeing Nanjing and were firing on any ships in the vicinity. The USS *Panay*, a gunboat that patrolled the Yangtze to protect American citizens and property, had reportedly been threatened by shellfire, along with three Standard Oil tankers, as they moved twenty-seven miles upriver to escape the fighting. In addition to the usual crew of around sixty-five, the *Panay* was carrying about fifteen American evacuees, including staff from the Nanjing embassy.

Grew didn't wait for instructions from Washington. He changed out of his golfing togs and arranged to meet Foreign Minister Hirota at 11:30. He showed Hirota the dispatches and reminded him that the Japanese military had been informed of the *Panay*'s whereabouts at every turn to prevent exactly this dangerous situation. He urged Hirota to intercede with the military before something disastrous happened.

Shortly before three o'clock, as Grew worked in the residence, Alice came in to say that Hirota had called the embassy and was en route to see him. Such a visit was unprecedented for a Japanese foreign minister. Grew told Alice it meant something terrible had happened. He walked down the hill and found Hirota already waiting in his chancery office. Hirota said that on the previous afternoon the *Panay* and the three oil tankers had been sunk by Japanese navy planes. He offered "the profound apologies and regrets" of the Japanese government.

Details remained scarce. Grew didn't know if there were casualties. His only information came from the Japanese Foreign Office, whose press release placed the American ships among a crowd of fleeing Chinese troopships. He wondered if he would be recalled pending a declaration of war by the United States. He and Alice began discussing what to pack if a quick departure became necessary, "precisely as we began to pack in Berlin after the sinking of the *Lusitania* in 1915."

The next morning's newspapers dutifully repeated the government's thin account. "Another strenuous day," wrote Grew. "Floods of telegrams about the *Panay*." Two British ships also had been fired upon. In Washington the British government was urging joint action, possibly including military action. It would suit Britain if the United States handled problems in the Pacific. Roosevelt was considering options ranging from an embargo to moving warships into the western Pacific. Secretary of the Navy Claude Swanson called for immediate war, and Secretary of the Interior Harold Ickes mused in his diary that this might be the right moment to fight Japan, before it got any stronger or more belligerent. Hull opposed all this as premature, not least because the American Congress and public wouldn't support it.

Grew knew little of this. He still had few facts from any direction. At 4:00 P.M. on December 14 he received a note from Hirota. The foreign minister apologized again for the incident, the damages, and—news to Grew—the casualties. The note supplied no numbers. Hirota said the Japanese navy ascribed the attack to "poor visibility." Even at low altitude the Japanese pilots "were unable to discern any mark" indicating that the ships were American. Therefore the incident "was entirely due to a mistake." Nevertheless, Japan intended to punish those responsible and to indemnify all American losses.

Just before this note arrived, Grew had received a dispatch from Hull with demands to be presented to the Japanese government. Grew couldn't get an appointment with Hirota until 8:30 P.M. His car crawled toward the Foreign Office through streets jammed with torchlight parades celebrating the fall of Nanjing. "At one time about a dozen students were standing on the floorboards of our car," wrote Grew, "yet all friendly enough."

"Tokyo went insane that night," wrote reporter Phyllis Argall. She went into the streets with her camera. The biggest crowds, as always, clogged the gardens and graveled walks alongside the imperial moat. "Every soul of the thousands there was carrying a lantern," she noted. When lantern lights danced onto the bridge over the moat, the crowd roared: the empress and the imperial princesses had come to the bridge to join the celebration at a royal distance. As Argall wandered the city she found torchlight processions everywhere. The delirious crowds thought the war was as good as over.

At the Foreign Office Grew told Hirota that his latest note had satisfied some of the US government's demands—apology, indemnification, and punishment of those responsible—but the government also wanted immediate assurances that Japan would not attack or unlawfully restrict American citizens and property in China in the future. Hirota promised a quick reply. "I wish to do everything in my power to maintain good relations with the United States," he said.

The Japanese public flooded the embassy with phone calls, letters, and even poems apologizing for the attack. They came to the embassy, sometimes in tears, to express the nation's remorse. One woman offered a traditional gesture of sympathy: she pulled scissors from her kimono and cut off a long strand of her hair, then handed it with a white carnation to an astonished embassy staffer. Donations for the victims and their families poured in, ultimately totaling about ten thousand dollars, which the US government gave to a Japanese charity to distribute. To Grew these responses demonstrated the existence of "two Japans," the chivalrous, warm-hearted country that he loved as opposed to the Japan of fanatical militarism.

Over the next few days American officials in China spoke to survivors and eyewitnesses. Facts emerged that contradicted Japan's version of events. Hull, incensed, wired Grew on December 16 to confront Hirota with these findings as soon as possible. The new details shocked Grew. He met Hirota at noon the next day and relayed Hull's message with cold formality, forgoing the smiles and small talk that typified their relationship.

Grew told Hirota that American reports had established that the *Panay* and the tankers were anchored far from Nanjing and any Chinese transports. The ships were adorned with large Stars and Stripes—draped horizontally across their decks, flying from their flagpoles, and painted on their sides. The Japanese planes had indeed flown at low altitude to bomb and strafe, but visibility that day had been perfect. The pilots couldn't possibly have missed the ships' huge multiple markings. Further, as the crew and passengers escaped from the sinking ships in sampans or by swimming toward shore, the planes strafed them as they sought refuge in the river reeds. Still further, the refugees watched from the reeds as Japanese army motorboats sped toward the *Panay* and machine-gunned it despite the American flags all over it, then boarded the ship, evidently looking for people to finish off. Planes likewise circled the riverbank looking for survivors to exterminate. From the *Panay* three were killed, two of them Americans, and about forty-three were wounded, some too seriously to walk. The number of casualties on the oil tankers was unknown, but at least one American was killed and many crewmen wounded.

The United States government, continued Grew, had no doubt whatsoever that the attack was deliberate and prolonged. The government now demanded to know, with greater urgency, what specific measures Japan was taking to punish those responsible and to protect Americans and American property from further attacks. Hirota "was visibly upset by the facts communicated and the gravity of the manner in which I presented them," wrote Grew. The foreign minister said he would question the naval and army authorities immediately.

Among the passengers evacuated by the *Panay* were several print journalists and newsreel cameramen. A reporter for the *London Times* wrote a story about the ordeal. The navy ministry called his firsthand account about Japanese soldiers machine-gunning the *Panay* and the survivors a hoax designed to anger Americans. (The cameramen later produced a newsreel of the attack and its aftermath, shown first to government officials in Washington in late December and then released to the public. It confirmed crucial details, including bombers attacking from perfectly clear skies.)

On December 20 the embassy received a report by the Japanese navy. It claimed that the pilots never saw the flags on the *Panay* and thought it was a Chinese vessel. The report added that if any future investigation established that survivors had been machine-gunned, the only possible reason was that the gunners had mistaken them for fleeing Chinese soldiers. Grew's comment: "Rot!"

On December 24 Hirota asked Grew to come at 7:00 P.M. to receive Japan's official response. Japan agreed to meet all US demands. The commanding admiral had been recalled—a severe shaming—and eleven other navy officers had been punished, including the commander of the air squadron that led the bombing. (Four years later this man, Minami Yoshimi, would again target ships flying American flags, at Pearl Harbor.) Despite all the contrary American evidence, the note also declared, "It has now been fully established that the attack was entirely unintentional."

Hirota appeared to be tired and worn down. "I am having a very difficult time," he told Grew. "Things happen unexpectedly." He didn't elaborate. He hoped the official note would settle the *Panay* matter. Grew said he would cable it to Hull immediately.

The next day the investigatory report from the United States Navy arrived. With methodical detail it demolished Japan's claim of an accidental attack. Grew delivered the report to Hirota. Later that day Hull sent the official reply to Hirota's note. The US government was pleased, it said, by Japan's quick admission of responsibility and offer to pay damages, and by its measures against those responsible and its pledge that nothing similar would occur in the future. As for the factual discrepancies, Hull drily noted that the United States would rely on the version in the US Navy's report. For the sake of peace and diplomacy, the American government was still willing to overlook Japan's alternative findings. The incident was closed, pending payment of damages. (In April 1938 Japan sent the United States government $2.21 million to settle claims.)

When Hirota finished reading Hull's note and looked up, his eyes were brimming. "I heartily thank your Government and you yourself for this decision," he said to Grew. "I am very, very happy. You have brought me a splendid Christmas present." Both men felt the elation that follows a brush with disaster.

"This was an eminently happy day," wrote Grew, "and it showed the wisdom and good sense of two Governments which refused to be stampeded into potential war in spite of the tendency of the one side to 'save face' at almost all costs, and in spite of an outrageous affront offered to the other." The incident also proved the value of an experienced diplomat who had earned the trust and respect of his host country's officials, and who had the confidence to act quickly in a crisis. Hull overlooked all that. In his *Memoirs* he took credit for resolving the *Panay* incident, with barely a nod toward Grew.

The emergency had passed. "Yet I cannot look into the future with any feeling of serenity," wrote Grew. A sudden exit remained a strong possibility. He ordered special boxes for his diaries in case he had to pack fast and go.

On December 28, two days after the resolution of the *Panay* incident, Grew received word from the Foreign Office in response to his latest protest about the bombing of another American mission hospital, this one in Nanchang, China. His weary summary: "Mistake, sincere regrets, rigid instructions for the future."

As the *Panay* crisis unfolded, the Japanese army massacred and raped the people of Nanjing in one of the worst atrocities of the twentieth century. After the city fell, the Japanese army was allowed to go berserk. Casualty estimates vary, but they murdered somewhere between 50,000 and 200,000 Chinese men, women, and children. Mutilations were common. The streets were heaped with mangled corpses. At least 20,000 Chinese females of all ages were raped and many were killed afterward. Much of the city was torched.

None of this appeared in Japan's censored press. The public knew little beyond the glorious victory at Nanjing. Yet there were clues. The Japanese newspapers followed two soldiers competing under the tradition of *bushido* (the way of the warrior) to reach 250 kills using a two-handed samurai sword. The coverage began with the occupation of Shanghai and continued to Nanjing but trailed off after each man had claimed more than 100 Chinese victims. Perhaps the obvious became apparent: swordsmen could only kill civilians who lacked weapons of their own.

"Of course the Japanese have an answer for everything," wrote Grew when reports of the massacres and rapes reached Tokyo. According to the Japanese, the raped women were Chinese prostitutes who had fled and were simply required to resume business. The few Japanese who had heard about the atrocities blamed missionaries for spreading false rumors to denigrate Japan.

Japan's consul general from Shanghai was visiting Tokyo and told Grew that the Japanese government hoped Nanjing's shopkeepers and families would soon return to the city and recommence normal life. The official was startled when Grew pointed out that "in the face of reports of whole sale executions, murders, and cases of rape it was perhaps not surprising that the Chinese inhabitants, especially those who had daughters, should be a little chary about returning."

STRENUOUS STASIS

THE EARLY MONTHS of 1938 were cold but clear, the best winter weather since the Grews had arrived in Tokyo. This was offset by a terrible flu season. Most people in the embassy caught it, including the Grews. Alice remained hobbled by a swollen knee. Nevertheless, diplomatic duties called and Grew responded with his usual energy. "Still very little formal entertaining, fortunately," he wrote at the end of February, then listed lunches, dinners, and concerts he attended on fourteen days that month.

Despite cold weather and recurring bouts of flu, his appetite for golf remained strong. On consecutive days in January he played twenty-seven, forty-five, and twenty-seven holes—ninety-nine holes in three days. "Very fair exercise for an old man nearing 58," he wrote. In September he played eighty-one holes in forty-eight hours. Golf momentarily relieved the worsening diplomatic pressures caused by Japan's conduct in China.

Most high army officers hadn't expected the "China incident," as it was called in Japan, to last more than a few months. But the occupations of Nanjing, Hangzhou, and other major cities didn't crush Chiang Kai-shek. Japan gave him until January 15, 1938, to accept its harsher new terms. Chiang waited until the deadline and then asked for more information, an obvious dodge. The next day Konoye announced to the Japanese public that the imperial government would have no further diplomatic relations with Chiang's government, which it intended to annihilate. Japan also planned to install a new Chinese government. Many young officers cheered the decision to expand the conflict.

Konoye was committing Japan to long-term war. Though the army's Supreme Command wanted peace with China, Konoye contended that settling with Chiang after so many Japanese victories would damage Japan's self-esteem and international image. Over the coming years, the cost of saving face would be financial deprivation, untold suffering, and millions of deaths.

Press coverage of Japanese bombings of Chinese civilians and American property roiled the American public. Hawks and internationalists clamored to punish Japan with an embargo or sanctions. Isolationists worried that such actions might lead to war. Humanitarians protested that the steel and planes used to bomb civilians were sold to Japan by American companies. All factions wanted to stop the killing and destruction. Hull rejected the idea of an embargo because he believed, as did Grew, that it could lead to war, but the reports from China incensed him. The State Department announced a "moral embargo" and notified manufacturers that the government "strongly opposed" the sale of airplanes or airplane parts to nations that bombed civilians.

While officials in Tokyo offered apologies and assurances, the bombings and depredations against Chinese civilians and American property accumulated. On February 4 Grew complained to Foreign Minister Hirota again about looting in Hangzhou, with dates and details. Hirota promised that Japan would pay for all losses and damages after an investigation. A week later his promises vanished in a cloud of excuses. He handed Grew a note stating that Japan had responded fast and fairly to the *Panay* incident and had instructed commanders in China to prevent any more accidents. It was unfortunate that the United States kept complaining, he wrote, because, after all, Japan had tried. Furthermore, after "a rigid investigation" the military had determined that the so-called looting in Hangzhou was merely "requisitioning" by troops in need of provisions. Yes, the foreign-owned buildings were marked with flags and notices, but Japanese troops might have missed them in the dark. And since foreign and Chinese buildings were intermixed, "it is possible that some of the requisitioning squads made mistakes." No indemnities would be forthcoming.

The endless loop spun on: the United States presented evidence, Japan provisionally apologized pending an investigation, then discarded inconvenient evidence for alternative facts that rationalized what had happened. Grew felt like a mouse on a wheel.

Viewed from the United States, Japan looked like a belligerent monolith, but its internal politics remained volatile. Right-wingers and hotheaded militarists still pressured the government to adopt their agendas. Marquis Kido, now minister of education, told Baron Harada that extremists had been visiting him to demand that he remove liberals and other suspect intellectuals from the universities. Ultranationalists wanted Hirota out because of his efforts to settle the China war and improve relations with Britain.

Ultranationalists also continued to push amnesty for jailed plotters and assassins. Fresh offenses committed under the guise of patriotism went unpunished. A group of nationalist thugs started harassing and punching members of the Diet for opposing the army, calling them "running dogs who are unpatriotic." Suetsugu, the extremist home minister who commanded the police, saw no need to hinder assaults against enemies of the state. When these thugs occupied the parliamentary building for ten hours to stop debate, Suetsugu did nothing.

In February the Diet opened debate on a proposed bill, the National Mobilization Law. This sweeping legislation, championed by ultranationalists, aimed to prepare Japan financially, materially, and psychologically for a long war with China by giving the central government control over almost everything—raw materials, businesses, the press, public discourse, and daily life, including shopping, entertainment, retail prices, even thought. Essentially the Diet was debating whether to neuter itself by ceding all power to a central government dominated by the military. The bill passed. The Diet became a vestigial appendage of government, and Japan took another leap toward totalitarianism.

While digging the country deeper into China and pushing for the National Mobilization Law, Konoye continued to feel blistered by moonbeams. He whined about resigning in January, February, March, and April. Totalitarianism attracted him, yet he shrank from its mantle. He reluctantly shouldered the burdens of office, then bleated that they crushed him while grumbling that his ministers didn't consult him. Japan's ruling class recognized that Konoye was weak and indecisive. That suited the army. His few decisive acts were often blunders he soon regretted, such as committing Japan to a long war with China.

Many advisors, including Harada, urged Konoye to be more independent and forceful, in hopes that he would grow into his anointed role. But a house cat never becomes a tiger. The nation, Konoye told Harada, needed someone strong "to take control of [the army], hold the reins." He knew that person wasn't him. No one doubted his intelligence, but he lacked the judgment and backbone necessary to lead a nation through crises. He was continually propped up by Prince Saionji, Harada, and Kido, who believed they were doing the nation a service. Eventually even Saionji threw up his hands. He told Harada that Konoye was acting like a servant, not a leader responsible for a nation.

Konoye was a prisoner of other people's expectations. Perhaps that partly explained his affinity with the emperor. Konoye visited the palace so often that the lord keeper told Harada, "There has never been a Premier who troubled us so much." Konoye talked to the emperor about affairs of state but also chattered and bellyached. "It is an extremely difficult thing," Konoye told Hirohito in March, "for a dreamy person like myself, who is popular yet has no power, to take charge of affairs indefinitely."

The emperor must have sympathized. He was the divine sovereign of Japan yet was a prisoner in his palace. His happiest hours were spent studying marine organisms in his lab. In December 1937 his ultranationalist military attaché, essentially a spy for the army, chided him for wasting time on scientific studies during a period of national emergency over China. Palace officials, fearful of the military right wing, told Hirohito to stop going to his lab. He obeyed.

The emperor fell ill in early 1938 and became noticeably weak. He desperately wanted to rest on the seacoast at Hayama, but the grand chamberlain and vice chamberlain refused to permit it. "They are worried," said the household minister to Harada, "over possible criticism on the part of the general public," who might blame him for convalescing at such a critical time. The lord keeper added that these same people were prohibiting the emperor from working in his lab.

Harada, irate and concerned, called Saionji, who said to use his name to reverse these absurd prohibitions and to remind those responsible not to put the public or the rightists above the emperor's health. The palace officials agreed to let the emperor go to Hayama, but only if the war and navy ministers entreated the emperor to do so. Harada arranged it. Relieved, the emperor asked the household minister if, when they reached Hayama, he might be allowed to go out in a boat to collect microorganisms. Hirohito was a god who needed permission.

On May 23 the worst earthquake since the Grews' arrival shook Tokyo. It reminded Grew of a pitching ship's deck, with rolling floors and objects flung about. Two weeks later another quake topped that one and stopped the chancery's clock. Then came a record-setting rainy season, causing fatal flooding and landslides. In late August a typhoon ripped up trees by the roots, with severe flooding that carried away homes and caused avalanches that closed roads. Earthquakes, floods, typhoons, tsunamis, and volcanic eruptions regularly devastated Japan. Calling the country volatile, as Grew often did, captured more than just its political instability.

Konoye's threats to resign alarmed his puppet master, the army. To placate him the army forced War Minister Sugiyama to resign in May, replacing him with General Itagaki Seishiro, one of the instigators of the Manchuria railway incident. General Tojo Hideki, Itagaki's new vice minister, previously chief of staff of the Kwantung Army, would soon become notorious to Americans. Foreign Minister Hirota fell next, replaced by General Ugaki, whom the army had blocked from the premiership the previous year for being too moderate. Ugaki considered China the nation's most urgent international issue. He took the post on the condition that Konoye would retract his refusal to negotiate with Chiang Kai-shek. Konoye exposed his increasingly right-wing leanings by appointing former war minister Araki, whom Grew called an "ultra-chauvinist and fire-eater," as minister of education.

On July 4, three days after the State Department announced the moral embargo, Grew had his first full meeting with Ugaki. Grew had spent two days preparing. The general had piercing eyes and a brushy white moustache. He would turn seventy in a few months but emanated vigor and command. He "speaks in crisp, staccato, peremptory tones as if he were giving military orders," noted Grew. Grew's official statement pressed the foreign minister on every American concern about China, in hopes the old general would take strong action. He began to read the statement out loud, one sentence at a time for the translator, who didn't know Grew and whispered his translations. "I had to jack him up," wrote Grew, "whereat the Minister observed that I was deaf." That pleased Ugaki, since he shared the condition.

Grew handed Ugaki a partial record of the indiscriminate bombings, destruction, and civilian casualties between July 1937 and June 1938. Twenty-two single-spaced pages with nearly three hundred entries documented the bombings of American hospitals, schools, missions, and churches, all of them clearly marked with American flags. Grew protested that Japan now prohibited American citizens from returning to their bombed-out or confiscated properties, an infringement that must be corrected immediately. The United States also expected Japan to indemnify all this. He moved on to examples of personal assaults against American citizens—slaps, shootings, ransackings, high-handed behavior. Next Grew protested Japan's schemes to close the open door, most recently by setting up "special companies" and monopolies in China to squeeze out foreigners. After delivering this battering, Grew told Ugaki that an ambassador, like a true friend, must speak the truth even if his remarks weren't welcome. He hoped Ugaki took his words in this spirit. He promised not to release any of this to the press.

The foreign minister had listened silently to all three thousand words. At the end he thanked Grew for the friendliness of his remarks and said that everything must be investigated. Meanwhile he could make a few preliminary replies. First, Japan wanted to end the war in China as soon as possible. Second, Japan and the United States must improve their relationship. After these innocuous statements, Ugaki turned slippery. Japan would maintain the open door, he said, but there might be "temporary difficulties." Echoing his predecessors, Ugaki assured Grew that indiscriminate bombings had been forbidden, so they could only be explained by lack of training among Japanese pilots—in short, they were accidents. American property would be returned as soon as possible, but at the moment that was unfeasible. Surely the United States understood.

The meeting ran for two and a quarter hours without discernible progress. They met three more times in July, essentially reprising this conversation and its strenuous stasis. After the last of these exercises in deadlock, Grew hustled to catch the noon train to Karuizawa for a solo vacation while Alice visited their daughter Elsie in China.

He needed the break, and not only because of diplomatic frustrations. After just seven years the embassy buildings all required resurfacing due to rot and staining. Some walls had been knocked out of plumb by earthquakes. Nearly one hundred workmen had turned the embassy grounds into a bedlam of hammering and chipping amidst piles of dirt, sand, and lumber. Despite the smothering heat and humidity of the Tokyo summer, windows had to be closed or boarded up. The chancery and residence became ovens. To accommodate the chippers and hammerers, an exoskeleton of staging enwrapped the buildings.

"I have become used to having Japanese workmen peer in while I am in embarrassing situations in the bathroom," wrote Grew, "but it is impossible to get used to the noise and lack of air." He was counting on eight relaxing days in Karuizawa, his only vacation of the year, to soothe his jangled nerves.

It rained almost without pause. He played golf every day anyway, sodden but determined to unwind. Back in Tokyo he wrote, "It will take two or three major wars to keep us from getting home next spring!"

Before he left for Karuizawa Grew had cabled two dispatches about a skirmish between Japanese and Soviet forces at Changkufeng, on the border between Russia and Korea. Neither side wanted war, so he expected the incident to fizzle. But factions within the army craved a fight. In mid-July, War Minister Itagaki and the chief of the army general staff asked for an audience with the emperor. Hirohito suspected they wanted an imperial sanction to attack in Changkufeng. To preserve the army's face, the emperor said to tell them not to come if they intended to seek a sanction, because they would fail. The generals insisted.

When admitted to the imperial presence they requested a sanction to attack. Irritated by this insolence, Hirohito asked if the army had conferred with other relevant ministries about this grave petition. Yes, said

Itagaki, with the foreign minister and the navy minister. Hirohito knew that both ministers opposed an attack against Russia. Anger replaced irritation. The army's methods, said Hirohito, were sometimes "arbitrary and sneaky which is altogether improper. . . . I feel that it is abominable in various ways." Then he addressed Itagaki directly: "Hereafter, you may not move one soldier without my command."

The army's face had received an imperial slap. Outside the chamber Itagaki said, "I can never look into the Emperor's face again." He felt compelled to resign, as did the chief of the general staff. Konoye talked them out of it.

After his disgrace in the palace, Itagaki told the army at Changkufeng to stand down. A few days later young officers disobeyed this direct order and commanded their forces to attack. The Soviets counterattacked and crushed the Japanese, inflicting casualties of at least twelve hundred dead and wounded. Both sides sought a quick settlement, and by early August the incident was resolved. The humiliating defeat stemmed from open insubordination, but instead of punishing the responsible commanders, the army saved as much face as possible by misrepresenting the attack as self-defense.

The army also wanted to settle with China. In early September, after more than a year of brutal fighting, the army general staff approached the navy general staff twice to ask its support to secure peace there. The navy was amenable but leery because factions inside the army constantly clashed and undermined one another. "The entire Army must agree or this problem cannot be settled," said Navy Vice Minister Yamamoto to Harada. He added that most of the nation was sick of this war.

The moment seemed promising for peace, but it was already passing.

22

APPEASEMENT

SINCE 1931 EVERY nod toward peace, democracy, or military constraint had been sabotaged by Japan's right wing. By 1938 its poisonous tentacles stretched far beyond the military and the patriotic societies into cabinet ministries and the palace. Totalitarian models of patriotism had been codified into laws and government agencies and had been normalized for the public by incessant propaganda and state-censored news. As in Germany during this decade, extremism infused national life while ordinary people worked and raised children and planned for a satisfying future under a government they assumed would protect them.

Some Japanese leaders, such as Prince Saionji and Baron Harada, worried about the growing influence of the right wing. Harada constantly spoke to people who either refused to see it or dithered about it. He reported these conversations and anxieties to Saionji. "This is extremely ominous," said the genro. The situation reminded him of the fall of the Ming dynasty. "There were many men of intelligence," said Saionji. "However, they all kept quiet, and there was no unity."

On the morning of August 28 Harada went to Konoye's villa to tell him about his plan to convene a small group to discuss strategies against the extremists. "I do not know whether it will have any effect," said Harada. "However, it is very necessary to have men of intelligence prepared, as much as possible, against these rumors and movements of the right-wing."

"Men of intelligence are all weak, and I don't think they'll be of any use," Konoye answered, in an apt self-description. He segued to what seemed a different subject. A few days earlier, Tomita Kenji, the ultra-nationalist former chief of the Police Affairs Bureau, had called on him. Shortly before, Tomita had jailed hundreds of leftists and union members for conspiring to damage the *kokutai* by rejecting Japan's rising milita-rism and nationalism. In February 1938 he had issued orders approving the transport of "comfort women" from Korea to service soldiers in China. Harada considered Tomita the most extreme fascist in a ministry filled with them. Tomita had been replaced after only six months and now was apparently angry.

"He told me," said Konoye to Harada, "'There might be circumstances in which you might become the victim. We do not want to make you the victim but depending on circumstances it might be unavoidable.' He threatened me quite a bit." The former head of Japan's national police was threatening to assassinate the prime minister unless he resigned. "If I am to continue," added Konoye, "I must make something that will include the whole right-wing." That wasn't the anti-extremist strategy Harada envi-sioned. "I came home a little worried," he wrote with his usual understate-ment. (Tomita was soon appointed governor of Nagano Prefecture and later was appointed chief secretary to the cabinet by the incoming prime minister—Konoye.)

The next day Harada spoke to several people about the right-wing threat, starting with Marquis Kido. Harada was especially worried about Home Minister Suetsugu. "I think matters may get out of control," said Harada. He felt compelled to do something "because of my anxiety for the nation and for society." Kido told him that speaking to the hard-liner Suetsugu was pointless. Next Harada met with Foreign Minister Ugaki, who shared his concerns and also felt them personally. Ugaki was under attack by ultranationalists for his efforts to mend relations with Britain and negotiate peace with China. But he told Harada that if he spoke out against extremists, "it would seem that I, who am already watched, am being forced to say such things and this would be very disagreeable." He would lose face.

Last on this long, frustrating day Harada spoke to Navy Minister Yonai Mitsumasa and Vice Minister Yamamoto about the need to push Suetsugu away from the right wing. To these military men the solution was simple:

Konoye should give Suetsugu direct orders. It troubled them that the prime minister was reluctant to rein in extremism among his own ministers.

While Harada was making his worried rounds about the right wing, five Japanese navy fighter planes forced down a commercial airliner owned by a Chinese American company, then strafed the plane after it crashed in a river near Guangzhou. The American pilot and three Chinese survived, but at least a dozen Chinese passengers and crew were killed on the ground in their seats. Grew filed a protest on August 26. Three days later the Japanese government denied all responsibility. The navy claimed the airliner displayed no visible markings and had taken evasive action. "Of course there could have been no doubt whatever as to the plane's identity," wrote Grew in his diary. "It was flying on a course and schedule followed almost daily for many months and the markings were over five feet high."

By late September the chimera of peace with China had nearly vanished. The political riptide was running ever stronger in one direction— rightward. It pulled in people who had once resisted. On September 22 Kido complained to Harada that the emperor "has too much of the scientist in him and has no sympathy for the ideas of the right-wing. It is very troubling because he is too orthodox." Surprised, Harada strongly disagreed. "In reality," he wrote, "the right has no substance." Their shallow agenda consisted of nothing beyond "reverence of the Emperor, the expulsion of foreigners, loyalty and patriotism. . . . They are only thinking of driving others out by feelings alone. Their slogan is: 'There are no others as loyal as we.'"

Japanese understood that resisting the riptide could be dangerous. Those dismayed by the country's direction were giving up or going silent, paralyzed by fatalism. Saionji was distressed that Japan was moving rightward but felt he could no longer make a difference. He was too old and tired. "There is nothing to do but to endure this," he told Harada.

In the last few days of September Grew worried about the meeting in Munich between Hitler, Mussolini, Prime Minister Neville Chamberlain of Britain, and Premier Edouard Daladier of France, to discuss Hitler's demand that Czechoslovakia either give him Sudetenland or suffer invasion. Europe seemed on the brink of another war. Grew, Alice, and embassy personnel gathered around radios for the afternoon, evening, and late-night news from London and Hong Kong, anxious to catch updates from Munich. Grew hoped for a last-minute agreement, "unless Hitler is utterly insane . . . the kind of insanity that would make him incapable of appraising the tremendous forces which war would ultimately have brought against him." On the twenty-ninth Grew listened to the radio news until after midnight and went to bed worried. At ten forty-five the next morning the British ambassador called to read him a Reuters dispatch of two words: "Agreement reached."

Grew and his staff were elated. Yes, Chamberlain and Daladier had submitted to Hitler's blackmail and handed him Sudetenland, but peace was saved. Hitler swore he wanted no more territory. Grew scoffed: "Appetites like Hitler's grow as they are fed." Hitler was a gangster, he wrote, who "held up Europe at the point of a gun." But like most people who remembered the horrific slaughter of World War I—twenty million dead and as many wounded—Grew was relieved. The Munich Agreement was soon notorious as appeasement with rapacious militarism.

A day earlier, Japan's political currents had swept away another resister. Ugaki abruptly resigned, exhausted by the military's opposition to his moderate stance and frightened by an assassination plot. Perhaps Ugaki, watching the Munich Conference, decided to get out before Europe exploded and Japan's ultranationalists pushed the nation into a disastrous alliance with Germany.

Konoye saw his own opportunity. If Ugaki could quit, so could he. Harada made a series of frantic phone calls to Kido, the lord keeper, the ministers of the navy and finance, and others, instructing them to change Konoye's mind. Even the emperor weighed in. After a long, tense day Kido called Harada near midnight. Konoye had agreed to stay.

After Japan signed the Anti-Comintern Pact, Tokyo became crowded with Germans and Italians. A steady flow of big black Mercedeses festooned with swastikas on streaming red pennants rumbled into the drive of the Imperial Hotel, where Japanese liaison officers awaited them. The hotel lobby resounded with German gutturals and the clicking of military boots. Photos of Hitler and Mussolini were popular in shops, as were flags with swastikas or the green, white, and red bars of Italy. Newsstand magazines featured stories about Germany and Italy. Bookstalls offered guides for learning German. Schools began including the language in curricula. Gestapo officers advised the Kempeitai and the Home Ministry police how to detect and purge subversives. The German embassy intensified its efforts to censor the local press. Starting in 1938 a press attaché there combed through the daily papers with a red pencil, marking articles offensive to Germany and sending them to Japan's Foreign Office with huffy demands to do something. The Germans were easily offended. Inundated with Nazi protests, the Foreign Office finally told the Germans to handle press complaints on their own.

Since early 1938 Hitler and Ribbentrop had contrived to lure Japan into a military alliance. Japan's military attaché in Berlin, General Oshima Hiroshi, championed the idea, but Japan's ambassador, Togo Shigenori, opposed it. So had Foreign Ministers Hirota and Ugaki. But the Japanese army wanted a pact and began scheming to remove the obstacles. Grew didn't hear about the proposed agreement until October 8, when Wilfrid Fleisher of the *Japan Advertiser* and *Herald Tribune* brought him the rumor. Grew doubted its accuracy because such a pact would be politically irrational for Japan. Yet that same day General Oshima, who admired Hitler, was installed as ambassador to Germany, a step toward irrationality.

After Ugaki resigned, Oshima urged the pact on the new foreign minister, Arita Hachiro. But Arita also disliked the terms. He instructed Oshima to seek an agreement aimed solely at the Soviet Union. Oshima, following instructions from the army, wrote back that the proposal must include Britain and France.

Arita didn't bite. He had powerful allies, including the navy minister, who knew that a war in the Pacific would fall mainly on his branch. The pact also alarmed the finance minister, who worried that Britain and the United States would cut off trade relations with Japan and ruin the nation's economy. Konoye neither supported the moderates nor discouraged the militants. The pact went dormant, but Oshima and Ribbentrop weren't finished.

A NEW ORDER

DURING THE MONTHLONG interim between Ugaki's resignation and Arita's appointment, Konoye served as acting foreign minister in addition to his role as prime minister. Protocol called for an ambassador to approach the host government through its foreign minister, so Konoye's dual role gave Grew an opening for direct communication with Japan's highest official. On October 3 he arranged a meeting. To avoid the press and other prying eyes, Konoye sent his personal car to fetch Grew. The ambassador was deposited at the back of Konoye's home and taken through the garden, then up the back stairs to Konoye's office. Grew read a litany of American complaints about Japan's violations of the open door and the promises by previous foreign ministers to abide by it. Konoye assured Grew the promises would be kept. Others had made the same pledge, but this time Grew heard it from the prime minister.

Three days later Grew followed up by sending Konoye a long note that listed examples of Japanese violations and asked for specific remedies. The list was head-spinning. On July 4 Ugaki had promised that American trade would not be restricted or blocked in China by Japanese monopolies or "special companies." Yet within a month Japanese authorities had established telephone and telegram monopolies in North China and Shanghai. A new navigation company was given a monopoly over all water transport in the Shanghai delta. Another monopoly appropriated the wharves at Qingdao and thus controlled all cargo traffic. In North China new monopolies were dictating all trade in wool and tobacco. Japanese authorities also had seized control over currency exchange rates and customs tariffs in key cities, putting all imports, exports, and trade transactions under Japanese rule. The open door was being slammed on American businesses.

There was more. Throughout China, continued Grew's note, Japan had prohibited Americans from reoccupying their property because of the war. Japanese censors were interfering with American mail and telegrams. American ships were forbidden to use the Yangtze on the pretext of military conditions, yet Japanese merchants cruised the river without restraint. Americans were restricted from trade, residence, and even travel on railroads and vessels. Grew pointed out that the United States had not imposed constraints on Japanese citizens or businesses in America, and had so far honored the 1911 Japanese-American Treaty of Commerce and Navigation—a statement with the whisper of a threat. He finished by asking Konoye to end the discriminatory monopolies and other violations of American rights. As always, he left a written summary of his oral remarks to forestall misunderstandings, whether innocent or deliberate.

Meanwhile, the Japanese army advanced through China. Japanese planes continued to bomb civilians and nonmilitary targets. By October 25 the major cities of Hankou and Guangzhou had fallen. Lantern parades lit up Tokyo's streets. The celebrants knew nothing about the atrocities in these shattered cities. Phyllis Argall's reportage brimmed with horrors: "Bodies and pieces of bodies twisted and charred beyond recognition as human, albeit all too heartbreakingly human, were the aftermath of Japanese bombing attacks on crowds of defenseless civilians, chiefly women and little children."

When Grew arose on October 26 he hadn't yet read these latest reports. He paused at the residence's upstairs window to admire the tranquil symmetry of snow-covered Mount Fuji, clear for the first time that autumn. That same day Japanese planes bombed an American Lutheran Brethren mission in Tongbai (Tungpeh). The building was clearly marked with American flags and was far from any military action. The Japanese authorities had known the mission's location for at least seven months. The bombing killed three-year-old Phoebe Nyhus and wounded her mother and sister.

In an atypically emotional entry, Grew seemed pushed to the brink. The death of Phoebe Nyhus, he wrote in his diary, made me even more sick at heart than usual, while first-hand accounts, supported by photographs, of the barbaric behaviour of the Japanese troops filled me with impotent anger. If we were not surrounded here in Tokyo with gentle Japanese who deplore these things as much as we do—even more perhaps, because it concerns their own country and their own honor—I should find it very difficult to remain at this post. Once in a while I do break loose and openly express my feelings, to such people as Kabayama, Baron Harada and other friends. I am sure they think I am being fed with Chinese propaganda and exaggerated tales because they themselves have no access to the facts. . . . Until they themselves go abroad, or talk with Japanese returned from abroad, they have no sources whatever from which to learn the truth. And the truth is sickening.

On October 29, two days after receiving this grim news, Grew had dinner with Baron Harada. "I had a long and very frank talk with him about the rotten condition of American-Japanese relations," wrote Grew. Harada also wrote about the evening and noted Grew's agitation about the killing of Phoebe Nyhus. Her story disturbed Harada as well. He called Navy Vice Minister Yamamoto and Foreign Minister Arita to ask them how it had happened. Neither knew anything about it.

Grew tried several times to meet with Konoye about the Nyhus case but settled for a meeting with Vice Foreign Minister Sawada Renzo. Grew "made emphatic representations," he wrote, "couched in vigorous terms." The loss of American life, he told Sawada, would enrage the US public. Sawada promised an investigation—another headstone in the graveyard of Japanese promises.

Grew had been feeling "rottenly" for weeks, with chronic indigestion and low energy. His doctor diagnosed mental strain and prescribed a month's rest in Honolulu. "But it would be even more of a strain," he wrote, "to be away from the job at a critical time when new developments are steadily occurring." He intended to press on until May and then rejuvenate himself with a furlough of at least four months.

· · ·

On November 3, 1938, at 9:10 A.M. Konoye addressed the nation on the radio for fifteen minutes. He announced a "new order in East Asia." Now that Japan had conquered China's major cities, he hoped the Chinese would awaken to their common mission with Japan "as an Oriental race." Unfortunately Chiang Kai-shek was fighting against Japan's benevolent plans. Chiang and the imperialist powers, not Japan, had caused China's problems. Now Japan had been "entrusted with the task of constructing a new Far East . . . in all fields of human life." To begin, Japan would install a more farsighted person to lead the true Chinese government. Japan would allow foreign powers to continue operating in China, said Konoye, as long as they "understand the real intentions of Japan" and change their attitudes "in accordance with the new situation in the Far East."

Grew understood Konoye's subtext: from now on Japan would call the shots in East Asia and control China's government, trade, and resources. Despite the rhetoric about common destinies and racial solidarity, Japan envisioned China exactly as the imperialist powers had—as a trove of raw materials and a huge market to be managed for the benefit of the superior nation, Japan.

Grew was dumbfounded. Only a month earlier Konoye had promised to honor the open door and equal opportunity. Days later, when Grew met Arita for the first time on November 7, they greeted each other as old friends. But circumstances had changed since Arita's first stint as foreign minister in 1936 and 1937. Grew began by asking if Arita would affirm his three predecessors' assurances that Japan respected the open door and American rights in China. Arita answered that Konoye's recent speech had laid out Japan's new policies. Grew asked Arita to clarify Konoye's statement that foreign powers must "adopt policies suitable for the new conditions." What new conditions? Arita hedged. They could have a long talk about that, he said, after he had settled into office. Grew suggested the next day. Maybe next week, said Arita. He advised patience because the situation was "very difficult." Patience, he repeated. Grew typically had a deep well of that virtue, but it was running dry.

On November 18, six weeks after Grew's request for a prompt response, Arita sent Japan's reply about the open door and American rights. The note denied or excused all of Grew's protests. Yes, Japanese companies had taken over many enterprises in China because they needed to be restored after war destroyed them. None of these companies would impair American trade if American companies operated "on the basis of the new conditions." Nor was Japan discriminating against the United States, argued Arita, because the restrictions applied equally to all foreigners. Japan was eager to lift the constraints on trade, travel, and residence, but unfortunately that wasn't militarily feasible. And frankly, Arita said, chiding, for Grew to complain about a few violations of American rights during a time of major military operations was excessively peevish. Japan would fully respect the rights of the United States and other foreign powers, he said, as long as they accepted Japan's plans for the present and future of East Asia based on the "new order." Welcome to the new open door, Arita seemed to say, heavily fortified and guarded by Japan.

The next day Arita invited his old friend Eugene Dooman, the American embassy's counselor and second-in-charge, to his private residence to discuss his note to Grew. As Dooman and Grew expected, Arita wanted to sound out Dooman about Grew's reaction. Dooman told Arita that the ambassador had read the note "with the best of good will" but found nothing responsive to the American government's concerns. "Well," said Arita, "I suppose not."

In mid-December the American government announced a $25 million loan to Chiang's government. The loan's obvious though unstated purpose was to help Chiang fight Japanese aggression. At a press conference Arita told foreign correspondents that the loan would prolong the war and increase unfortunate incidents affecting foreign citizens.

On December 22 Konoye issued another statement about China. Though short, it managed to combine threat, condescension, equivocation, self-justification, arrogance, and unreality. Konoye declared that Japan would pursue "the complete extermination" of Chiang's government while simultaneously establishing "a new order in East Asia." After extermination would come "neighborly amity," economic cooperation, and mutual defense against communism. "The spirit of renaissance is now sweeping over all parts of China," claimed Konoye, "and enthusiasm for reconstruction is mounting ever higher." To advance this renaissance, he said, China must cast aside all resentment about Japan's past actions. That long list included Japan's theft of Manchuria and Hebei, the invasion of China south of the Great Wall, the seizure of Chinese resources, and the incessant bombings, atrocities, and carnage against Chinese civilians. Amity and economic co-operation would be enforced, continued Konoye, by the presence of Japanese troops. But he insisted that Japan had no desire to control China and would welcome foreign powers "who grasp the meaning of the new East Asia and are willing to act accordingly."

Where could a diplomat start with such a mess of contradictions? That same day Grew sent another note to Arita asking for a reply to all his unanswered protests about bombings and violations of American rights, including the death of Phoebe Nyhus. The ambassador and the foreign minister met on December 26. Arita claimed that the ten or twelve incidents involving Americans and American property were still being investigated, but he did wish to express the regrets of the Japanese government for the death of an American citizen in the accidental bombing of Tongbai. Grew, containing himself, noted that the number of incidents wasn't a dozen but between two and three hundred. He suggested that the foreign minister consult the list given to him months ago. Two days later Grew sent Arita an updated count of the bombings, assaults, injuries, and lootings: 296.

Somehow Arita had a response ready for Grew that very day. Investigating such incidents was difficult, he wrote, but Japanese forces always exhausted "every possible precautionary and technical measure" to protect noncombatants and avoid damaging their property. "Accordingly," he went on, completing his false syllogism, "if, as reported by the American Embassy, damage was done to the property of American citizens in China, it must be surmised that such damage was caused by stray shells or bomb fragments from bombing operations."

In short, accidents. Since Japanese forces were meticulous about avoiding noncombatants, wrote Arita, the only explanation for accidental bombings was that the owners had marked their properties poorly. In either case Japanese forces were not at fault. An addendum specifically addressed about thirty of Grew's protests. After thorough investigations, Japanese authorities had concluded that every case, without exception, was accidental. Japan's pilots, like Japan, were entirely and comprehensively blameless.

Once again Japan had obliterated pages of factual details and had substituted fabrications. The more facts that accumulated, the more preposterous became Japan's denials of reality. Grew seemed to be stuck in an infinity loop of futility.

On December 30 he received the State Department's response to Japan's declaration of a new order in East Asia. Grew delivered it to the vice minister at his residence at 11:30 A.M. on the last day of 1938. The note was firm, clear, and cool. The United States rejected Japan's claim to special rights in China. It rejected Japan's decree that a new situation in China had nullified all previous rights and agreements. It disputed Japan's power to control China's raw materials and other resources, a grab that would lead to conflict and instability. The note acknowledged that the situation in East Asia had changed, but added that "many of the changes have been brought about by the action of Japan." Japan could not appoint itself the maker of arbitrary rules for a self-proclaimed new order. The United States was willing to revise existing agreements with the participation of all parties, and welcomed proposals from Japan. "Meanwhile," ended the note, "this Government reserves all rights of the United States as they exist and does not give assent to any impairment of any of those rights."

Firm and clear. But Japan didn't seem to care about assent from the United States. The note was another warning without teeth.

On December 31 Konoye called Harada. The prime minister had tried to resign in November and December of 1937, and also in January, February, March, April, September, and October of 1938. This time he was adamant. He was determined to flee the war he had started in China. He and his cabinet were resigning on January 4.

In the coming year Grew would test one of his favorite adages: a pessimist sees a difficulty in every opportunity, while an optimist sees an opportunity in every difficulty. Many opportunities lay ahead.

MANEUVERS FROM ALL DIRECTIONS

BARON HIRANUMA KIICHIRO, the seventy-one-year-old president of the Privy Council, replaced Konoye as prime minister. Hiranuma, gaunt and severe, with a permanently downturned mouth, had strong advocates within the military and Japan's right wing, and had angled for the premiership for years. Yuasa Kurahei, the lord keeper, recommended him and consulted Prince Saionji in the usual way, honoring the protocol of decades. Saionji considered Hiranuma a dangerous fascist and had always opposed his ambitions, but this time he neither approved nor objected, too worn down or fatalistic to fight the tide.

Hiranuma retained most of Konoye's cabinet, with the exception of the far-right home minister, Suetsugu, replaced by Kido, who had begun to tilt rightward. Arita agreed to remain foreign minister, but only if Hiranuma promised not to expand the Anti-Comintern Pact with Germany into a military agreement against Britain and France. That suited Hiranuma. He didn't trust any of the European powers or the United States and didn't want to entangle Japan in Western conflicts. Less easily swayed than Konoye, Hiranuma told Arita that if the army tried to force him into a broad military pact, he would quit. But when War Minister Itagaki demanded that Japan strengthen its military ties with Germany and Italy, he acceded. This contradiction planted a time bomb inside the cabinet.

Japan's recent turbulence, especially the shock of the February 1936 insurrection, had tempered Hiranuma's extremism. He still rejected democracy and individualism as unsuitable for Japan, but he also rejected

European totalitarianism as contrary to Japan's national spirit and reverence for the emperor. He still believed absolutely in Japan's imperial Asian destiny, yet he recognized the practical sense of good relations with Britain and the United States, if possible.

Hiranuma's nuanced stance on Japan's role in the world order could be put to use by attentive diplomacy but Hull pigeonholed Hiranuma from the outset. The new prime minister was "a Japanese counterpart of the European Fascists and Nazis," wrote Hull. "The change, therefore, could only be for the worse."

The Grews began 1939 with a six-day vacation in the coastal resort of Kawana. Grew called it a badly needed rest cure. He played golf every morning, napped every afternoon, solved double-crostics in the evening. He returned to Tokyo feeling recharged, but in mid-February bronchitis and strep throat knocked him and Alice to their knees for two weeks. Adding to their doldrums, their oldest friends in the diplomatic corps— the Belgian ambassador and his wife and the Romanian minister and his wife—were leaving Tokyo. The Romanians had been sacked for having "some Jewish blood." The Grews had stopped accepting invitations from the German embassy because of Kristallnacht and other Nazi outrages in Germany. Now anti-Semitism had touched them in Japan.

In February Japan invaded the Chinese island of Hainan, further undercutting their rhetorical commitment to peace and territorial contentment. Situated in the Gulf of Tonkin between French Indochina and Hong Kong, Hainan was a critical link in Chiang's supply chain. On February 17 Grew called on Arita to remind him of Japan's repeated denials about territorial ambitions in China. The maneuvers were strictly military, replied Arita. He added that the occupation "will not go beyond military necessity." "Which of course," commented Grew, "means precisely nothing."

A few weeks later Japan annexed the Spratly Islands, a sprawling, sparsely populated archipelago south of Hainan between French Indochina and the Philippines. Japan also claimed sovereignty over the waters framing the islands—about one hundred thousand square miles of the South China Sea. The Japanese flag was now planted within striking distance of the resource-rich Southeast Asian colonies of Britain, France, and the Netherlands, as well as of the Philippines, a US protectorate. All these nations protested. You don't understand, replied Japan.

On March 15 Hitler honored his Munich promises of peace and territorial contentment by invading Czechoslovakia. Arita wired German foreign minister Ribbentrop that the occupation would "contribute to the peace of Europe and ultimately to the peace of the world." Germany and Japan occupied alternative realities where war was peace and territorial greed was altruism. Each considered itself the master race of its hemisphere, destined to rule over lesser peoples.

On April 14 Roosevelt sent public messages to Hitler and Mussolini asking them to pledge nonaggression toward thirty-one European and Near Eastern nations. Mussolini responded with ridicule. On April 28 the Grews listened to Hitler spew scorn and mockery about Roosevelt's message for nearly two and a half hours in a radio broadcast from the Reichstag.

Hitler and Ribbentrop wanted Japan on Germany's flank. A new cabinet meant new opportunity. Ribbentrop and Ambassador Oshima renewed their pressure, with help from War Minister Itagaki and Germany's ambassador in Tokyo, General Eugen Ott. Many in the army and the Foreign Office also wanted a military pact with Germany, but Arita still opposed it and Hiranuma had promised to support him. Neither the navy minister nor the finance minister wanted a military entanglement with Germany and Italy.

The sane view seemed to be prevailing. Grew heard from the British ambassador that Arita swore to him that the revised pact wouldn't be military. The next day the president of Domei, the official news agency, visited Grew to assure him that Oshima and other extremists clamoring for a military pact "are in the minority and are steadily losing ground." At a private dinner on April 16 Harada told Grew not to worry about the possibility of a military alliance with Germany because he "was in a position to assure me that I need have no further anxiety on that score." A few evenings later Grew and Dooman attended a formal dinner for American and Japanese naval officers. After the food and flowing sake, after some juggling and dancing by pretty Japanese women, Navy Minister Yonai pulled Dooman aside. In Japanese, Yonai asked him to tell Grew that the rumors of a military alliance with Germany and Italy were untrue. The cabinet had just set a policy to stay out of European conflicts. Japan also wanted to improve relations with the United States. Dooman repeated all this to Grew in English. When Grew thanked him, Yonai smiled and said the issue of a pact was settled.

"This is one of the most important and significant conversations that we have had," wrote Grew, "and I regard it as marking a new trend, indeed a milestone, in Japanese-American relations, for Yonai can be trusted."

Three weeks later, on May 8, Grew sent Hull a long summary of Japan's internal squabbling over the subject of a military pact with Germany and Italy. He had harvested an impressive amount of information and knew that the cabinet had agreed to revise the Anti-Comintern Pact without committing Japan to anything beyond opposition to the Soviet Union. But he warned that "there are at work in this country powerful and sinister influences" supporting a military pact. He believed these forces had failed, at least momentarily, and cited the statements of Arita and Yonai.

The next night the Grews gave a dinner for Arita and his wife, along with others from the diplomatic corps. Aside from an official banquet in April, Arita hadn't accepted another foreign invitation all year, another indication that Japanese felt more comfortable in the Grews' residence than in any other foreign home. After dinner and before the evening's movie, Arita emphatically assured Grew again that Japan would not form a military alliance with Germany and Italy.

On May 19 the Grews sailed for home on a leave of five months. The Japanese press, reflexively anti-foreign, made an exception for Grew, praising him as someone who tried to understand Japan and whose return would be welcome. Grew departed feeling confident he had helped to preserve the distance between Japan and Germany. He had collected guarantees from the highest levels of the Japanese government.

The day after Arita told Grew the policy toward Germany was settled, Navy Minister Yonai asked Harada to suggest a secret place for him to meet with War Minister Itagaki. Yonai wanted to find some way of reducing the army's unrelenting pressure for a military pact with Germany. Despite what Arita and Yonai had told Grew, they had been fending off serious attacks from the right wing for months.

In Berlin and Rome, Ambassadors Oshima and Shiratori Toshio had defied Arita's instructions. They were the diplomatic equivalent of the Kwantung Army, attempting to set foreign policy without consulting the central government. Both ambassadors threatened to resign if Japan didn't accept Germany's proposal for a military alliance. They hoped War Minister Itagaki would resign with them and cause the cabinet to collapse. The right wing also instigated a campaign to undermine Arita and intensify the public's pro-German, anti-British feelings. "There are all kinds of maneuvers, from all directions, taking place," wrote Harada.

In early April, Ribbentrop asked Oshima if Japan would support Germany in a war against Britain and France. Oshima, disobeying direct instructions, said yes. Shiratori told the Italian government the same thing. Arita, infuriated, ordered the ambassadors to retract this pledge. They balked. Yonai backed Arita, but Hiranuma began to waffle. On April 11 the emperor weighed in. He summoned War Minister Itagaki and chided him for two hours for supporting the defiant ambassadors. These two insubordinates, said the emperor, were infringing on his supreme authority in matters of war, and the German proposal was unacceptable.

Despite his promise to Arita and the emperor's opposition, Hiranuma moved to Itagaki's side. Through Marquis Kido, he attempted to persuade the emperor to accept the army's position. Kido told Harada about this plan, adding, "The present Emperor is a scientist and very much of a liberal as well as a pacifist. Therefore, if the Emperor's ideas are not changed, there will exist quite a gap between His Majesty and the Army and rightist groups. . . . We must also make it appear as if we understood the Army a little more."

Harada was dumbfounded and angry. He and Saionji expected Kido to protect the emperor and Japan from extremists, not narrow the gap between them. Rightists, he reminded Kido, were sowing disunity and chaos. They were the problem, not the solution. Kido and Hiranuma had strayed from their sworn commitment to their country and their emperor, and the typically coolheaded Harada was furious. In a desperate, seething passage unlike any other in his diary, he wrote of telling Kido, "I am thinking of possibly killing five or six of these men who will become obstacles in the future." Kido, alarmed, promised to think more about the issue.

In early May, Arita informed Germany and Italy through Oshima and

Shiratori that Japan was rejecting their proposal. The Germans instantly sent a new draft that preserved many of the rejected terms. Arita discovered that the document had been written by Oshima. The ambassador's insubordination infuriated Arita. At a heated cabinet meeting he, Yonai, and the finance minister voiced their alarm about Oshima's actions and his pledge to Ribbentrop. Itagaki and Hiranuma supported the ambassador. Arita threatened to resign. Hiranuma said that would cause the cabinet to fall, but Arita wouldn't budge. Two days later at another meeting, Hiranuma and Itagaki pressed again to support Oshima's pledge. Yonai had heard enough. If Germany attacked another country and Japan joined in, he said, the navy would sit it out. Hiranuma, shocked, agreed to study the issue further.

That same day, Itagaki asked for an audience with the emperor. Hirohito responded that if his aim was to seek support for the war pact with Germany, the answer was no. Itagaki, fearing another imperial slap, sent Prince Kanin, chief of the army general staff, to promote the pact to the emperor in his stead. Irritated by the army's impertinence, Hirohito repeated his veto and spoke to the prince "quite severely."

Perhaps that explained Arita's confident assertion to Grew the next day that the military pact was dead. But it still had a pulse. On May 22 Germany and Italy grew tired of Japan's equivocations and signed a military pact between themselves. In late May, Arita again declined Germany's terms and sent a revised draft for Oshima and Shiratori to present to Ribbentrop. The two ambassadors refused to do so without including a military pledge to assist Germany. When Arita complained about this defiance to Hiranuma, the prime minister recommended using whatever wording the army wanted—that is, to surrender foreign policy to the military. Arita refused. Yonai told Harada, "It is very abominable for the Premier to support the Army and the Ambassadors who take action contrary to the will of the Emperor."

"From this time on," wrote Harada, "the Rightists became active again and as usual, rumors were rampant." Members of patriotic societies poured into Tokyo to protest the stalled pact. Reports said the extremists intended to assassinate Arita, Yonai, and palace officials blocking the agreement.

The Kempeitai promised to safeguard them, wrote Harada, but "it cannot be ascertained whether [the Kempeitai] are the protectors of the officials or the agents of the rightists."

To Prince Saionji the desire for a military pact with Germany was perplexing and irrational. "I can never reason it out," he told Harada. "It does not make any sense diplomatically nor politically."

ABROGATION

IN MAY 1939, as Prime Minister Hiranuma was advocating a military alliance with Germany and Italy, he played a stratagem from another direction. He invited Dooman to a secret dinner at his private home on May 23. The date was a few days after Grew would sail for America, when Dooman would be in charge of the embassy. Grew cleared Dooman to accept the invitation and investigate the premier's thinking.

On the evening of the dinner, Hiranuma's assistant picked up Dooman and drove to the modest suburb of Shinjuku. To avoid detection by the press, they parked a few blocks from Hiranuma's small house, which Dooman noted was as unpretentious as a shopkeeper's. A few policemen stood guard at the gate. Inside, after some brief small talk, Hiranuma got to the point. He said that the possibility of a European war horrified him. It would inevitably embroil the entire globe and destroy civilization. Certain groups in Japan wanted "special relations" with Germany and Italy for the nation's security, but he believed the best security was peace. The only powers with a chance to preserve it in Europe were Japan and the United States, working together. He wondered how the American government might respond to these views.

In other circumstances, said Dooman, the American government would gladly collaborate with Japan to lessen the threat of war in Europe, but Japan's actions in China were threatening the very unity and peace the premier professed to want. Dooman couldn't imagine the American government working with a nation that bombed and violated American citizens and property.

The prime minister wondered if the United States understood Japan's "very real feeling of grievance against the Occidental powers, especially Great Britain." He recited the litany: the West's lack of appreciation for helping win World War I, the refusal to let Japan keep its territorial rewards in Asia, the complacency as China repeatedly violated Japanese rights, which led to the occupation of Manchuria and North China. For these reasons, said Hiranuma, Japan sympathized with Germany and Italy, other "have-nots" who had been mistreated by the Western powers. If the United States insisted that the China problem must be resolved before anything else could happen, he added, then his proposed plan for peace would have to be abandoned because Chinese resources were essential to Japan's security "in a world of sanctions, embargoes, closing of markets to foreign competition, and lack of free access to raw materials." Then he remarked that if these discriminatory trade practices were corrected and the world's resources became more equally accessible, Japan wouldn't depend so much on China, and Germany and Italy wouldn't be driven to take what they needed by force. Peace was impossible, he continued, until the conditions that caused the problems were acknowledged and addressed by the other powers.

It was time to eat. A maid passed dishes through a sliding door to Hiranuma's daughter, who served them. During dinner they discussed Chinese philosophy. Afterward, in his study, Hiranuma summarized his earlier point: Japan and America were the only powers capable of halting the slide toward war in Europe, but to stop it, the economic and political conditions that generated the friction would have to be addressed. Hiranuma suggested an international conference. Japan would be glad to include the China issue in the negotiations, he said. If such a conference appealed to the American government, he would sound out Germany and Italy while Roosevelt sounded out Britain and France. If all were willing, Roosevelt could call the nations together.

The idea was astonishing. It bristled with possibilities and risks for all sides, as well as great obstacles. The prime minister asked Dooman to convey his proposal to Hull. Hiranuma's assistant drove Dooman back to the embassy, where he sent a telegram that night. He wrote that Hiranuma's proposal reflected Japan's growing anxiety about how developments in Europe would affect the nation. Hiranuma evidently believed Japan couldn't stand alone and must ally itself with either the totalitarians or the democracies. His motive for offering to collaborate with the United States, wrote Dooman, wasn't affinity for democracy but "stark facts." If war came, Hiranuma expected the rich democracies to win. Dooman asked for a prompt response.

Hull asked Joseph W. Ballantine, chief of the department's Japan desk, to analyze the proposal. Ballantine had spent time in Japan, spoke the language, and was far more sympathetic to the country than Hull and Hornbeck, but also deferential to them. On June 7 he sent Hull a long memo. He acknowledged that a conference might hasten peace in China, avert a war with Japan, prevent the complete economic and political collapse of Japan and/or China, and give Japan an alternative to a military alliance with Germany and Italy.

On the other hand, he wrote, if the United States took the initiative for a conference, Japan would gain leverage for negotiating about China. Japan also might use the conference to save face with the Japanese public while ending the China war—a good thing—but that would preserve the Japanese military's prestige and the likelihood of more destructive blunders. He suggested that a better strategy might be to wait until the consequences of Japan's war with China undermined the Japanese public's view of the army, a stance that echoed Hornbeck's. Ballantine also cautioned that neither Japan nor China would be satisfied with any settlement and would blame the United States when it failed. He recommended declining Hiranuma's proposal. Hull tabled the idea. He didn't inform Dooman.

After two weeks without a reply, Hiranuma sent an assistant to ask Dooman to send another telegram for Hull's urgent attention. Dooman did so. Another two weeks passed. The assistant visited Dooman again, looking for news. Dooman sent a third telegram asking for an immediate answer. The department replied that its response was coming by diplomatic pouch, a delay of another two or three weeks.

Hull's answer finally arrived at the end of July, more than two months after Dooman's secret dinner with Hiranuma. Hull thanked the prime minister for his interest in world peace and said Japan could start by withdrawing from China. That was his entire response. He ignored the idea of a conference. On July 31 Dooman asked Hull what he should say to Hiranuma about his proposed summit. Was the department declining the idea? Studying it? Dooman reminded Hull that the proposal was a direct invitation from Japan's prime minister.

The next day Acting Secretary of State Sumner Welles replied that Hull's answer was clear and no further explanation was necessary. Two days later Dooman wired Hull again to make sure the secretary of state understood that the Japanese would interpret the department's silence as a snub signifying that relations with the United States couldn't improve unless Japan ended the war with China. Hull understood perfectly. He let his silence stand. "I was more than skeptical of Hiranuma's approach," he wrote in his *Memoirs*. A collaboration with Japan, he wrote, "would have the effect of sanctioning all her brazen expansion in the Orient up to that time."

The probability of the powers gathering in 1939 to correct international inequities and prevent war was always slim to none. A conference would have required prodigious diplomacy and political flexibility. Equally implausible was the idea that Hitler, Mussolini, and the Japanese military would abandon their messianic paths. Maybe Hull was right that Hiranuma was trying to play him, though Dooman, an experienced Japan hand, considered the prime minister sincere. Neither Dooman nor Hull knew that Hiranuma was simultaneously advocating a military pact with Germany. Nevertheless, an acute diplomat might have sensed an opening in Hiranuma's gesture. It suggested that Japan's civilian government was still capable of acting outside the military, a space closing fast. Hull didn't bother consulting or even informing Grew about any of this until his return to Tokyo. Grew later wrote, "The nature of [Hull's] reply to Baron Hiranuma's momentous step was interpreted by him as in no way an encouragement but, on the contrary, as a rebuff, and the matter was not pursued."

Hiranuma's proposal arrived in the State Department stillborn because Hull and others believed Japan couldn't be trusted, for reasons constantly supplied by Japan. The news that flowed into Washington from Japan following Dooman and Hiranuma's secret dinner had given Hull no reason to change his mind.

• • •

In the summer of 1939 the Kwantung Army provoked skirmishes with Soviet and Mongolian forces on the disputed border where Russia touched Mongolia and Manchuria. Both sides massed troops there. In late June, in a signature move, the Kwantung Army bombed a Soviet air base without getting permission from the central command in Tokyo.

Then on July 6 and 7 Japan intensively and indiscriminately firebombed Chongqing (Chungking), where Chiang had moved his capital after Nanjing. Most of the casualties were civilians. Bombs damaged an American mission church and fell a few hundred yards from the residences of the American ambassador and counselor. Bombs also exploded two hundred yards from the American gunboat *Tutuila* on the Yangtze, narrowly avoiding a reprise of the *Panay* incident.

A week later Arita responded to the latest batch of US protests about bombings of American people and property throughout China, including another bombing of the mission where Phoebe Nyhus had been killed six months earlier. Japan had investigated the bombings, wrote Arita, and "the actual facts" proved that all of them were accidents brought on by the victims themselves, either by marking their properties poorly or by allowing Chinese forces proximity.

All these actions did alarm some leaders in Japan. After the first night's bombing of Chongqing, Foreign Minister Arita told Baron Harada, "In this condition, diplomacy and everything else is impossible." During a two-hour meeting with War Minister Itagaki about the Soviet incident and the bombings, the emperor barked, "There is no one as dumb as you." The lord keeper also was disgusted with Itagaki. "It's not only his brains that are bad," he told Harada. Itagaki also lied and blamed others to save his own face. "There are only a few men doing the agitating," continued the lord keeper, "and they all resort to personal feelings. They only think of winning or losing, and whenever the Army's proposal does not pass, they consider that they've lost and become infuriated. These circumstances might lead them to misjudge the main issues and it is very dangerous." Prince Saionji lamented to Harada that he had been following political conditions since age thirteen, "but there never was a period when politics was so difficult as at present."

Within days British ambassador Robert Craigie agreed to give Japan "special rights" in China, including the right to maintain security for its forces and to "suppress or remove" anything that obstructed Japan or benefited its enemies. Britain, anxious about an impending war in Europe, had caved in to Japan's "new order." The Japanese press crowed. Hull and Roosevelt worried that Japan would take Britain's submission as clearance to do whatever it wanted in East Asia.

The situation was spiraling. Bombings and attacks on Americans and their interests had worsened. The Yangtze River remained closed to foreign navigation. Harbors were restricted all along China's coast. Trade barriers kept proliferating, as did assaults on foreigners. The Japanese military was gnawing its way toward the South China Sea, claiming land and ocean that controlled important shipping lanes.

Hull knew the American public was angry about Japanese atrocities and bombings in China. In June a Gallup poll found that 66 percent of Americans now favored a boycott of Japanese goods and 72 percent wanted an embargo on war materials to Japan. It was time for the United States to flash a caution light. Japan's small domestic market and lack of natural resources made it vulnerable to trade controls. America was Japan's foremost trading partner. Hornbeck and a few members of Congress had previously floated the idea of ending the bilateral Treaty of Commerce and Navigation, signed in 1911, which gave Japan most-favored-nation status. Hull advised the president to use his authority to abrogate the treaty. Roosevelt agreed. On July 26 the State Department told Japanese ambassador Horinouchi Kensuke that the United States was giving Japan the required six months' notice. The treaty would end on January 26, 1940, leaving Japanese imports and exports subject to punitive tariffs and duties.

The psychological shock in Japan was immediate. Most in the military, government, and business had assumed the United States would continue its high-minded neutrality and take no concrete action to hinder Japan's plans. They believed what they read in their censored press: that Americans were soft isolationists with no appetite for conflict. In Tokyo and Washington, Arita and Horinouchi asked why the United States had taken this drastic action without warning, as if Grew and Hull hadn't been protesting Japanese actions for years. The decision also surprised Dooman, still in charge during Grew's absence. He got word of it afterward, another instance of the department keeping the Tokyo embassy in the dark about vital issues.

Arita and Horinouchi were eager to know what the United States intended to do when the treaty ended in January. "I was careful to give them no enlightenment," wrote Hull. "I felt that our best tactic was to keep them guessing, which might bring them to a sense of the position in which their flagrant disregard of our rights and interests in China was placing them." He dismissed the idea that desperation might lead to rash action rather than submission.

GALLONS OF VINEGAR

IN JULY 1939 the Kwantung Army mounted another attack on the Soviet-Mongol forces at Nomonhan on the border between Russia, Mongolia, and Manchuria. On August 20 the Soviets counterattacked with tanks, demolishing the Japanese. They trounced them a second time on August 31. It was another military and diplomatic debacle instigated by insubordinate officers acting outside their orders. Nomonhan also shattered the myth of an invincible imperial army ready to take on the Soviet Union in the "northern advance" urged by some in the army.

"Somehow it doesn't make sense," said Prince Saionji when Harada reported this. "It is like a dream." That evening the phone rang in Harada's home. A reporter told him Germany and the Soviet Union had just signed a nonaggression pact. If this stunning betrayal by Germany was true, noted Harada, a military alliance between Japan and Germany was kaput and so was the Hiranuma cabinet. In Berlin, Ambassador Oshima got the same news when Ribbentrop called him at 11:00 P.M. on August 21 from Hitler's mountaintop villa. Oshima exploded. Ribbentrop said Germany had to protect its eastern flank against "encirclement" by Britain and France. This lesson about Hitler's trustworthiness was soon forgotten by the Japanese.

Hiranuma and his cabinet resigned on August 28. Saionji was consulted about a new prime minister but once again was too disgusted and confounded to recommend anyone. "The next Cabinet is beyond me," he told Harada. "Our foreign policy is our biggest failure since the beginning of our history." He said Japan should ally itself with Britain, the United

States, and France. He told the lord keeper that anyone who got the imperial mandate was qualified only if he had "tasted the bitter suffering" of drinking gallons of vinegar through his nose.

After the usual maneuvering, the palace advisors nominated a compromise candidate for prime minister who was acceptable to the army: General Abe Nobuyuki. Abe's political views were undefined but not extremist. The emperor summoned him to the palace to form a cabinet and surprised him by issuing several imperial commands: respect the constitution; pursue friendly relations with other countries, especially Britain and the United States, which meant appointing a foreign minister sympathetic to those goals; and select a home minister who would follow these same guidelines in domestic affairs. The emperor wanted to nudge the government and the army away from fascism and back toward the democracies.

Three days later, on September 1, Hitler's blitzkrieg hit Poland from the west. On September 3 Britain and France declared war on Germany. On September 17 the Soviet Union invaded Poland from the east.

Abe vowed that Japan would not join a European war. The defeat at Nomonhan had momentarily silenced Japanese proponents of a northern advance against Russia. Germany's betrayal had embarrassed the army and made swastikas temporarily unpopular in Tokyo. The Nazi cabal retreated into the shadows. Ambassadors Oshima and Shiratori were recalled to Tokyo. Abe repulsed intense lobbying to name Shiratori as foreign minister and instead appointed Admiral Nomura Kichisaburo. This appointment signaled that the new prime minister accepted the emperor's commands and wanted to improve relations with the United States. Nomura was known to be pro-American. During World War I he had been a young naval attaché in Washington, DC, where he knew a young assistant secretary of the navy named Franklin Roosevelt. Abe hoped that would be useful for Japan's foreign policy. Considering all this, it seemed faintly possible that Japan might change its direction.

But many in the Japanese military had other plans, despite these temporary setbacks. They saw the European war as Japan's golden opportunity. With Britain, Germany, and the USSR preoccupied in the West, East Asia was unprotected and ripe for plucking. To them, this was not the time to shrink from Japan's imperial destiny. The Abe cabinet had to go.

• • •

After Grew left Tokyo for home in mid-May, much had gone haywire. He kept track of developments while making his usual rounds in Boston, the North Shore, Hancock, Washington, and New York, where he visited the World's Fair. He delighted in golf, music, theater, and family time with his children, grandchildren, and brothers. In Hancock Alice had two mild heart attacks. While she rested Grew barely slowed down. He socialized almost nonstop and wrote 246 letters.

He met with Hull and Hornbeck several times and with Roosevelt twice. He found their attitude toward Japan considerably hardened since his last visit. They were distrustful and resentful, poor mindsets for diplomacy, and were losing patience with the Japanese. Grew told Roosevelt that if the United States cut off oil to the Japanese, they would likely invade the Dutch East Indies. The president replied, "Then we could easily intercept her fleet." After another visit with Roosevelt, Grew wrote, "I do not think that we shall let ourselves be crowded out of China." The State Department didn't consult him about Hiranuma's proposal or the commerce treaty, deepening his conviction that his on-the-spot knowledge of the country rarely penetrated the department's stiffening viewpoint.

As Grew traveled he asked Americans from all social strata about Japan—businesspeople in the smoking cars of trains, stewards on airplanes, gas station attendants, taxi drivers, farmers, men and women behind counters in city shops. As in the State Department, the depth and breadth of their anger startled him. He was often asked to speak at private dinners and began giving an off-the-record talk that addressed this worsening attitude. He started by condemning Japan's international bad faith, military belligerence, and atrocities in China. American anger at Japan was justified, he said, if aimed at the extremists responsible for these actions. Yet Japan did have legitimate grievances against the Western powers, he continued, and the threats to its economic survival were real. He reminded his audiences about recent history in which Western nations hadn't hesitated to take what they wanted by force—which in no way justified Japan's actions, he added, but did put them into a wider perspective. He noted that Americans tended to lump all Japanese together, but this was inaccurate and unfair. He and Alice had lived among many nationalities during their thirty-five years in the Foreign Service, but none were finer than the Japanese for high principles, courtesy, and chivalry. "These are the people we live among," he said, "people whom we admire, respect and love. It would be utterly biased and prejudiced and blindly unwilling to accept the truth to fail to give them their proper due."

Considering that American feelings were running high against Japan, Grew's speech was brave as well as broad-minded. But he saw that his first-hand perspective wasn't denting the animosity toward Japan in the State Department or his audiences. He realized that if this surprised him, with his access to American newspapers, Japanese moderates must be completely in the dark about how the bombings and rights violations were pushing the United States to the limits of its tolerance. The termination of the commerce treaty had given Japan a flash of insight into the American mood, but Grew felt a stronger strategy was necessary to avert major trouble.

He told Hull that when he returned to Tokyo he wanted to give the Japanese a blunt wake-up speech. They needed to hear that Japan's atrocities in China and its high-handed violations of American rights there were turning Americans against Japan. The extremists wouldn't listen, but the moderates might still be capable of alarm. Hull approved the idea. Department staff wrote a draft that Grew heavily revised.

By the end of Grew's visit home, the future in Japan looked even more uncertain and unpredictable. He decided to leave his diaries in Washington for safekeeping.

THE HORSE'S MOUTH

"ON THE JOB once more and quite ready for it," wrote Grew after arriving in Tokyo on October 10, 1939. "I feel very fit and keen to get going." On the return voyage he had spent hours revising his speech, scheduled for the America-Japan Society on October 19. In the interim he met briefly with new foreign minister Nomura, an old acquaintance, and other Japanese friends. Grew told all of them that American attitudes toward Japan were growing bitter. He was told, in turn, that the new cabinet wanted a better relationship with the United States.

This information altered Grew's plan. He wanted his speech to change the dialogue, not shut it off by embarrassing Abe and Nomura. He hoped the speech would create a fresh basis for talks with the new foreign minister and was pleased when the State Department, in a sign of trust, cleared him to use his own judgment. It was "a ticklish business," he wrote, to clang the alarm without alienating the people he needed to reach. He opted to steer clear of threats and "Jovian thunderbolts" about principles in favor of hammering home the facts—the bombings, the trade violations, the personal assaults. Most of this would be news to his audience.

Grew was breaking protocol by exposing these issues in a public speech, but this was not a time for muted private messages. He needed to convey the growing anger within the American government and public to a wide Japanese audience. The American government had tried not to irritate Japan, but this had created the dangerous misimpression that America would always back down. It was time to disabuse the Japanese of that misjudgment.

At the America-Japan Society luncheon, more than two hundred people, evenly split between Japanese and Americans, settled into their chairs. They were influential diplomats, government officials, palace courtiers, financiers, business leaders. Count Kabayama's introduction of Grew, like the count himself, was effusive and optimistic. He called the Grews "the true symbols of American-Japanese amity."

Grew began with his customary charm. He said he and Alice were pleased to be home in Japan with their friends. He waxed about his family reunion in Hancock and the World's Fair in New York, and praised Japan's lovely pavilion at the Golden Gate International Exposition. He hoped America and Japan would always be friends. Yet there were serious problems, he continued, pivoting. An ambassador was an interpreter between cultures. During his leave he had given the Japanese perspective to many Americans, including the president and secretary of state. He also had listened to their perspectives on Japan, and now it was crucial for the Japanese to hear what the president and others had told him. He was relaying news, he said, "straight from the horse's mouth."

He did so masterfully, mixing rhetorical questions, disturbing facts, concern for Japan, hope. He waded in by summarizing the views of one Japanese friend in particular. This friend believed that the Japanese military in China took every precaution to avoid bombing American properties and that all damage was accidental. Stories about physical assaults against Americans were exaggerated. Violations of trading rights were minor. Any reports that contradicted these descriptions were anti-Japanese propaganda. Most Japanese in Grew's audience shared this friend's views.

"Alas," said Grew, "the truth is far otherwise. . . . And in the interests of the future relations between Japan and the United States those facts must be faced."

For instance, Japanese often dismissed America's objections to Japan's actions in China as "legalistic." Yes, treaties and agreements were legal documents that Americans expected other nations to respect, because discarding them signified scorn for the harmony and friendship such documents were meant to preserve. Japanese also insisted that Americans simply didn't understand "the new order in East Asia." Yet Americans of all stripes understood it precisely, said Grew, as "depriving Americans of their long-established rights in China." Most Japanese didn't know how horrified Americans were by the constant bombing of civilians and how angry they were at the contempt for treaties and rights, the constant insults to American citizens. Grew himself believed, as did the American government and people, that all these damaging actions were *"wholly needless."* From every point of view—economic, commercial, political, cultural, historical—it was illogical for Japan to keep injuring its friendship with the United States. He stressed that his frankness was motivated by deep affection for Japan.

The audience was silent. No polite applause interrupted him. One retired Japanese army officer walked out. No diplomat in Japan had ever spoken so bluntly in public.

Grew came to his ending. Upon his return to Tokyo, he said, a Japanese reporter had asked whether he was concealing a dagger or a dove in his bosom. "I have nothing concealed in my bosom," he told his audience, "except the desire to work with all my mind, with all my heart and with all my strength for Japanese-American friendship." Then he added forcefully, *"If it can be preserved."* The dove was gripping a dagger.

Grew had been speaking for forty minutes. The audience hadn't made a sound. Stories filed by correspondents in Tokyo described the audience as "stunned," "shocked," "startled," "dumfounded," "rocked." Now the room erupted with prolonged applause from both nationalities. Hugh Byas of the *New York Times* had been reporting from Japan for more than twenty years. He later told Grew no other ambassador could have given this speech "and gotten away with it," by which he meant "and lived." Grew's affection and respect for Japan had created a well of goodwill toward him that allowed him to criticize Japan without affronting face. Reports about the speech ran on the front page of newspapers across the United States. They almost universally praised it, reinforcing Grew's belief that Americans were reaching the end of their patience with Japan.

After the initial shock wore off, the Japanese press resumed its usual righteousness. The major papers complained that the United States still didn't understand Japan or the facts about China. They called the speech propaganda. Japan's policies in China were unalterable and its conduct was blameless, so if America wanted to adjust relations, it must correct its attitude.

But Grew's message did reach its target. A week after the luncheon, Count Kabayama told Grew that his "epoch-making" speech was being studied by Prime Minister Abe, Foreign Minister Nomura, and palace officials. Kabayama had talked to each of them for more than an hour. All agreed that the moment was ripe for Japan to change its relationship with the United States. Grew had heard similar reactions in person and by letter. A leading member of the Diet told him, "You have started the ball rolling and we shall keep it rolling."

If so, it was a pinball. It ricocheted crazily throughout November and December. All eyes were on Grew's upcoming talks with Nomura. For the foreign minister the risks were high. Grew's speech gave Nomura a reason to change direction, but the criticisms in it required some pushback to save face and placate the extremists. Stress was also rising in Japan about the impending termination of the commerce treaty. Less than two weeks after Grew's speech, the Foreign Office announced that Nomura's top priority was Japan's relationships with America and Britain.

This encouraging overture was immediately nullified by a prerequisite for negotiations: the United States must admit, as Britain had, that "allowances must be made for the conduct and behavior of Japanese troops" in China. Grew knew the United States was finished with allowances. The next day the Foreign Office also announced that talks couldn't begin until the new Chinese government was installed, fronted by the Japanese puppet Wang Jingwei, onetime rival of Chiang Kai-shek. All negotiations about China must start from this new reality—an unreality certain to be rejected by the United States. These announcements had the army's fingerprints all over them.

Nomura and Grew met on November 4. Nomura had read the horse's mouth speech and wanted to hear what else Grew had to say. Plenty. Grew handed him some documents. First, a chronological list of 382 protests about bombings and violations in China. Second, excerpts from conversations with previous foreign ministers who had repeatedly promised to respect American rights in China. He told Nomura that Japanese-American relations couldn't change until the bombings and violations of American rights stopped. He also suggested that Japan make some friendly gesture, such as opening the Yangtze to commercial traffic. Nomura was noncommittal, but it was a start.

That same day the US Congress amended the Neutrality Act to allow military sales to certain nations at war. It was aimed at supporting Britain and France against Germany, and China against Japan. The amendment alarmed Japan. The next day Nomura told Harada he was determined to improve relations with America and Britain. But the day after that, November 6, brought more whiplash. The Foreign Office sent Grew a note about nine bombing incidents, dismissing responsibility with the usual excuses and rationales.

Grew was constantly frustrated by the barrage of fake news in the nation's press. The Japanese saw "black as white and white as black," he wrote. "They have broken no treaties, the door is wide open in China, any injuries to American interests have been purely accidental. . . . The United States simply doesn't understand." Yet he stayed focused on the possible. On November 6 he wrote to Roosevelt that Abe and Nomura strongly desired better relations, as did the emperor, but they were hamstrung by the army and ultranationalists who had convinced the Japanese public that negotiating required a kowtowing loss of face. If any improvement came, Grew predicted, it would be slow. He told the president that Nomura wouldn't agree to anything that weakened Japan's economic grip on China, "because no Japanese Government could make such concessions and survive." He foresaw better luck in smaller steps, such as stopping the worst violations against Americans and their property. Grew also warned Roosevelt that if the United States declared an embargo, "we must expect to see American-Japanese relations go steadily downhill thereafter."

On December 1, before he began his talks with Nomura, Grew sent Hull a four-thousand-word analysis of the situation. In the wake of his speech and the new cabinet's desire for better relations, Grew sensed a fragile diplomatic opportunity threatened by contrary forces, most of them in Japan. The dispatch offered blunt truths delivered again from the horse's mouth, this time aimed at the State Department in hopes of convincing Hull of the moment's promise and urgency. The key issue, wrote Grew, was finding a way to align the high principles of American foreign policy with the realities in the Far East.

Reality: every level of Japanese society, including the moderates, was committed to the "new order in East Asia" and the "holy war" in China. Nothing but total military defeat would oust Japan from that country. Since no Western power could risk war in the Far East, the "new order" was an accomplished fact. "However sugar-coated the pill may be," he wrote, "that term means China for the Japanese."

Economic analysts and certain observers—Grew had in mind Hornbeck and American hawks—believed that financial pressures would isolate Japan, kneecap its army, and wreck its China policy. No one in the embassy agreed. The Japanese army was embedded in the nation's identity and couldn't be cut off like a dog's tail. Some Japanese resented the army's heavy expenditures of money and sons, but the idea that economic deprivation would end the military's dominance struck Grew as "an hypothesis which I believe no one intimately conversant with Japan and the Japanese would for a moment entertain"—a jab at the department's frequent dismissal of analysis from the man on the spot. Statistics might predict that Japan would be defeated by embargoes, continued Grew, but numbers didn't account for psychological factors. "Japan is a nation of hardy warriors." They were accustomed to cataclysms, natural and human. Endurance and regimentation were ingrained. Privations would never buckle them.

So, Grew asked, what to do about the conflict between principle and realism? To compromise principle was unacceptable. That left two possible courses. One was "complete intransigence." The United States could demand that Japan change its policies and leave China, could refuse to negotiate a new commerce treaty, and eventually could impose an embargo. This option, he wrote, would send American-Japanese relations downhill toward war.

Grew recommended "a wiser course": continue to insist on all rights in China but maintain decent relations on the condition that Japan take measures to stop the bombings and the worst commercial violations. Once the US government had evidence of these changes, negotiations could begin on a new commerce treaty, whose implementation and future would depend on Japan's progress toward correcting matters in China. As long as Japan was taking verifiable steps, an embargo would be postponed.

Good relations with Japan, he wrote, were in the best interests of the United States politically and commercially. He advised realism. Barring a war, the open door policy was finished. "There is no use whatever in quibbling about this," Grew continued, "no use in refusing to face facts." Diplomacy, however, might be able to reduce the bombings, indignities, and flagrant commercial violations. "We have the choice of losing everything or of saving something from the wreckage while opening the way to a potential building up of our relations with Japan."

To start the salvage operation, Grew suggested a modus vivendi—a temporary agreement—to replace the commerce treaty until a new one could be negotiated, pending concrete improvements by Japan. The alternative—sanctions, embargoes, eventual war—showed a lack of imagination and statesmanship. "There will be time enough to speak of sanctions when the resources of diplomacy will have been exhausted," he wrote. "By nature not a defeatist, I believe that those resources may yet win the day."

Because of the memo's length, Grew sent it by pouch. For unknown reasons it didn't leave Tokyo until December 23 and didn't reach Washington until January 10, 1940. That was far too late to influence Hull's decisions during this critical moment.

On December 4, three days after Grew wrote his analysis about how American-Japanese relations might be mended, he and Nomura had the first of three consequential meetings. Nomura told Grew that Japan wanted to resolve American protests about bombings and indignities and would take steps to reduce them. He also trotted out the usual lines about unavoidable accidents and America's misunderstanding about trade practices. Unofficially he offered to reopen the Yangtze to commercial traffic in "about two months." As a quid pro quo for these hypothetical future concessions, Nomura wanted a new commerce treaty now. Grew reported all this to Hull, who responded that he appreciated Nomura's willingness to start rectifying a few matters, but even if he actually followed through and took action, such efforts "little more than touched the fringe of the problem."

Their second meeting, on December 18, echoed the first. Nomura made vague promises about the bombings and the Yangtze, then asked for a new treaty. Hull responded to Grew's report that same day: the United States couldn't negotiate a commerce treaty with a nation actively discriminating against American commerce.

Grew agreed with this principle but worried that Hull was sacrificing a vanishing opportunity to it. "The simple fact," he wrote to Hull at midnight, "is that we are here dealing not with a unified Japan but with a Japanese Government which is endeavoring courageously, even with only gradual success, to fight against a recalcitrant Japanese Army, a battle which happens to be our own battle. The Government needs support in that fight." Rejection of the government's gestures, small as they were, would discredit the Japanese cabinet and boost the army. The cabinet might fall. By contrast, offering a conditional modus vivendi would bolster the government with the public. Grew urged Hull not to close the door on Nomura. "I am convinced," he wrote, "that at this juncture we are in a position either to direct American-Japanese relations into a progressively healthy channel or to accelerate their movement straight down hill."

Hull's brush-off of Nomura was understandable. Nomura acted as if his government was making extraordinary concessions by pledging to reduce flagrant violations in China and perhaps to reopen the Yangtze at some indefinite date—infringements that shouldn't have happened in the first place. Yet most Japanese were astonished by Nomura's generous offer, especially about the Yangtze. The Foreign Office's spokesperson told the press that Japan had done everything possible to meet American requests. Some Japanese newspapers agreed, praising the nation's "magnanimity" and "extraordinary sacrifice" for offering these hypothetical concessions. Other papers controlled by the army and extremists also were astonished, for different reasons. Reopening the Yangtze would be a "stain on Japanese diplomacy," they claimed, made by a "supine" government. One paper argued, without irony, that reopening the Yangtze would violate Chinese sovereignty and undermine Japan's noble policy of freeing China from exploitation.

This was all absurd, but Japan had disregarded international rules and censure for nearly a decade, so the Japanese saw Nomura's offer as momentous. Hull saw it as minor and indefinite. So did Grew, but he also recognized it as a seed with potential to grow and to stop the erosion of American-Japanese relations. Not all seeds sprout, but why not water this one and see what it produced?

Hull looked at Japan's gesture politically, Grew diplomatically. Hull was thinking globally, Grew locally. Hull wanted immediate sweeping changes before the United States would consider any negotiations, while Grew saw the long-term value of small changes and negotiations tied to evolving circumstances. Grew favored the incremental over the all-encompassing, imperfect evolution over perfect stasis. He was willing to take a risk by giving Japan another conditional chance.

A lot was riding on Hull's answer to Grew's proposed modus vivendi. On December 20 Grew tried one last time to sway him. He wired that Japan's follow-through on promises might be slow or feeble. "Nevertheless," he continued, "it is unquestionably clear that the Japanese Government is now embarked upon a new orientation, namely a policy of respecting American rights and interests in China." A small gesture such as a modus vivendi would "tide over this most critical period in American-Japanese relations." If the Japanese didn't keep their promises, the agreement could be revoked.

In Washington, Hornbeck attacked Grew's recommendation of a modus vivendi as naïve appeasement. From seven thousand miles away he declared that almost every Japanese was demanding expansion of the empire. He dismissed the recent gestures of Nomura and Abe, neither of whom he knew: "There is a change neither of attitude nor of heart." Hornbeck advised Hull that instead of conciliation the United States should "put the screws on the Japanese."

Hull chose a middle path. On December 20 he wrote to Grew that the State Department would neither close the door on Nomura nor offer a modus vivendi. The United States couldn't consider a new treaty until Japan stopped discriminating against American commerce, but in one month, when the current treaty expired, the United States would suspend punitive tariffs and duties—for the time being. Hull was holding to his plan to make the Japanese wait and wonder. Like Hornbeck, he doubted the Japanese government's sincerity.

On December 22 Grew climbed the stairs to Nomura's office to deliver

Hull's response. Nomura "was obviously bitterly disappointed, in fact rather crushed by what I told him." The foreign minister thanked the US government for suspending customs duties but noted that this left Japan in commercial limbo with its most important trading partner, an intolerable condition. "For the first time in our meetings," wrote Grew, "he did not accompany me downstairs."

That same day the State Department expanded the moral embargo to include rare materials used in weaponry, such as aluminum and molybdenum, and technical information about the manufacture of high-octane aviation fuel. The Japanese felt that their friendly offer of concessions had been met with suspicion and insults. Japan's press intensified its attacks on the United States and the Abe cabinet. On December 27 a majority of the Diet presented Abe with a petition asking him to resign. He refused, but his fate was clear. Two weeks earlier German ambassador Eugen Ott had worried that Japan was tilting toward an alliance with the United States. On December 31 he reported to Berlin that Abe's cabinet would fall by mid-January and that Oshima and Shiratori were "working hard for the overthrow of the present cabinet."

The opportunity offered by Nomura, like Hiranuma's before it, died from neglect. Despite Hull's enduring willingness to listen to the Japanese, he was incapable of overcoming his deep-seated suspicion of them, an opinion fortified by Hornbeck, his chief political advisor on Asia. The two men didn't share Grew's faith in diplomacy, or at least they viewed its purpose differently. For Grew diplomacy meant a meeting of minds to find self-interested compromise. For Hull and Hornbeck it meant bending others to American principles, a stance the Japanese mirrored distortedly. Hull, Hornbeck, and Grew all considered themselves reasonable and realistic, but only one of them understood the Japanese and grasped that nothing except military defeat would remove them from China. Only one of them believed that refusing to concede anything in acknowledgment of Japan's legitimate fears would lead to war.

FIRE-EATERS ON ALL SIDES

ON NEW YEAR'S Day 1940, millions of Japanese rose early to honor gods and ancestors at Shinto shrines. At exactly 9:00 A.M., as instructed by the government via radio and newspapers, these millions bowed as one toward the Imperial Palace and shouted "Banzai! Long Live His Majesty the Emperor!"

Throughout 1940 the government scheduled twelve other precise moments of reverence. All commemorated the anniversary of twenty-six hundred years of Japan's imperial dynasty, a fable invented in the nineteenth century. To celebrate the anniversary, Japanese volunteered for fifteen thousand public works projects and thronged twelve thousand events—patriotic rallies, parades, ceremonies, contests, movies, exhibitions. They tuned in to a stream of special programs on the nation's sole radio station, state-owned NHK (call sign JOAK).

In addition to honoring Japan's ancient divine origins, this choreographed mass patriotism was aimed at boosting the public's faltering enthusiasm for the war in China. The quick early victories and the installation of a puppet regime hadn't crushed Chiang or turned the Chinese people against him. His army faded into the country's vast interior and kept fighting. The war became a grind. The Japanese army needed more and more bodies. To get them it lowered standards for draftees' health and age. In early 1940, one million Japanese soldiers were fighting in China. Almost every house in Japan displayed a small plaque designating it an "honor home" for sending someone to the war. More than a hundred thousand Japanese soldiers had been killed and hundreds of thousands wounded.

The government withheld such bleak statistics from the public, but evidence was in plain sight. Train after train departed Tokyo with fresh troops for China, seen off by families and female patriots from the National Defense Women's Association wearing white aprons. Many other trains arrived packed with soldiers bandaged and shattered. They wore white kimonos, the uniform of the wounded, and were common sights on city streets, ghostly reminders of the war's toll. Trainloads of white wooden boxes also arrived, bearing human ashes. A soldier carried each box to a grieving family, who placed it on a tiny altar holding a photo of the deceased alongside offerings of cakes, oranges, and sticks of burning incense.

Japan's commitment to the defeat of China was ruinous. The military consumed half of the national budget and grabbed all resources considered necessary for the war effort, which covered almost everything. Scarcity and rationing followed. Gas was first, in March 1938. Private transport became unfeasible. The government converted buses to run on charcoal. Charcoal-burning taxis smoked and wheezed around Tokyo, stalling on hills. Their drivers periodically hopped out to stoke the fire in the trunk. Most Japanese used charcoal to cook and to heat their homes and baths, so by the end of 1940 it also was scarce and rationed.

The list of shortages lengthened: not only basics, such as coal and oil, but also small luxuries, such as sugar, sake, beer, cigarettes. Shortages even hit the foundation of the Japanese diet: polished white rice, most of which was reserved for the military. Store shelves emptied, food lines grew. The government declared the twenty-second of each month national fruitless day. Students and workers ate frugal, patriotic "rising sun box lunches"—a pickled red plum on a rectangle of rice. The military requisitioned leather, so consumer goods such as shoes were made from stiff sharkskin or whale skin, and the government encouraged civilians to return to traditional wooden footwear. The military commandeered all metals. Appliances such as iceboxes and washing machines vanished from stores. New phones and other equipment became unobtainable as copper was requisitioned for planes, ships, and weaponry.

As the military and wartime industries swallowed more and more workers, students were assigned public service projects, such as cleaning parks or collecting charcoal and scrap metal. They were encouraged to donate their savings to the war effort. For exercise, schoolchildren now did military drills. Workers' unions were supplanted by associations dedicated to "industrial patriotism." Everything promoted single-minded war psychology.

Shortages and rationing worsened throughout 1940. To divert public resentment, the government's propaganda apparatus stressed that material sacrifice was patriotic, a strategy later familiar to Americans. Deprivation and discomfort became emblems of self-disciplined toughness, spiritual and physical, in contrast to the softness of Westerners. A government slogan proclaimed, "Extravagance is the enemy."

To spread the gospel of national willpower and patriotic sacrifice, the Japanese government saturated the country, including rural villages, with free AM radios. The radios received one station, state-controlled NHK, which broadcast from 6:00 A.M. to 11:00 P.M. Many Japanese blasted the station all day at full distorted volume. "Radio is, in fact, one of the major curses of living in Japan," wrote one observer. "There is no escape from the noise; it assaults one from all directions."

Programming included censored news bulletins, patriotic speeches, and broadcasts from Germany and Italy, including speeches by Hitler. Groups did calisthenics outdoors or at work to directions shouted from the radio. The station aired lectures on Japanese culture and "spiritual mobilization." By 1940 the daily language lesson had switched from English to German. Jazz and American popular songs, once pervasive, mostly disappeared.

NHK controlled all foreign radio news as Domei controlled all foreign print news. Shortwave radios, which could penetrate this shield and deliver information from the outside world, were banned. By 1940 the Japanese were living in a nationalistic media bubble.

Nevertheless, Grew started 1940 with his customary faith that diplomacy could prevail.

On January 4, 1940, the Kempeitai arrested an army major and several dozen coconspirators who were about to blow up the British and American embassies, assassinate the ambassadors, and murder several palace advisors for being pro-Western. The army kept the plot out of the papers, but Reuters and UPI called Grew to ask about the rumor of an assassination attempt on him. "I hadn't noticed any, yet," he said.

In early January the Diet passed a resolution of no confidence in the Abe cabinet. The army and the right wing also had been scheming against Abe and Nomura. The cabinet's life expectancy dwindled to days. The army wanted the malleable Konoye back as prime minister, but he demurred. "He is hopeless," the lord keeper told Baron Harada, "because he always seems to be running away." The Abe cabinet fell on January 14.

The consensus replacement was sixty-year-old Admiral Yonai, former navy minister. Nearly six feet tall and 190 pounds, he conveyed strength. He was also known for his pale complexion, deafness in one ear, and easygoing personality. He strongly opposed a military pact with Germany and Italy, so his nomination was seen as a gesture toward the democratic West. The emperor summoned War Minister Hata Shunroku to stress that the army mustn't sabotage the new cabinet by refusing to appoint a war minister. The army grumbled but submitted. (Of Japan's last eight prime ministers, three had been generals, two admirals.) Arita returned as foreign minister and immediately became a target because he still opposed a military pact with Germany and Italy. Yonai and Arita wanted to strengthen the new order in East Asia while avoiding an entanglement with Germany or clashes with Britain and America. The goals conflicted.

Grew saw the incoming ministers as proof that diplomatic opportunities remained alive. He wrote to Roosevelt that the Yonai cabinet "is about as good, from our point of view, as any that could have been made." Perhaps, but "good" was a relative assessment. Yonai and Arita would need to fight off the pro-Nazi factions in the military and the Foreign Office, and they would need to temper Japan's belligerence in China. Further, Hull would need to grasp that Yonai's new cabinet represented the moderates' endangered resistance to massive pressure from the ultranationalists. After eight years in Japan, Grew's definition of promising had been reduced to a list of improbabilities and conditionals.

At the end of January the commerce treaty expired, leaving Japan dangling in uncertainty, its future in another nation's power—the desperate psychological position that had led it to invade China. The Japanese press raged, accusing the United States of insulting Japan and trying to wreck the new order in East Asia.

Grew watched with dismay. "Just now I seem to be fighting two Governments at once," he wrote. "There are unfortunately fire-eaters on both sides of the fence." That included Stanley Hornbeck. He had written a snarky letter to Grew about Grew's paraphrase of an analysis by the British ambassador that contained some criticisms of American policy. Hornbeck intimated that Grew was disloyal for sending in such criticisms and implied that they were unwelcome. In a sharp reply Grew wrote that he assumed the department wanted to hear all significant views about Japan, since ignorance about dissenting opinions or unwillingness to grapple with them would be disastrous. Likewise, he continued, if embassies only reported what might please the department, "I would fear for the future of our Foreign Service."

He didn't back off of his previous advice to the State Department to retain some semblance of friendly relations with Japan, which he knew Hornbeck disapproved. Any drastic measures against Japan at this delicate moment, he wrote, would kill the "unmistakable budding of a more moderate trend and policy in Japan. . . . That trend may or may not develop progressively. I merely wish to give it a fair chance to do so."

A GOLDEN OPPORTUNITY

ON FEBRUARY 2, 1940, in the wood-paneled chamber of the Diet's House of Representatives, the new cabinet sat on benches facing fan-shaped rows of seated lawmakers. The cabinet was there to answer questions, an annual tradition. A diminutive sixty-nine-year-old named Saito Takao, a leader of Japan's largest political party, Minseito, rose and asked some simple questions. What are the real facts about the war in China? What is the government's plan to end it? The Japanese people had been told the incident would be contained locally and end soon, he said, but nearly three years had passed. He doubted that Japan could ever win a war in such a huge country. He called Wang Chingwei, China's ersatz ruler, a Japanese puppet with no army and no chance of controlling China. Why did the cabinet and the military spout bombast about imperial benevolence and a "holy war" instead of being honest about Japan's material reasons for occupying China?

Saito challenged the cabinet to answer the most basic question of all: What was the war's point? He described the tremendous sacrifices the war had imposed—two million conscripts, one hundred thousand deaths, hundreds of thousands of casualties, economic hardship—and then dared to ask what all this sacrifice had accomplished and if it ever would be worthwhile. Last, Saito warned that though the Japanese had willingly sacrificed for the China war, their patience wasn't limitless.

He spoke for two hours, occasionally interrupted by cheers and jeers. The public expression of such blunt doubts stunned the army and their

Diet lapdogs. The army banned the press from covering Saito's speech, though too late to stop the first editions. But the Diet itself handled the demolition of what remained of free expression in the nation's parliament. The army's allies in the Diet called Saito a traitor and demanded his expulsion. The body voted overwhelmingly to oust him, and two-thirds of his speech was erased from the official record.

The episode demonstrated again that the Diet would never check Japan's militarism. Yet Saito's bold speech and its positive reception in some quarters also showed that, in contrast to Germany and Italy, the nation's fervent militarism hadn't completely silenced critics.

Throughout February Diet members also grilled Foreign Minister Arita. He was attacked for his "obsequious diplomacy" toward the United States and Britain. Furious interpellators pounded their desks and swarmed the rostrum, shaking their fists and shouting "Coward!" Guards cleared the room. In other sessions Arita was attacked for not giving military support to Germany and Italy. He explained that Japan needed to focus on establishing the new order in East Asia, and besides, Germany's victory was certain.

Grew discerned glimmers of diplomatic opportunity in all this, faint signs of resistance to military extremism. "The bombings of American property and the indignities to American citizens have almost, but not quite, ceased," he wrote to his predecessor, W. Cameron Forbes, in America. "I want to give this new trend a chance to develop. It may not go far but it can go a considerable distance—if not rebuffed by us." He approved Hull's strategy to keep Japan guessing without imposing trade penalties or an embargo, which gave the Japanese "a chance to implement their constant assurances." He knew the odds were slim that Japan would do so. "I have no reason to be optimistic," he wrote Forbes, "but at least something can be accomplished by the resources of diplomacy and I want to see those resources used to the full before we throw up our hands in final despair and begin the rough stuff."

As usual, China was the rub. Everyone affected wanted the war settled—Japan's army, navy, government, and public, as well as the American and British governments and the business interests in all three countries, not to mention Chiang Kai-shek and the Chinese communists. But the proposed solutions were incompatible. The Japanese government wanted to solidify Japan's gains without antagonizing the United States, an impossible contradiction. Arita didn't help by offering Chiang three unacceptable choices: surrender; merge with Japan's puppet government; or make the puppet your partner. From the other direction, the United States angered Japan by giving Chiang another $20 million loan, against the background threat of an embargo.

Meanwhile, the perennial right-wing plots about assassinations and martial law kept sprouting. In February and March Baron Harada heard about half a dozen schemes and an emergency escape plan for the emperor.

Seven months had passed since Germany invaded Poland, but military action had been rare. That changed on the morning of April 9 when German warships slipped through British mines into Norway's major port cities and landed thousands of Nazi soldiers. German troops simultaneously occupied Denmark.

No one expected Hitler to stop there. His next likely targets were Belgium and the Netherlands. That possibility rang alarm bells in Japan. If Germany took the Netherlands, what would become of the Dutch East Indies, a crucial Japanese source for oil, tin, and rubber? Foreign Minister Arita tried to get out in front diplomatically. On April 15 he declared that Japan and the Dutch East Indies were "economically bound by the intimate relationship of mutuality." No matter what happened in the European war, he continued, Japan would consider any attempt to alter the status quo of the Dutch East Indies a threat to the peace and stability of East Asia.

Was this a shot at Hitler's territorial greed? A warning to Britain and the United States not to play protector? An opening move in a plan to scoop up the Dutch East Indies if the Netherlands fell? Or did Arita simply mean what he said? Given Japan's habit of talking about peace while seizing territory, Hull smelled deceit and acquisitiveness. Nevertheless, he responded with a measured statement that seconded Arita's commitment to the status quo of the Dutch East Indies. Spokespeople from Japan's Foreign Office and navy said they were pleased that the two countries agreed, but the Japanese press, goaded by the army, managed to be outraged. The fate of the

Dutch East Indies was purely an Asian matter, they barked, and despite Arita's statement, a new order must replace the status quo.

The agitation rippled outward. Japanese forces bombed two distinctly marked American properties in China, including a hospital. American citizens in Tianjin who wanted to enter the British or French Concessions were stopped, searched, and forced to exit their cars and walk past a line of jeering Japanese soldiers. "Makes my blood boil," wrote Grew. For the first time in four months he had reason to visit the Foreign Office and protest.

The distortions and belligerence also frustrated Arita. Like Grew he was dealing with fire-eaters on all sides. In a meeting on April 26 he implored Grew not to take his planned leave of absence in May because the public would see it as a rupture in diplomatic relations. Grew cabled the department the next day to cancel his precious leave. In a speech on May 3 Arita repeated his goals of settling the war with China and preserving peace with America, Britain, and Russia. He denounced the "reckless proposals" of the extremists and their "sheer stupid blustering."

But reckless stupidity was in the ascendant. A week after Arita's speech, Hitler invaded Belgium, the Netherlands, and France. The blitzkrieg ripped through Western Europe. After five weeks Nazi troops marched through the Arc de Triomphe in Paris.

Half a world away the blitzkrieg made the Japanese military giddy with land lust. The newspapers urged Japan to grab the Dutch East Indies. On May 24 the navy conducted a war-planning exercise and determined that invading the colony would spark war with Britain and America. The exercise also determined that the United States would respond to an invasion by embargoing oil, and that Japan could wage war for a year on its reserves, but beyond that "our chances of winning would be nil." Despite the conclusion that attacking the colony would be a disaster, the navy decided to develop a secret plan anyway, without informing Yonai or the cabinet.

On June 6 Japan notified the Dutch East Indies that it now expected the colony to sell it one million tons of oil per year, triple the previous amount. To Hull, that didn't sound like a commitment to the status quo. The United States responded with a small embargo on machine tools and motors. The Dutch East Indies made plans to destroy its oil wells if Japan invaded.

As German victories piled up, Japan's newspapers renewed calls for an alliance with the Axis, to smash the status quo in Asia as Germany was doing in Europe. "It is only too obvious which course Japan should take," declared the *Asahi Shimbun* in a typical assertion, "as between destruction of the old world order or maintenance of the status quo." Japan must "walk in the footsteps of the Axis powers, Germany and Italy." The foreign policy of Arita and Prime Minister Yonai to seek better relationships with Britain and America came under stronger attack. Grew analyzed all this in dispatches to Hull and asked for approval to countermand the drift toward Germany by approaching Arita about building better relations.

Hornbeck dismissed Grew's analysis and vehemently opposed any gestures smacking of appeasement. Japan was incorrigibly untrustworthy, Hornbeck wrote to Hull. Any pledges its leaders made were worthless. A friendly approach by America would be seen as a tacit admission—Hornbeck called it "a 'go' signal"—that the United States wouldn't oppose Japan's plans in East Asia. The argument was self-fulfilling and self-defeating, a circle with no exit. Diplomacy was pointless because Japan would break its promises, so giving Japan a chance to modify its actions was pointless because that would never happen, so why attempt pointless diplomacy that would instead foster aggression and make the United States look weak?

Hull, with his eye on collapsing Europe, was willing to see if Japan could be contained on the war's sidelines. He told Grew to resume talks with Arita under the same conditions as before. If Japan demonstrated that it accepted the principles of national sovereignty and international law by eliminating violations in China, the United States might reconsider a commerce treaty. Hull required Japan to abide by broad principles before any specific concessions could be discussed. Grew preferred to start with small specifics—fewer bombings and indignities—and work up to principles. But he accepted Hull's conditions because they got him back through Arita's door.

Grew and Arita had four long conversations in June. To avoid the media they met at the homes of mutual friends. On June 10 Grew laid out the recurrent problems and reiterated his case that Japan's future would be brighter as America's ally than as Germany's. He handed Arita a partial list of bombings and infractions committed since late December—thirty-three typed pages. After Grew finished his presentation Arita said, "I agree in spirit and in principle with everything you have said." He added that his government was under pressure from factions urging an alliance with the Axis. He implied that he and Yonai preferred closer relations with the United States. Arita had three requests for the United States: restore the commerce treaty; stop aiding Chiang; and agree to split the Pacific into two spheres of influence. Only the first wasn't impossible, but Grew left feeling hopeful. The door was open again.

During the nine days before Grew and Arita's next meeting, military developments demolished most of that optimism. Japan's reckless bombing in China intensified again, particularly around Chiang's new capital of Chongqing. Bombers destroyed residential areas, killing hundreds of civilians and wounding thousands. Hull instructed Grew to protest. In response Japan warned foreigners to leave Chongqing or risk attack, then bombed the city four more times before the end of June, destroying the Soviet embassy and the consulates of Britain and France.

On June 18 France sued Germany for peace. Japan instantly demanded that France stop shipping military supplies to Chiang from French Indochina. That same day Japan's War Ministry and general staff met to discuss Indochina. One group wanted to invade immediately; another wanted to wait. They postponed a decision. The next day the Foreign Office told the French ambassador in Tokyo that France must allow Japanese inspectors at the Indochinese border, and that all goods moving into China, not just military goods, would now be stopped and scrutinized.

When Grew and Arita reconvened on June 24, the rapid political shifts were apparent. Arita now doubted that Japan could change anything in China until a new commerce treaty was in place. As usual the Japanese wanted payday before doing any work. Four days later an American hospital and two missionary schools in Chongqing suffered direct hits by Japanese bombs. That night at nine o'clock Arita summoned Grew to a private home (the press had staked out his). Arita wanted to respond to the issues laid out by Grew in previous meetings.

"At first sight," he said, Japan and America appeared to differ, but in fact he saw "no differences in opinion practically." This preposterous statement required elaboration. For instance, both nations followed a policy of nondiscrimination in trade. After absorbing this jaw-dropper Grew pointed out that Japan discriminated against the United States constantly. Arita, completing his trifecta of absurdity, said that Japan only did that in China and would stop it when the war ended. Arita wanted to alter reality with words. He clearly had been unable to withstand pressure from the right. The talks had completed a circle to nowhere. When Grew asked him to reaffirm Japan's pledge to maintain the status quo of territories, including the Dutch East Indies and French Indochina, Arita scuttled away from the subject as "a somewhat delicate matter."

It wasn't delicate at all. The next day the Foreign Office informed the Dutch minister that Japan had changed its mind. Instead of one million tons of oil, as requested on June 6—already three times the allotment in previous years—Japan now expected two million tons. Similar increases would be necessary in war materials such as rubber, tin, bauxite, manganese, tungsten, and molybdenum. Japan also told the colony it must open itself to unrestricted Japanese immigration and businesses, effective immediately. The Dutch minister told Grew that the quantities of resources demanded by Japan would give it a virtual monopoly in all of them, shutting out the United States and other countries. Meanwhile Japanese businesses would penetrate all aspects of the economy. As in China, Japan would gain complete control.

The Foreign Office was on a roll that day. It also formalized demands to the British ambassador, euphemistically called "requests," to close the Burma Road into China, shut down shipments to China from Hong Kong, and withdraw all troops from Shanghai. Immediately.

That afternoon at two thirty Arita addressed millions of Japanese over the radio. His subject was the nation's changing foreign policy. Japan would neither involve itself in the European war nor allow it to embroil East Asia. He described "a new vast aggregation of satellite States in East Asia and the South Seas revolving harmoniously around Japan." These states would form a "co-prosperity sphere" and "a new world order" linked by geography, race, culture, and economics. But some nations, Arita said, were obstructing Japan's great undertaking by aiding Chiang Kai-shek, whom Japan intended to eradicate. Some nations, he continued, disapproved of "a change in the status quo by force of arms"—a shot at the United States.

But Japan, he said, used force only to create peace and justice. "The sword [that Japan] has drawn," said Arita, "is intended to be nothing other than a life-giving sword that destroys evil and makes justice manifest."

The Japanese press applauded this nationalist megalomania. EAST ASIATIC RACES WILL COOPERATE—JAPAN REJECTS FOREIGN INTERFERENCE, said one headline. JAPAN SEEKS WORLD PEACE THROUGH NEW ORDER IN EAST ASIA, said another. "The new order includes emancipation of the peoples of East Asia and the South Seas from European oppression," shouted the anti-West organ *Nichi Nichi*.

One Japanese group was irate: the army. Its leaders were outraged that Arita hadn't consulted them about this foreign policy statement. On the afternoon of the speech, a group of right-wing generals met, including Masaki, Araki, and War Minister Hata. They complained that Arita's global vision had been too timid. Creating a new world order through cooperation was weak-kneed nonsense. Arita also had failed to declare Japan's willingness to tear down the old order by joining the Axis. War Minister Hata told the assembled generals that Japan must "not miss such a golden opportunity."

June had been a whirlwind. American-Japanese relations were no longer mired, they were shredded. "The vicious circle is complete," wrote Grew in his diary, "and how to break it is a puzzle which taxes the imagination."

He found some slight comfort in a Buddhist funeral on June 11 for Prince Tokugawa Iesato, a pro-democratic politician and diplomat. Grew, Alice, and Dooman were the only Westerners present. That night Grew wrote,

> After eight years in Japan, I had the feeling today of being not outsiders but an intimate part of that group, almost as if the gathering were of old family friends in Boston and not in Tokyo. We knew well a great many of the Japanese and their wives who were sitting around us, members of the outstanding families and clans. The Tokugawas, Konoyes, Matsudairas, Matsukatas might have been Saltonstalls and Sedgwicks and

Peabodys. We knew their positions, their influence and reputations, their personalities, and their interrelationships as well as those of a similar group in Boston. And we felt too that they regarded us as a sort of part of them.

For Grew, the solemn, friendly intimacy of this gathering exemplified what he called "the other Japan," the one passing away before his eyes.

HELL-BENT TOWARD THE AXIS

ON JULY 11, 1940, Grew traveled to another secret meeting with Arita at a private residence. The ambassador's mind whirled with the latest proliferation of bad news. France was crushed, Holland was impotent, Britain was preoccupied by its fate in shattered Europe. Japan was dazzled. "The German military machine and system and their brilliant successes," wrote Grew, "have gone to the Japanese head like strong wine."

More than a hundred Japanese planes had bombed the Chinese capital of Chongqing again, the nineteenth time in two months. Twice in the previous week Japan had demanded that Britain close the Burma Road or risk attack on Hong Kong. Britain had resisted so far, but its survival was at stake in Europe and it couldn't afford a war in Asia. A few days earlier Japanese police had arrested fifty members of the right-wing Shimpeitai (God-Sent Soldiers) on the verge of assassinating Prime Minister Yonai, Arita, and other politicians and palace officials. Baron Harada was on the kill list as a "pro-British messenger." He was awakened by a call at 4:20 A.M. on July 4 alerting him to the plot and advising him to leave his house quickly. The government forbade the press from publishing any details about the conspiracy.

Yonai's cabinet was teetering. The army and its media mouthpieces were agitating for a one-party totalitarian state modeled after Germany and Italy, with Prince Konoye as leader. Inspired by Germany, the army was impatient to exploit the moment and strike. Grew didn't yet know it, but on July 3 the army ministry and general staff had drafted a policy called

"Outline of the Main Principles for Coping with the Changing World Situation." It called for Japan "to seize the most opportune time to solve the problem of the South" by invading the Dutch East Indies, Hong Kong, Singapore, and Malaya while the European powers were crippled and the United States was irresolute. The outline called for plans to be completed by the end of August.

In America Roosevelt had responded to the catastrophe in Europe by appointing two hard-liners to his cabinet, Henry Stimson as secretary of war and Frank Knox as secretary of the navy. The Japanese still hated Stimson for his denunciation of the Manchuria incident. Knox, publisher of the *Chicago Daily News*, had previously been general manager of the Hearst newspaper chain, notorious for its "yellow peril" attacks on Asians. In 1933, as a precaution against expected hostilities with Japan, Knox had recommended interning all Japanese Americans in Hawaii. Stimson and Knox would not be receptive to Grew's perspective on Japan.

The situation was collapsing from all directions, jeopardizing the possibility of better relations between the two countries. Grew felt this meeting with Arita might be his last chance to shore up American-Japanese relations. He suspected Arita felt the same gravity.

After the usual greetings Grew told Arita that today's presentation "was one of the most important that I had made to the Japanese Government since I had been Ambassador to Tokyo." The United States government, he continued, believed that Japan must now answer a basic question: Would it cooperate with other nations to develop poorer countries, share resources, and encourage free trade, or would it seize other countries by force and exploit them for its own benefit? One path led to collaboration and peace, the other to isolation and war, and eventually to economic ruin.

Grew wooed Arita with statistics about Japan's heavy reliance on trade with North America, in hopes that facts still mattered. A war against the democratic West would vaporize this trade and Japan's economy. Nor would the United States stand by if Japan tried to commandeer the natural resources of Asia. Japan had thrived through close ties with America and participation in the world economy, said Grew. The country would wither inside a closed Asian bloc. Grew repeated the American government's belief that Chiang Kai-shek represented the legitimate government of China and was supported by the vast majority of Chinese. The war couldn't end until Japan recognized that fact. A few small good-faith changes by Japan now, said Grew, would lay the foundation for bigger changes later. He had made the same plea many times, but today it had a desperate edge.

Arita carefully read through Grew's presentation again. So, he finally asked, the United States intended to keep supporting Chiang Kai-shek? Not the response Grew had hoped for. Yes, he said, but the aid and money sent to Chiang were tiny compared to the amounts pouring into Japan from America. Arita said he and the prime minister would study Grew's statement. Before leaving, Grew commented that Japan was "seething with unrest." Arita agreed, and added that the government was under great pressure to change its policies.

That evening at six Grew wrote to Hull. Frustration crackled beneath his usual tact. At a moment when Japan was leaning toward the Axis and lured by "golden opportunities," he wrote, debating with Japan's Foreign Office about principles "cannot be expected of itself alone to exert concrete effect on Japanese policy." He had started the current talks with Arita, he wrote, in hopes of finding some way to break the impasse, but the attitudes of both governments were deadlocked and the conversations had devolved into "a vicious circle."

To keep Japan out of the Axis, he again suggested a modus vivendi that could lead to a new commerce treaty. The Japanese press would crow that this was a sign of American weakness, but it would buoy the current cabinet and other Japanese leaders trying to resist the pull of the Axis. The cabinet's survival was doubtful, Grew wrote, but without some gesture by the United States, the tide would "flow toward the totalitarian camp with increasing momentum." Negotiations for a modus vivendi should occur only in conjunction with specific actions by Japan. "I do not advocate a surrender of principle," he wrote, trying to preempt charges of appeasement by Hornbeck and others.

No matter. Time had run out. Five days later, on July 16, the army made its play. Hata resigned as war minister to protest the policies of Yonai and Arita. The army refused to recommend a replacement, which toppled the cabinet. Following tradition, Baron Harada traveled to Okitsu to tell Prince Saionji that the lord keeper would be consulting him about a new

prime minister, though the army intended to reinsert its man, Prince Konoye. Saionji, old and ill, felt that current events had overwhelmed not
only his influence but his comprehension. "Truthfully, I am unable to
accurately understand what is going on in the world," he told Harada.
"Therefore I cannot say anything. I would like to be excused from answering this inquiry."

The emperor commanded Konoye to form a new cabinet. He brought
in a plan for totalitarian one-party rule and a resolve to join the Axis. His
new war minister was General Tojo Hideki. Tojo, five foot four, bald, and
moustachioed, had a reputation for decisiveness. His nickname was "the
Razor." He had been commander of the Kempeitai in Manchuria, then
chief of the Kwantung Army there. In 1934 he had called for a military
totalitarian state. He deified the emperor and revered the sacred mission of
spreading the imperial way beyond Japan.

For the post of foreign minister, Konoye ignored warnings from many
Japanese leaders by choosing the brash and flamboyant Matsuoka Yosuke,
hero of the League of Nations walkout. Matsuoka admired Hitler and
totalitarianism.

Grew wrote in his diary that the new cabinet "gives every indication of
going hell-bent towards the Axis and the establishment of the New Order
in East Asia, and of riding rough-shod over the rights and interests, and
the principles and policies, of the United States and Great Britain." He
called the cabinet changes a typhoon that obliterated his previous work.

Grew was deeply experienced, adept at surfing diplomatic tsunamis,
but this particular wave exasperated him because he felt it could have been
diffused. The American government's admirable insistence on principles,
he told his diary, had turned into an "intransigent and rigid policy" that
left no flexibility to offer the cabinet any incentive or leverage against the
extremists. He didn't send these thoughts to Washington. "It is too much
like saying 'I told you so,'" he confided to his diary, "and no good soldier
says that to his superior. The record speaks for itself."

A diplomatic pouch had arrived with recent clippings about Japan from
American newspapers. They helped explain Hull's unwillingness to bend.
A truculent tone predominated, reflecting the public's growing animosity
toward Japan. The idea of negotiating a new commerce treaty was de-

nounced as "appeasement" akin to groveling before Hitler in Munich. The word and the comparison offended Grew. He had recommended gradual steps requiring reciprocal actions by Japan—not appeasement but "constructive statesmanship." The clippings suggested that the American press and public—and by implication the State Department—"do not differentiate between 'appeasement' and that form of adjustment of mutual problems which should not be beyond the wit and good will of man to bring about consistently with our honor, our interests and our obligation to third countries."

As in Japan, the American public and government were moving away from Grew's perspective and approach. When Konoye took over, hawks in Roosevelt's cabinet, such as Knox, Stimson, and Treasury Secretary Henry Morgenthau, with support from Hornbeck at State, urged the president to impose an embargo on oil and other essential materials. Their insistence increased after Britain caved in and agreed to close the Burma Road on July 18. The hawks, despite scant knowledge of Japan, were certain that the country's civilian and military leaders were all bluster and that nothing would push them into war. But Japan's military didn't need a push; it was already planning for conflict. The hawks discounted Grew's repeated warnings that an oil embargo would spark a crisis and drive Japan to attack the Dutch East Indies.

On this Hull agreed with Grew. He wanted to stick with a policy of principled distance in reaction to Japan's transgressions. Morgenthau sneered at what he considered Hull's appeasement. Near the end of July Roosevelt exasperated the hawks by taking a middle path. He ordered an embargo on aviation fuel and high-grade scrap iron, both vital war materials. When the Japanese ambassador complained, he was told the embargo was for US military purposes and not aimed at any single nation.

A typhoon seething in Japan, a storm gathering in Washington, years of diplomacy blowing away. "But maybe it is not all scrapped," wrote Grew to his daughter Anita on July 23 with his habitual resilience. "We shall see."

THE MATSUOKA HURRICANE

IN JANUARY 1940 James R. Young, an American correspondent living in Japan, left Tokyo to report on the war in China. When he returned he gave a talk at the American Club, where hidden Dictaphones recorded conversations and at least two waiters worked for the Kempeitai, charting who sat with whom. A few days later Young was arrested and charged under the army's criminal code with spreading false and slanderous rumors, more typically called facts.

Young's first call was to Grew. The ambassador's authority didn't extend into Japanese law, but he made clear his keen interest in the case by sending Young his trademark fur coat to wear in the unheated jail. Grew was over six feet tall and Young was not, so Young could turn up the collar and stay cozy from forehead to ankles. More important, the coat was "a diplomatic formula of secret protection," wrote Young, because all the policemen knew it was Grew's. That may be why they slit the lining to look for hidden messages. During his two months in jail Young never took the coat off, and he wore it throughout his trial. His defense was that he had written the truth, which the judge dismissed as immaterial. Young was convicted but given a suspended sentence, perhaps partly thanks to Grew's coat.

Young's arrest sent a chill through the foreign reporters in Tokyo, but chill turned to fear after the Konoye cabinet took over in July. A spigot opened wide, spewing xenophobia and hatred of the Western media. On July 27 the Tokyo police arrested a British correspondent for Reuters named James Cox. After two days in police custody he jumped out a fourth-story window—a suicidal leap, according to the police. His wife and colleagues scoffed at that. His arms and legs had been repeatedly punctured by hypodermic needles. Grew suspected he had thrown himself out the window, or been thrown out, after days of torture. Cox was posthumously charged with eight counts of espionage for possessing, though not publishing, common military information, such as troop strength in China and Manchuria.

Censorship of the press took many forms. By 1940 most Japanese newspapers were servants of the government. To make the press easier to manage, the government had choked off the supply of newsprint, which it controlled. Between 1937 and 1939, hundreds of papers shut down. By 1940 most prefectures had only one paper, with dwindling pages. The number of magazines and journals plummeted as well. The government further chilled free expression by arresting reporters and suspending permits to publish.

In a separate category were the few independent English-language periodicals in Japan, and the correspondents for American and British media, but the Japanese government tightened its control of them as well. Into the mid-1930s the correspondents could send their stories home via international telephone, but as events in China and Japan got uglier, the government censors who monitored the phone calls began refusing to put them through. When the correspondents asked the government to investigate censorship of their stories, they were told that censorship didn't exist in Japan so no investigation was necessary. Reporters were banned from writing about certain topics or events, and they also learned to steer clear of some subjects to avoid arrest, but the criteria and enforcement weren't predictable, which kept reporters off-balance. The effect was self-censorship on top of official censorship. Nevertheless, the best correspondents managed to get strong stories through.

The police paid janitors to bring them the contents of newspaper staffers' wastebaskets. Investigation into the James Cox incident revealed that the police had taped his phone conversations and banter at the American Club, where he liked to play cards, and had monitored all his movements and contacts. Grew assumed that the embassy's servants and chauffeurs reported all visitors and anything overheard to the police. Few Japanese dared to visit the embassy anymore, fearful that they would draw police attention. Grew had his walls swept for microphones and protected the secrecy of important office conversations by smothering his phone with a thick pillow.

On August 9 the British government suddenly announced the withdrawal of its troops from China, shocking its citizens there and in Britain's Asian colonies. France had withdrawn its troops from the International Settlement in Shanghai in June. Only one small group of foreign troops remained in China: twelve hundred US Marines stationed in Shanghai to protect American interests in the International Settlement. They immediately became the next Japanese pressure point.

All this agitation—the German victories, the ascension of Konoye's Axis-friendly totalitarian cabinet, the government crackdown on reporters and foreigners, the buckling of France over Indochina and of Britain over the Burma Road and China—churned up waves of arrogance, xenophobia, and spy mania in Japan. New laws allowed the police to arrest anyone who criticized Japan's foreign or domestic policies or its armed forces. Anything written, said, or filmed that might disparage Japanese soldiers, citizens, or the Japanese economy was a crime. Anything that touched upon military matters—and in a totalitarian military state this included almost everything—violated the Military Secrets Act. Anyone who criticized the laws themselves was, of course, a criminal. The Kempeitai began "spy hunts" that radiated outward from Tokyo to China, Korea, and Manchuria. Some speculated that the purpose of these measures was to curry favor with Germany, but Japan didn't need external motivation to stir up its native xenophobia and paranoia.

The government's propaganda apparatus warned the public against foreign espionage networks disguised as innocuous organizations. The ministry of education announced that all foreigners teaching in Japanese schools or universities, about five hundred people, would be replaced "as a precaution against espionage." On August 6 the Kempeitai arrested the leaders of the Japanese Salvation Army. The military couldn't stand by, it explained, while organizations, "under the cloak of religion, become the tools of spies as well as propagate foreign anti-Japanese thoughts." The organization included about half a dozen foreigners among its 250 members. Those arrested also were charged with damaging the war effort by preaching that Christ was superior to the emperor.

Later in August the government began a campaign to push out Western missionaries by requiring all religions to submit to new controls over acceptable teachings. Missionary groups had spent millions of dollars on hospitals, schools, and charities in Japan, all soon forfeited under the government's crackdown. At the same time, the Kempeitai, heavily influenced by Gestapo advisors, labeled Japan's forty-seven Rotary Club chapters "a hotbed of espionage" operated by Jews and communists. Many Rotary chapters dissolved. The others cut ties with the club and barred foreigners.

The once robust flow of Western tourists became a trickle, further slowed by Japan's inhospitable treatment. Before being allowed onshore, travelers had to list the books and pamphlets in their luggage, which the police screened for anti-Japanese or pro-communist sentiments, leading either to seizure or scissoring. All travelers were tailed by a detective, a creepy practice that foreign residents knew well. In summer the detectives were easily spotted, since they wore the same uniform: black alpaca coat, white flannel trousers, black bow tie.

A number of foreign officials lived in the Imperial Hotel, a hive of police spies. One official lost patience with the obvious rifling of his papers during his absences by his obvious watchdog. The official baited his desk with chocolate candies, irresistible in a country with sugar rationing. The candies immediately disappeared. So did the watchdog. The chocolates were potent laxatives nicknamed "dynamite pills." Such were the small retaliations possible by foreigners in Tokyo in 1940.

That summer Grew's beloved Karuizawa offered less escape, partly because he had little time but also because Nazis had inundated it. Swastika flags fluttered throughout the village. Crowds of Germans filled the two hotels and greeted one another on the streets with Nazi salutes and shouts of "Heil Hitler." Uniformed Hitler Youth trained in side lanes. The Grews didn't go to Karuizawa at all that August.

At five foot two, Matsuoka Yosuke was short even for a Japanese. Grew towered over him. The new foreign minister had cropped hair, round eyeglasses, and a neatly clipped brush moustache. He vibrated with energy, physical, mental, and especially verbal. He had strong ideas about foreign policy and expressed them freely.

In an interview with *Herald Tribune* correspondent Wilfrid Fleisher, Matsuoka had made clear where he stood on the issue of Japanese-American relations. They sat in Matsuoka's home study, surrounded by his Chinese art. He wore a summer kimono. Drinking iced tea and fanning himself against the ninety-five-degree heat, Matsuoka declared that any improvement in Japanese-American relations depended solely on America's willingness to stop clinging to the status quo and accept the great changes occurring in East Asia. Fleisher was so amazed by Matsuoka's harangue that he went straight to Grew to talk about it, though it was a Sunday afternoon. Democracy was finished, the foreign minister had assured Fleisher. Totalitarianism would soon rule the world, and the Axis was Japan's natural partner.

So Grew knew what he was facing. In their first meeting Matsuoka characteristically tacked between swagger and pushy affability. He admired Secretary Hull, he said in excellent English. (The two had met in 1933 when Matsuoka was traveling back from the League of Nations. Hull later wrote, "I had long considered him to be as crooked as a basket of fishhooks.") Matsuoka warned that Grew would find him very frank, sometimes to the point of being undiplomatic, because he believed that if their countries ever went to war, the reasons should be clear to both.

Grew parried by agreeing that straight talk was best, but "we might rule out the word 'war.'" Matsuoka countered that in a rapidly changing world, history was often shaped by uncontrollable blind forces—familiar Japanese fatalism. Grew partly agreed. "But I added that one of the primary duties of diplomacy and statesmanship is to direct those forces into healthy channels." He was confident that the two of them could give "helpful directive to the blind forces he had in mind." The world was evolving so fast, said Matsuoka, peace couldn't be preserved by guarding the status quo. It must now be based upon "a new order."

In a press conference a few days later Matsuoka explained how the new order applied to foreign policy. "The Japanese Government is through with toadying," he said. Japan would no longer "make vain efforts to shake hands with countries who cannot be turned into friends."

Matsuoka was born in 1880, the same year as Grew, but chasms separated them. The foreign minister began life poor in a small town. At
thirteen, to better himself and his family, he was shipped to Portland,
Oregon. He lived with an American family and converted to Christianity.
He memorized the Declaration of Independence. He knocked around
a little on the West Coast before ending up back in Portland. During
the day he worked at a lumber company; in the evenings he took classes
at University of Oregon School of Law, graduating in 1900. After nine
formative years in America, Matsuoka returned to Japan in 1902. He professed to love America and to understand it completely. Neither would be
apparent during his time as foreign minister.

Matsuoka entered Japan's foreign service and returned to the United
States from 1913 to 1916 as a secretary in the Washington, DC, embassy.
He also took trips across the country before and after the Paris Peace Conference in Versailles, and again to and from his performance at the League
of Nations. On this second trip he stopped in Portland to visit the grave
of the woman who had given him a home. The grave was poorly marked,
so he bought an attractive granite headstone and inscribed it with tender-
ness and self-absorbed loquacity: "Raised by the loving hands of Yosuke
Matsuoka in token of the lasting gratitude for the sympathy and gentle
kindness of a woman who, next to his mother, shaped his mind and character." After returning from the league he became president of the South
Manchuria Railway, an important Japanese enterprise.

Opinions of Matsuoka were mixed. He was a cock-a-doodle-do who
craved the spotlight. His higher ambitions were as well known as his im-
pregnable self-confidence and garrulous bluster, unusual in Japan and
attractive to some. "Matsuoka is a person who is likely to fall into paradoxes," said Prince Saionji with his usual acuity. Arita told Harada that
making Matsuoka foreign minister might be dangerous. Matsuoka was
an early Japanese admirer of Hitler and Mussolini and affected a similar
strut. He was also an early advocate of one-party totalitarianism, which
recommended him to Konoye. When Konoye appointed him, moderates comforted themselves with the thought that at least Matsuoka wasn't
as fanatical as Konoye's other candidate for the position, the notorious
Shiratori—and then Matsuoka appointed Shiratori as his special advisor.

In early August, Marquis Kido, who was now lord keeper, told Harada that Matsuoka had asked for a one-hour audience with the emperor, then stayed for two, lecturing all the while. "I don't know what the fate of Japan will be in the hands of Matsuoka," said Kido. "He is a troublesome fellow." Harada was worried. He told Saionji that some people thought Matsuoka was insane.

In what became known as "the Matsuoka hurricane," he purged the Foreign Office of pro-Western staffers. He recalled forty diplomats, including two dozen ambassadors and ministers, among them the ambassador to the United States. The purge exemplified the spirit of the new cabinet, said his vice minister: "The whole Japanese race rolled into a ball of fire and sweeping everything before it—that is the character of the new regime."

GREEN LIGHT

ON SEPTEMBER 12, 1940, Grew sent "what I can only call my 'green light' telegram, perhaps the most significant message sent to Washington in all the eight years of my mission to Japan." The twelve-page dispatch marked a swerve in Grew's thinking since the Konoye cabinet took over. It expressed his accumulated frustration with Matsuoka and Matsuoka's vice foreign minister, Ohashi Chuichi.

A meeting with Matsuoka triggered it. After much fruitless dialogue, Grew asked him how long he had been in office. Fifty days, said the foreign minister. Then you must be aware, said Grew, of all my past and recent protests about the ongoing bombings of American property in China. "Astonishment was expressed," commented Grew drily. Matsuoka asked for details, which Grew promised to provide in grim abundance. The two had been jousting for an hour and twenty minutes. Grew left, he wrote, "with a reluctant feeling of complete frustration."

At nine o'clock that evening Grew sent his green-light telegram. It had been vetted, amended, and endorsed by the embassy's key staff. All his previous telegrams, he wrote, had been "red lights" recommending "constructive statesmanship through conciliatory methods and the avoidance of coercive measures." After dealing with Matsuoka, he no longer believed those approaches could alter Japan's direction. "Diplomacy," wrote Grew, "has been defeated by forces, both at home and abroad, utterly beyond its control." Germany's victories had made Japan delirious with territorial ambition. Japan's leaders were certain Britain would soon fall, freeing the imperial forces to gobble up East Asia.

Japan, Grew continued, must now be grouped with Germany and Italy among "the predatory nations." They wanted to destroy democratic values and countries. "In attempting to deal with such powers," wrote Grew, "the uses of diplomacy are in general bankrupt." At best, diplomacy could only delay this rapacity. Patience, restraint, negotiation, adherence to principles, expressions of disapproval—these no longer met the situation. Japan doubted the United States had the stomach for anything stronger, Grew reported, which made the current policy more dangerous than a policy of firmness. To prevent war Japan's leaders must be convinced that their present course would be too costly. They could be jolted into that awareness only by a genuine and frightening threat—for example, an oil embargo. That risky step might sober up Japan but also might provoke its military into some rash step that led to war.

Grew acknowledged that his view from Japan was limited. He didn't know how his piece of the puzzle fit into the overall design of American foreign policy. But he knew Japan deeply. The risks of firmness, including war, were indisputable. Yet the alternative—more toothless warnings—was also perilous because it guaranteed that Japan would rampage through East Asia and ultimately require the United States to fight. The United States must also support Britain in the Pacific and maintain the status quo there until Germany was defeated, which Grew was certain would happen despite current evidence. At that point, Grew argued, Japan would find itself in different circumstances and diplomacy might be possible again.

Grew heard that his telegram had stirred up the department. The dominant opinion—almost certainly Hornbeck's—took the dispatch as confirmation that forceful actions against Japan entailed no risk of war. This crude misinterpretation puzzled Grew. The explanation was confirmation bias. Hornbeck and his allies felt certain that nothing could push Japan into the stupidity of a war with the United States. Japan's leaders, especially Matsuoka, had the same misconception about America.

On August 2 the navy ministry and general staff met to discuss war planning for the army's proposed southern expansion into Southeast Asia and the Pacific Islands. The brass heard reports that the fleet wasn't ready. They were told that if Japanese attacks caused an American oil embargo, the navy would run out of aviation fuel in one year and crude oil in two. If America and Britain cut off trade in vital war metals, Japan's stocks would be gone within a year and a half. "Such a situation would finish us," concluded the navy's chief of procurement. "The navy could barely fight for one year."

Yet two days later the navy general staff decided to move ahead quickly with war plans. Yoshida, the navy minister, pointed out that the plan seemed flawed. He advised the navy not to be "pulled by the army." Nevertheless, the navy set November 15 as the target date to complete preparations. In late August, navy planners again reported that Japan probably could win a quick war with the United States, but if the war was prolonged, as expected, "then we are not very confident of our capacity for endurance." Yet if the nation stayed resolute and gave the navy all the money it wanted, they added, maybe pessimism was unjustified. This willingness to sweep aside facts and replace them with faith in some mystical destiny exemplified the wishful thinking that culminated at Pearl Harbor.

In early September the stress of opposing this irrationality put Yoshida into the hospital with a nervous breakdown. His replacement was Admiral Oikawa Koshiro, a pliable man. The progression of navy ministers from Yonai to Yoshida to Oikawa epitomized Japan's spiral into delusion. Yonai had flatly declared that Japan would not join the Axis and could not defeat the United States. Yoshida had damaged his mental health trying to insert reality into the military's plans for war. Oikawa dismissed the navy's own findings and endorsed the war plan, and also supported Matsuoka's desire to join the Axis.

Matsuoka had been pushing Japan to sign a pact with the Axis, but the navy had balked, reluctant to tie Japan to Germany's military plans. On September 16, at a "liaison conference" between high officials from the government and the military, Matsuoka overcame the navy's objections by deleting a clause in the draft agreement that obliged Japan to provide military support if the United States attacked Germany. The revision preserved Japan's autonomy about when to enter the war.

The emperor knew bits and pieces about the military's plans to move south despite the risks of war with the United States. He had heard that whenever the navy gamed out a war, Japan lost. "Is everything all right?" he asked Konoye. "Since we have come so far, we cannot turn back. But, Mr. Prime Minister, are you prepared to walk this path with me, sharing my joys and sorrows, wherever it may lead?"

"When I heard these words," Konoye later told Baron Harada, "my eyes became dimmed with tears." Konoye left the palace for a cabinet meeting, where he related this exchange. Matsuoka burst into loud sobs. The rest of the room fell into anguished quiet at the thought of distressing their emperor.

Nevertheless, irrationality was on full display at the imperial conference of September 19, called to seek the emperor's sanction of the liaison conference's decision to join the Axis and expand southward. The emperor sat at the head of a small conference room on an elevated dais in front of a gold screen. The ministers and the military faced one another across long tables running lengthwise down the room. The president of the Privy Council asked questions about the liaison conference's decision on behalf of the emperor, who listened in silence.

Konoye and Matsuoka spoke strongly in favor. The director of the planning board outlined the ominous consequences if America embargoed vital materials such as oil. He then built an air castle on wishful ifs—if this and this and this all worked out simultaneously, he said, Japan would be fine. When the navy chief of staff questioned these tenuous assumptions, Matsuoka jumped in with more pipe dreams. Germany had promised to help Japan with oil, he said, and Japan also could get all the oil it wanted from the Soviets—Japan's bitter enemy—"after adjustment of Japanese-Soviet relations." Matsuoka believed he could make obstacles vanish through sheer self-confidence.

The president of the Privy Council noted that when Japan announced its membership in the Axis pact, the United States probably would increase aid to Chiang, ban exports of iron and oil as Grew had warned, and stop trading with Japan "so that we will not be able to endure war." Japan would have to get oil from the Dutch East Indies, with violent consequences. Matsuoka played the German card again. Hitler would compel the Dutch East Indies to provide oil peacefully. Once Hitler conquered Britain, he wanted friendship with America, and Matsuoka was confident that the tens of millions of German and Italian Americans would ensure US friendship toward the Axis. Matsuoka also said Japan was joining the Axis "to prevent the United States from encircling us." Standing firm now would frighten the United States against taking action when Japan moved south. At that point America would either "arrive at a reasonable attitude" or cause a conflict. "I would say that the odds are fifty-fifty," Matsuoka said.

In Matsuoka's peculiar thinking, Japan was joining the Nazis to defend itself against a paranoid delusion—encirclement by the United States—and also to prevent a war with the United States—a disaster made more likely by aligning itself with nations determined to destroy America's allies. Further, if joining the Axis led America to embargo oil, Japan would have no choice but to take oil from the Dutch East Indies. If the United States couldn't accept that, then the United States would be responsible for any conflict. The odds that Japan's decisions might cause a war were a coin toss, fifty-fifty, which Matsuoka blithely called an acceptable risk. This was his dicey foreign policy.

Though the officials had been discussing and debating for three hours, an imperial conference was a ritual with a predetermined outcome, another illustration of the emperor's impotent power. The president of the Privy Council, on the emperor's behalf, always sanctioned the liaison conference's decision, giving it the inviolable authority of the throne although the emperor literally had no say in it. So at the end of the September 19 conference, the president of the Privy Council confirmed the decision to join the Axis and advance southward. If Indochina and the Dutch East Indies refused Japan's peaceful overtures, the ensuing violence would be their fault. Hirohito never spoke.

Matsuoka presented the imperial decision to the Germans as a triumph. When they objected to his deletion of the key clause about entering the war, he said that altering an imperial sanction was impossible.

The day after the imperial conference, Japan gave Indochina an ultimatum: agree to our demands to station our troops in the north and use your airfields or we will invade—you have two days to decide. Grew reminded Matsuoka about Japan's pledge to protect the status quo. Matsuoka's written reply was a confounding blend of lies, self-justification, and insolence.

While trying to settle the China incident, he wrote, "Japan has been avoiding conquests and exploitation, and has been employing brotherly love, mutual existence and mutual prosperity as guiding principles." Japan didn't want "undesirable changes to the status quo," but conditions were changing so quickly that "past rules and norms rapidly become inapplicable to actual conditions." Matsuoka advised the United States to drop its "meddlesome attitude." He also told Grew, with a straight face, that after China surrendered, Japan would leave Indochina and everything would return to normal. As promised, Grew handed Matsuoka a partial listing of the bombings of Americans and American property since 1937. It ran for thirty single-spaced pages.

On September 22 France's Vichy government, having no choice, agreed to let Japanese airplanes and six thousand troops into northern Indochina, with tens of thousands more to follow. In Washington, cabinet members Morgenthau, Stimson, Knox, and Harold Ickes, secretary of the interior, furiously demanded an oil embargo, as did Hornbeck. Hull fended them off, worried that an embargo would lead to war before the US military was prepared. He recommended bans on scrap iron and steel. Roosevelt agreed, partly because anything more drastic might jeopardize his reelection in six weeks. He was already being accused of warmongering by the isolationists, gutlessness by the hawks, and dictatorship by the Republicans for seeking a packed Supreme Court and a third term.

The embargo was announced on September 26. The news on the following day that Japan had joined the Axis barely seemed to ruffle the American government. Hull's bland statement noted that the agreement had been expected and changed nothing. Matsuoka thought he could apply Hitler's Munich strategy to America. He expected the pact to deter the United States from aiding Chiang and Britain, and believed it would help defeat Roosevelt by frightening the American public back toward isolationism. Instead of the timid flinches Matsuoka expected, the US government announced another $25 million loan to China, the permanent berth of the American fleet at Pearl Harbor, and a tightened bond with Britain.

To Grew, Japan's embrace of the Axis confirmed his green-light recognition that diplomacy had failed. "My heart is heavy as I close the diary for September," he wrote. "This is not the Japan which I have known in the past."

Baron Harada was angry. In the past, whenever the emperor had been pressured to approve a pact with the Axis, he had always said, "I absolutely shall not permit it." Why this reversal? Harada learned that Konoye, Matsuoka, and Lord Keeper Kido had convinced Hirohito that allying Japan with Nazis and Fascists was the only way to preserve peace with the United States. Konoye and Kido had kept Harada and Saionji in the dark about the Axis negotiations. Harada demanded an explanation. It was their duty to inform the genro of all crucial matters so he could advise the emperor. "I felt too sorry for Prince Saionji to report the matter to him," said Kido.

The true reason, Harada knew, was that Saionji would have urged the emperor to withhold his consent. The old ways, like the ninety-year-old genro, were obsolete. So was good judgment. Making enemies of Britain and the United States, Saionji told Harada, was "a glaring diplomatic blunder." It was his final political judgment. Saionji died on November 24.

Admiral Yamamoto, now commander in chief of the Combined Fleet, agreed with Saionji about the pact. "It is indeed outrageous," he told Harada one night at dinner. Yamamoto expected a ruinous war against the United States, Britain, and probably Russia as well. But his duty was clear. "I shall exert my utmost efforts," he said, "and will probably die fighting on the battleship *Nagato*," his flagship. He agreed that Japan's only hope was a quick war. A military genius who loved gambling, Yamamoto would soon start devising his audacious strategy to surprise the American fleet at Pearl Harbor. But he didn't expect victory.

"Tokyo will probably be burnt to the ground about three times," Yamamoto told Harada that night, "and tough times will ensue. Moreover, in the end, although it is pitiful for Konoye and others, they may be torn limb from limb by the public. It is indeed a perplexing matter, but as long as it has come to this point, it is inevitable."

A week after joining the Axis, still swollen with certainty about their power to intimidate the United States, Konoye and Matsuoka doubled down on bluster and arrogance. On October 4 Konoye declared to the news service Domei that if the United States opposed the new world order, "there will be no other course open to [the Axis] than to go to war." That same day Matsuoka gave an interview that went out over the International News Service. "I fling this challenge to America," he said. "If she in her contentment is going to blindly and stubbornly stick to the status quo in the Pacific, then we will fight America."

"Apparently the interview went off like a ton of dynamite at home," wrote Grew. Matsuoka immediately retreated, claiming he had been misquoted. He also invited Grew to his private home for tea, where he assured Grew that he would never say such crazy things because he only wanted peace and understanding. Matsuoka also harangued Grew about Japan's purely peace-loving reasons for joining the Axis. The meeting dragged on for more than two hours. "About 95% Matsuoka and 5% Grew, because the Minister's volubility flows on by the hour with little or no punctuation," wrote Grew, "and his monologues can be broken into only by forcible intrusion." Grew suspected Matsuoka had spoken exactly as quoted. It sounded just like him.

Matsuoka's diplomatic strategy was to bully, bullshit, and bewilder. His brainstorms could verge on the preposterous. On October 7 he publicly urged Chiang Kai-shek to join the Axis. A week later, at a rally of fifty thousand people in Hibiya Park, he invited the United States to join the Axis and create "one great family" living under the new order, each power dominant in its home sphere. "However," he added, "we are firmly determined to eliminate any nation that will obstruct our order."

The war talk by Matsuoka and Konoye prompted the State Department to issue an advisory that all nonessential American citizens should immediately evacuate Japan, China, Manchukuo, and Hong Kong. To the Japanese this was even more stunning than the embargoes and the abrogation of the commerce treaty. Was the United States planning an attack? "For the first time," wrote Grew in his diary, "a totally new conception is dawning on the Japanese, namely that the initiative as to whether there shall be war or peace between the United States and Japan may no longer rest with Japan. This thought has come as a profound shock." As a precaution he shipped home his diaries, letters, and other papers in a diplomatic pouch. But shock also opened opportunities for diplomacy. He sent a note reminding Matsuoka about those thirty pages of bombings and his pledge to do something about them.

That same day Roosevelt made a campaign speech in Boston, responding to his opponent Wendell Willkie's attacks on him as a warmonger. Roosevelt had been tiptoeing between isolationist neutrality and support of Britain and China. "I have said this before, but I shall say it again and again and again," he told the crowd. "Your boys are not going to be sent into any foreign wars." A week later Roosevelt won a third term in a landslide, with 449 electoral votes to 10 for Willkie. Grew was elated. The Japanese press saw the election as the American public's surprising endorsement of Roosevelt's deplorable views—pro-Britain, pro-Chiang, anti-Japan, anti-Axis— and a complete refusal to understand Japan's noble intentions.

In late October, Japanese warplanes attacked two more commercial airliners over China. One of them was the same plane shot down by Japanese pilots in 1938. This time they pursued it until it landed, machine-gunned it on the ground until it burst into flame, and strafed the passengers frantically trying to escape. The plane's American pilot was killed along with several passengers. Others were wounded. Grew protested to Matsuoka on November 8. Misidentifying this commercial plane, with its lumbering profile and five-foot-high markings, said Grew, was inconceivable. Now another American citizen had been killed by out-of-control Japanese pilots.

Two days later, on November 10, Matsuoka asked Grew to his private home for tea. Grew arrived well armed with a long menu of the latest issues. Matsuoka pledged to respond quickly to all concerns. The United States, replied Grew, would be impressed by acts, not official statements. He protested the newest bullying and insults to American citizens in China, the newest restraints on American trade, the killing of the American pilot, and other matters including, of course, the most recent bombings of American properties in China. Unless these bombings stopped, added Grew, the American government might feel compelled to start publicizing them.

Oh, don't do that, said Matsuoka with his bottomless chutzpah—it might damage Japanese-American relations.

A GRIM AND CRUEL YEAR

THE CELEBRATION OF the Japanese empire's 2,600th birthday culminated on November 10 and 11, 1940. For months workers had been building an open-air pavilion to hold fifty thousand invitees on the plaza facing the palace. Banners and heaps of flowers decorated the space. The weather on the morning of the tenth was sunny and crisp. Cabinet members and diplomats arrived for the opening ceremony wearing formal frock coats, military officers their full ornamental uniforms. Princesses shimmered in brightly colored silk kimonos. Hitler Youth wore khaki festooned with swastikas. The office buildings beyond the plaza had been emptied so no one could look down on the emperor. By ten thirty everyone was in place, waiting in total silence.

At the prescribed moment the palace gate opened. A bearer carried the imperial standard, a golden sun suspended on a field of red. The emperor's crimson Rolls-Royce followed slowly. They crossed the moat on the double-span bridge as bands played the national anthem. The emperor and empress took their seats on an elevated dais draped with brocades adorned with the imperial chrysanthemum. Princes and princesses stood to their right, cabinet members and military leaders to their left.

Prince Konoye bowed to the imperial couple and announced into the microphone that the ceremony was open. Millions of Japanese were listening by radio. Konoye bowed to the imperials again. The crowd, already standing, bowed in rough unison. Konoye unrolled his speech. He praised the emperor's glorious achievements, such as sending conquering armies into a foreign land and forming an alliance with like-minded European powers to promote world peace. Konoye bowed again, followed by 50,000 simultaneous bows. The music swelled. When it ended at precisely 11:25, Konoye went to the microphone and led the crowd, plus 70 million people in Japan and 105 million Japanese outside it, in three banzais, flinging his arms into the air with each repetition.

The second day of celebration in the pavilion included a feast, ceremonial dancing, band music, chorales singing patriotic songs, and more speeches. Grew, as dean of Tokyo's diplomatic corps, gave a short address to honor the emperor. Hirohito had been sitting motionless and expressionless throughout the two days but nodded throughout Grew's speech, emphatically at the last sentence, in which Grew hoped Japan would keep contributing to the well-being of humankind. The French ambassador told Grew afterward that the emperor's nods were messages to Japan's leaders that he wanted peace and friendship. The palace's official summary of the day specified, unusually, that Grew's speech had pleased the emperor. The foreign press reported these as tiny signs that hopes for peace weren't quite dead.

The appointment of a new ambassador to the United States added another small ray of hope to the festivities. Admiral Nomura, onetime foreign minister, had turned down Matsuoka three times, alarmed by Matsuoka's ideas and judgment. "In my view," wrote the sixty-two-year-old Nomura, "it is utterly out of the question to try to improve Japanese-American relations while attempting to strengthen the Tripartite Alliance." But Matsuoka had persisted, certain that Nomura could use his friendship with Roosevelt to Japan's advantage. The navy's leaders, worried about war with the United States, had begged the sane old seadog to accept the position. He had reluctantly given in, on condition of wide latitude. Nomura was known to be sympathetic to the United States and to oppose a war, so Matsuoka and the Japanese press hailed the appointment as a grand gesture of friendship and compromise.

Just before Nomura's appointment was announced, Joseph Newman, Tokyo bureau chief for the *New York Herald Tribune*, talked with him at the Tokyo Club. Nomura was cheerful by nature, but that night he seemed pessimistic about his mission. As they parted, walking down the club's stone steps, Nomura said something Newman never forgot: "Everything is now out of our hands. The outcome will be decided in heaven." Even for a Japanese, wrote Newman, "that struck me as an unusually fatalistic remark." Newman wrote that Nomura would return to Japan "either a great hero or a tragic failure."

Grew was often exasperated by the ignorance of American isolationists and pacifists about the situation in Japan. They seemed to believe the warmonger in question was the United States. If they could read the stories in the Japanese press, he wrote, they "would realize the utter hopelessness of a policy of appeasement." The Japanese newspapers reflected the topsy-turvy thinking of the nation's newest leaders, Konoye, Matsuoka, and Tojo. They were all stuck in a reality warp. The new guard and their propagandists fed fake news to the Japanese media, which regurgitated it for the public and reinforced their leaders' own disinformation. American ignorance exasperated Grew, but the ignorance among Japan's leaders about facts and contradictory information was dangerous. They read censored papers and listened to censored radio, which constantly assured them that America was a nation of pacifists and appeasers who would never support a war with Japan.

Japanese media also claimed that the country's deteriorating relations with the United States were caused by America's refusal to compromise, by which they meant defer to Japan. The immutable starting assumption was that Japan was right and the United States must change. America, they said, acted like it had a monopoly on rectitude, which carried some truth. Yet the United States wasn't the country seizing territory, bombing civilians, imposing repression, and stealing resources. Grew began handing out American editorials and op-eds that contradicted the picture painted in the Japanese press. The Japanese response was always astonishment followed by denial. Their proof: stories in the Japanese press.

Grew's job now consisted of constantly reminding Matsuoka and other influential Japanese that Japan was flirting with disaster by overestimating American tolerance. On December 17, in another two-hour meeting with the foreign minister, Grew's agenda listed eleven issues. All the usual suspects were on it. Like all the foreign ministers before him,

Matsuoka listened, occasionally expressed indignation, promised to look into things.

He also read an eleven-page oral response to Grew's thirty-page compendium of bombings. Earlier conversations had sparked dim hopes in Grew that Matsuoka might actually address American concerns. The foreign minister began by saying he had carefully studied Grew's list of "so-called" infractions. The response went downhill from there. A war had been raging in China for more than three years, said Matsuoka, so it was "extremely unrealistic" to think that American economic interests wouldn't be disturbed. He didn't mention that Japan had started the war and caused the economic disturbances, and that Japan was ruthlessly shutting out American businesses.

Next Matsuoka said it was "unreasonable, to say the least," that the US government refused to provide Japan with war materials but objected when Japan took measures to get them. He didn't mention that the US government had embargoed certain materials in response to Japan's constant violations of international law and American rights, or that Japan's measures to replace these materials included threat and force. Continuing the theme of victimhood, Matsuoka said Americans "totally ignore both the sincere intention and the earnest endeavors" of Japan's military to prevent "untoward incidents." Such complaints, he implied, showed ingratitude for Japan's efforts. Further, the allegation that these incidents "are willfully and maliciously inflicted upon Americans," huffed Matsuoka, "is altogether unfair as it is unfounded."

As for the alleged insults and assaults by Japanese soldiers, Matsuoka complained that the American government acted as if these soldiers hadn't been forbidden to do such things. This again seemed unappreciative of Japan's sincere efforts. The American government should try to understand that most of these soldiers were simple rural men trying to do their duty, he said, yet this was often made difficult by the insulting superior attitudes of Westerners. In other words, seen correctly, the real victims were the malicious soldiers.

Grew didn't record his reaction to this performance, but his dispatch to Hull noted that Matsuoka's statement "fails to offer any redress and only expounds the usual explanations and excuses."

• • •

Two mornings later Grew met his old friend Count Kabayama at the To-kyo Club. Kabayama wanted to warn Grew about a speech to be given that day by Matsuoka at a farewell luncheon for new ambassador Nomura at the America-Japan Society. Matsuoka had shown Kabayama his speech beforehand. The count was dismayed. He tried to convince the foreign minister to revise it, without success. At the Tokyo Club, Kabayama handed Grew a copy of the speech to forewarn him. "So I had to go to the luncheon 'loaded for bear,'" wrote Grew, "and the Minister got both barrels."

The event was relocated to the Imperial Hotel to accommodate a large turnout. As honorary president, Grew welcomed Matsuoka, who sat beside him. The foreign minister spoke next. After some conventional luncheon praise for Nomura, Matsuoka said he now wanted to speak frankly. The fundamental cause of poor relations between America and Japan, he said, was "American misapprehension of Japan's aims and aspirations."

The guests sat up a bit. Surely Matsuoka wasn't going to sully this rare moment of good feeling between America and Japan. "Contrary to impressions current in America and elsewhere," he continued, "Japan is not waging a war of greed and aggression in China. . . . We are engaged in a moral crusade."

People snickered. "You may, if you like, ladies and gentlemen, laugh or shrug your shoulders," continued Matsuoka, "but I am sure time will prove it." He kept delivering laugh lines, though no one laughed again. Japan's China policy, he said, "shut the door nowhere and to no one." Japan stood "for peace and order." The nation's new order in East Asia would tolerate "no conquest, no oppression, no exploitation." As Matsuoka rumbled on, one observer noted that it became apparent why a Chinese newspaper had nicknamed him "Yap-Yap." All Japan wanted, droned Matsuoka, was to carry on "our constructive work unhindered," but he worried that America might bring on Armageddon and destroy civilization. He hoped for peace but also wanted every American citizen to understand that Japan would honor its commitments to the Axis. "This, of course, implies no threat." Nomura must have felt his pessimism curdling into gloom.

Grew slowly stood and faced the silent, chagrined crowd. Everyone agreed with the foreign minister's desire for peace, he said. With barely detectable sarcasm he also welcomed the news that Japan's policies in China offered an open door to all, and that the new order condemned conquest and exploitation. The minister must know from his time in America, added Grew, that Americans believed in justice and equity, and would uphold both their obligations and their rights. What mattered in international relations today, he said, wasn't words and speeches but "concrete evidence of facts and actions."

Grew paused and looked around the banquet room, then stared down at Matsuoka. "Let us say of nations as of men," he said directly to the foreign minister, "'By their fruits ye shall know them.'"

Afterward the chief of the Foreign Office's American Bureau complained that the ambassador no longer seemed interested in improving American-Japanese friendship. "That remark is completely typical," wrote Grew. "If one doesn't accept the Japanese point of view, hook, bait and sinker, one isn't friendly." Grew's retort to Matsuoka made news all over the United States, in papers from Maine to Atlanta, Milwaukee to Knoxville, North Dakota to Kansas, New York to San Francisco. All praised Grew for speaking firmly and frankly.

The Japanese press, on the other hand, praised Matsuoka for speaking firmly and frankly about Japan's goals and America's stubborn misapprehension. *Asahi* hoped America would learn from Matsuoka's speech. The paper added that Japan could not be expected to compromise its goals beyond appointing Nomura. *Kokumin* headlined its story AMERICA'S ATTITUDE TOWARD JAPAN IS RIDICULOUS, and warned that opposing Japan's southward advance would be a "fatal blunder." *Hochi*, always bellicose, said Matsuoka had been too diplomatic—the time had come to show courage in the Pacific. None of the papers reported Grew's remarks.

On December 14 Grew wrote a personal letter to Roosevelt. He enclosed four Japanese stamps for the president's collection, including two commemorating the 2,600th anniversary. Most of the letter repeated his analytical dispatches, as if he wanted to make sure the president received his views without the filter, or perhaps the barrier, of the State Department. He wrote that diplomacy had failed and Japanese moderates were helpless to stop the extremists. Germany was doing everything possible to push Japan into war. He told Roosevelt a showdown with Japan was inevitable, the only question was when. He emphasized, as he had with Hull, that the best chance of preventing that showdown from becoming a war was to convince Japan that the United States wouldn't shrink from fighting.

"If you are willing to give me even a cue [sic] to your thoughts," wrote Grew, "either in a personal ultra-confidential letter or orally by some trustworthy person coming out here, it will be of tremendous help."

Roosevelt's long response thanked Grew for his helpful assessments, "based as they are upon a rare combination of firsthand observation, long experience with our Japanese relations, and masterly judgment. I find myself in decided agreement with your conclusions." As for clues about his thinking, he wrote that threats were multiple, linked, and worldwide. They had to be considered together. Britain's survival was key in both Europe and the Far East, and required American support. His letter was so long, he explained, "because the problems which we face are so vast and so interrelated that any attempt even to state them compels one to think in terms of five continents and seven seas."

By the time Grew got this letter he and Alice had listened to a staticky broadcast of Roosevelt's fireside chat of December 29, his "arsenal of democracy" talk. Its power and determination heartened Grew. He read the text five times, almost memorizing it, and sent copies to influential Japanese because the national press printed only brief excerpts. Roosevelt had described the situation bluntly. "The Nazi masters of Germany have made it clear that they intend not only to dominate all life and thought in their own country, but also to enslave the whole of Europe, and then to use the resources of Europe to dominate the rest of the world." If Britain fell, the Axis would control Europe, Asia, Africa, southern Asia, and the seas. "The Americas would be living at the point of a gun," he said.

Isolationists and appeasers believed that oceans and nonaggression pacts with the Axis could keep America safe, the president continued, but that was folly. Hitler had broken every agreement. "There can be no appeasement with ruthlessness." The parallels with Germany's ally Japan were obvious. The United States must become "the great arsenal of democracy," said Roosevelt, by providing Britain with the war equipment, munitions, and supplies to resist and defeat Germany, and to keep the oceans secure. Doing so would save democracy—he was certain Britain would win—and might also keep America out of the fighting.

The speech chimed perfectly with Grew's thinking and gave him a dose of hope. Despite what he called "a grim and cruel year," he somehow found cracks of light. Matsuoka's blustery threats had backfired. Congress would pass Roosevelt's Lend-Lease Act, allowing America to aid Britain. That would eventually reverse Germany's momentum. Nazi glitter would no longer bedazzle Japan. Roosevelt was pursuing the strong policies Grew believed would give Japan second thoughts about aggression toward the United States and Britain.

On New Year's Eve he and Alice listened to a broadcast of a Japanese orchestra playing Beethoven's Ninth Symphony. The performance was mediocre, he wrote, yet the "Ode to Joy" still stirred his spirits. "It conjures up visions of better things to come," he wrote. "My incurable optimism leads me to believe that they will come in 1941. This time I believe that good ground for optimism is offered by the facts."

DARKENING

AFTER PRINCE KONOYE resumed the premiership and committed the nation to totalitarianism, daily life in Japan changed drastically. Voltage for electricity unrelated to the war effort was cut, dimming streets, neighborhoods, and moods. The Ginza's neon dazzle got unplugged—too frivolous and wasteful. Brightness of any kind was discouraged as inappropriate extravagance. Women in colorful kimonos or chic Western fashions were scolded on the street by patriots and were handed cards printed with government slogans: "Deny the self, serve the public" and "Indulgence in luxuries is our enemy."

The list of enemies kept lengthening, especially for women. Rouge, lipstick, nail polish, hair treatments. Watchdogs monitored beauty parlors. One woman was told that her usual hairstyle of five curls in front and fifteen in back was now illegal, the maximum number being three. Men were expected to shave their heads in the military style to avoid the opulence of hair oil. The Japanese Barbers' Association announced that its members would refuse to cut hair "in styles contrary to the national spirit and unbecoming to present conditions."

This was all part of Konoye's "new structure," soon dubbed the "new stricture." Not much escaped the stern gaze of the killjoys. Children were forbidden to catch dragonflies, "this being out of key with the spirit of the times." Double features were banned as excessive, and the government advised theaters to run propaganda films from Japan or Germany. The Grews had once kept up with new American movies on the rooftop of the

Imperial Hotel, but those dangerously entertaining imports disappeared. The new rules shut down clubs and dance halls as immoral distractions from the nation's holy mission. Restaurants were forbidden to serve expensive food. Cars couldn't be used for recreational purposes. Geishas, epitomes of lavish entertainment, were too revered and traditional to ban but were renamed "national policy girls."

"The police and gendarmes are busy," wrote Grew, "cracking down hard on all who violate the principles of the 'new structure' which involves an economical way of life and a general frowning upon most forms of light-heartedness, bright colors, fun, sport and general gaiety, so much loved by the Japanese, and, of course, 'dangerous thought.'" It reminded him of his favorite definition of totalitarianism: "Everything Not Forbidden is Compulsory."

To the grinches who sniffed out pleasure and frivolity, sports carried a stink. Athletic activities were permitted only to improve physical stamina for the war effort. Anyone displaying delight would be reprimanded. "There are many insincere skiers who ski purely for enjoyment," complained the newspaper *Asahi*, "and there are some who go to resorts and do not ski at all." The fusspots were especially hard on golf. Since better fitness was its only justification, caddies were eliminated. Players were allowed two new balls per year. All silver trophies had to be surrendered to the government for melting down. Grew played through it all, complaining, but had less and less time for the game. People noticed. "Your golf is the thermometer which measures the temperature in the Diplomatic Corps," said the French counselor in February 1941. "If a week goes by without your playing golf, the fact is cabled to every chancellery the world over, for the situation is then indeed critical!"

To combat luxury and incidentally to fund the war machine, the government required citizens to turn in their gold, even wedding bands. Jewelry and expensive watches became illegal accoutrements and disappeared from public view, though many Japanese hid their treasures instead of subsidizing another tank. Grew had to rush to get a dental bridge made (his "bridge of sighs") before the end of February, when gold would no longer be available for nonpatriotic uses. The empire claimed other metals as well. Streetlights, railings, and decorative ironwork were torn out and sent to the munitions factories. Manufacture of household items made from metal, such as appliances, can openers, tongs, and cuff links, ceased. Even metal buttons had to be cut off and turned in, replaced by glass or bone.

The military commandeered most cotton, textiles, and silk. That pushed men and women to give up fashion for the government's alternative: drab, shapeless garments made from *sufu* or "staple fabric," wood pulp mixed with scraps of cotton or wool. After a few washings *sufu* clothing disintegrated into splintery mush with holes. *Sufu* soon became slang for "lousy substitute."

Lousy substitutes were the norm. Many Japanese showed desperate ingenuity: flour made from crushed acorns or dried radish leaves, sausage made from whale or seal meat, coffee made from roasted barley or soybeans. For Japanese the worst *sufu* was partially polished brown rice instead of white, most of which went to the military. Less rice also meant less sake. Beer, another Japanese favorite, wasn't an alternative. In May 1941 a newspaper ran the headline GOOD NEWS! BEER TO BE RATIONED OUT; 2 BOTTLES MONTHLY TO EACH HOUSEHOLD.

Small things taken for granted suddenly became precious. Matches got thinner and shorter and finally were rationed at four per person per day, or one box a month per family. Housing construction stalled for lack of wood, not to mention nails, which required a police permit. Even pencils became rare because of their three precious elements: wood, brass, rubber.

The government's restrictions were moralistic cover for acute shortages. Milk, eggs, meat, fish, rice, fruit, soap, fuel—the list grew longer every month. Stomachs were empty, houses were cold. The government's advice: eat less, sacrifice more, toughen up. The government assured the public that if the nation could maintain a "rock bottom subsistence level" for just ten years, Japan would dominate the world. Most Japanese did eat even less, did sacrifice even more, became even tougher. Grew had been telling Washington for years that Japan could never be starved or squeezed into submission because the people would endure anything their emperor asked of them.

Yet even imperial devotion and the "new structure" couldn't stop the human urges to hoard, racketeer, and make a few yen under the table. The government set the price of all commodities, from food to clothing, usually too low to allow any profit. The government also set wages in wartime factories, also low, but shifts were long so workers had money but little to spend it on because of scarcities. These were perfect conditions for a black market. Many in this nation of scrupulous rule followers turned outlaw. Trains arriving from the countryside were crowded with farmers hauling crates of vegetables, chickens, and rice sold directly to waiting housewives or grocers willing to pay higher prices. Hikers took trains into rural areas, not to improve the empire's physique but to stuff their empty rucksacks with black market produce.

The government employed squads of "economic police" to track down scofflaws, sometimes going house to house to inspect what people were eating and wearing. Since Japan was also the empire of the slogan and the poster, the government promoted better citizenship through campaigns such as Good Commercial Morals and Shady Transaction Prevention Week, with inspiring slogans such as "No soul looking up to the Rising Sun flag will besmear itself with dishonor doing shady business."

As the military devoured Japan's resources and the "new structure" snuffed joy, Toyko changed from vibrant to shabby and sullen. Civic life frayed. Potholes deepened, sidewalks buckled. Buildings and streets turned dingy with neglect, gloomy with reduced electricity. In summer Tokyo began to stink. Few of the city's one million households had flush toilets, so waste was picked up by night-soil men and transported by truck to the countryside. The gas shortage soon made that impossible, so the transport switched to carts pulled by bikes or other non-combustion devices. The system got backed up, and Tokyo reeked. Japanese could endure almost any hardship, but tempers shortened like rationed matches. Newspapers carried stories of moviegoers fighting in line at theaters. Restrict joy, noted Grew, and people were bound to get ugly.

Westerners in Japan were useful scapegoats. Grew received regular reports of Americans elbowed in the streets by Japanese. In January, queuing for a train ticket, he was shoved out of line. "Luckily I counted ten before hitting him," he wrote, "and then discretion overcame valor. There are roughnecks in every country, but in Japan they now seem to predominate. One's blood boils but there's nothing to be done about it."

The "new structure" also took measures to reverse the related trends of delayed marriages and the declining birth rate. These were caused partly by the military's voracious appetite for young men and partly by insidious notions about female autonomy promoted by foreign movies. But the retreat into feudal nationalism crushed the frail women's suffrage movement and pushed women back into traditional roles. (Japanese women couldn't vote until 1946.) The government began a campaign to encourage patriotic marriages, starting with posters and slogans: "Early marriages are a benefit for the nation" and "Children are the country's hope and treasure." The marriage age was lowered. Official matchmaking agencies sprang up. For couples who couldn't afford wedlock, government programs funded trousseaus and offered loans and subsidies, plus bonuses for large families. Birth control was banned.

Male Japanese colonists in Manchukuo and North China also needed brides, so the government opened training schools that churned out hundreds of women who took three-month courses in farming and housekeeping. Tokyo's famed Takarazuka Revue dramatized the rewards of this connubial mission with an operetta entitled *When Spring Orchids Bloom*, about Japanese women who patriotically ventured to Manchukuo to marry. Brides had to be exported to avoid mixed marriages between Japanese colonists and Chinese or Manchu women, which would dilute the "Nippon race." Otherwise Japan might end up like the United States. An editorial in *Hochi* mocked America's so-called melting pot as a stew of races that led to bigotry and a "fickle and frivolous civilization" that couldn't be saved by the descendants of Germans. "Such racial heterogeneity is a grave weakness in time of war," said the paper.

The "new structure" also reorganized the Japanese educational system. Every school was assigned army officers whose power rivaled the principal's. Military training became compulsory for boys, five or six hours per week, which gradually expanded into time once devoted to academic subjects. The training included drills, long marches, and lectures about the glory of dying for the emperor. It was common to see primary school students bayoneting straw dummies on the playground. The school year was shortened to accelerate the flow of bodies into the military.

The government distracted the public from discontent over strictures and deprivations by firing up paranoia, xenophobia, and war fever. No nation had threatened to bombard Japan, but sirens regularly announced air-raid drills. At night this meant extinguishing all lights and covering windows with heavy black paper.

The propaganda campaign against anything foreign intensified, starting with the English language, common in Tokyo. Signs and labels—for the Miss Tiger bar, Golden Bat cigarettes, the W.C.—were replaced with Japanese equivalents. On the radio American music was edged out by patriotic songs and marches. Announcers at baseball games had to find patriotic Japanese substitutes for *foul ball* and *bunt*. Students who wanted to learn English were monitored as potential spies by the Bureau of Moral Principles and Science. The language eventually was dropped from the curricula, and English-language schools were pressured to close. Japanese who spoke English in public might be detained and questioned.

The government intensified its anti-spy campaigns, flooding the public with pamphlets, speeches, radio programs, and posters (BEWARE OF FOREIGN SPIES!) that warned Japanese against talking to foreigners, all of whom were suspected of collecting data for espionage. Any mail going abroad had to be submitted to the post office unsealed for the censors, with stamps attached but unaffixed so secret messages couldn't be hidden underneath.

New laws permitted a death sentence for anyone who gave a foreigner vital Japanese information, which included almost all information. Japanese employed by foreigners were the laws' primary targets, though many were already working as spies for the Kempeitai or the Home Ministry police. The laws put an axe over the heads of foreign correspondents. Police regularly tossed the offices and residences of foreigners, searching for subversion. They didn't touch the American embassy, but Grew assumed his Japanese staff reported to them. If he left his office for even a few minutes, he put all important papers into the safe.

Japanese suspected of straying from the imperial mission—"thought offenders" who might spread "contagious thoughts"—were sent to "preventive detention" for psychological reorientation. The government proudly noted that this approach differentiated Japan from Germany's brutal treatment of dissidents. Japan, a nation of racially pure conformists, didn't need death camps.

Japanese leaders at all levels preached that dying for the emperor was a privilege to be celebrated. In April 1941 the government paid for the parents and widows of 14,500 dead soldiers to travel to Tokyo for five days of ceremonies at the Yasukuni Shrine. Nearly 30,000 grieving relatives, most of them rural peasants, wore black kimonos with special armbands while walking to the shrine of the war dead. Despite the nation's desperate shortages, food and drink were piled high to honor the lost patriots.

In January 1941 the government announced that even greater sacrifices would be necessary to fulfill Japan's imperial destiny. That same day War Minister Tojo issued his *Instructions for the Battlefield*, a pamphlet given to every soldier. Among its sermons on discipline, honor, and imperial loyalty was a stark exhortation: "Do not suffer the shame of being captured alive." The Japanese army didn't train medics to rescue the wounded, didn't erect field hospitals behind the front lines, because its soldiers were under orders not to surrender or refuse a heroic death.

No, the Japanese would not be pushed into submission by deprivation or suffering.

A RUMOR OF PEARL

"THERE IS A lot of talk around town," wrote Grew on January 27, 1941, "to the effect that the Japanese, in case of a break with the United States, are planning to go all out in a surprise mass attack on Pearl Harbor. Of course I informed our Government. I rather guess that the boys in Hawaii are not precisely asleep."

Grew heard the rumor from one of the embassy's third secretaries, who got it from the Peruvian minister. The minister called it "fantastic" but passed it along for Grew because the same rumor had reached him from several sources, at least one of whom overheard it from a tipsy Japanese admiral. It sounded implausible to Grew as well, but the minister was a friend whose judgment he respected, so he reported it.

The rumor was too far-fetched to alarm anyone at the State Department, which duly sent it on to the army and navy. The navy had already studied the possibility and judged it improbable. Even if the Japanese were foolish enough to start a war with Britain and the United States, a surprise attack would likely target Singapore, Hong Kong, the Philippines, or the Dutch East Indies.

A few weeks earlier Admiral Yamamoto had started devising his strategy to cripple the American fleet.

In his Christmas message Hitler had promised Britain's defeat in 1941. In a New Year's message Ribbentrop had assured Matsuoka that Britain would be wiped out by fall. The Japanese press lapped up this bravado. Germans were flooding into Tokyo. "The hotels are crammed with them," wrote Grew. The Nazis were prodding Japan's army, navy, and Foreign Office to invade Singapore and Hong Kong simultaneously with Germany's invasion of Britain, rumored for early spring. Hitler was tired of Japan's loitering and its obvious plan to mop up the Pacific spoils of German victories. His message was to fight or lose those spoils to Germany. The extremists were eager to attack, but saner leaders knew that invading British territories probably meant war with America. Matsuoka covered all bets, insisting that the Axis's Tripartite Pact was strictly peaceful while waving it like a gun to warn America to stay out of Europe and East Asia.

Like Grew, the Japanese media were inspired by Roosevelt's "arsenal of democracy" talk, but in the opposite direction. They called it an implicit declaration of war. They complained that the president's State of the Union address on January 6 was more of the same. On January 15 Hull testified before the House Foreign Affairs Committee to support the lend-lease bill, which would give Roosevelt the power to send aid to Britain, China, and other nations threatened by totalitarian assault. (It passed in March.) The bill alarmed Germany and panicked Japan. If American aid kept Britain and China afloat, Japan's plans to control East Asia were jeopardized.

On January 21, in a defiant speech to the Diet, Matsuoka warned that the United States must not interfere with Japan's new order in East Asia, must stop supporting Chiang, must lift trade restrictions, and must cede Japan economic primacy in Indochina and the Dutch East Indies. In short, the United States must agree to everything Japan wanted despite everything Japan had done. If America failed to concede, he threatened, the consequence might be war, which would be America's fault since Japan wanted peace. A few days later Matsuoka declared that the United States refused to understand that Japan's actions were based on the harmonious concept of *hakko ichiu*, "the eight corners of the universe under one roof." The roofer, of course, was Japan.

In reply Hull issued a press statement: "We have threatened no one, invaded no one, and surrounded no one. We have freely offered and now freely offer cooperation in peaceful life to all who wish it."

• • •

In late January, Eugene Dooman, the embassy's counselor in Tokyo, was about to return to Japan after a long furlough in America. He had been trying to get permission to see Roosevelt for five months without success, despite carrying a personal letter of introduction from Grew. Grew and Dooman often wondered whether their views from inside Japan were surviving the State Department's bureaucracy and reaching Hull, much less the president. The paperwork pipeline crossed the desks of Joseph Ballantine (Dooman's replacement on the Japan desk), Maxwell Hamilton (chief of the Far Eastern Division, who had served in China prior to working under Hornbeck for six years), and finally Hornbeck (now Hull's special advisor on the Far East).

Grew and Dooman suspected, correctly, that the embassy's viewpoint was being undermined in Washington, principally by Hornbeck. Dooman's furlough offered the opportunity for an unfiltered connection to the president. Grew's letter asked Roosevelt to give the counselor just a few minutes, "for it would be very much as if I were talking to you myself. Dooman can give you in brief compass a clear picture of the scene and our analysis of the situation." Following protocol, Dooman sent a note to Hull asking for permission to see the president on Grew's behalf. "That application was refused," said Dooman. He saw Hornbeck's hand in it. Whether Roosevelt knew about Grew's request was unclear.

Now Dooman was about to return to Japan. Grew was so intent on putting his views before Roosevelt and getting the president's in return that he tried again. He sent another note to Roosevelt, this time by wire, asking him to see Dooman. He cabled Hull the same request. "It must be difficult for the Administration to visualize just how much we feel out on a limb with regard to many matters of high policy intelligence and tentative plans," wrote Grew in his diary. "Naturally information along those lines might, and probably would, have an important bearing on my work out here. If Ambassadors are something more than messenger boys, they must be allowed to see behind the scenes."

Hull sandbagged the new request, though he did brief Dooman in late

January. If Grew's telegram reached Roosevelt, he ignored it. For much of 1941 Grew sent increasingly urgent messages into the black hole of Washington and felt more and more like a messenger boy kept on call outside the stage door. In spare moments he had started making notes toward a book about his time in Japan. Its tentative title: *Failure of a Mission*.

On February 7 Grew sent Hull a long analysis of Japan's southward strategy, which he called a "nibbling policy." Japan had nibbled south through Huizhou, Hainan, and the Spratly Islands. Now, encouraged by Germany's aggression, Japan had taken over airfields in northern Indochina. Its navy was patrolling the Gulf of Thailand and Cam Ranh Bay, and troops had mobilized in Thailand. All of it pointed to Japan's next snack: French Indochina.

When France fell, Thailand began demanding the return of previously annexed territories in Laos and Cambodia. France refused. According to Matsuoka, Thailand and Indochina were in Japan's Greater East Asia Co-prosperity Sphere. Without being invited, Matsuoka appointed himself mediator of the conflict. As payment for his unbiased and benevolent peacemaking, he demanded that Indochina sell Japan 80 percent of its rice.

Matsuoka also announced that the Dutch East Indies was in the Co-prosperity Sphere and thus "should be in intimate and inseparable relationship with our country." The colony was on Japan's nibble list. But the leaders of the Dutch East Indies rejected Matsuoka's invitation and added that if Japan insisted, they would fight. The two governments had been negotiating for several months about Japan's demands, which included selling Japan large amounts of resources, such as oil, tin, and rubber. The Dutch kept throwing up obstacles. The Japanese press accused them of "insincerity" and condemned their poor attitude. The press also said negotiations should focus on removing "the White Peril" from the Pacific. Extremists clamored for Japan to stop talking and simply take what it needed.

The Japanese army and navy had approved attack plans for the Dutch East Indies and Indochina. Admiral Yamamoto, alarmed by the navy's intentions, forced the general staff and war college to do map exercises, which concluded that assaulting Indochina or the Dutch East Indies would mean war with the United States, a war Japan couldn't win. The navy's leaders were unfazed.

Japan's ultimate target appeared to be British Singapore, wrote Grew in his analysis of February 7. Singapore would give Japan and Germany control of Southeast Asia—a disaster for Britain, the Dutch East Indies, China, and ultimately the United States. The question, repeated Grew, wasn't whether the United States should stop Japan's southern advance, but when. He advised now, even at the risk of war, before Japan nibbled any more. American passivity, which the Japanese counted on, would be calamitous. "The moment decisive action should be taken, if it is ever to be taken," wrote Grew, "appears to us to be approaching."

On February 14 Dooman called on Ohashi Chuichi, vice minister of foreign affairs, to brief him on what he had learned during his recent furlough. Attitudes were changing, said Dooman. Most Americans and their leaders still didn't want war, but all were fully committed to helping Britain. Any action that blocked supplies to that country, whether from the United States or from Britain's colonies, would not be tolerated. For instance, said Dooman, if Japan invaded the Dutch East Indies or Malaya, it would endanger Singapore and trigger conflict with the United States.

Ohashi looked astonished. "Do you mean to say," he asked after a few moments, "that if Japan were to attack Singapore there would be war with the United States?"

"The logic of the situation would inevitably raise that question," replied Dooman.

Ohashi, agitated, went on a tirade, citing the usual litany of Japan's mistreatment and victimhood. Was Dooman saying that to avert war Japan must let itself "be tied hand and feet by the United States and Great Britain?" Dooman could have replied that he hadn't said any such thing. Instead he said America couldn't dictate Japan's actions, but unless Japan started to match America's restraint and forbearance, war would be hard to avoid.

That didn't calm Ohashi. He said the Foreign Office was eagerly awaiting Ambassador Nomura's reports about his upcoming talks with Roosevelt and Hull.

That same day, Hull took Nomura to the White House so the ambassador
could present his credentials to Roosevelt. Hull had told Roosevelt beforehand that he was pessimistic about reaching an accord with Japan. "I estimated right at the outset," he later wrote, "that there was not one chance of
success in twenty or one in fifty or even one in a hundred." Hull noted that
Nomura was tall and vigorous, with limited English. He bowed frequently.
The president greeted him like an old friend, recalling their time together
twenty years earlier in the service of their countries' navies. He hoped they
would always be candid, as friends should be. Then he followed his own
advice. Relations between their nations were getting worse, he said. He
listed the Japanese actions that had caused the deterioration. War would
senselessly harm both their countries, so he hoped Nomura would work
with Hull to see if relations could be improved.

Nomura nodded earnestly at all of it. He wasn't obsequious; he agreed
with most of Roosevelt's points. Before leaving for Washington he had
written two memos that laid out his views. Like Admiral Yamamoto,
Nomura believed that war with the United States would destroy Japan,
yet Matsuoka and the military extremists were whipping Japan toward
confrontation. To avoid that, he wrote, Japan should offer concessions
on every significant issue. Give all countries equal commercial access in
China. Pledge to make Japan's southward advance an economic strategy,
not a military one. Assure the United States that if it joined Britain in the
European war, Japan wouldn't automatically reinforce Germany under the
Tripartite Pact.

Nomura's views inverted Matsuoka's. That was why Nomura had refused the ambassadorship so many times. But he believed his views were
Japan's only path away from devastation. Matsuoka would never agree to
propose them to Hull, but perhaps opportunities would pop up in Washington. Nomura's meeting with Roosevelt confirmed his belief that the
United States wanted peace but hadn't been intimidated by Matsuoka's
bluster or Japan's embrace of the Axis.

That same week brought two more signals that Matsuoka's diplomacy of threat wasn't working. The United States announced the fortification of Guam and Samoa, and again advised all remaining nonessential citizens in Japan to evacuate. These were signs of preparation, not fear. The families of consulate and embassy officers packed for home. The occasion for most parties was farewells. "The American embassy in Tokyo during 1941," wrote Third Secretary John K. Emmerson, "was a bachelor establishment." Even so, Alice stayed.

NEGOTIATIONS

IN MID-FEBRUARY 1941 Matsuoka sent a note to his British counter-part, Foreign Secretary Anthony Eden, offering his services as an international peacemaker. A couple of days later, at a small luncheon for several foreign correspondents at his home, Matsuoka revealed another far-fetched peace plan. He intended to persuade Roosevelt to advise Chiang Kai-shek to negotiate directly with Matsuoka or else lose American aid—that is, he wanted Roosevelt to blackmail Chiang into throwing China onto Matsuoka's mercy. "If President Roosevelt would only trust me," he said, "I can guarantee that I will not fail."

Both peace proposals furnished more evidence of Matsuoka's boundless self-confidence and schizophrenic diplomacy. His services as peacemaker bristled with threats. His letter to Eden advised Britain to adopt a "prudent attitude" and to stop its "elaborate military moves" in the Pacific, a reference to the mining of Singapore's harbor against the threat of Japanese invasion. Matsuoka's offer was mentioned and discarded in Parliament, where it was seen as a sign of Germany's worry about the blitz's failure to break Britain. That interpretation thoroughly irritated Hitler and Ribbentrop. After a scolding from German ambassador Ott, Matsuoka scurried away from his offer and claimed he had been misunderstood.

A few days later Matsuoka had to yank his foot from his mouth again. Japan needed territory for its excess population, he told the Diet, and had a "natural right" to Oceania as part of the Co-prosperity Sphere. Oceania, said the minister, included the East Indies, the Philippines, and Malaya, plus a few islands he generously exempted—Australia, New Zealand, and Hawaii. This vast territory, he added, shoving his foot beyond his tonsils, should be ceded by whites to Asians.

This sentiment wasn't uncommon among extremist Japanese but had never been expressed in public by a foreign minister. It caused a kerfuffle overseas. Japan's Foreign Office tried to suppress Matsuoka's remarks, then denied them, then issued a statement with the soothing clarification that "White men occupying Oceania are due to return it to the Asiatics." More kerfuffle. Matsuoka insisted he had been misquoted again.

Shiratori, former ambassador to Italy and now Matsuoka's special advisor, was more blunt. Two weeks later he told the press that one goal of the new order in East Asia was to drive out whites. After that honest clarification of government policy, posters quickly appeared on Tokyo's streets, white lettering on a black background: ASIA FOR THE ASIATICS! DRIVE THE WHITE MAN OUT OF ASIA! and SOUTHWARD HO—BY FORCE!

When Grew met with Matsuoka on February 26, the foreign minister was more hyped up than usual, perhaps because his mediation of the Thailand-Indochina dispute wasn't going well. Nor were Britain and America wilting under his threats. He had been complaining in the press about "Anglo-Saxons" creating a menace by taking defensive precautions in Singapore, British Malaya, Guam, and Samoa. The Western powers were "crying wolf," he said, pretending that Japan was dangerous. Now Matsuoka was grousing to Grew about these Anglo-American incitements. Grew said it was extraordinary to twist defensive measures into offensive menaces. Matsuoka didn't want to hear that or anything else. He wanted to talk. Grew listened for an hour and a half.

"Afterwards," noted Grew in his diary, "I wrote thirteen separate memoranda on the subjects touched upon, and even they were not enough to cover all he said. One emerges from such a conversation with one's head feeling like a whirlpool."

Matsuoka had promised that his mediation of the Thai-Indochina dispute with France would respect Indochina's territorial integrity. The day after meeting with Grew he told the French ambassador in Tokyo that Vichy had until the next day to accept Japan's final proposal. This wasn't an ultimatum, insisted a Foreign Office spokesperson, because mediators didn't issue ultimatums. On March 2 as troops and ships massed near Indochina, France accepted Matsuoka's gunpoint arbitration. Thailand received five large territories, including important producers of rice and rubber, rumored to be promised to Japan.

One of the topics Matsuoka had sprayed at Grew during their meeting was his upcoming trip to Berlin, with stops in Moscow and Rome. Hitler had summoned Matsuoka and Ambassador Ott for "all-embracing talks," no doubt focused on pushing Japan into the war. Matsuoka was eager to unleash his diplomatic prowess on Hitler, Mussolini, and Stalin—giants, in his view, yet his equals. He would act for the sake of peace, he told the Japanese press, as when mediating the Thai-Indochina dispute. Next he intended to hypnotize Churchill and Roosevelt. He believed that great men working together could solve the world's problems.

The Japanese press seemed proud of the invitation to Berlin (though Matsuoka insisted the trip was his idea) but nervous about what their unpredictable and loquacious foreign minister might say, and also about how America and Britain would react. The cabinet and high command held four liaison conferences just before Matsuoka left to make clear to him that he couldn't promise Japan's military support to Hitler.

On the evening of March 12, Prime Minister Konoye, the entire cabinet, and several hundred well-wishers and reporters crowded Central Station to see Matsuoka off. "I am going to explain *hakko ichiu* to the leaders of Germany and Italy," he said, "and to tighten Axis cooperation towards a lasting peace and a new world order." His express train pulled out to the roar of banzais.

In late January 1941 Roosevelt and Hull met for two hours with several amateur diplomats with a plan to mend relations between Japan and the United States. This odd group, soon dubbed the John Doe Associates, consisted of a Japanese banker named Ikawa Tadao, US postmaster general Frank C. Walker, and two Maryknoll priests, Father James M. Drought and Bishop James E. Walsh. Walker had gotten the group into Roosevelt's office by assuring the president and Hull that they were backed by the highest echelons in Japan. This statement, like their proposal, was lightly connected to reality. Matsuoka had dismissed their plan, but Konoye and the army encouraged it, while doubting the United States would accept anything so favorable to Japan. For instance, part of their proposal called for strengthening Japan's position in Indochina and the Dutch East Indies.

Like Konoye, Roosevelt and Hull didn't expect much to come from the group but were willing to see if their alternate route led anywhere. Ultimately the group gummed up the diplomatic works, with additional gum provided by Nomura. The new Japanese ambassador didn't learn about the John Does until he reached Washington, but he then coordinated with them to insert revisions that made their proposal both more and less acceptable to the United States. To advise Nomura, the army sent Colonel Iwakuro Hideo to Washington. Iwakuro had his own strong ideas about the terms of a potential agreement, such as affirming Japan's loyalty to the Axis. He occasionally cabled his suggested provisos straight to Konoye, bypassing Matsuoka, whom he disliked, and Nomura, whom he sometimes patronized.

Meanwhile, Hornbeck was papering Roosevelt and Hull with memos about the dangerous futility of any agreement with Japan. "The effects," he wrote, "would be those of a super-colossal political bombshell: tremendous repercussions in all directions." Hornbeck dismissed the possibility that Japan's leaders would risk war. "That those authorities will embark upon a war in the southwestern Pacific," he pontificated, "in the event of and because of lack of success in a 'negotiation' with the United States in the near future, I do not for one moment believe."

No one at the State Department asked what the man with the deepest knowledge of Japan's political intricacies believed. Grew learned about the John Does and their proposal in a summary dispatch that didn't seek his opinion. Hornbeck occasionally sent Grew updates on the talks without asking his reaction. Grew felt sidelined. Nevertheless, in March he canceled his scheduled furlough again in case the deteriorating situation needed him.

Hull soon decided he would deal only with Japan's appointed representative, Ambassador Nomura, not the John Does. Nomura wanted to announce that the Japanese drafts toward an agreement were the basis of a negotiation, but Hull said their countries were too far apart for that term. Their talks, he insisted, were "unofficial, exploratory, and without commitment."

During the first months of 1941, Matsuoka didn't know that Nomura, Iwakuro, and the John Does were working at odds with his instructions to Nomura. Hull was often unsure if Nomura was speaking for Matsuoka or the John Does. More than once Nomura also submitted a proposal to Hull on his own, separate from those of Matsuoka and the John Does, without making that point clear to Hull or telling Matsuoka. Nomura tended to report the encouraging parts of Hull's responses to Tokyo and to leave out the tougher bits. He did the same thing in the other direction, scrubbing out the worst of Matsuoka's bluster. So the Japanese embassy misled the Japanese Foreign Office about American responses to their requests and delivered contradictory messages to both governments. The result was a mess of miscommunication and misunderstanding that worsened reciprocal mistrust.

As his special train clattered across Siberia, Matsuoka drank vodka and ate caviar provided by the Soviet government. Alcohol expanded his robust self-regard. He boasted to his retinue that his diplomatic finesse would turn Stalin and Hitler into his puppets. The journey to Moscow took a week. He arrived amidst snow flurries on March 23 and spent two days there. He met with Foreign Minister Vyacheslav Molotov, who had signed more execution lists than Stalin, and also with the Soviet leader himself.

Matsuoka harangued Stalin for forty minutes. (Other accounts said sixty or ninety minutes but were unanimous that it was a monologue. Grew wondered if Matsuoka would blast Hitler with a similar torrent. "It would take a superman to outtalk Matsuoka," he wrote.) Matsuoka expatiated to Stalin about the supposed ideological differences separating imperial Japan from communist Russia. In fact, he claimed, their countries were allied as "moral communists." This brilliance was meant to soften Stalin's stance toward Japan. On his trip back to Japan through Moscow, Matsuoka intended to ask the Soviets for a nonaggression pact. He also assured the American ambassador to the Soviet Union, Laurence Steinhardt, that he detested communism. He added that "under no circumstances" would Japan attack Singapore or anyplace else in southeastern Asia. "I wish Roosevelt and Hull would trust me," he told Steinhardt.

At the border with Germany Matsuoka transferred to a special Nazi train. It took him into Berlin on the evening of March 26. Ribbentrop and other Nazi dignitaries met him at the station. A huge crowd, ordered there by Minister of Propaganda Joseph Goebbels, waved Japanese and Nazi flags as throngs of Hitler Youth shouted, "Heil Hitler! Heil Matsuoka!" Matsuoka, delighted, stuck his arm out the window in the familiar salute. Cheering crowds lined the route to his lodgings. The Germans' flattery was meticulous. The local cinemas were showing *The Daughter of the Samurai*, a Japanese movie about a young woman who tries to throw herself into a volcano but is saved to lead a happy life on a Manchukuo farm.

Matsuoka basked in the royal treatment, despite knowing that he couldn't deliver its objective. Ribbentrop and Hitler pressed for Japan to help defeat Britain by attacking Singapore, preferably before summer. Matsuoka gushed to them and to the German press about Japan's loyalty to the Axis. Unfortunately, he told Hitler and Ribbentrop, military commitments were beyond his power, but he promised to champion Germany's case when he got home. The irritated Nazis wondered why he had bothered to come. The answer was simple: Japan had its own agenda, which didn't include involvement in the European war.

The strongest potential obstacles to Japan's imperial plans were America and the Soviet Union. Japan's worst nightmare was a treaty between those two countries, putting Japan within their jaws. Since a Japanese agreement with America looked unlikely, Matsuoka wanted a partnership with the USSR. That would protect Japan's northern flank and free troops for a move south. Even better would be a three-way alliance with Germany and the Soviets. Matsuoka tried to interest Ribbentrop in such an arrangement. Impossible, said the German foreign minister. In that case, said Matsuoka, he might seek a nonaggression pact with the Soviet Union on his way home. Ribbentrop vaguely advised against it. He didn't mention Operation Barbarossa, Germany's ripening plan to invade Russia.

Matsuoka traveled on to Rome. His reception rivaled Hitler's in 1938. A thin line of cheering Fascists stretched for eight miles along the route to his accommodations. He met with Mussolini, newly dimmed by Italy's defeats in Abyssinia and Eritrea, and also prayed for peace in the Vatican with Pope Pius XII. On April 4 Matsuoka returned to Berlin. Hitler and Ribbentrop pressed him again about Singapore, with the same result. Two days later, he left for Moscow, where, in meetings over several days, Foreign Minister Molotov repeatedly rejected the idea of a nonaggression pact.

Matsuoka also wanted to meet with Britain's ambassador to the Soviet Union, Sir Stafford Cripps, but Cripps had treated Japan's ambassador so shabbily that Matsuoka felt Japan would lose face if he invited Cripps for a talk. Instead Matsuoka asked Ambassador Steinhardt to arrange a meeting at the American embassy. Not possible, said Steinhardt, because of the Soviets' intense surveillance. Cripps had a message for Matsuoka from Churchill, but no way to deliver it, also because of Soviet surveillance. Steinhardt discovered that all three of them would be at the Moscow Art Theatre one evening, so he devised a plan to "accidentally" introduce the two men there. Cripps secretly passed Churchill's message to Matsuoka, who pocketed it without a glance.

Churchill's note questioned the wisdom of Japan's allegiance to Germany. Britain was growing stronger every day thanks to American aid, wrote Churchill, and the two nations were likely to form a military partnership. Did Japan really want to tie itself to a weakening Reich? And did Japan understand the stark implications of the fact that in 1941 Britain and the United States together would produce ninety million tons of steel versus Japan's seven million tons?

Matsuoka had sensed that Hitler and Ribbentrop were pushing for an attack on Singapore because their campaign against Britain had stalled. They had dodged his direct questions about when Germany would invade. He also sensed Germany's growing hostility toward the Soviet Union but didn't think Germany would risk a two-front war. He certainly knew about Japan's shortage of steel, and understood the military's opinion that the nation couldn't sustain a long war against the resources of the United States. Nevertheless, he answered Churchill's pragmatic questions with blather about *hakko ichiu* and Japan's commitment to peace, while also asserting that its policy was anchored to the Axis and the new order in East Asia.

By April 11 Matsuoka was ready to leave Moscow without a nonaggression agreement. That evening a message from Stalin invited him to meet the next day at 5:00 P.M. Stalin immediately suggested a neutrality pact. They agreed on terms in less than half an hour and signed the agreement the following afternoon in the Kremlin. For Matsuoka it was proof that great men could make quick transformative decisions.

The celebration began. Stalin proposed a toast to the emperor. "I will drink anything," said Matsuoka, "if it is for his Majesty the Emperor." He drained his glass and soon demonstrated that alcohol could loosen his tongue even further. "The treaty has been made," he said to Stalin after an unknown number of toasts. "I do not lie. If I lie, my head will be yours. If you lie, be sure I will come for your head."

"My head is important to my country," said Stalin. "So is yours to your country. Let us use care to keep our heads on our shoulders." A toast to leaders who keep their heads!

"You are Asiatic," Stalin continued. "So am I."

"We are all Asiatics!" declared Matsuoka. "Let us drink to the health of the Asiatics!"

Eventually the Japanese entourage staggered for their train. It was delayed. After an hour the reason appeared. Stalin wanted one more farewell with his ebullient Japanese partner. They reaffirmed the pact with "back-slappings, bear hugs, and even kisses," wrote American ambassador Steinhardt, adding, "The behavior on the station platform while awaiting the departure of the train can only be described as frolicsome."

On the long traverse of Siberia, Matsuoka felt elated, only partly because he was again supplied with vodka and caviar. The trip had been a glorious success. He had avoided committing Japan to the European war while matching wits with Ribbentrop and Hitler, whom he considered a genius. He had prayed with the pope. He had signed a treaty with Japan's archenemy that protected Japan in the north and eased its expansion to the south, admittedly a move he had promised Steinhardt would never happen.

The pact also killed the threat of an agreement between the Soviet Union and the United States. Now America would be forced to negotiate with Japan—that is, with Matsuoka. He had asked Steinhardt to cable

Roosevelt and urge him to take a gamble: invite Matsuoka for a summit. The foreign minister envisioned traveling to Washington, where two great leaders would resolve the China problem, settle claims to East Asia, and become beacons of world peace as flashbulbs popped. He began working on his homecoming speech. It was almost time to make his move for prime minister.

BAD DRAFTS

ON APRIL 22, 1941, Matsuoka landed at a military airfield just out-side Tokyo. Grew later heard he was drunk. A retinue of reporters had covered the foreign minister's triumphant journey, and he got a delirious welcome. A huge crowd shouted banzais as Prime Minister Konoye and other dignitaries greeted him. But Konoye was anxious. A new proposal had arrived from America. Nomura and Iwakuro had been conducting important talks on their own, without Matsuoka's knowledge.

"Since [Matsuoka] is an extraordinarily sensitive man," Konoye wrote later, "I had intended to explain the proposal to him in the automobile on the way back to Tokyo." But Matsuoka had decided that a returning hero should go directly to his emperor, so he snubbed Konoye's offer. "To [Vice Foreign Minister] Ohashi was entrusted the delicate task of discuss-ing the American Proposal," wrote Konoye. "I was told afterward, that as expected, the Foreign Minister was extremely annoyed and showed no interest whatsoever."

Five days earlier Nomura and Iwakuro had sent Konoye a draft under-standing with the United States. They urged the government to act on it quickly. Under the draft's main provisions, Japan would not enter the war unless Germany was attacked by a country not yet involved, clearly the United States. Roosevelt would ask Chiang to negotiate with Japan. If Chiang refused, the United States would cut off aid to China. (Hull had deleted this, though Tokyo didn't yet know it.) Japan would agree to ad-vance in the Pacific only by peaceful means. The open door would resume under terms to be worked out later. The United States would recognize Manchukuo, renew the commerce treaty, and guarantee nondiscrimination for Japanese immigrants.

A liaison conference had discussed this draft on April 18. The military disliked some of its limits, but overall the cabinet and the military were agreeably surprised by the terms. Konoye told Vice Minister Ohashi to telegraph Nomura that the Japanese government accepted the draft in principle. Ohashi disobeyed, pending Matsuoka's return. Now, as their car headed into Tokyo past cheering crowds lining the streets, Ohashi described the draft to Matsuoka. The foreign minister's exhilaration soured into anger. The proposal wasn't his and therefore wasn't acceptable.

He didn't know the half of it. Iwakuro had written Konoye that the draft came from Hull, a flat deception that led Konoye and others to call it the "American proposal." Nor had Nomura mentioned that Hull hadn't agreed to any of it, or that he was insisting real talks couldn't begin until Japan accepted his "four principles": respect for every nation's territory and sovereignty; noninterference in the internal affairs of other nations; equality among nations, including commercial equality; and no alterations in the Pacific's status quo except by peaceful means. Japan was violating all four.

After arriving at the palace, Matsuoka rattled on about his trip for two hours until the emperor, worn down, ended the audience. "He is a strange character," said Hirohito, "in that he would always oppose any plan started by others." When Matsuoka learned that the new American proposal had nothing to do with his invitation to Roosevelt, he "made everything about the negotiation very hard," said the emperor. After exhausting Hirohito, Matsuoka extolled his European triumphs in a radio broadcast.

Konoye was so eager to respond to the proposal that he called a liaison conference for that night. It began at 9:20 P.M. and lasted three hours. First Matsuoka "talked endlessly about his European trip," wrote Konoye. When the subject changed to the draft understanding, Matsuoka disparaged it and said he would need between two weeks and two months to study it. Konoye wrote, "He interpreted the American proposal"—which none of them knew was largely Japanese—"as being 70% ill-will and 30%

good-will." Pleading fatigue, Matsuoka abruptly left at 11:00. The rest of the group decided that any delay in response to the draft was unwise, but they also felt they couldn't act without the foreign minister's approval.

Over the next few days, ministers and military officials called on Matsuoka to mollify him and promote the draft, but he sulked and feigned sickness. On April 26 Matsuoka gave a radio address at a huge rally in Hibiya Hall. Mimicking his Axis idols, he shouted and pounded the table while expressing total devotion to the Tripartite Pact. He heaped praise on Germany and Italy for their strongman leadership, which he contrasted with the Japanese government's weakness and bureaucracy. The implicit message was that Japan would benefit if Matsuoka assumed a Hitler-like role as prime minister.

Konoye and the cabinet weren't pleased. Because of his European feats Matsuoka was momentarily too popular to chop down, but bureaucrats were adept at whittling. The government had printed one hundred thousand copies of Matsuoka's Hibiya Hall speech, but Home Minister Hiranuma banned its distribution, with Konoye's approval. The cabinet also set up a commission, aimed at Matsuoka, to guard against "dangerous thoughts" by public officials. The foreign minister's dream to visit Roosevelt was firmly nixed. His disruptive ambition, combined with his volatility and aversion to opposing opinions, were alienating the cabinet. They were also subverting a small move toward peace.

On April 18, the same day the liaison conference agreed to move forward with Nomura's draft understanding with the United States, Hornbeck sent another memo to Hull repeating his leitmotif: Japan's incorrigible belligerence and deceit. Japan could never be trusted, and the United States shouldn't consider signing an agreement until Japan changed its military nature, which unfortunately appeared to be unchangeable. So talks were pointless, because Japan could never be trusted. The circular, self-defeating logic was a perfect repellant against diplomacy. Meanwhile, Japan's leaders reasoned that an agreement was impossible because the United States wanted the nation to change its imperial plans and renounce the Axis, but that would mean loss of territory and face, which wasn't acceptable.

Both Grew and Nomura tried to nudge their governments toward flexibility and small steps in the direction of better relations. Neither government seemed capable of thinking that way. "Although it is nearly impossible to eradicate in one stroke the serious and complex issues that have accumulated over many years, between the two countries," wrote Nomura to Matsuoka in May, "once both sides begin to move toward an understanding, grudges will be gradually dispelled, to be followed by the growth of friendly feelings. . . . Consequently," Nomura continued, "I have taken up matters of substance in the belief that it would be to our advantage to put first priority on achieving practical results."

Nomura's appeal to reason failed. Matsuoka was furious with him and had no interest in any agreement that didn't star himself. He was determined to regain total control of foreign policy. Matsuoka had quashed the liaison conference's plan to respond quickly and positively to the "American" proposal and then disappeared.

When he finally agreed to attend another conference on May 3, he blew it up. The agenda was to discuss "adjustment" of diplomatic relations with the United States. Matsuoka spoke first. He wanted to sign a neutrality pact with the United States to keep the country out of the war. He also wanted to tell the United States that Germany was certain to defeat Britain, so entering the war would only delay the inevitable and destroy civilization. They also needed to understand that Japan would honor the Axis pact. "Almost all members expressed their disagreement," wrote the army's official note taker. Matsuoka persisted, but the majority continued to disagree, "and there was silence for a while."

Next, as he had promised Hitler and Ribbentrop, Matsuoka suggested attacking Singapore to scare off America. Army Chief of Staff Sugiyama, appalled, rejected the idea as tactically difficult, even with extensive planning. It also was politically unwise. "Germany says she can beat Russia in two months," sniffed Matsuoka. "Singapore should not be difficult."

Careening on, Matsuoka demanded revisions in Japan's draft understanding with the United States. America must acknowledge that the Tripartite Pact was aimed strictly at peace. Yet he also wanted to delete the clause specifying that Japan wouldn't enter the war unless the United States attacked Germany. And though Nomura had called the clause banning force in Southeast Asia "the basis of the entire Draft Understanding," Matsuoka scrapped it as "inappropriate and unnecessarily critical," since Japan had already pledged itself to peace. The United States also must agree not to assist any nation against another. That meant halting aid to Britain and China and pledging not to enter the war unless attacked. The new draft still required the United States to mediate between Japan and China, and to cut off aid if Chiang balked, but it added that peace terms would be set solely by Japan. In this "Matsuoka draft," flexibility was replaced by overblown demands with no chance of acceptance in Washington. Nevertheless, Matsuoka's forceful intensity triumphed over reason. The liaison conference approved his revisions. At his insistence they also agreed to let Germany vet the draft before dispatching it to Nomura.

Despite the conference's rejection of a neutrality pact with the United States, Matsuoka immediately instructed Nomura to float the idea to Hull. He also told Nomura to deliver an "oral statement" that repeated the blustery remarks rejected by the conference, including a warning that if Roosevelt didn't accept Japan's terms, he would be responsible for the destruction of civilization that followed. The statement verged on the unhinged. Nomura was dismayed, but on May 7 he followed instructions and suggested a neutrality pact to Hull. Hull swatted it away as an attempt to get carte blanche in East Asia. Next, still embarrassed, Nomura mentioned the oral statement but paraphrased it because many of its remarks, he said, "were wrong." He offered to show it to Hull, who waved it off.

Hull had already read it. In an operation called Magic, American analysts had broken Japan's code for diplomatic cables. (The Japanese military used a different code, not yet broken.) Starting in early 1941, Hull read all the diplomatic traffic between Tokyo and Washington, and also between Tokyo, Berlin, and China. He knew beforehand what Nomura would be proposing, the strategy behind the proposals, and Tokyo's reactions to Washington's replies. This tremendous advantage also deepened Hull's distrust of the Japanese, because as 1941 wore on, Tokyo's messages often contradicted Nomura's representation of them. Because the intercepts were so valuable, and because the State Department wasn't completely confident that its own codes hadn't been broken, Grew didn't learn about Magic until he returned to the United States after internment. So though he often knew more than the State Department about the political currents in

Japan, he also often knew far less, and Hull gave more weight to Magic's intercepted cables than to Grew's distant judgments.

Under pressure from the cabinet, Matsuoka gave the Germans a deadline to review and respond to his revised draft. The Nazis were angry that Japan was considering an agreement with America, and disregarded Japan's deadline. So the foreign minister sent the Matsuoka draft to Nomura on May 12 anyway. Hull told Nomura that the revisions were a step backward, especially the deletion of Japan's pledge not to advance by force in Southeast Asia.

Ribbentrop finally responded to Japan's draft on May 13 with demands that he repeated a week later. Japan must tell the United States that sending supply convoys to Britain would be an act of war that would force Japan to join the fighting. Germany also wanted "total participation" and veto rights in any potential agreement. "Such were the high-handed representations of the Germans," wrote Konoye. Hull knew all this from Magic intercepts.

TOO MUCH MATSUOKA

THE DAY MATSUOKA returned from Europe, Grew requested a meeting. Matsuoka kept him waiting for three weeks. They finally met on May 14, 1941. "The ensuing conversations and correspondence," wrote Grew, "will afford an astonishing chapter in diplomatic history, certainly unprecedented exchanges between a Foreign Minister with a foreign Ambassador."

Matsuoka had spent the previous weekend at a resort with the German and Italian ambassadors, who prodded him to get tough with America. He was in a foul mood and also had a bronchial cough, all of which worsened his predisposition to bully. Matsuoka told Grew he wanted to speak to him as "an American friend and not as the American Ambassador," but his remarks, wrote Grew, "were bellicose both in tone and substance." He began by forcefully repeating the threats he had sent to Hull. Next he praised Hitler's "patience and generosity" in overlooking America's provocations. If the United States were "manly, decent, and reasonable," he said, it would declare war on Germany instead of cowering behind neutrality. Matsuoka developed this theme, wrote Grew, "at considerable length." When he took a breath, Grew took offense at calling America's conduct unmanly, indecent, and unreasonable, and then proceeded to dispute every point Matsuoka made. "We finally agreed that such debate was profitless," wrote Grew, "and that a meeting of minds was impossible."

Matsuoka turned to Japan's plans. The southern expansion would be peaceful, he said, "unless circumstances render this impossible." What circumstances? asked Grew. Provocations, said Matsuoka, such as Britain's reinforcement of troops in Malaya. Grew again pointed out that these measures were strictly defensive, necessitated by Japan's aggressions. Matsuoka brushed that aside. "The whole future of the world and of civilization now lies in the hands of one single man," said Matsuoka. "President Roosevelt." Japan took no responsibility for the state of affairs and disavowed any control over whatever happened next.

As Grew was writing to Hull about this strange conversation, a rambling handwritten letter arrived from Matsuoka, partly an apology but mostly self-justification. Grew sent him a thank-you but also regretted "the grave and far-reaching implications" of his remarks during their conversation. Matsuoka replied that same day with an emotional note marked "entirely private." It approached the bizarre. "I very often forget that I am a Foreign Minister," he wrote. "Especially, I am apt to lose the sense of nationality when I converse with Your Excellency, pouring out my heart as man to man." Matsuoka often wished Grew would "forget that you are representing your country, laying aside, so to speak, the Ambassadorship, so that I may feel that I am addressing only a friend to whom I can bare my thoughts."

The note went on, "I wonder if Your Excellency can understand how intensely my innermost soul is troubled and even agonized these days." Matsuoka was praying to God day and night, as he had prayed with the pope, that Roosevelt would "refrain from exasperating Germany by further acts of provocation finally exhausting the patience of Herr Hitler." He worried about Armageddon. "I often indulge in thoughts in terms of one thousand or two or even three thousand years," he wrote. "It may strike Your Excellency as if it were a sign of insanity but I can not help it as I am made that way. . . . Of course it is very hard to judge whether or not a man is truly unsound in his mind."

Grew didn't find it hard to judge. "His letters to me might be regarded as merely laughable if the situation were not so terribly serious," he wrote, "and in such a situation to have in office a Foreign Minister who by all criteria can only be considered as mentally unbalanced is a profoundly dangerous thing."

A few days later Matsuoka invited Grew to his private residence for tea and talk. They sat in his garden for two hours smoking pipes. Matsuoka had been surprised to learn that Grew reported their previous conversation to Washington, since he considered the talk private. Grew replied that his job was to discover Japanese policy and report it to his government, especially when that policy was expressed by the foreign minister. Matsuoka repeated his hope that America wouldn't keep testing Hitler's patience, since the führer just wanted peace with the United States. Grew had come armed with examples of Hitler's threats and read them aloud. For instance, "We shall soon have storm troopers in America. We shall have men whom degenerate Yankeedom will not dare to challenge." Matsuoka dismissed the quotations as fake. Hitler himself had told him he wanted friendship with America.

After the liaison conference rejected his suggestion to attack Singapore, Matsuoka moved his target to the Dutch East Indies. On May 22 he told the group it was time to seize the oil and tin Japan needed from there. Someone pointed out that attacking the Dutch East Indies would bring trouble, perhaps war, with Britain and America. Matsuoka erupted. "If we do not make up our minds, won't Germany, Britain, the United States, and the Soviet Union be united in the end and bring pressure to bear on Japan? It is possible that Germany and the Soviet Union may form an alliance and turn against Japan, and also possible that the United States may begin a war with Japan."

Navy Minister Oikawa asked, "Is Matsuoka insane?"

As for the talks with the United States, continued Matsuoka, no progress. Hull had rejected the Matsuoka draft. The foreign minister put the chances of an agreement at three in ten. To Konoye it was becoming obvious that Matsuoka alone among the cabinet opposed an agreement. The next day the foreign minister called on Konoye to deliver another tirade. The army and navy seemed willing to make an agreement with the United States even if it betrayed Germany and Italy. "What could be accomplished by such a weak-kneed attitude?" he shouted. Konoye worried that Matsuoka had made a secret deal with Hitler, though Matsuoka denied it. "The problem remained as to what was the truth," wrote Konoye, partly because "it was extremely difficult to comprehend the Foreign Minister's actual intentions."

• • •

In confidential rush cables on May 24 and May 26, Hull surprised Grew by finally asking for his views. Hull's questions were basic and speculative. If Japan pledged to renounce expansion by force, settle the China war fairly, respect economic equality, and adjust its relationship to the Axis, would the government keep its commitments? Could it? Essentially he was asking whether Japan could be trusted if the two sides somehow found common ground.

An ambassador must work in two directions, toward the home and host governments. Offered a chance to influence Hull, Grew seized it. Grew believed, correctly, that with the exception of Matsuoka the Japanese government was momentarily susceptible to negotiation. The war in China continued to drain Japanese men and money. The public was war-weary and tired of deprivation. Germany wanted to pull Japan into another war but couldn't be trusted, nor could the Soviet Union, despite the new agreement. Matsuoka's strategy to bully the United States into passivity had instead pushed Japan toward conflict with America and Britain. To Grew this uncertainty and discontent created openings for diplomacy.

"I drafted it early in the morning," he wrote about his telegram to Hull, "after a night of most careful and prayerful thought." Dooman read it and seconded it. The telegram went out that afternoon, May 27, Grew's sixty-first birthday, which he hoped was an augury.

"There can be no doubt," began the dispatch, "that any Japanese Government which assumed a bilateral commitment of the nature under reference, with the approval of the Emperor, the Cabinet and probably the Privy Council, would carry out the provisions of the settlement in good faith to the best of its ability." The rest of the telegram explained that confident opening. The only possible impediment was the military, but no agreement would be possible in the first place without their support. The emperor also wanted peace, and if he issued an imperial rescript that approved an agreement, no Japanese government would dare defy it. Though Japan might look monolithic to outsiders, Grew knew that its politics were fluid and volatile, changing with new circumstances. He felt the time was ripe to explore an understanding.

Last, he pointed out that even if Japan violated an agreement, the United States could withdraw from it without serious damage. So the United

States had much to gain and very little to lose. "The alternative," Grew wrote, "might well be progressive deterioration of American-Japanese relations leading eventually to war."

Hornbeck vehemently disagreed. In May as in April, he barraged the secretary of state with memos about Japan's treachery and untrustworthiness. Hornbeck dismissed with scorn the possibility that Japan had even a shred of sincerity in seeking an agreement. He warned Hull not to get fooled or make America look foolish. He preached about the moral dangers of any affiliation with Japan. An agreement would strengthen Japan's military leaders and their territorial greed, weaken China, and sully the United States.

On May 23, perhaps because he knew Hull was about to ask Grew's opinion, Hornbeck bombed the secretary with a preemptive twelve-hundred-word screed denouncing the Japanese as irredeemably devious. On May 24 he fired off another critical memo about proposed revisions to the draft agreement with Japan. His suggestions, Hornbeck wrote with typical pomposity, "should under no circumstances be construed as implying that this project in any way has or could by any process of drafting or redrafting be made to have my favorable opinion." On June 10 he informed Hull that an agreement was "something which neither the Japanese nation nor the people of the United States want and which, if consummated, will be distasteful to both." His qualifications to speak in absolutes for the people of both nations were unclear.

Hornbeck's certainties about Japan didn't stem from his knowledge and experience of the place, which were sparse, distant, and secondhand. His opinions were rooted in bias, intellectual arrogance, and self-righteousness, dubious bases for foreign policy.

In his bones Hull agreed with Hornbeck. Still, he honored his weighty responsibilities by seeking other views. Hull was often silent in department meetings, listening to his experts discuss an issue before he made a decision. To his credit, despite Hornbeck's hostility toward talks with Japan, Hull kept them going, and he did send the telegrams asking Grew's opinion. But it would have taken a far more acute statesman than Hull to see past Japan's actions and detect diplomatic opportunity. He was willing to hear Grew's views, but he was also predisposed to shelve them. He didn't reply to the ambassador's prayerful telegram, didn't change anything about his approach to the talks with Nomura, didn't even keep Grew informed about those talks or ask his opinion again. In the State Department, Hornbeck was the man on the spot, and his view prevailed.

Throughout May and June, as talks between Hull and Nomura went in circles, Japan kept supplying fresh grounds for distrust. In a statement on May 30 Matsuoka affirmed Japan's total commitment to all its responsibilities under the Tripartite Pact, a clear warning that Japan would join Germany if the United States made a wrong move. Matsuoka repeated Japan's promise to advance southward by peaceful means, but he immediately qualified it with a rhetorical marvel: "Should, however, untoward international developments render the execution of such policy impossible, it is a possibility that Japan may have to reconsider her attitude in the light of the changed situation."

Matsuoka's new book, *The Great Undertaking in East Asia*, added to Hull's mistrust. Matsuoka wrote that Japan's heaven-sent mission was to save humanity. "Japan should take over management of the continent on a large scale, and propagate Hakko Ichiu and the way of the Emperor in Asia and then extend it all over the world." Posters appeared around Tokyo promoting Matsuoka for prime minister.

Matsuoka's belligerence was infecting the government. Most troubling were Japan's escalating threats against territories in Southeast Asia. In late May the Foreign Office demanded that the Netherlands reconsider its "insincere" attitude toward trade talks. The Japanese press was astounded that the Dutch East Indies had declined Japan's invitation of co-prosperity and emancipation from oppression, and outraged that Japan's reasonable demand to get everything it wanted had been rejected. The Dutch had refused to understand Japan's true intentions. Since persuasion hadn't worked, it was time for more effective measures. Grew heard that Germany was pressing Japan to invade.

Liaison conferences convened on June 11 and June 12 to discuss what to do about the Dutch East Indies and French Indochina. The army and navy chiefs of staff dropped their earlier caution, calling for force if necessary. Army Chief of Staff Sugiyama advocated sending troops into southern Indochina. Matsuoka suddenly became the voice of caution, a bad sign about where Japan was heading. He noted that Britain and the United States might react poorly to a military occupation of Indochina. Yet he didn't want to lose face by retreating from what he had provoked, so he joined the others in approving the "Acceleration of the Policy Concerning the South." The declaration called for sending troops to southern Indochina after some sham negotiations. The policy also declared that if Britain or the United States tried to obstruct this plan, Japan would "not refuse to risk a war with Britain and the United States." Bluster was solidifying into policy.

Japan's standing with Hull was also worsened by more bombings of American assets in China. On June 5 Grew protested to Matsuoka about a bombed Methodist mission in Chongqing. Either the Japanese aviators were deplorably unskilled, said Grew, or they intentionally hit buildings marked with large American flags. Grew cited a new saying in China: The most dangerous place to be during a Japanese air raid was an American mission. Matsuoka promised to look into it.

Ten days later Japanese bombers struck so close to the American embassy in Chongqing that windows exploded and the nearby office of the military attaché was wrecked. Other bombs rocked the anchored American gunboat *Tutuila*, and shell fragments shattered the pilothouse windows. After getting this news Grew went straight to Matsuoka's private residence. The Japanese were "playing with fire," he told the foreign minister. If the out-of-control pilots killed an American ambassador or sank another gunboat, the American people "would simply blow up, and rightly."

"I agree with you," said Matsuoka. He promised to look into it. A few days later the Japanese naval commander in China called the bombing an unfortunate error. Matsuoka sent a note to Grew regretting that "stray bombs" had caused an accident. He suggested that the United States move the boat. The entire incident was banned from publication in Japan.

At a liaison conference on June 16 Matsuoka expressed second thoughts about the new policy to accelerate the southern expansion and occupy Indochina. Army Chief Sugiyama now disagreed. The Vichy government, he said, didn't seem to understand that occupation by Japan "will protect Indochina from American and British oppression."

"How can we say that a forceful occupation is not an occupation?" asked Matsuoka. He added that Japan's ambassador in Berlin was warning that Germany intended to invade the Soviet Union. Matsuoka didn't believe such a betrayal was possible, but if true, Britain and the Soviets would become allies and the United States might join them. The new southern policy should be reconsidered in light of these possibilities. Sugiyama and War Minister Tojo opposed delay, but everyone agreed to study the matter for a few days.

Grew noticed these signs of fracture and disarray and saw diplomatic opportunity amidst Japan's bellicosity. The Japanese press had described friction between Matsuoka on one side and Konoye and Home Minister Hiranuma on the other, illustrated by the pulping of Matsuoka's speech. The press occasionally expressed doubts about the wisdom of tying Japan's fate to Germany's, and also about the aping of Nazism as a model for Japan. The Japanese press, the public, and government officials also increasingly resented German arrogance. Grew heard rumors about divisions within the cabinet over policy, particularly concerning the Dutch East Indies.

The Japanese government seemed to be adrift, treading water. Such indicators, wrote Grew to Hull, "strongly suggest the lack of unity in the nation. They also imply that the direction of Japan's diplomatic policy has not been finally determined and that a sudden change is not impossible." But in Washington these indicators looked alarming, not promising.

Three days later the calculus changed completely.

A BETRAYAL AND A PURGE

MATSUOKA AND THE visiting puppet ruler of China, Wang Chingwei, were watching a Kabuki performance when Matsuoka's secretary rushed in and whispered in his ear. Matsuoka hurried to the Foreign Office. The shocking news was true. The Nazi army had smashed into the Soviet Union.

Matsuoka was stunned, but he shouldn't have been. Germany had betrayed Japan before. In 1939 Hitler signed a nonaggression pact with Russia less than two years after Japan and Germany signed the Anti-Comintern Pact against the Soviets. But this new duplicity felt personal. Matsuoka had cajoled Japan into the Tripartite Pact the previous September, and he had clinched the neutrality pact with Stalin just two months earlier. His Axis partners, Hitler and Ribbentrop, had kept him in the dark about their plans for the Soviet Union. Now his greatest diplomatic victories were burning to ash on the Soviet border. He looked like a fool.

German ambassador Ott arrived to placate him. The conflict would be over in two or three weeks, said Ott, and Japan would benefit. Ribbentrop didn't expect Japan to violate its treaty with the Soviet Union. Ott didn't mention that the invasion violated the Tripartite agreement. In a telegram from Berlin, Japan's ambassador Oshima said the German High Command predicted victory within four weeks and considered the invasion a mere police action.

Matsuoka was desperate to recover face. Always a gambler, he decided on a long shot and went straight to the emperor. Matsuoka told Hirohito that Japan must join Germany and attack the Soviet Union immediately.

The southward expansion would be delayed, but eventually Japan would fight there as well, and if necessary would fight the USSR, Britain, and the United States simultaneously. He seemed to be hoping that Hirohito would save him with an imperial order for war.

"The Emperor was greatly astonished," wrote Konoye. Hirohito ordered the foreign minister to consult with the cabinet. Matsuoka called on Konoye at ten o'clock that night in delirious logorrhea. "What he said was not very clear," noted Konoye, except that he was adamant about attacking the Soviet Union and undertaking war with the United States. Konoye learned that Matsuoka also had been ranting to other high officials "and had caused quite a stir." The premier postponed a liaison conference to give Matsuoka time to subside, then held six conferences over the next week to discuss the new chessboard created by Germany's move into the USSR.

To Grew the attack revealed that Germany had abandoned plans to invade Britain and was running out of resources, especially oil. Hitler was taking a desperate gamble to replenish Germany with the Soviet Union's immense natural wealth. The invasion was either a masterstroke or a fatal blunder, depending on the Soviet military. Grew also saw the moment as a crucible that burned away impediments to better relations with Japan. The invasion gave Japan's leaders an excuse to exit the Axis without losing face. "This is the time, if ever," he wrote, "for Japan to adopt a new orientation of conciliation with the United States."

Konoye was thinking along the same lines. He sent an official to sound out War Minister Tojo on the possibility of using Germany's betrayal as a way to abandon the Tripartite Pact and move toward peaceful relations with Britain and America. The idea offended Tojo's code of loyalty. "Do you really think," he asked angrily, "we can act in such an immoral way, against justice and humanity?"

In Washington, Hull sensed an opening as well. When Ambassador Nomura visited him on the day of the invasion, Hull suggested that Germany's action allowed Japan to withdraw from the pact. For Hull, separating from the Axis was a barometer of Japan's seriousness about reaching a peace agreement. Nomura had opposed the pact from the start. He said he would ask his government to consider the matter.

Matsuoka and Tojo rejected any talk of repudiating the Axis, but Konoye worried that Hitler's newest surprise would motivate an alliance between the Soviet Union, Britain, and the United States, a nightmare for Japan. "The policy which was proper in the fall of 1940," he later wrote, "became a dangerous one in the summer of 1941." Konoye transmitted this view in weak signals picked up by Grew's diplomatic antennae. The prime minister sent a mutual friend to tell Grew he was hoping for better relations, an atypical gesture. Equally atypical, on June 29 he gave an interview to an American reporter and repeatedly emphasized that Japan was "very anxious to maintain friendly relations with the United States." He also insisted that Japan wasn't Germany's partner in world conquest, a direct reference to a statement by Hull. Konoye emphasized that the Tripartite Pact was strictly defensive, intended to keep Japan and America out of the war.

To Grew these were all clues, but the State Department read them differently. Matsuoka's threats had invalidated Konoye's latest interpretation of the Axis pact. Ballantine, head of the Japan desk in Far Eastern Affairs, wrote a memo to Hull dismissing the prime minister's statements as the usual Japanese blather. Konoye's comment that Japan didn't share Hitler's desire for world conquest, wrote Ballantine, "might be read as implying a denial that Germany is planning world conquest."

Hitler had given Japan an easy way out of the pact, a path away from war and perhaps toward better relations with Britain and the United States. But Konoye was too weak to make that case among leaders infatuated by a dream of imperial destiny. Within a week he was agreeing with them that Hitler's invasion left Japan only two possible paths: north to fight the Soviet Union alongside Germany, or south to seize the riches of the South Seas while the USSR was preoccupied. Matsuoka's preference, delivered with his usual force, was to go north, right away. The pact called for it, he insisted. Besides, if we want any of the Soviet Union's wealth, Japan had to join Germany. "We have to either shed blood or engage in diplomacy," he told the liaison conference on June 25. "It's best to shed blood." Reminded that he had recently insisted on attacking Singapore and Indochina in the south, he said, "Great men will change their minds."

The army, with fresh memories of its spankings by Soviet troops at

Changkufeng and Nomonhan, didn't share Matsuoka's confidence that Germany would overrun the Soviet military. But Matsuoka wanted to tell Ott that Japan would live up to its moral obligations without delay.

"It's fine to talk about integrity," said Sugiyama, "but we can't actually afford it."

"I would like a decision to attack the Soviet Union," insisted Matsuoka.

"No," said Sugiyama.

Since Germany's invasion of the Soviet Union, Ambassador Ott had been visiting Matsuoka frequently to push Japan toward war. On June 30 Matsuoka told the conference that Hitler now wanted Japan to break its pact with the Soviets and attack. The conference held firm. Japan would stay neutral unless the USSR moved most of its troops west and gave Japan an irresistible opportunity to invade. Otherwise the government would proceed with earlier plans to expand south and finish the war in China. All this was solidified on July 2 in an imperial conference that approved the "Outline of National Policies in View of the Changing Situation." The policy included a clause affirming that Japan would stick to this course even if it brought war with the United States and Britain.

The document alarmed Nomura. The next day he warned Tokyo that if Japan was determined to use force in the south, "there seems to be no room at all for adjusting Japanese-American relations." The United States would embargo oil. War would result. Nomura's insider's perspective, like Grew's, was ignored. A week later Nomura asked permission to be relieved from his post. Matsuoka said no.

All of Japan was wondering about the purpose of the recent imperial conference. The government announced that a crucial national policy had been approved, but it was secret. Nevertheless, the public must mobilize behind it and trust their leaders. On July 6 the government launched the Great Japan East Asia League at a mass meeting in Hibiya Hall. Konoye, Tojo, and other high officials attended. All swore an oath to eradicate the "root evil" in East Asia—white people, especially Anglo-Americans—and to establish the Greater East Asia Co-prosperity Sphere based on "Hakko Ichiu and the August wishes of His Majesty the Emperor."

• • •

Nomura had sent Hull's revised proposal to Tokyo the day before Germany attacked the Soviet Union. The invasion preoccupied the liaison conference for more than a week. When they finally got around to Hull's draft, it shocked them. Nomura had misled Konoye and Matsuoka into thinking that the earlier, softer drafts came from Hull. Nomura also had avoided mentioning factors that he knew would be unacceptable, such as Hull's "four principles." For the first time the cabinet was seeing Hull's basic stipulations, which had never changed. Before serious talks could begin, Hull insisted, Japan must accept his four principles: leave the Axis; repudiate forceful expansion; and agree to fair settlement terms and commercial equality in China.

The Japanese were also taken aback by Hull's attached oral statement. He criticized certain unnamed Japanese leaders who supported Nazi Germany's policy of world conquest and who declared that Japan would join Germany if America entered the European war. Hull implied that talks were pointless while such leaders remained in the cabinet. His obvious target was Matsuoka, who was enraged. He denounced Hull's draft and said Japan must demand the withdrawal of this arrogant attempt to interfere with the cabinet. Matsuoka also wanted to break off negotiations with the United States. The other members agreed that Hull's oral statement must be rejected but objected to ending talks. They preferred to restate Japan's terms. Matsuoka wanted to send a stinging rejection of the oral statement first and delay the reply to the draft for a few days. Konoye and the military vetoed that as too combative, especially on the eve of Japan's planned occupation of southern Indochina. Konoye ordered Matsuoka to send the replies simultaneously.

Instead Matsuoka did it his combative way. On July 14 he sent a demand, by itself, to withdraw Hull's oral statement. The next day he gave Japan's new counterproposal to the Germans for their approval but didn't send it to Nomura. Someone in the Foreign Office, upset by Matsuoka's defiance of the liaison conference, cabled the revised draft to Nomura without his boss's permission. Nomura, too, disobeyed instructions and followed his own judgment. He didn't deliver either document for fear of upsetting talks that were already shaky. Hull saw it all via Magic.

Konoye soon heard that Matsuoka had disobeyed the conference's instructions. The foreign minister's insubordination and destructive behavior infuriated the prime minister and finally drove him to act. At noon on July 16 he called a secret meeting with the army, navy, and home ministers to plan Matsuoka's purge. The only surefire tactic was for the entire cabinet to resign, which they did that day. A messenger informed Matsuoka, who was ill in bed, that he was out. "The Foreign Minister was taken unawares," wrote Konoye, "and showed great annoyance." Konoye's revised cabinet contained only one new member, Admiral Toyoda Teijiro as foreign minister.

The next day Matsuoka sent Konoye a bitter, belligerent letter. He cawed that his revised draft for Hull was written for maximum offensiveness. It "runs completely counter to the demands of the United States," Matsuoka wrote. "Your Excellency, I am certain, is well aware that there is not one chance in ten thousand that the United States will accept our proposal."

So ended Matsuoka's year of strutting upon the world stage. His chaotic diplomacy had pushed Japan closer to war.

THE FREEZE

WITH MATSUOKA GONE, Grew thought diplomacy might again stand a chance. He suggested as much in cables to Hull and Under Secretary Sumner Welles and noted that he was relying partly "on observation at close hand of factors to which the Department may not be sensitive." The department felt sensitivity was irrelevant compared with Japan's many offensive actions. They didn't bother responding to Grew's suggestion.

He resented being kept in the dark. On July 10 he wrote a restrained but angry note to Welles after once again hearing about vital matters from the British ambassador. Grew was embarrassed and fed up. He was already "groping in the dark," he wrote, because his Japanese contacts didn't dare meet him anymore, "yet at the same time I am deprived of intelligence or clues available in Washington pertinent to issues which I am asked to deal with or to estimate here." Grew noted "the very great handicap and discouragement" of this situation, which he hoped wasn't caused by mistrust.

The next day Welles cabled a conciliatory response that lifted Grew's spirits and briefly improved communications. The department didn't intend to withhold vital information from him, wrote Welles, but some material was so sensitive, the department couldn't risk sending it by cable or radio. Welles no doubt had in mind the damage being done to Japan by Magic, the code-breaking operation that was unknown to Grew. For instance, by the time Grew wrote that Matsuoka's ejection might offer diplomatic opportunities, Welles and Hull knew from intercepts that Japan was about to occupy southern Indochina, with the further goals of taking Singapore and then the Dutch East Indies.

Part of Matsuoka's last act had been an ultimatum on July 14 to the Vichy government. It called for the "joint defense" of French Indochina while also guaranteeing respect for the colony's territorial integrity. The note said Japan's decision to occupy yet respect Indochina was final. Vichy had until July 20 to agree.

Welles, acting for Hull, who was ill, warned Nomura that if Japan proceeded with this occupation, further talks were pointless. Nomura seemed distraught. He urged patience. Japan's new government wouldn't have approved the occupation, he said, but couldn't change what it had inherited. Konoye expressed this same preposterous idea to former foreign minister Arita, who criticized him for occupying southern Indochina while negotiating with the United States. Konoye agreed it was a mistake, but the troopships had already departed. "It was as if an arrow had already been shot," he wrote, "and nothing could have been done to stop it." Japan's leaders acted as if they were pawns of their own decisions. This psychological detachment from their actions allowed them to act shocked and angry whenever they were called to account.

After speaking with Welles, Nomura telegraphed Tokyo to report that if Japan advanced into Indochina, talks with the United States would end and diplomatic relations might be severed. The liaison conference on July 24 discounted this, as well as Nomura's warnings that invasion would cause a freeze of assets and an embargo. "One can't help being amazed at how hysterical the telegram from Nomura is," said the army's War Guidance Office. Despite Grew's warnings, Konoye and the cabinet assumed that dumping Matsuoka was enough to pacify the American government into overlooking another military occupation.

That same day, Roosevelt tried once more to appeal to Japan's reason. At 5:00 P.M. he summoned Nomura and Welles to the Oval Office and went straight for Japan's vulnerability—oil. To preserve peace, said Roosevelt, the United States had been allowing Japan to buy American oil. But if Japan invaded the Dutch East Indies to seize oil, war was likely. He then made a remarkable proposal, which he said had just come to him. If

Japan refrained from occupying Indochina, or withdrew its forces if they had already moved in, he would do everything possible to convince the other powers in East Asia to declare Indochina a neutral territory, like Switzerland, provided Japan agreed. Roosevelt's proposal destroyed Japan's rationales for taking Indochina. It guaranteed military security and full access to buy food and raw materials to alleviate the deep deprivations suffered by the Japanese people. It removed the threat of retaliation by the United States. The proposal was another opening for Japan to choose peace. Nomura said he would present the idea but his government probably wouldn't agree to it "on account of the face-saving element involved."

Nomura was right. In Tokyo, Konoye and the cabinet acted as if they had no power to stop the plan they had designed, approved, and put into motion. Japanese troopships were already en route to Saigon and other ports in southern Indochina. Turning them around would make the government look weak. The troops landed.

On the evening of July 25 Roosevelt froze all Japanese assets in the United States. Within days Britain, Canada, and the Netherlands followed suit. The Japanese were stunned that the United States had carried through on its threat. The Japanese press screamed about America's outrageous disturbance of the peace in Asia and the so-called ABCD plot (by America, Britain, China, and the Dutch) to encircle Japan.

The day after the freeze, Toyoda Teijiro asked Grew to call on him. The new foreign minister, fifty-five and reserved, was slender and wore a sparse moustache. He had served as vice minister of the navy and as Konoye's minister of commerce and industry. Grew had known him for years and found him "sound and sensible." But Toyoda had no experience with foreign affairs or diplomacy, a serious deficit at this delicate moment. Now, speaking to Grew, the foreign minister was upset. He blamed everything on the failure of the United States to understand Japan's "real purposes." Grew flared at this tired lie. Japan's broken promises, he told Toyoda, had made it impossible for the American government and public to swallow any more nonsense about Japan's "true intentions."

The next day, a Sunday, Grew finally received a cable notifying him about Roosevelt's proposal to make Indochina neutral ground. It was an electrifying possibility for peace. He immediately called Toyoda at home and rushed there at 11:30 to discuss it. Toyoda looked bewildered. He had no idea what Grew was talking about. Toyoda left to call the Foreign Office for information. He returned with nothing. Either Nomura hadn't sent the proposal or hard-liners in the Foreign Office had buried it. Grew excitedly presented the gist. Toyoda regretted that the proposal was too late. Grew couldn't let another potentially transformative opportunity slip away. "I then urged the Minister with all the strength and earnestness at my command" to rise above the problem of face and seize this opening. This was Toyoda's chance, Grew told him, to go down in history as one of Japan's greatest statesmen. But nothing could turn Toyoda into that, and the opening for peace was soon slammed shut.

On July 30 in Chongqing, Japanese bombs again damaged the American gunboat *Tutuila* and shook the residence of the American ambassador. Observers saw the planes change course to fly directly over the *Tutuila* and the embassy to drop their bombs. At a moment when the United States was already angry about the occupation of Indochina, wrote Grew, the intentional bombings showed "the utmost stupidity." But the young pilots were angry too. The raid was retaliation for Roosevelt's freeze of Japanese assets. Toyoda offered deep regrets for this "accident."

Roosevelt responded to the bombing by embargoing any oil or gas that could be refined for aviation. He also limited Japan's access to certain grades of oil by requiring export licenses. Treasury Secretary Morgenthau and Assistant Secretary of State Dean Acheson, who had long lobbied for a total embargo, manipulated the licensing requirements to stop any oil from going to Japan. Neither Hull nor Roosevelt knew of this ploy for several months. The Japanese press howled, incensed that America had dared to penalize Japan for doing precisely the things that America had warned would bring penalties.

By the end of August Grew's deep well of optimism was nearly pumped dry by Japan's broken promises, belligerence, self-justifications, and refusal to alter its conduct. The United States had finally reached its limit and was hitting back. "The vicious circle of reprisals and counter-reprisals is on," wrote Grew. "The obvious conclusion is eventual war."

He wasn't ready to surrender all hope. "Meanwhile I am taking no defeatist attitude here and am doing what little can be done to avoid catastrophe." Grew still believed Germany would fail, especially now that Hitler had blundered into the Soviet Union, though so far no evidence supported this faith. German ambassador Ott had assured Toyoda that Germany would mop up the Soviets by the end of August and invade Britain in September. But if Germany did collapse, wrote Grew, everything in the Far East would look different. Japan couldn't face the world alone and would need peace to survive. "We must leave nothing undone to avoid a break with Japan," wrote Grew, "in hopeful anticipation of such an eventuality."

In late July and early August 1941, the Japanese government held four liaison conferences to craft a new proposal in hopes of reopening talks with the United States. After declining Roosevelt's proposal, invading Indochina, and suffering the freeze and the oil embargo, the Japanese government offered what it considered a reasonable compromise: the United States must stop defensive preparations in the Philippines; help Japan secure resources from the Dutch East Indies; recognize Japan's "special position" in Indochina; force Chiang to settle the war on Japan's terms; halt aid to Britain, China, and the Netherlands; and lift the freeze, the oil embargo, and all trade restrictions "promptly." In return Japan would guarantee the neutrality of the Philippines and wouldn't station troops beyond Indochina. Japan wanted to keep everything it had taken and cancel all consequences imposed because of its actions.

On August 8, two days after receiving this oblivious document, Hull handed Nomura the American response. It barely mentioned the Japanese draft. It said the United States had made clear what steps Japan must take for talks to reopen. "America will resume the conversations only if Japan suspends the use of force," Nomura cabled to Tokyo that day. "In this respect, the other side will never retreat and so long as there is no change in our policy, there is no longer any room for proceeding with the talks."

For Hull, Japan's new draft, combined with the gaping discrepancy between the Magic intercepts and Nomura's hollow talk about peace, were a tipping point. "From now on," he wrote, "our major objective with regard to Japan was to give ourselves more time to prepare our defenses. We were still ready—and eager—to do everything possible toward keeping the United States out of war; but it was our concurrent duty to concentrate on trying to make the country ready to defend itself effectively in the event of war being thrust upon us."

THE CROSSROADS
OF PEACE AND WAR

COURAGE AND IMAGINATION weren't qualities associated with Prince Konoye, but in August 1941 he devised a plan that demonstrated both. For it to work he needed the support of Japan's true power, the military. Konoye summoned the ministers of war and the navy and told them that he wanted to resolve the intractable misunderstanding between Japan and the United States by meeting secretly with Roosevelt in Honolulu. He said their duty to the emperor and the Japanese people obliged them to try everything possible before descending into war. If Roosevelt refused to understand "the true intentions of the Empire," the Japanese people would accept war as necessary and the world would not condemn Japan. The meeting must be held soon, Konoye said. If the German army stalled in the Soviet Union before winter or failed to defeat Britain, the United States would have less reason to negotiate with Japan.

Both ministers listened intently, then took this extraordinary idea to their services. Within hours Navy Minister Oikawa gave his full support. War Minister Tojo sent a note. A meeting with Roosevelt, he wrote, would weaken the Tripartite Pact and agitate the Japanese public, so it wasn't "a suitable move." Yet he admired Konoye's willingness to try this for Japan's sake, so the army would offer tentative support. But if the talks failed, Konoye must lead Japan into war. "Failure of this meeting is the greater likelihood," wrote Tojo.

Foreign Minister Toyoda approved the plan next. On August 7 Konoye sought the emperor's sanction. Hirohito was enthusiastic. Everyone essential had agreed. Konoye, Toyoda, and Nomura felt great optimism, and Nomura presented the idea to Hull on August 8. The timing was poor. Hull was feeling sour about Japan. A few minutes earlier he had handed Nomura the statement replying to Japan's oblivious draft agreement. Until Japan changed its policies, Hull now told Nomura, "I lack confidence in relaying this proposal to the President." Nomura, crestfallen, telegraphed Toyoda to ask for Grew's help.

Konoye's proposal was astonishing. No Japanese prime minister had ever left the country for any reason, much less to meet a possible enemy in the enemy's territory. But considering Japan's recent actions, the proposal seemed to drop from the blue. Hull, Hornbeck, and Ballantine were instantly suspicious. Why now? Was it a trap? A stunt? Did Japan's jingoistic military leaders sanction this? If so, what was their scheme?

New Japanese offenses soon dented the idea's promise. Heavy bombing resumed in Chongqing. On August 15 Grew handed Toyoda six pages detailing recent mistreatments of Americans all over Japan, China, and Manchukuo in retaliation for the freeze. Most were petty—travelers hassled, phones cut off, properties occupied by the Kempeitai, deliveries of food and coal halted, mail opened or censored (including at American consulates), even prohibitions against Americans using taxis.

Japanese extremists also continued to undermine Hull's confidence in the ability of the nation's leaders to control Japan's direction. A thug named Nakano Seigo led the fascist party Tohokai, which regularly threatened to assassinate moderate Japanese officials and advisors. When Home Minister Hiranuma ordered the arrest of some Tohokai members, Nakano phoned Hiranuma and said if the police came for him, the minister would be killed the next day. Hiranuma began wearing a bulletproof vest. On August 14 a man went to Hiranuma's residence and asked for a sample of his calligraphy (his autograph). The guards let him in. As Hiranuma calligraphed, the man pulled a gun and shot six times, wounding the minister in the neck and jaw.

Roosevelt had been away at a secret meeting in the Atlantic with Churchill, hammering out the Atlantic Charter. Both leaders wanted to focus on Germany and keep Japan out of the war, but they also were determined to stop Japan's expansion in the South Seas. Roosevelt wired Hull that he wanted to speak to Nomura immediately upon his return to Washington on August 17.

On that day in the Oval Office, Nomura again proposed the secret meeting with Konoye. Instead of answering, Roosevelt read two statements worked out during his summit with Churchill. The first warned that if Japan continued to move south by force or threat, the United States "will be compelled immediately to take any and all steps." Second, the resumption of informal conversations about peace in the Pacific was impossible as long as Japan kept violating the very reason for the talks. Further, Japan's leaders and press were inflaming the public against the United States with nonsense about encirclement and other fake conspiracies. Conversations couldn't restart until Japan made clear how it would correct these matters. Roosevelt added that if Japan did so, he was open to meeting with Konoye. He even suggested a place and time: Juneau, Alaska, in mid-October.

Nomura left feeling anxious but hopeful. He wrote Toyoda, "Today we are at the crossroads of peace and war." He suggested acting fast, "before this opportunity is lost."

Grew didn't know about any of this. The State Department hadn't informed him about Konoye's invitation or sought his insights about what it meant.

The day after Roosevelt's meeting with Nomura, Foreign Minister Toyoda summoned Grew for a meeting at 4:00 P.M. Grew had been told beforehand to expect something momentous. Toyoda began by saying he had a far-reaching proposal that must remain absolutely secret, especially from the Germans and Italians. That got Grew's full attention. Over the next two and a half hours—Grew's longest meeting ever with a foreign minister—Toyoda read an oral statement in Japanese, pausing as it was translated. Grew wrote it all down in English, cramping his hand.

As Toyoda droned on, Grew's hopes waned. The foreign minister was hitting the same tired points. Japan's occupation of Indochina was strictly peaceful and defensive. The United States had refused to understand Japan's real intentions. The freeze was unfair. The United States had misunderstood Japan's revised draft. As Grew waited for the next translation, he felt restive. It was all stale fiction. None of it required secrecy from Nazis or anyone else.

The day was hot and humid, and both men were dripping with sweat. After an hour Toyoda ordered cold drinks and cold wet towels. He mimed taking off his coat. Grew nodded. They shed their jackets and rolled up their sleeves. Toyoda resumed reading.

After the rationales and complaints came the high bunkum. Japan's leaders, said Toyoda, only wanted peace. Japan and the United States had a duty to save their friendship and thus save the world. And so on.

Then came a remarkable pivot. To resolve the differences between their countries, said Toyoda, their leaders must talk directly to each other. Grew listened with growing excitement. Toyoda was proposing a secret face-to-face meeting between Konoye and Roosevelt. Konoye, said Toyoda, wouldn't be bound by Japan's revised draft of August 6. In other words, Japan was open to true concessions. Toyoda pointed out that Konoye's offer to go abroad had no precedent in Japanese history, but the prime minister was determined to try for peace despite objections within Japan.

To avoid the misimpression that Konoye had caved in to American pressure, continued Toyoda, the United States should lift or moderate all economic penalties right away. This was the usual Japanese tactic of expecting a concrete benefit today in return for a misty promise about tomorrow. Nevertheless, Grew was elated. For the first time in years Japan seemed serious about reconsidering its direction. Now Grew understood Toyoda's concern about secrecy. If Konoye's plan leaked, extremists would try to kill him and probably Toyoda as well.

Grew rushed back to the embassy and began writing his report to Hull. Near 10:00 P.M. he finished his long dispatch and gave it to the coders, who worked until dawn to send it. After handing off the dispatch, Grew returned to his desk and wrote Hull and Welles a short impassioned plea, partially tamed into the third person by State Department coders. The ambassador, said the note, didn't know how the president would respond to Konoye's proposal.

The Ambassador urges, however, with all the force at his command, for the sake of avoiding the obviously growing possibility of an utterly futile war between Japan and the United States, that this Japanese proposal not be turned aside without very prayerful consideration. Not only is the proposal unprecedented in Japanese history, but it is an indication that Japanese intransigence is not crystallized completely owing to the fact that the proposal has the approval of the Emperor and the highest authorities in the land. The good which may flow from a meeting between Prince Konoye and President Roosevelt is incalculable.

The next day Grew sent Hull another urgent dispatch. He wanted to make sure the department understood how extraordinary Konoye's proposal was from a Japanese perspective. First, the invitation showed great courage because Konoye was risking assassination. Second, the offer acknowledged for the first time that peace was impossible unless Japan made far-reaching concessions. Third, it suggested Konoye's determination to take government back from the extremists. Grew called the proposal "an act of the highest statesmanship. If viewed in that light it deserves to be met with magnanimity." Echoing Nomura, he advised rapid action, before America's economic sanctions weakened the cabinet and strengthened the extremists.

Then Grew came to the delicate issue of expectations. Hull's were high and inflexible. If the secretary of state insisted on rigid specifics before the meeting, wrote Grew, Konoye's proposal would die in the cradle. Lowering expectations now could pay off in the long run. Even if the meeting's results were imperfect or slow to materialize, the momentum toward conflict would be slowed. "This desideratum alone," he wrote, "would seem to justify acceptance of the Japanese proposal in some form or other." If the United States rejected "this outstanding and probably final gesture" by Japan, Grew warned, the cabinet would fall, replaced by a do-or-die military clique. War would be inevitable.

At the State Department Hornbeck wrote furious memos to undercut Grew, the Japanese, and the proposed meeting. He believed Grew had gone native, was being duped, was keen to appease the Japanese. Hornbeck bloviated for twenty-one hundred words on the theme of "the hazard-ous futility of placing any reliance upon a pledge by Japan's diplomats." He wrote seven more pages mocking Grew's dispatches about Konoye's proposal. In another memo he sneered at Grew's description of Konoye as courageous: "A jump from frying pan into fire does not prove that he who makes that jump is exhibiting extraordinary courage." Hornbeck sug-gested that the "kindest" course toward Japan wasn't to make peace but to do everything possible to discredit and eliminate the military leadership.

Two more memos by Hornbeck in late August and early September, in response to several dispatches from Grew, further illustrated the wid-ening divide between the State Department and the Tokyo embassy. On August 27 Grew warned that the freeze and embargo were creating "a psy-chology of desperation." Japan was beginning to see that Germany proba-bly wouldn't defeat Britain and the Soviet Union before Japan's dwindling resources ran out. "In Japan," wrote Grew, "a psychology of despair leads characteristically to a do-or-die reaction."

He followed this on August 29 with two important dispatches. The first expanded his previous analysis of Japan's changing atmosphere. Tension was rising. Newspapers, instructed by the military, were drumming up war fever over conspiratorial encirclement by the ABCD powers. After invent-ing this fiction, the Japanese government had ordered mass mobilization of men and materials. Air-raid drills, air-raid shelters, and anti-aircraft em-placements all were multiplying. Among the public Grew detected growing dread of another conflict. The Japanese were feeling drained by four years of war and worsening deprivations. The government had responded with a publicity campaign—patriotic posters and newspaper photo spreads of battleships and airplanes—which didn't put rice in the pot or bring their sons home. Nevertheless, Grew concluded that if war came, the Japanese public "will go into it blindly, doggedly, desperately."

In a second dispatch that same day, Grew reported another furor in Japan caused by a media leak. Ambassador Nomura, in another bungle, had stepped out of a conference with Roosevelt and Hull on August 28 and spilled to reporters that he had just given the president a personal note from Konoye suggesting a meeting. This news electrified the Japanese press, and the German and Italian ambassadors in Tokyo demanded an explanation from Toyoda. The foreign minister sent word to Grew that extremists were riled up, the risk of assassinations had risen, and all this bad publicity might wreck the proposed meeting between Konoye and Roosevelt. Grew reported all this to Hull on August 29 and wrote, "Time is now of the essence."

From seven thousand miles away Hornbeck disparaged Grew's first-hand observations and insinuated that he was too eager to appease. Hornbeck doubted that Konoye was in danger of assassination now or ever, and jeered again at Grew's notion of his courage. He repeated his view, always presented as indisputable, that Japan would never start a war with the United States. "The simple fact is," he wrote, "that Japan is already more than half beaten. . . . The Japanese Government has no intention of making war on the United States." Hornbeck wrote that the worse things got in Japan, the less Japan would menace the Pacific, further illustrating his ignorance of Japanese psychology.

He scoffed at Grew's conviction that Japanese-American relations were at a moment of crisis. "By way of comment, it is submitted that this concept is in considerable degree out of perspective," he wrote from his perspective in Foggy Bottom. The crisis existed in the press and perhaps in the minds of some Japanese "but does not exist in reality." The only true crisis was within the Japanese government. That didn't concern the United States, he continued, which should do nothing to help Konoye's cabinet survive. Hornbeck did get one thing right: "Worse things could happen in Japan and between Japan and the United States than the fall, by whatever process, of a Japanese premier, a Japanese cabinet, a Japanese 'government.'"

Hornbeck equated the proposed secret meeting with the Munich Conference. The talk about peace and courage and visionary statecraft was nonsense. The United States would be seen by the predatory nations as weak and compromised. A meeting between Konoye and Roosevelt would resolve nothing and only encourage Japan to greater aggressions. Hornbeck's prophetic powers were again on display. "We are not in great danger vis-à-vis Japan," he wrote, "and Japan is not capable of doing us any great injury."

Hornbeck was blind not only about the situation in Japan but about the dangers posed to the United States by an imperiled, desperate Japanese government. Yet he was Hull's chief advisor on the Far East. He showed a disdain for the lived insights of front-line diplomats, perhaps because he had never been one. Hornbeck flooded Hull's in-box with these confident errors in judgment for the next three months, until Japanese bombers blew them to smithereens.

ROUGH WINDS AND WAVES

ON SEPTEMBER 3, 1941, Roosevelt, Hull, and Nomura met secretly at the White House. Nomura asked if Roosevelt was still agreeable to meeting with Konoye. Yes, said the president, but first Japan needed to commit to the four principles Hull had been emphasizing. Japan also must clarify its position on three sticking points: withdrawal of troops from China, withdrawal from the Axis, and nondiscrimination in commerce. Nomura got the impression that Roosevelt's enthusiasm for the summit had been dampened by his State Department.

That day in Tokyo a liaison conference met for seven hours, from 11:00 A.M. to 6:00 P.M. They approved a new draft agreement for the United States that moderated several positions in hopes of reviving the talks. The conference also discussed a new policy developed by the military without civilian participation. "The Essentials for Carrying Out the Empire's Policies" was the bland title for this disastrous plan. Japan would continue to negotiate with the United States, the document declared, but also would ramp up war preparations. Unless the two countries came to terms by early October—just over a month away—Japan would go to war with America, Britain, and the Netherlands. The military justified this shocking rush with risky logic: if Japan had to fight the United States, better to do it before America got stronger.

This was the conference's first look at this reckless plan, yet even Konoye and Toyoda, who opposed war with the United States, approved it to avoid looking weak. Maybe they and the military felt safe endorsing the document's bravado because they expected Konoye's meeting with Roosevelt to resolve all issues. In any case, none of Japan's leaders objected to putting their nation's fate on a short deadline.

That evening Toyoda, probably anxious about the policy he had just approved, sent a subordinate to the embassy to urge Grew to advocate for the summit meeting, perhaps by September 20. Toyoda sent for Grew again the next day with the same agenda. The foreign minister told Grew that he and Konoye "would leave no stone unturned" to make the meeting happen soon, because if it failed, "he was afraid further efforts would be useless." Toyoda gave Grew the new draft agreement and asked him to send it to Hull. The foreign minister had already wired it to Nomura but wanted insurance, given Nomura's unreliability.

Toyoda sent for Grew again the following day, anxious to know Roosevelt's answer, but Grew hadn't heard anything. They also discussed Japan's revised draft agreement with the United States. In his report to Hull, Grew pointed out that if the United States wanted to adjust relations with Japan, "some risk must be run." No agreement could be completely satisfactory, but the United States could retain leverage by lifting sanctions in stages as Japan met its promises. The risk of Japan's noncompliance, he said, was far less serious than the risk of war if no agreement was reached. This was Grew's usual practical plea not to kill off the good for the sake of the perfect.

That same afternoon Konoye visited the emperor to report the liaison conference's plan to end diplomacy in early October. He asked the emperor to call an imperial conference the next day to sanction the new policy to escalate preparations for war. The document appalled and angered Hirohito. He called it a war plan that put diplomacy second, and told Konoye to summon the chiefs of the army and navy at once. General Sugiyama and Admiral Nagano appeared.

How long did the army expect a war with the United States to last? asked Hirohito.

About three months to mop up the South Pacific, said Sugiyama.

When the China incident began, said the emperor, you were minister of war and you said it would be over in one month, yet Japan is still fighting four years later.

China opens onto a vast hinterland, replied Sugiyama, and military operations could not be conducted as planned.

If the hinterland of China is vast, said the emperor, his voice rising in anger, isn't the Pacific Ocean even more vast? What convinces you to say three months?

Sugiyama bowed his head, silenced by embarrassment. Hirohito wanted one thing clear before tomorrow's imperial conference. Did both Sugiyama and Nagano understand that diplomacy must take precedence over war? The question was an imperial rhetorical. Yes, said the general and the admiral.

September 6 was a pivotal day in both Tokyo and Washington. An imperial conference to sanction Japan's new military policy began at 10:00 A.M. Its first sentence blamed the necessity for war planning on "the offensive attitudes" of the United States, Britain, and the Netherlands. Representatives of the cabinet and the military services had prepared a series of questions for the conference. The answers began soberly, then swiveled into fantasy. Question: What is the outlook for a war with America and Britain, and how would Japan end it? Answer: A war is likely to be long and hard, and the United States is unlikely to surrender. Then the fantasy began. "However, we cannot exclude the possibility that the war may end because of a great change in American public opinion, which may result from such factors as the remarkable success of our military operations in the South or the surrender of Great Britain. At any rate, we should be able to establish an invincible position."

Question: What is the status of our homeland defenses? Answer: Not too good, and not good at all against air raids. Then the swivel: "However, the Army and the Navy will try to destroy the enemy air forces by taking the offensive. Therefore, it is believed . . . the losses from air raids can be limited to a point where no great difficulties will be encountered in carrying on the war."

All the main players spoke. Sugiyama and Nagano warned that a war with the United States would be prolonged unless Japan struck soon and hard. They implied that Japan couldn't defeat the United States but could cripple it into agreeing to Japan's demands. Toyoda summarized the Hull-

Nomura talks, which had stalled after Japan occupied Indochina. The United States refused to understand, he said, that invasion prevented war and occupation was self-defense. Japan had recently presented its basic conditions for a meeting between the two heads of state and was hoping for an answer soon.

The director of the planning board, Lieutenant General Suzuki Tei-ichi, reported that Japan had abundant supplies of manpower and morale. "The only problem," he added, "concerns material resources." Japan had always depended on America and Britain for trade and raw materials, now cut off, so "our Empire's national power is declining day by day." Then the swivel. If Japan kept the war as short as possible, said Suzuki, "I believe that we shall not run into serious difficulties in maintaining and strengthening our national power."

Everyone was pretending that these assumptions weren't as flimsy as shoji walls. Before the conference, the emperor had worried that things might descend into exactly this kind of dangerous nonsense. He had told Lord Keeper Kido that he wanted to break protocol and ask some questions himself. Kido vetoed the idea. The divine emperor must not risk soiling the throne by saying anything that might later be construed as taking responsibility. The president of the Privy Council, as always, would ask questions for him.

So Hara Yoshimichi began by asking Nagano and Sugiyama the emperor's key question: Was Japan's main priority diplomacy or war? The new policy seemed weighted toward the latter. Neither chief spoke, evading the previous day's pledge to the emperor.

"The question Hara has just asked makes sense," blurted Hirohito, stunning everyone by speaking and also by sounding angry. "Why doesn't the high command answer?" Hirohito pulled a paper from his breast pocket and read:

> In all four seas all are brothers and sisters
> Then why, oh why, these rough winds and waves?

Hirohito said he hoped this revered poem by his grandfather, Emperor Meiji, would instill these times with Meiji's "ideal of international peace."

"Everyone present was struck with awe," wrote Konoye, "and there was silence throughout the hall." When Nagano and Sugiyama found their voices, they pledged complete agreement with Hara's request to support diplomatic efforts for peace. Hara, speaking for the emperor, gave the imperial assent to the new policy.

No one suggested removing the policy's ticking deadline.

That evening near five o'clock, a car driven by Konoye's private secretary picked up Grew and Dooman at the embassy. The prime minister had invited them to a secret dinner. To avoid attention, the car's diplomatic plates had been switched out for normal ones. In another layer of secrecy, they met at the house of a friend, who had dismissed the servants for the evening. The only people present were Grew, Dooman, Konoye, Konoye's private secretary, and an attractive young woman, Konoye's mistress, who served them dinner.

The invitation broke protocol. Prime ministers rarely met directly with ambassadors and never in secret. But Konoye, fresh from the imperial conference, knew that Japan had only a month to reach an agreement with the United States. He needed to pull every lever to arrange a meeting with Roosevelt.

Relations between our nations have become so strained, said Konoye, that mending them through normal diplomatic channels has become nearly impossible. Many Japanese were loyal to the Axis and opposed reconciliation with America. These included members of the Foreign Office who would instantly inform the Germans and Italians about any diplomatic moves toward America and would try to subvert them. For that reason, Konoye told his guests, tonight's meeting was secret even from the foreign minister, to prevent a damaging leak.

Konoye then stressed several points. First, he was determined to do whatever was necessary to overcome the differences between their countries. He was the only person who stood a chance of doing that. He accepted Hull's four principles, he said, though problems could arise when applying them to actual conditions. These were the very problems that could be resolved in a meeting with Roosevelt. Their nations wouldn't settle everything quickly, but Konoye was confident that he and Roosevelt could work out a strong basis for moving forward.

Second, Konoye acknowledged that Roosevelt and Hull doubted he could implement a peace policy before extremists ousted his cabinet. But he had the full support of the military, and they would quash any opposition. The ministers of war and the navy knew about tonight's meeting and had already chosen officers to represent them at the summit. Third, extremists and worsening economic conditions were creating resentment and eroding support for his cabinet, so the summit should happen soon. If their nations missed this opportunity, another wouldn't arise.

Grew reminded Konoye of Japan's many broken promises. Any agreement must be based on actions, he said, not words. Konoye repeated that he was determined to make real commitments and meet them even at the risk of his life. He intended to propose actions that Roosevelt "could not afford to reject." As soon as he and Roosevelt reached an agreement, he would radio the news to Tokyo, and the commander in chief in China would be instructed to suspend the fighting.

After his secretary translated this remark into English, Konoye turned to Dooman and spoke in Japanese. "Now I am going to tell you something that I don't want you to repeat to Mr. Grew or in any way disclose," said Konoye. Once he and Roosevelt came to terms, Konoye intended to radio directly to the emperor, who would issue the command to break off hostilities. Even the extremists and Axis loyalists within the military wouldn't dare defy an imperial order. It was a slight but momentous addition to the plan he had just described.

The conversation ended after three hours. As he was leaving, Grew told Konoye he was about to write the most important dispatch of his diplomatic career. He and Dooman both left the dinner convinced of Konoye's earnestness and sincerity. The issue was how to convince Washington.

That same day, in Washington, Nomura handed Hull Japan's revised draft agreement, which the liaison conference believed was sweetened with concessions: suspension of force; no expansion to the north or south; withdrawal of troops from China after peaceful settlement; commercial fairness for all nations in China; assurance that Japan itself, not the Tripartite Pact, would determine whether Japan entered the European war. The Japanese government hoped the draft would provide a basis for the meeting between Konoye and Roosevelt.

For Hull the draft "fell far short of any possibility of acceptance." Where Japan saw concessions, he saw the usual slipperiness and deceit. The promise to suspend force and expansion had an escape clause: "without justifiable reason." The assurance about the Tripartite Pact didn't foreclose the possibility of aiding the Nazis. The draft mentioned no terms of settlement with China or a timetable for withdrawing Japanese troops, leaving room for whatever Japan wanted. Japan agreed to the American demand for commercial fairness in China if "pursued on an equitable basis," no doubt defined by Japan. In return Japan expected the United States to cut off its aid to China, halt defensive improvements in the Pacific, let Japanese vessels use the Panama Canal, and lift the freeze and trade restrictions.

Hull had just received Grew's enthusiastic dispatch about the secret dinner with Konoye. Grew had written, in excited oversimplification, that Konoye and his cabinet "conclusively and wholeheartedly agree with the four principles." To Hull this sounded like tricky sweet talk. Later, when Hull learned that Konoye expected the four principles to be tempered by circumstances—his actual words at the secret dinner—Hull called it more backtracking and deceit. To confuse things further, on September 4 Nomura had handed Hull a different draft agreement, written himself without clearance from Toyoda, which deepened Hull's skepticism about Japan's motives.

Hull's devotion to honorable principles made him inflexible and blind to nuance. This trait and his knee-jerk suspicions about Japan left him unable to see past the smoking heap of Japan's offenses and broken promises. "To me," he wrote, "it seemed there was still only one chance in fifty of reaching a real agreement with Japan. My major hope was to hold off Japan's next advance, which would probably bring war to the Pacific, as long as possible."

TENSE SILENCE

TOYODA OR AN assistant checked constantly with Grew and Dooman for an answer from the State Department about Konoye's invitation to meet with Roosevelt. The embassy never had one. Patriotic groups, egged on by Nazis, were rallying opposition to a summit meeting. Rumors multiplied about plots to kill Konoye, Toyoda, Grew, and others.

On September 18 as Konoye's driver pulled out of the premier's private residence, four assassins armed with daggers and short swords jumped onto the running boards and tried to attack Konoye. But the doors were locked and the driver sped up and swerved, spilling them off. The government suppressed the story, but Grew heard about it and started carrying a gun. "I feel somewhat 'Wild West' these days," he wrote in his diary. "I don't like heroics but have no intention of letting a group of roughnecks carve me up without a reasonable attempt at repartee."

A menacing atmosphere pervaded Tokyo. During one of his many visits to the American embassy about Konoye's invitation, the head of the Foreign Office's American Bureau grabbed Grew's hand and placed it over his heart. "I thought he meant to convey the idea that his heart was in the right place," wrote Grew, "but it felt like a very hard heart and I soon grasped the idea that the hardness wasn't his heart at all but a very businesslike gun."

On September 19 Grew sent another urgent telegram to Hull. The Japanese government was alarmed by the American silence about Konoye's offer to Roosevelt, and also worried about rumors that extremists were plotting a coup to coincide with the anniversary of the Tripartite Pact on September 27. Grew hoped the State Department would expedite its consideration of a meeting between the two leaders to deflate the rising support for the Axis. That same day War Minister Tojo gave a national radio address to commemorate the ten-year anniversary of the invasion of Manchuria. He called the incursion "a divine revelation which revealed to the world the epoch-making dawn of East Asia." Using the feverish rhetoric of imperial destiny, he exhorted the Japanese to sacrifice for "the historical holy national task" of building the Co-prosperity Sphere and destroying any "third powers" who tried to thwart them.

Another liaison conference convened on September 20. More than three weeks had passed without an answer to Konoye's invitation. The military felt insulted and submitted a harsh new draft agreement to replace the earlier one. The draft withdrew the pledge not to move north without good reason and declared that Japanese troops would stay in China at multiple locations "for such periods as may be necessary." The conference approved it. Toyoda knew it would damage chances for a secret summit between Konoye and Roosevelt and didn't send it for five days. The new draft stoked the fire under the foreign minister. On September 22 he summoned Grew to ask for news about the summit. Grew still had none. Toyoda again fretted that Axis supporters wanted to kill the idea and were gaining strength. Time was running out.

Toyoda's urgency energized Grew. He returned to the embassy and wrote a personal appeal to his friend and president. He wasn't sure his dispatches were making it from the State Department to Roosevelt's desk, especially recent ones about the pressing need to respond to Konoye's invitation. A direct telegram would settle that. He wrote that Konoye was responsible for much of the strain between their countries, but despite his past failings Grew was convinced that Konoye now desired peace and good relations.

> It seems to me highly unlikely that this chance will come again. . . . The alternative to reaching a settlement now would be the greatly increased probability of war,—*Facilis descensus Averno est*—and while we would undoubtedly win in the end, I question whether it is in our own interest to see an

impoverished Japan reduced to the position of a third-rate
Power. I therefore must earnestly hope that we can come
to terms, even if we must take on trust, at least to some
degree, the continued good faith and ability of the present
Government fully to implement those terms.

Roosevelt ignored this urgent appeal for more than a month. On October 29 he finally asked Hull to handle it. The next day a staffer sent a generic reply over Roosevelt's name. By then it didn't matter.

The deadline for ending diplomacy with the United States had been left indefinite—early October—but the military had lost patience with American silence. At a liaison conference on September 25 the military chiefs, Nagano and Sugiyama, proposed a hard deadline of October 15. This shook Konoye. He told Toyoda to cable Ambassador Nomura right away to push for a meeting between October 10 and October 15.

Konoye's fragile courage was beginning to crack. He had pushed Japan into a disastrous war with China, entangled Japan with the Axis, ruined Japan's economy, and overseen a military expansion that took Japan to the edge of war with the West. His belated regrets had led to his invitation to Roosevelt. Now Konoye was horrified that the United States might reject his gambit for peace, leaving him responsible for another tragic mistake. His old instincts kicked in: he fled. He told Lord Keeper Kido he might resign, then secluded himself from September 27 to October 1 at his villa in Kamakura, forty miles from Tokyo.

In August and September the German army had churned through Russia toward Moscow. Yet the Axis had lost much of its allure to the current Japanese government, which tamped down celebrations of the Axis anniversary, permitting only one small rally of five thousand people and forbidding pro-Axis demonstrations. Toyoda held a subdued luncheon for Axis officials. His speech emphasized the Tripartite Pact as a tool for peace. German ambassador Ott brushed that off, insisting that all Axis partners must unite in military action against Soviet communism and "Anglo-Saxon world intrigue."

As soon as the luncheon ended Toyoda asked Grew to call. Grew took that as Toyoda's signal that the pact wasn't dictating Japan's relations with the United States. They talked for two hours, mostly about the proposed summit. Grew was struck by Toyoda's earnestness. As always the foreign minister asked if Grew had news; as always Grew said no. Toyoda had summoned Grew, he said, to stress "the anxiety of Prince Konoye and the entire Cabinet lest the proposed meeting between the heads of our two Governments might be indefinitely delayed." Japan had completed all preparations. The delegation had been appointed, including full admirals and generals to show the military's support. The ship was ready to sail. The opportunity might soon vanish. Toyoda said he would be grateful if the American government would reply at its earliest convenience with a specific place and date, perhaps between October 10 and 15, though "the Japanese mission is ready to leave at any time."

Grew put all this urgency into his next dispatch. It had the same effect as all the others.

Hull sent Roosevelt a draft statement of the State Department's objections to the latest Japanese proposal, including advice to delay any meeting with Konoye until Japan accepted certain principles and actions as preconditions. On September 28 Roosevelt instructed Hull to "reemphasize my hopes for a meeting" but to ask the Japanese to start over. That suited Hull and Hornbeck's strategy of serial postponements. Hornbeck had convinced Hull that delays would weaken Japan and subdue its government's tendency for rash action.

When Nomura visited Hull the next day to press for an answer about the summit, Hull had none. Nor did he expect to. Hull didn't bother to tell Nomura or Grew, but the idea was as good as dead. Hull now put the odds of a successful agreement at one hundred to one. The fault, he judged, was entirely Japan's. He believed that agreeing to the summit could "have negated principles on which we had built our foreign policy and without which the world could not live in peace." But this noble sanctimony, rather than keeping the peace, was another obstacle to it.

That same day Grew sent a last-ditch appeal to Hull. He had spent his entire Sunday working on it before handing it to the coders at noon the next day, September 29. At fifteen pages it was among his longest telegrams ever. His argument was logical, practical, and desperate.

He began by noting that his recent dispatches made clear the intensifying efforts by the Japanese government to set up a meeting between Konoye and Roosevelt. Konoye's proposal, he wrote, gave diplomacy with Japan new life and shouldn't be snubbed. The chaos in Japanese politics and social conditions made the timing propitious for adjusting relations. If Roosevelt and Konoye met, wrote Grew, the United States might be able to stop Japan's expansion without going to war. If the leaders didn't meet, the risk of war would skyrocket.

Some in the US government argued—Grew was thinking principally of Hull and Hornbeck—that Japan was seeking an agreement to gain breathing room for its next conquest, so the smart policy was to stall negotiations and strangle Japan economically because Japan wouldn't dare take action against the United States. Grew disagreed. Japan's plans might be nefarious, but why not try conciliation—not appeasement—before escalating things further? If negotiations failed or Japan reneged, the United States could always lower the economic hammer.

Grew emphasized that understanding Japanese psychology was essential. If the United States demanded commitments to principles and concrete details before the meeting, the preliminary talks would falter and the Konoye cabinet would lose face. Anti-American feeling would swell. The cabinet would fall, replaced by a military dictatorship not disposed to avoid war with the United States. Grew said it was riskier for Konoye and Roosevelt not to meet than to meet and disagree—the reverse of Hornbeck's calculus.

Grew agreed that the Japanese proposals were "so abstract or equivocal as to create confusion rather than to clarify the commitments which the Government is prepared to undertake." This partly reflected Japanese psychology but also Konoye's fears that Matsuoka's supporters, who still infested the Foreign Office, would leak any specific details to the extremists and the Germans. Grew had been assured, he wrote, that when Konoye came face-to-face with Roosevelt he would offer far-reaching commitments that would satisfy the United States. Grew had no way of knowing if that was true, but he doubted Konoye would risk the terrible loss of face entailed by coming home a failure.

Grew knew Hull was adamant about Japan ending its affiliation with the Axis. Japan's internal politics and the importance of face made such a public disassociation difficult, Grew wrote, but he hoped Hull would be satisfied by Japan's clear signals of withdrawal from the Tripartite Pact. Its main champion, Matsuoka, had been expelled by the entire cabinet. Japan's leaders had rejected Germany's demands to fight, and their draft proposals to the State Department had distanced Japan from any military obligation to the Axis. Last, he wrote, Konoye's invitation to Roosevelt had reduced the pact "to a dead letter."

At this point "the only wise alternative" was "constructive conciliation." Grew asked Hull, "Is it not the better part of wisdom and statesmanship" to make such efforts before the opportunity disappeared?

The telegram was powerful and persuasive. And ignored. A few days later Grew complained in his diary that sending dispatches to the State Department "is like throwing pebbles into a lake at night; they disappear and generally one doesn't even see the ripples."

KABUKI

ON OCTOBER 1, 1941, Konoye stirred in his hideaway in Kamakura. The Japanese army seemed bent on war, but Konoye knew that the navy, which would bear the brunt of a conflict with the United States, was uneasy. The prime minister invited Navy Minister Oikawa to visit. Oikawa knew Konoye wanted peace. The navy minister also may have heard about the meeting two days earlier between Navy Chief Nagano and Admiral Yamamoto, commander in chief of the combined fleet. Yamamoto was deep into the top-secret planning for an attack on Pearl Harbor, and his staff had been war-gaming what might happen afterward.

"The war would continue for several years," Yamamoto told Nagano, "our supplies would be exhausted, our ships and arms would be damaged, and ultimately we would not be able to escape defeat. Not only that, as a result of the war, people of this nation would be reduced to abject poverty. . . . We should not venture on such an imprudent attempt that offers little hope of success." But mere facts couldn't deter Nagano. He told Yamamoto to keep planning.

Oikawa wanted to avoid war. "We must be prepared to do nothing less than swallow whole the United States proposal," he said to Konoye. If the prime minister would lead, the navy would follow. He thought the army would prefer a settlement as well, and Foreign Minister Toyoda clearly wanted peace.

"That's a relief," said Konoye. "That's also where my thinking lies." They agreed to look for a way to alter the imperial conference's new deadline of October 15. They ignored the obvious solution—ask the emperor to nullify the decision made in his name—because that would remove the emperor from his cocoon of divine immunity.

At nine the following morning, October 2—Hull's seventieth birthday—Nomura called on the secretary of state at his apartment in the luxurious red-brick Wardman Park Hotel. Many of their forty or fifty meetings took place there or at Hull's previous apartment in the Carlton Hotel, usually in the evening to avoid the press. Joseph Ballantine, the department's main Japanese expert, typically attended as Hull's interpreter and note taker. Hull handed Nomura the American reply to Japan's last harsh draft agreement. The reply met harshness with harshness. It required Japan to make multiple specific commitments before any meeting could occur between Roosevelt and Konoye—exactly the strategy Grew had advised against. The statement said Japan must embrace the four principles, openly renounce the Axis, and withdraw troops from China and Indochina. It essentially required Japan to accede to the entire American position in advance.

As Nomura read the statement, his spirits sank. Hull asked for his comments. Nomura said his government "would be disappointed because of its very earnest desire to hold the meeting." He knew Tokyo would never agree to these preconditions, which offered no means to preserve face. No Japanese leader who suggested accepting them could possibly survive. Hull said, absurdly from Nomura's point of view, that the United States had "no desire whatever" to cause delay. Hull must have known the proposal would be rejected and kill the summit.

Nomura telegraphed Tokyo. "It is my sense," he wrote, "that Japanese-United States negotiations have finally reached a 'deadlock.' . . . I think there will be no change in [US] policy toward Japan unless there is a great change in the world political situation and unless Japan does an about-face in its policies."

Nomura was right about the reaction in Tokyo. At a liaison conference on October 4, the army and navy chiefs, Sugiyama and Nagano, pushed for immediate military action, while Konoye, Toyoda, and Oikawa wanted to keep talking to the United States. The split played out for several days in a flurry of high-level meetings. The result was tense stasis. Sugiyama and War Minister Tojo saw no way around war, but if the navy lacked confidence, the army would reconsider. Nagano, a blusterer, supported the army. Oikawa didn't want war but lacked the spine to stand up alone against military colleagues who equated caution with cowardice. Likewise, Konoye opposed war but refused to voice a strong opinion either way, hoping the services would fix the problem for him.

This Kabuki continued into the night of October 7. In a second meeting that day between Tojo and Oikawa, Tojo said, "We have lost 200,000 souls in the China Incident, and I cannot bear to give it all up just like that. But when I think of all the lives that will be further lost if there is a war between Japan and the United States, we must even think about withdrawing troops." This hint from the usually rigid Tojo implied that if the navy declared no confidence in war, he and the army would moderate their stance about troops in China and give diplomacy another chance.

Tojo went from this meeting to Konoye's house at 9:00 P.M. "With regard to the problem of stationing troops," Tojo told Konoye, "I find it absolutely impossible to make concessions." With Konoye, Tojo had hardened back into rigidity. The war minister also insisted that the decisions of an imperial conference couldn't be changed. Konoye remarked that Tojo seemed to be taking the possibility of war too lightly. "Sometimes," said Tojo, "a man has to jump with his eyes closed from the veranda of the Kiyomizu Temple"—an idiom meaning "take the plunge." This rash fatalistic remark appalled Konoye. "A person in a responsible position," said the prime minister, "when he considers a 2600-year-old national polity and a hundred million subjects, cannot take such a risk."

Konoye, desperate, tried another tack. He called a ministers' meeting for October 12—his fiftieth birthday—at his house. He didn't invite the pro-war Sugiyama and Nagano. Konoye had a plan to avoid both war and responsibility. Late on the night before the meeting he sent Tomita Kenji, chief cabinet secretary, to Oikawa's home. Tomita asked Oikawa to speak clearly against war at the ministers' meeting. Like Konoye, Oikawa was adept at dodging responsibility. He told Tomita he couldn't voice his opposition to war openly because "it is proper that the prime minister should decide." If Konoye opposed war strongly, said Oikawa, the navy would support him.

Next Tomita phoned Military Affairs Bureau Chief Muto Akira to share the navy's stance, in hopes it would budge the army. "If the navy is loath to go to war," said Muto, "then I want them to say that clearly, straight from their own mouths. If they do that, we will put a stop to the pro-war arguments in the army." The army, too, knew how to pass the buck. Tomita called Muto's counterpart in the navy, Oka Takazumi. "If the navy says 'no can do,'" Tomita told Oka, "we will get the army under control one way or the other." No, said Oka, the navy will not say that. Tomita told Muto to call and ask again. No, repeated Oka.

The ministers gathered at Konoye's home at 2:00 P.M. and stayed for four hours. Tojo said negotiations were pointless. Oikawa left the decision to Konoye. Konoye asked Toyoda about the prospects for talks with the United States. "I cannot say with absolute confidence," said Toyoda.

"There are risks in taking either road," said Konoye. "The basic problem is which one involves the greater risks, which one we have greater confidence in. I myself have greater confidence in negotiation and therefore want to take that road."

"That's the prime minister's subjective view," said Tojo. "I can't convince the high command on such a basis as that."

Konoye repeated that he had greater confidence in diplomacy. "If, in spite of this, you say go to war, I for one cannot take the responsibility."

Tojo blew up. "At the Imperial Conference it was decided to resolve on going to war in the event that diplomacy did not work," he said. "The prime minister was present, was he not? And did he not agree with this? It is hard for me to understand how, in spite of this, he can now say he cannot take responsibility for going to war."

"I am saying," said Konoye, "that I cannot take responsibility if, in spite of my having greater confidence in one route, you tell me to take the other in which I have none."

When the meeting adjourned neither side had shifted. Everyone had implied willingness to delay war, but no one was willing to lose face by saying so, and no one wanted responsibility for the next move. Instead of coming out strongly against war, Konoye had threatened to quit. Tojo had refused to bend. Oikawa had stayed silent despite his belief that a war with the United States would be unwinnable and devastating.

Suzuki, director of the cabinet planning board, knew Japan's waning resources couldn't bear the strain of a war. After the ministers' meeting he suggested the obvious to Konoye: the prime minister should ask the emperor to cancel the decision made by the imperial conference. That would remove the deadline and allow negotiations with the United States to continue. Konoye asked Suzuki to sound out Tojo on the idea. The war minister said that nullifying the decision of an imperial conference would be impossible unless the entire cabinet first resigned in shame for failing to carry out the imperial will. Next Konoye told Suzuki to ask Lord Keeper Kido about approaching the emperor. Kido said Konoye must first secure approval from the war and navy ministers. It was the old Kabuki.

A cabinet meeting was scheduled for October 14. Beforehand, in a private meeting at Konoye's house at 9:00 A.M., Konoye made one last attempt to sway Tojo. The prime minister said he felt great responsibility for the war in China and didn't want to further jeopardize the nation with another devastating conflict. "On this occasion, we ought to give in for a time," he said. He asked Tojo to agree to withdraw troops from China. Tojo refused, saying that would make America "more high-handed." Withdrawing troops also would be difficult, he said, "from the point of view of maintaining the fighting spirit of the Army." Angry, Konoye asked him to reconsider, but Tojo remained adamant. His voice filling with emotion, the war minister said, "All this must be due to the difference in our characters."

Tojo opened the cabinet meeting with an impassioned speech about ending negotiations with the United States and proceeding toward war. The cabinet remained divided. That afternoon Muto visited Tomita. "If the Navy will openly come to the Army," said Muto, "and say that 'The Navy at this time does not wish war,' then the Army can easily control its command. I wonder if you can not manage it so that the Navy will come and say something along this line." Tomita went straight to Oka, Muto's naval counterpart. Oka soon phoned back with Oikawa's response: the army knew how the navy felt, so an open statement was unnecessary. In short, the same deflected responsibility and gutless cowering behind face.

The day's backstage maneuvers weren't over. After the cabinet meeting Tojo went to the palace to see Kido, where he took a position very different from his latest rant to the cabinet. Peace with the United States was impossible, Tojo told the lord keeper, unless the deadline disappeared and troops were withdrawn. The only solution was for Konoye to resign so a new prime minister could discard the imperial decision and order the withdrawal of troops. Kido agreed.

That night Tojo sent Suzuki to Konoye's house with a message and a proposal: the navy didn't want a war, but since Oikawa wouldn't say this to Tojo, the army couldn't reconsider its position. By refusing to make up its mind, the navy was prohibiting the cabinet and the Supreme Command from obeying a decision sanctioned by the emperor. The only way out was resignation en bloc so that the next prime minister could annul the imperial decision. Tojo's surprising recommendation to replace Konoye: Prince Higashikuni Naruhiko, the emperor's uncle-in-law and an army general strongly opposed to war with the United States. Tojo seemed willing to avoid war, but only through private sideways tactics that preserved face for himself and the army.

Suzuki reported back to Konoye around midnight. Konoye was determined to resign, and he lunged at the suggestion of Prince Higashikuni. He went to the palace later that day to propose it to the emperor. Hirohito seemed enthusiastic about putting his anti-war uncle in charge. He gave Konoye permission to approach him. But early the next morning, October 16, Lord Keeper Kido vetoed the idea. The imperial family must not get tarnished by political responsibilities, he told Konoye, regardless of the possible benefit to the nation.

These maddening evasions, including his own, had frazzled Konoye and drained his small store of courage. Without bothering to plan a safe path forward for his country, he went to the palace at 5:00 P.M. and presented his resignation. Kido told him that the best candidates for premier, owing to the volatility of the military services, were Tojo and Oikawa. Did Konoye have a preference? Konoye recommended Tojo on the dubious theory that the position's weight might shift his views toward prudence.

On October 17 the emperor summoned Tojo to the palace and asked him to form a government. As Grew had forewarned, Japan's new prime minister was a hard-core anti-American militarist. Tojo also retained his position as minister of war.

The idea of a summit with Roosevelt had died in Washington weeks earlier without Grew's knowledge. Its death was now also official in Tokyo.

A DEADLINE FOR DIPLOMACY

LORD KEEPER KIDO carried a message from the emperor to Tojo and Oikawa: resolve the differences between the army and the navy, and do not feel shackled to the imperial decision of September 6. It was an indirect request to find a way out of war. Kido, however, failed to inform the Supreme Command of the emperor's wishes. The army and navy didn't take orders from their cabinet ministers, and since their chiefs, Sugiyama and Nagano, hadn't been officially informed, the services chose to assume that the old deadline of October 15, 1941, still applied.

The new foreign minister was Togo Shigenori. "Togo was a person completely devoid of any personal charm," said Dooman, who had known him since the 1920s. "He was the closest thing that I have ever known to a piece of ice." Slender and dour, with a brush moustache and round eyeglasses, Togo had studied German literature in college, served in the Berlin embassy as a young man, and married a German. In 1937 he returned to Germany as ambassador, but he detested Nazism and opposed Japan's decision to join the Axis. In 1938 he was reassigned as ambassador to the Soviet Union, but two years later he became a victim of the "Matsuoka hurricane" that purged moderates from the Foreign Office. Back in Japan, Togo was disturbed by the rising enthusiasm for the Axis and imperial expansion. He vocally opposed war with the United States.

When Tojo first asked Togo to become foreign minister, he declined because the new prime minister had said withdrawal of troops from China was impossible. In Togo's opinion that ended the prospects for diplomacy.

Tojo backed up and implied that his position might not be irrevocable, so Togo eventually relented, on the understanding that he had full diplomatic license to pursue peace. He hibernated for a week to read the Foreign Office's thick files about the talks with the United States. Several things shocked him: the "hopeless muddle" of the negotiations, the intransigence of the United States, and the constant intrusion into foreign affairs by the military. His task was far bigger than expected.

In Washington Nomura was worn down and pessimistic. He believed the change of cabinets killed any chance of an agreement. On October 18 he asked to be recalled, and asked again on October 21. "I am now, so to speak, a skeleton of a dead horse," he wrote to Togo. "It is too much for me to be a sham existence, cheating others as well as myself. I do not mean to run away from the battlefield, but I believe that this is the course I should take as a public man." Togo, determined to restart the talks without delay, denied Nomura's request.

Between October 23 and November 1, Prime Minister Tojo held liaison conferences almost daily to decide between war and peace. The conferences were exercises in bravado and self-delusion, with glimmers of sanity. On October 23 Tojo began by telling the conference about the emperor's wish to "wipe the slate clean" and reexamine the imperial conference's decision of September 6. The chiefs of the army and navy, Sugiyama and Nagano, both objected. The deadline for diplomacy had passed, they insisted. "We can't devote four or five days to study," said Sugiyama. "Hurry up and go ahead."

Foreign Minister Togo was stunned. The conference eventually decided to follow the emperor's wishes and reconsider the deadline, but Togo realized that the Supreme Command's desire for war remained strong, "like a mine in the path of diplomatic activity." As the liaison conferences proceeded, Japan's lack of preparation and raw materials, such as oil, gas, and steel, became alarmingly apparent, especially compared with the immense capacity of the United States. Sugiyama was unfazed. "The deficiency of materials," he said, "can be overcome by taking advantage of changes in the situation, and by clever strategy."

On October 30 the conference revisited the main American demands to see whether concessions were feasible. Membership in the Axis? No change possible. Acceptance of the four principles? No change possible. Commercial equality in China? "Let's show our generosity," said Nagano. They agreed to consider nondiscrimination.

Last, they discussed the issue of withdrawing troops. From Indochina? No change possible. And from China? Togo argued—"forgetting reality," according to the army's official note taker—that troops should be withdrawn immediately to preserve Japan's welfare. This caused an uproar. Eventually, as a "diplomatic gesture," the military agreed to withdraw troops from China after a "reasonable period." Their first suggestion was ninety-nine years, but they finally agreed to what they considered a compromise, twenty-five years.

The agenda also asked, "What would happen to Japan if the American proposals were accepted in their entirety?" Everyone except Togo agreed that Japan would sink into third-rate status. Togo suggested that if both sides softened their conditions, "everything would turn out for the better." The official note taker recorded, "[Togo] gave everyone a strange feeling." The Supreme Command, impatient, again requested a decision for war, but Togo and Finance Minister Kaya Okinori, whose anxiety about Japan's financial state had risen throughout the conferences, asked for a pause to deliberate.

Prime Minister Tojo consented. He told the group to weigh three alternatives: peace and the hardships it would cause; immediate war; or preparation for war while also continuing diplomacy. In two days, at the next liaison conference, they would decide Japan's future.

At the end of October, Grew, too, was swathed in self-delusion. On the evening of October 25 his best friend and informant in Japan, Count Kabayama, told him about the events leading to the formation of the new cabinet, including the emperor's directive to reconsider the imperial deadline. Kabayama's dramatic story fanned the guttering flame of Grew's optimism. These events, wrote Grew in his diary, "may in future be regarded as one of the really big moments in Japanese history." He sent Hull two excited dispatches about it with Kabayama's sunshiny assessment: "For the first time in ten years the situation at present and the existing political set-up in Japan offer a possibility of a reorientation of Japanese policy and action."

But Kabayama had enhanced reality. In the count's telling, the emperor hadn't given slantwise hints to Sugiyama, Nagano, and Tojo. Instead, wrote Grew about his conversation with the count, "in an unprecedented action [the emperor] ordered the armed forces to obey his wishes." Upon this fictitious imperial command Grew erected a castle of mistaken assumptions, among them that the emperor chose Tojo as prime minister for his commitment to peace with the United States. Kabayama also assured Grew, who informed Hull, that the virulent anti-American, pro-Axis tone of the Japanese press "gave no real indication" of the true feelings of the Japanese public or the political leaders. But Grew knew those leaders controlled the press.

Grew embraced these desperate fantasies partly because they restored his hopes, partly because his corps of Japanese informants had dwindled as anti-American hostility rose, and he lacked better intelligence. Kabayama had entrée to the palace and the cabinet, and his information was usually reliable. But as Grew often noted, the old count's interpretations of that information generally skewed toward the rosy. After a visit from him just four days earlier, Grew had written, "Good old Kabayama, one of the dearest men in any country. For him the rainbow is always just around the corner."

For two weeks in late October, Grew willed himself to mistake lightning storms for rainbows.

The liaison conference to decide between peace, war, and deadline diplomacy began at 9:00 A.M. on November 1 and lasted nearly seventeen hours. The conference opened with a demand by Admiral Shimada Shigetaro, Oikawa's replacement as navy minister, for a massive increase in the navy's share of the allocation for steel in 1942. That was the navy's price for agreeing to consider war. Army Chief Sugiyama accepted the deal. Suzuki, head of the planning board, pointed out that since estimates of available steel were far too high, the navy would be increasing its share of what didn't exist. The conference began in fantasy.

On to the three options. First, peace—quickly discarded. Next, war. Sugiyama presented the army's proposal in favor, to start on December 1. Foreign Minister Togo said he needed time to negotiate in good faith.

The military huffed, which brought the group to the third option, a deadline for diplomacy. The argument got so heated that Prime Minister Tojo, who supported this choice, called a twenty-minute break. The army staff huddled. Their goal was war in early December. After the recess they said negotiations could continue until November 30, five days before Japan would declare war. If diplomacy succeeded before then, war would be called off.

At 10:00 P.M., after thirteen hours of stress and squabbles, the discussion turned to the terms of negotiation with the United States. Tojo and the military assumed that the foreign minister would use the proposal previously given to Hull, called Plan A. But Togo played a hole card, a backup plan that he thought stood a better chance of quick acceptance, which he needed under his tight deadline.

"I believe that there is no hope for Proposal A in the short time that is left," the foreign minister told the group. If the United States rejected Plan A, Togo wanted to submit his Plan B. It called for both countries to abjure force in the South Seas and to share commercial access to resources from the Dutch East Indies. The United States would then lift economic sanctions and reopen the flow of oil. In return Japan would pull its troops from southern Indochina to northern Indochina, and would remove them entirely upon settlement of the China incident, which Japan would handle without US involvement. Togo hoped these partial concessions would be enough to prevent war and extend the talks.

"We absolutely cannot withdraw our troops from southern Indochina," shouted Army Vice Chief Tsukada Osamu. He was angry about both Togo's ambush and the proposed concessions. Sugiyama and Nagano joined in. Togo shouted back that he would resign if the military insisted on war. Someone called for another recess. The army huddled again. If Togo resigned, the cabinet would fall and the next one might oppose war. At best, war would be further delayed. The army agreed to accept Plan B if necessary. The deadline remained November 30.

Afterward Tsukada told the official note taker, "In general, the prospects if we go to war are not bright. We all wonder if there isn't some way to proceed peacefully. . . . On the other hand, it is not possible to maintain the status quo. Hence one unavoidably reaches the conclusion that we must go to war. . . . The moral spirit of Japan, the Land of the Gods, will shine on this occasion."

Inspired by his rainbow rhetoric, Tsukada built imperial fantasies from snowballing ifs. If Japan took the south, he said, China probably would surrender. That probably would help Germany defeat Britain. Meanwhile Japan probably could take the Soviet Union. Next Japan probably could cripple America's Pacific defenses and encircle Japan's enemies with "an iron wall," destroying them one by one until Britain was defeated and thrown out of the Far East. And then, said Tsukada, overcome by visions of unstoppable empire, "America will have to do some thinking."

On November 3 Count Kabayama visited Grew again. He brought inside news straight from Togo. The liaison conference had made a firm decision about how far Japan could go to meet the emperor's desire for an understanding with the United States. Togo had implied to Kabayama that he had the support of the navy minister as well as Prime Minister Tojo, who was also war minister and home minister. As usual Kabayama was amazingly well informed. Everything he said was true but incomplete, leaving room for optimistic embroidery. In his interpretation the liaison conference was stacked with military doves eager to obey the emperor's direct command for peace.

Grew reported Kabayama's news to the State Department but sent a second dispatch the same day that made clear the rainbow was fading for him. Grew repeated his warning against the notion that economic sanctions would cripple Japan and prevent war, or that Japan would never attack the United States. He labeled those ideas—championed by Hornbeck—as not only mistaken but "hazardous," "dangerous," and "perilously unsure." Such ideas were more likely to cause war than prevent it, Grew warned. If the talks failed, he continued, Japan would move back toward the Axis. If the United States tightened the economic screws, Japan's leaders might make "a 'do-or-die or all-out' effort to make Japan invulnerable to foreign economic measures, even to the point of risking national suicide. . . . It is apparent to us who are in daily contact with the sentiment here that such an eventuality is not only a possibility but a probability." The dispatch ended ominously: war "may come with dangerous and dramatic suddenness." In his diary Grew wrote, "That important telegram is on the record for all time."

Hornbeck felt the sting. He attacked Grew's analysis with his usual snark, calling it flawed, weak, and appeasing, and he accused Grew of advising the United States to avoid pressuring Japan because that might cause war, "in which case the fault would be ours." It was an ugly distortion of Grew's telegram and beliefs. Hornbeck scoffed at any suggestion of flexibility toward Japan. "A firm or even bold course on our part," he wrote to Hull, "is and will be better strategy than would be a course giving any indication or implication of weakness or anxiety."

OFFERINGS

JUST AFTER MIDNIGHT on November 3, loud knocking awakened Kurusu Saburo. Foreign Minister Togo had sent a policeman to fetch him. When Kurusu walked into the foreign minister's home, he found Togo and several staffers, all looking tense. Togo got right to the point. He wanted Kurusu to go to America to help Nomura with the talks. He felt the ambassador was unreliable, and with less than a month to the deadline, Japan couldn't afford mistakes.

A dapper fifty-five-year-old with the usual moustache and round glasses, Kurusu was one of Japan's most seasoned diplomats. He had recently served as ambassador to Belgium and then Germany, where he had signed the Tripartite Pact on Matsuoka's orders despite his personal opposition. He was married to an American and spoke perfect English.

Togo filled him in on the difficult state of the negotiations, as well as Japan's growing economic desperation. He explained Plan A and Plan B but didn't mention the deadline. If the talks failed, he said, war was likely. Reluctant but dutiful, Kurusu accepted the assignment. He spent the day studying documents and packing. At 7:00 P.M. he called on Tojo at home and found the prime minister in a kimono and hakama. Tojo estimated the talks' likelihood of failure at 70 percent. Of the three main issues, he said, no concessions were possible on the issue of withdrawing troops. In that case, said Kurusu, your estimate of failure is optimistic.

After visiting Tojo, Kurusu called on Grew. The two men and their families had known each other for ten years. Kurusu's daughter Jaye was a good friend of Grew's daughter Elsie. "I had negotiated with him, played golf with him, played poker with him," Grew wrote about Kurusu. "Such close association helps one to size up any man." Grew considered him pro-American. He didn't hold Kurusu's signing of the Axis pact against him. Ambassadors followed orders from their governments regardless of their own beliefs.

Kurusu thanked Grew for arranging his flight from Hong Kong to San Francisco on the Pan Am Clipper. Togo had asked for Grew's help to delay the flight for two days so Kurusu could catch it. Otherwise the wait was two more weeks, unthinkable given the November 30 deadline. Grew sensed the urgency behind Togo's request and pulled strings to delay the plane.

Grew asked Kurusu if he was taking a new proposal to Washington. No, said Kurusu. In that case, said Grew, it was useless to go. But maybe negotiations have fallen into a rut, said Kurusu, and he would detect some way out. Grew brightened a bit at that. Alice came in to say goodbye, tearful as she shook the special envoy's hand.

Kurusu got to bed after midnight. At 4:00 A.M. he rose to start his journey. Fearing assassination, he asked his son Ryo, born in Chicago and now in the Japanese army, to escort him to the train station. Only twenty hours had passed since he had accepted his bleak mission. In ten days he would be in Washington.

An imperial conference convened on November 5. Japan's highest political and military leaders all spoke in support of the decision for a deadline followed by war. No one suggested changing the cutoff date. Everyone, including Foreign Minister Togo, claimed victimhood for Japan. After more than four hours of self-righteousness and swagger, the decision received the emperor's pro forma sanction. Hirohito didn't speak. It was too late for poetry.

The imperial conference and Kurusu's departure for Washington led to fresh gouts of anti-American vitriol in the press. Grew usually shook off such outbursts, but now he was fed up. "I have about given up hope of the Washington conversations making any progress," he wrote in his diary on the day of the imperial conference. If a complete breakdown could be avoided until Germany's defeat, Japan might come to its senses. "That is about the best we can hope for now."

In Washington Grew's telegram about the possibility of national suicide reached Hull's desk along with a Magic intercept that reinforced it and finally made the possibility of a Japanese attack real. On the day of the imperial conference, Togo had instructed Nomura that circumstances made it "absolutely necessary" to complete an agreement by November 25. To Hull the implication was clear: either America met Japan's demands within twenty days or Japan declared war. At a cabinet meeting on November 7 Hull called the situation "extremely critical," and warned, "We should be on the lookout for a military attack by Japan anywhere at any time." That evening Nomura came to Hull's apartment and presented Plan A. Hull quickly pegged it: nothing new, no chance of acceptance.

Nomura was anxious for Hull's official response to Plan A, but Hull kept putting him off. Nomura wired his daily non-news to Tokyo. On November 12, five days after the delivery of Plan A, Togo sent his secretary to Grew with an urgent message. The foreign minister was "shocked" that the United States "does not fully grasp the urgency of successfully concluding the current conversations in the shortest possible time." Togo wanted Grew to stress the need for speed in Washington. The foreign minister also asked the British ambassador to push his government to pressure the Americans. Covering his bets, Togo told General Sugiyama to begin revitalizing ties with Germany in case the talks failed. The Nazis had been peeved by Kurusu's assignment to America.

Nomura finally got a response to Plan A on November 15 in Hull's Washington apartment: no. But Hull also offered a surprising new inducement—a commercial treaty under which Japan and America would cooperate to reduce trade barriers, eliminate discrimination, and give all nations access to the raw materials they needed. This treaty, noted Hull, "would have given [Japan] much of what her leaders professed to want." But he didn't expect the offer to change anything because Japan also wanted China, Indochina, and the Greater East Asia Co-prosperity Sphere. Nomura's constant protestations of peace were undercut by Magic intercepts from Tokyo filled with belligerent messages.

On the morning of November 17 Nomura and Kurusu went to Hull's office, where a road-weary Kurusu met the secretary of state for the first time. They all walked across the street to the White House, where they would meet with President Roosevelt. Hull could imagine only two roles for Kurusu at this stage: to pressure the United States into signing an un-fair agreement or, if that failed, "to lull us with talk until the moment Japan got ready to strike." To Hull, Kurusu also was stained as the signer of the Tripartite Pact. "I felt from the start that he was deceitful." Never-theless, Kurusu and Nomura left the meeting encouraged by Roosevelt's openness. The president had even recited an old saying, "There is no last word between friends." They sent optimistic telegrams to Togo.

Hull had arranged to meet the Japanese the next day. He dashed their fresh hopes. Progress was impossible, he told them, until Japan addressed the three obstacles: the Axis pact, troops in China and Indochina, com-mercial inequality. The diplomats went around and around, deepening the diplomatic rut. Then Nomura and Kurusu surprised Hull by suggesting a modus vivendi. The Japanese proposed turning back the clock to the situation as it had stood in late July. Japan would withdraw its troops from southern Indochina, and the United States would lift the freeze.

This wasn't Plan B, it was Nomura going rogue again, desperate to un-block the talks. Hull's knee-jerk response was suspicion. How can we be sure, he asked, that you won't just put the troops somewhere "equally ob-jectionable"? Kurusu said they simply wanted to do something to stop the slide toward hostilities. Hull doubted he could convince his government to remove the freeze unless Japan took a clear new direction, away from conquest. Japan, said Kurusu, was "tired of fighting China and would go as far as she could along a different course." Hull, unenthusiastic about solutions that didn't solve everything at once, said he would consult with the British and the Dutch.

On the following evening the three diplomats met again at Hull's apart-ment. If we adopt a modus vivendi, asked Hull, would the conversations to resolve the other outstanding issues continue? Yes, said Nomura, but Japan couldn't nullify the Axis pact. To Hull that looked like the same old direction. He also knew from new Magic intercepts that Nomura had been instructed to listen for a code on the Japanese shortwave newscast, a signal to destroy all codebooks and secret papers—another portent of war.

Togo strangled Nomura's offer as well. He scolded his envoys for free-lancing a modus vivendi. Present Plan B immediately, he instructed, and make clear that it must be accepted "in its entirety," which included halting aid to China. Nomura and Kurusu handed Plan B to Hull on November 20, Thanksgiving Day. Hull had already read it via Magic. Despite the concessions in it, he called the plan "extreme." In his view, "It was an ultimatum."

On November 13 Grew had wired a report by the embassy's commercial attaché to Washington. Grew asked Hull to consider it alongside his warning ten days earlier about the probability of a sudden attack. The report noted Japan's worsening desperation and dwindling options to avoid war with the United States. According to the attaché's report, Japan's leaders felt they were confronting a stark choice: lose face by abandoning imperial goals and conceding to the United States or take a suicidal gamble on war to preserve empire and status. Japan's military leaders, said the report, firmly supported the latter. The State Department never acknowledged the document.

Grew followed this with a similar dispatch on November 17. The embassy's military and naval attachés could no longer provide reliable information about Japanese troop and ship movements, he wrote, because their contacts had dried up and personal observation was no longer possible. Japan could send its forces in any direction without detection, and was likely to exploit "every possible tactical advantage, such as surprise and initiative."

As Grew wrote this, the Pearl Harbor Striking Force was underway from Japan to its fogbound hideout in the Kuril Islands.

DECISION FOR WAR

ROOSEVELT AGREED WITH Hull that Plan B was a nonstarter, but he had been thinking about a modus vivendi of his own. He outlined it for Hull on November 21, 1941. The State Department quickly turned it into a simple, reasonable proposal. Both the United States and Japan would forgo force or threats in the Pacific. Japan would withdraw its troops from southern Indochina and reduce the troops in northern Indochina to twenty-five thousand. The United States would partially lift the freeze and economic sanctions to allow limited trade, including oil for civilian purposes. This bridge agreement would last three months but could be renewed.

It was a gradualist approach, as Grew had been advocating. Hull didn't think the Japanese would accept it—he put the odds at one in three—but it would show the world that America wanted peace. Even if Japan accepted it but failed to comply, the United States would gain three more months to prepare for war. Hull didn't bother to inform Grew about this proposal.

The next day, Friday, November 22, Hull called the ambassadors of Britain, China, Australia, and the Netherlands to his office. He summarized the modus vivendi and asked for their reactions. All found it promising except the Chinese ambassador, who objected that loosening sanctions could worsen his country's situation. They agreed to consult their governments and meet again on Monday.

That same day Magic intercepted a message from Foreign Minister Togo to Nomura and Kurusu. It extended the deadline for diplomacy to

November 29. (Togo hadn't told his envoys the true deadline or what would happen afterward, and still didn't.) The message urged the envoys to "spare no effort" to conclude the talks by the cutoff date. "This time we mean it, that the dead line absolutely cannot be changed," wrote Togo. "After that things are automatically going to happen."

Togo's telegram was on Hull's mind that evening as he welcomed Nomura and Kurusu into his apartment. "It was almost unreal," he wrote, "to see these representatives come to my home smiling, courteous, and outwardly friendly. It was a strain to talk to them in the same tone and on the same level, knowing what I did of Japan's nefarious plans from the intercepted messages, and knowing that Nomura and Kurusu had the same information. There they sat, bowing agreeably, Nomura sometimes giggling, Kurusu often showing his teeth in a grin."

Hull told them about his meeting several hours earlier with the ambassadors but didn't mention the modus vivendi. The Japanese envoys pressed him for an answer about Plan B, but Hull put them off until Monday. First he wanted to hear from the other governments.

Togo called Grew to his office on November 24. He was puzzled and agitated that the United States hadn't accepted Japan's new proposal to end aggression in the South Seas and to withdraw Japanese troops from southern Indochina in return for the lifting of economic sanctions and the oil embargo. Togo said he had written the proposal himself as Japan's best offer. Hull's silence baffled him. America had imposed the freeze after Japan moved troops into southern Indochina, so shouldn't removing those troops alter America's stance?

That same day, the Allied ambassadors reconvened in Hull's office. This time Hull handed out copies of the modus vivendi. They began to read and grumble. Hull, his temper rising, noted that stopping hostilities in the Pacific for three months would benefit all of their countries, which had far more at stake in the Pacific than did the United States, yet they seemed to expect the United States to shoulder the burden of defending the region. Instead of cooperating, he said, the Allied nations were carping. Hull decided to ask Roosevelt to send a telegram directly to Churchill asking him to support the modus vivendi.

At a meeting the next morning at nine thirty Hull showed the modus vivendi to Secretary of War Stimson and Secretary of the Navy Knox. Hull said he intended to give it to the Japanese later that day or tomorrow. As the day progressed, the Allied ambassadors began reporting their governments' responses. The reaction from China, wrote Hull, "was violent." Chiang himself sent outraged cables to Churchill, Stimson, and Knox, protesting any easing of economic sanctions to appease Japan at China's expense. As the Chinese ambassador relayed all this, Hull's dander rose again. The generalissimo and Madame Chiang, he noted, had been flooding Washington with cables begging for more aid, yet when the United States wanted to guarantee peace in Southeast Asia for three months, Chiang fulminated.

Hull's mood wasn't improved by Britain's ambassador, Lord Halifax. Halifax said Foreign Secretary Anthony Eden had complete confidence in Hull, of course, but wanted to suggest a few modifications. Japan should remove all troops and military equipment from southern and northern Indochina and halt all operations in China. America should continue all economic sanctions, including the embargo on oil, until all troops were withdrawn. Hull was astounded. Such "modifications" would gut the modus vivendi and assure its failure. To Hull it seemed that everyone, friends and foes, wanted everything without giving anything up.

Hull talked into the night with his Far Eastern staff about whether to offer the modus vivendi despite the Allies' objections and the slim chance of Japanese acceptance. He finally decided to present it the next day. "It would help emphasize for all time to come that we were doing everything we could to avoid war," Hull wrote, "and a Japanese rejection would serve more fully to expose their predetermined plan for conquest of the Orient." That was his plan when he went to bed on November 25.

During the night Churchill's reply to Roosevelt arrived. Of course the choice was America's, began the prime minister, and no one wanted another war. Then came a paragraph of artful nudges. "There is only one point that disquiets us," wrote Churchill. "What about Chiang Kai-shek? Is he not having a very thin diet? . . . We are sure that the regard of the United States for the Chinese cause will govern your action." The modus vivendi had postponed the huge issue of China for later because of its complexity. Churchill wanted it to be determinative.

That day in Tokyo several leaders addressed a mass rally. Their speeches were broadcast to the nation. Prime Minister Tojo urged the Japanese people to keep reducing consumption and to work harder on war production. "Our daily life is war," he said, "and we are all warriors even without guns." Suzuki, head of the planning board, said that Anglo-Saxon domination of the Far East would soon end because "the racial spirit of the Japanese people" had been aroused. Finance Minister Kaya echoed the call to "emancipate East Asia from the bondage of the white races. Japan," he said, "is standing at the threshold of her rise or fall."

When Hull rose on November 26 he saw Churchill's telegram. This message, plus the lack of support from other allies, abruptly changed his mind about offering the modus vivendi. Other news that morning hardened his decision. Stimson called around nine thirty to tell him that a Japanese convoy carrying an estimated fifty thousand troops had been sighted south of Taiwan, heading for Indochina. Roosevelt blew up at the news. Japan was sending more troops while supposedly negotiating their withdrawal. Hull told Stimson he was dropping the modus vivendi and would offer nothing in its place. But he changed his mind again, unwilling to give up completely. At the White House he told Roosevelt the bridge agreement was off the table but he would give the Japanese a comprehensive ten-point proposal. Roosevelt agreed. Neither Hull nor Roosevelt consulted Grew.

Nomura and Kurusu called on Hull at the State Department that afternoon. He handed them what became known as the Hull Note. As the Japanese read it, gloom settled over them. Among its ten points, the proposal required Japan to renounce the Axis, withdraw all military and police forces from China and Indochina, and give up any territorial rights there. It also required Japan to halt aid to any Chinese government except Chiang's. Such absolute demands could not be accepted by any Japanese government. The shame would be too great. Nomura and Kurusu saw the proposal for what it was: an ultimatum. As Hull later said, "We had no serious thought that Japan would accept our proposal of November 26."

Hull believed the talks had failed because Japan became progressively more unreasonable and inflexible—precisely how Japan saw America. He was incapable of imaginative diplomacy, but no one could fault his doggedness. He had met with Nomura dozens of times and given Japan every opportunity to comply with American requirements. But he had reached his limit. He was exhausted from sixteen-hour days of terrible strain, worsened by deteriorating health. The Magic intercepts had inflamed his chronic suspicions about Japan and destroyed any possibility of trust in Nomura and Kurusu.

Kurusu finally said that if this was the American answer to Japan's modus vivendi, he didn't see how any agreement was possible. Nomura, desperate, asked for a meeting with Roosevelt. Hull arranged it for the next day.

Early that morning Stimson called Hull to see how things had gone with the Japanese diplomats. "He told me now that he had broken the whole matter off," wrote Stimson in his diary. "As he put it, 'I have washed my hands of it and it is now in the hands of you and Knox—the Army and the Navy.'"

Later that day Hull and the Japanese envoys met Roosevelt in the Oval Office. The president, as usual, was cheerful and welcoming. He offered cigarettes, reaching out to light Nomura's. But Roosevelt had seen the intercepts and had run out of patience with Japan's two-faced diplomacy. When Nomura said he was disappointed that the United States had rejected Japan's latest proposal, Roosevelt pointed out that throughout the conversations, Japan's leaders had constantly flouted the central goal of peace by word and deed. Even in the last two days they had given bellicose speeches and ordered more troops to Indochina, poisoning any chance for negotiations.

Hull, his frustration boiling over, railed against Japan's slogans about co-prosperity and a new order, which everyone knew were smokescreens for "force and conquest by Japan and the domination by military agencies of the political, economic, social, and moral affairs of each of the populations conquered." Nomura and Kurusu could offer little in defense. Nomura wired Togo that the conversations couldn't succeed because of an obvious contradiction: "When we are endeavoring to arrive at a peaceful settlement, the high officials in Tokyo are, on the contrary, advocating the establishment of a new order."

The Hull Note delighted Hornbeck. On November 27 he wrote a memo for the State Department offering his "Estimate of Situation and Certain

Probabilities." As smugly vatic as ever, he assured Hull, "There is no warrant for any feeling on our part that the situation in the Pacific has been made worse" by refusing to make any concessions to Japan. In fact, he continued, "there is less reason today than there was a week ago for the United States to be apprehensive lest Japan make 'war' on this country." He felt so confident, he offered odds: five to one against war before December 15. He read things wrong up to the end.

The chiefs of the American army and navy were told to advise their commanders in Hawaii and elsewhere in the Pacific that negotiations had ended and Japan might strike at any moment.

On the same day that Hull delivered his note, the Japanese fleet weighed anchor in the Kurils.

"I can never forget the despair which overpowered me," wrote Foreign Minister Togo about his reaction to the Hull Note. "I could feel no enthusiasm for the fight thereafter." The Japanese army and navy, by contrast, were elated. The Hull Note obliterated the possibility of postponing war.

A liaison conference began on November 29 at four o'clock. The decision was for war against the United States, Britain, and the Netherlands. The group called for an imperial conference two days later to get the emperor's sanction. "Tell me what the zero hour is," said Togo. "Otherwise I can't carry on diplomacy." Nagano leaned over and said in a low voice, "December eighth." (In Hawaii, December 7.) Togo asked if he could inform Nomura and Kurusu. No, said the military, the diplomats would have to be sacrificed. Diplomacy was now a weapon of war whose purpose was to camouflage the surprise attack. Togo wired Nomura and Kurusu to keep talking to Hull as if Japan was still interested in negotiations. Magic intercepted the instruction.

On November 30 at a mass rally in Hibiya Hall broadcast to the nation, an announcer read a speech by Prime Minister Tojo. America and Britain must be "purged with a vengeance" from East Asia, he said, to make way for the sphere "decreed by Providence."

Against all evidence and most opinions, Grew insisted that the Hull Note wasn't technically an ultimatum since the sides were still talking. He spent several evenings at the Tokyo Club trying to persuade influential Japanese of his view in hopes they would carry it upward.

On the afternoon of December 1 the imperial conference approved the decision for war. The emperor didn't speak. That night Grew and Dooman met Count Kabayama at the Tokyo Club. The old optimist looked haggard. "I have just heard something which has made me sick," he said. He told them the cabinet had decided to end negotiations. As they talked, the evening editions came out carrying stories planted by the government that the conference had ruled for conversations to go on. "But my friend seemed crushed," wrote Grew. Kabayama's information, as usual, came from the inside.

The department sent Grew a confidential telegram advising him to make an evacuation plan. Despite all the ominous signs, including his own warnings about sudden strikes, he willed himself to look beyond these troubles. "I firmly believe that we shall surmount them, as we have in the past," he wrote in his diary. "I haven't packed a thing and do not intend to."

On December 2 Togo wired Nomura to destroy one of the embassy's two code machines and to burn the codebooks and all secret papers. He sent the same instruction to diplomatic posts in London, Manila, Hong Kong, and Singapore. In Washington, Magic decrypted the messages. An intelligence officer sent someone to observe the Japanese embassy on Massachusetts Avenue. Smoke and paper ash drifted skyward behind the embassy's walls.

On December 3 Grew attended the funeral of the Dowager Princess Kaya. The day was bitter cold. Since no overcoats were permitted in the imperial presence, beneath his formal attire Grew swaddled himself with two sets of underclothing and a sweater. Waiting for the hearse, he found himself standing next to the German ambassador. He eased the stiff moment by asking after Frau Ott. Grew, as dean, led the diplomatic corps to the altar to lay branches of japonica, then filed out just behind Prime Minister Tojo. Afterward, as people waited for their cars, Foreign Minister Togo approached Grew. "I am very much disappointed," he said.

"Let us continue the conversations in any case," said Grew.

That day, the Pearl Harbor Striking Force crossed the international date line toward Hawaii.

INFAMY

ON THE EVENING of December 6, Hull sent a triple-priority telegram to Grew. It contained a message from Roosevelt to Emperor Hirohito, and Grew was instructed to present the message at once. After reading it he understood why. But it wasn't delivered until 10:30 P.M. on December 7 (in Hawaii it was 3:30 A.M.). Grew didn't notice until the next day that the Tokyo telegraph office had held Roosevelt's message for ten hours. The army general staff wanted to ensure it arrived stillborn.

Roosevelt's note was another eleventh-hour attempt to rescue peace. Grew grabbed it. He asked Dooman to come to the embassy immediately. Urgent matters, even late at night, were guided by protocol. Dooman phoned Togo's private secretary and asked for a meeting at once between Grew and the foreign minister. It was set for midnight at Togo's house.

The embassy's Japanese chauffeurs had long since gone home, so Grew roused one of the under secretaries to drive him. They sped through the streets of Tokyo, once vibrant and sparkling with nightlife even at this late winter hour. But tonight, because of energy shortages and a ban on clubs and dance halls, the streets were silent, dark, and empty. The Tokyo Grew had grown to love had been smothered by dreariness and nationalistic fervor. He touched the telegram in his pocket and felt a flicker of hope. Perhaps this direct appeal from one supreme commander to another could avert disaster, or at least delay it.

The car pulled up to Togo's home at 12:15 A.M. The foreign minister, always dour and unreadable, seemed even more grim than usual. Grew apologized for inconveniencing him at such a late hour, but speed was essential. He asked Togo to arrange an audience with the emperor so he could present Roosevelt's pressing message. Then he read it aloud. Roosevelt opened by reminding Hirohito that their nations had been friends for almost a century. He was writing now, he continued, "because of the deep and far-reaching emergency which appears to be in formation"— specifically the flood of army, navy, and air forces pouring into southern Indochina. "Those developments contain tragic possibilities," wrote Roosevelt. If Japan would withdraw its forces from Indochina, the conversations between their nations could continue. Roosevelt ended by reminding the emperor that as leaders they had "a sacred duty to restore traditional amity and prevent further death and destruction in the world."

Togo curtly agreed to convey Grew's request and the president's message to the throne. By 12:30 A.M. Grew was back in his car.

Ten minutes later Togo called Lord Keeper Kido about Roosevelt's telegram. Kido said of course the emperor would see the foreign minister at any time of night on an urgent matter. He also advised Togo to inform the prime minister. When the translation was ready, Togo brought it first to Tojo. The prime minister dismissed it as irrelevant. "It's a good thing the telegram arrived late," he said. "If it had come a day or two earlier we would have had more of a to-do." He and Togo composed the emperor's reply.

At the palace Togo was shown in to Hirohito at 3:15 A.M. Togo read Roosevelt's letter. The emperor listened and approved the answer written for him. A palace official escorted Togo down dim corridors, quiet at this hour. Emerging from the Sakashita Gate, "I gazed up at the brightly shining stars," wrote Togo, "and felt bathed in a sacred spirit. Through the Palace plaza in utter silence, hearing no sound of the sleeping capital but only the crunching of the gravel beneath the wheels of my car, I pondered that in a few short hours would dawn one of the eventful days of the history of the world."

An hour later, his home telephone rang. The Navy Ministry was calling. The surprise attack on Pearl Harbor had been a complete success.

At 7:00 A.M. a phone call from Togo's secretary awakened Grew. The foreign minister wanted to meet as soon as possible. Grew, surprised at the emperor's fast response, dressed quickly and was admitted to Togo's residence at 7:30. Togo, stern and stiff, entered the room and slapped down a long memo. He said it had already been sent to Nomura in Washington for delivery to Hull. Japan was ending talks with the United States. Togo thanked the ambassador for his efforts and ushered him to the door. Grew assumed the memo was a bigger bump to be smoothed out later.

He returned to the embassy, shaved, ate breakfast, and dashed off his report about Togo. The morning was bright and warm for December. He was looking forward to a round of golf, and the bags were piled in the chancery foyer. Then someone rushed in with that day's *Yomiuri*, Tokyo's biggest daily newspaper. The headline shouted that the imperial empire had declared war on the United States and Britain. Grew didn't believe it—he had just left Togo—but the news was soon confirmed. Newspaper boys in the streets around the embassy were crying out special editions. Grew learned the details later. While he slept, 350 Japanese aircraft had killed more than 2,400 Americans in a surprise attack on the fleet anchored at Pearl Harbor. Other Japanese forces assaulted Guam, the Philippines, Singapore, Hong Kong, and Malaya.

A minor official from Togo's office came to the embassy seeking Grew but had to settle for First Secretary Edward Crocker. As embassy staff gathered to listen, the official began reading. The paper trembled in his hands. It was Japan's official declaration of war.

"This is a very tragic moment," said Crocker.

"It is," said the official, "and my duty is most distasteful."

At 11:00 A.M. the embassy's gates were closed and guarded by armed police. Other police entered and began searching every room for radios and transmitters. They walked past embassy staffers shoving documents into fires. Immediately after confirming the attack Grew had ordered his staff to start burning all codebooks and confidential correspondence. Papers blazed in every fireplace, in wastebaskets, in bonfires in the courtyard.

"The code room looked as if it had been gutted," wrote Grew, "with six or seven fires going in the baskets and pails of water emptied on the floor to prevent conflagration. The air was full of floating black pieces of soot and the courtyard, towards dusk, looked like a veritable inferno." He was relieved that the police let the burning proceed instead of seizing everything.

At 6:45 he and Alice invited the entire exhausted staff, some sixty people, to the residence for cocktails. They were prisoners of war.

On the evening of December 6, Togo sent a wire to Nomura telling him to expect a subsequent telegram in fourteen parts. The entire document was to be delivered to Hull at an exact time to be wired later. Magic intercepted the first thirteen parts disjointedly. Around nine thirty that night the decoded document was delivered to Roosevelt, Hull, Stimson, and Knox. The president read it and handed it to his advisor Harry Hopkins. When Hopkins finished, Roosevelt said, "This means war." Hopkins agreed.

The fourteenth part came through in the early hours of December 7, followed by several telegrams from Togo. One instructed Nomura to deliver the fourteen-part document at exactly 1:00 P.M. that day. The second thanked Nomura and Kurusu for their service. The third instructed them to destroy the remaining encryption machine and codebooks.

To American officials these final intercepts were ominous but opaque. Nothing in the long memo expressed a clear declaration of war. It said only that Japan's hope to "preserve and promote the peace of the Pacific through cooperation with the American Government has finally been lost." An attack seemed imminent sometime after 1:00, but where? The guesses were Southeast Asia, Singapore, Hong Kong, or the Philippines. Roosevelt, Hull, Stimson, and Knox received these last intercepts at about 10:30 that morning. In Hawaii it was 5:30 A.M.

At noon in Washington, Nomura called Hull's office and asked for an appointment at 1:00. But the Japanese embassy was slow to decrypt, translate, and type the lengthy document, so at 1:00 Nomura called back and asked to reschedule for 1:45, an hour almost to the minute after the first bombs would fall. Nomura and Kurusu finally reached the State Department at 2:05 and were shown into the diplomatic waiting room. At nearly the same moment, Roosevelt called Hull. "There's a report that the Japanese have attacked Pearl Harbor," he said.

Hull could barely contain his fury. He waited fifteen minutes before calling Nomura and Kurusu into his office. He didn't invite them to sit. Nomura gave Hull the memo from Foreign Minister Togo. The ambassador said he had been instructed to deliver it at one o'clock but decoding had delayed him. Why precisely one o'clock? asked Hull, seething. Nomura said he didn't know. Hull pretended to read what he had already seen. Kurusu noticed the hand holding the memorandum begin to shake with anger.

"In all my fifty years of public service," said Hull, "I have never seen a document that was more crowded with infamous falsehoods and distortions—infamous falsehoods and distortions on a scale so huge that I never imagined until today that any Government on this planet was capable of uttering them."

The Japanese envoys were shocked. Hull's virulent response seemed far out of proportion to the document they had just delivered. Nomura, recovering his composure, began to speak, but Hull held up a hand and jerked his head at the door.

The anxious bafflement of the Japanese diplomats deepened as they approached their embassy and saw an angry crowd gathering. After their car passed into the compound, police closed the gates and surrounded the grounds. That was when the envoys learned what had happened ninety minutes earlier.

Within days the American embassy in Tokyo had organized itself around the new reality. Embassy personnel could no longer live outside the compound. The police ordered the Japanese staff to leave. Eventually sixty-five people, including about fifteen women and one child, were living on the grounds. Beds, or at least mattresses, were found for all. The group organized chores. For dining they divided themselves into nine messes. Grew's table seated fourteen, and the staff rotated through. Food wasn't plentiful, but they didn't go hungry. Grew refused to leave his extensive wine cellar for the Japanese, so he assigned a staffer to keep all the messes well supplied. (Nevertheless, seven months of internment didn't exhaust his stock.) They were permitted enough fuel to run the furnace only two hours per day.

As cold set in, Grew's embassy staff worked hard to keep up morale. They organized tournaments for chess, bridge, badminton, mah-jongg, and Ping-Pong. They sang at the piano and played poker. Someone laid out a nine-hole chip-and-putt course on the embassy grounds, soon dubbed the

Greater East Asia Black Sulphur Springs Golf Course, a sardonic reference to the luxurious internment of the Japanese diplomats at the Greenbrier resort in White Sulphur Springs, West Virginia. Some of the holes required hitting over the embassy's three-story apartment houses. A running sweepstakes awarded a cash pot to whoever correctly predicted the next person to break a window. They celebrated Christmas and New Year's Eve. On February 19, 1942, Grew marked the tenth anniversary of his appointment to Japan, writing that he wouldn't have given up the experience "despite the final failure of my mission."

At first the days passed quickly. Grew worked in the mornings until eleven thirty, often on his final report to Hull, then played the embassy golf course and participated in all the tournaments. He read lots of books. He wrote letters of recommendation for the laid-off Japanese staff, many of whom had worked at the embassy for more than a decade, and he asked the State Department to keep paying the older workers during the war.

Aside from food, fuel, and the presence of insolent police who treated them like criminals, the embassy's main focus was repatriation. Grew met daily with the Swiss minister, the embassy's representative to the Japanese government. The prisoner exchange had to be coordinated between officials in Tokyo and Washington. Plans moved glacially. Grew lost a ten-dollar bet that they would be evacuated by Valentine's Day.

The war news, relayed by the Swiss minister, was always bad: Singapore, the Dutch East Indies, Borneo, Burma, Java, the Philippines, all fallen. Yet Grew's confidence never wavered. One day in April as he was saying goodbye to the Swiss minister, they heard explosions and low-flying planes. Looking out the windows from the hilltop residence, they saw big fires and black smoke on the horizon. The sky was filled with buzzing Japanese fighters and lumbering bombers trailed by black puffs of anti-aircraft fire. It was the Doolittle Raid, the first American planes to demonstrate Japan's vulnerability. Morale inside the embassy soared. At the Memorial Day celebration, the staff sang patriotic songs. Grew kept his Memorial Day tradition, reciting the Gettysburg Address by heart.

On June 18 the embassy staff and other Americans who had been imprisoned since the previous December finally boarded a ship. They left Japan behind on June 25. On July 20 the ships carrying the evacuees west from Japan and east from America rendezvoused at Lourenço Marques in Portuguese East Africa (now Maputo in Mozambique). The evacuees began switching boats to complete the exchange of prisoners.

As he strolled down the town's main street, Grew saw Nomura and Kurusu walking toward him on the opposite side. He had planned for this. They were old friends, but now their countries were at war. Grew had no intention of giving the news photographers a shot of them chatting amiably. Nomura spotted Grew and started over, smiling with his hand outstretched. Grew smiled thinly and doffed his hat but didn't slow down. The Japanese diplomats, in quick comprehension, raised their hats and passed by.

Like Grew, Nomura and Kurusu felt like failures, but Japan greeted them as heroes. They had an audience with the emperor, dinner at the palace, a luncheon with Tojo. At the luncheon Kurusu was seated next to the prime minister. Tojo turned to him and said that if Roosevelt's telegram to the emperor had arrived two or three days earlier, the war might never have happened.

BACK HOME

HULL SENT GREW barnstorming around the country, making speeches to boost the war effort—about 250 in his first year home. He made headlines everywhere, his audiences eager to hear his firsthand knowledge of the enemy. Despite his stressful decade in Japan, he remained fit, energetic, and dashing, though his hair had turned silver. His short book, *Report from Tokyo*, published the year he returned to the United States, quickly sold more than 100,000 copies. Grew aimed his message at several popular misconceptions. First, stop underestimating the Japanese. Japan's soldiers and people were tough beyond belief, willing to make any sacrifice for their emperor. Defeating them would be long and difficult. Second, the nation was controlled by fanatical militarists who must be crushed and rooted out before peace was possible.

In his earliest speeches and in *Report from Tokyo*, Grew also mentioned "the other Japan," the one he loved, marked by fine people and ancient culture. "They are not the people who brought on this war," he wrote in *Report from Tokyo*. "As patriots they will fight for their Emperor and country, to the last ditch if necessary, but they did not want this war and it was not they who began it." But those nuances didn't fit with the war-effort message, and the Office of War Information asked him to drop them.

In late December 1943, when the war's momentum had turned against Japan, Grew returned to his dual portrayal, drawing a line between Japan's military cult and its general population. He wanted to address how foreign powers should treat Japan after its inevitable defeat. Grew's new speech cut against wartime depictions of Japanese as uniformly brutal and deceitful, predicting that the majority would embrace peace. He also wrote that the militarists had deformed Shintoism and the emperor's role to suit their warmongering fantasia, and that once the military was destroyed, those ancient Japanese beliefs could be channeled to help rebuild peace. For expressing this perspective, Grew was attacked in the press as an appeaser and emperor lover. Hull canceled Grew's assignment as a speechmaker.

On May 1, 1944, Grew was appointed director of Far Eastern Affairs in the State Department. That same month, he published *Ten Years in Japan*, the edited diary of his time in Tokyo. The book spent more than two months on the *New York Times* bestseller list. In the foreword Grew wrote that readers would find fresh evidence of "the fanatical determination, the utter cruelty and brutality, of the Japanese military." But he added that the book would fail if it didn't also make clear that many Japanese had tried to restrain the militarists. "In the heat and prejudice of war," he wrote, "some will deny that there can be any good elements among the Japanese people." Yet those critics, he continued, didn't know or understand the Japanese. Such knowledge would be crucial for establishing a stable peace.

After Hull resigned from the State Department in late November 1944 because of illness, the new secretary of state, Edward Stettinius, appointed Grew his second-in-command as under secretary. In the tumultuous period between late December and the end of the war, Grew often served as acting secretary of state while Stettinius and his successor, James F. Byrnes, were away.

In 1945 the United States began carpet firebombing Japanese cities. The practice had outraged Americans when Japan deployed it in China, but after Pearl Harbor and years of horrific fighting in the Pacific, including countless stories of Japanese brutality, the tactic was now central to US military strategy. The bombing of Tokyo on March 9 and 10 incinerated the city and killed more than one hundred thousand people, still the deadliest aerial assault in history. By June 1945, American firebombings had destroyed more than sixty Japanese cities. The war was lost, but the Japanese fought on. Germany had surrendered in May 1945.

During spring and early summer of that year, Grew worked on a surrender plan for Japan with the secretaries of war and the navy, Henry Stimson and James Forrestal. President Harry Truman, who had assumed office in April after Roosevelt's death, intended to take a draft surrender proposal to his summit in July with Churchill and Stalin in Potsdam, Germany. American government and military leaders knew that invading Japan would be a horror show. Fanatical loyalty to the emperor meant that all Japanese, not just soldiers, would fight and die rather than surrender. Grew believed this nightmare could be avoided if the Japanese were presented with surrender terms allowing them to preserve the throne as an institution, even if Hirohito had to go. Otherwise, he warned, the Japanese were likely to fight to self-annihilation. Grew persuaded Stimson to imply in the draft that the throne could be preserved.

On July 16 all calculations changed when the first atomic bomb was detonated at Alamogordo, New Mexico. Invading Japan wouldn't be necessary. On July 26 Truman, Churchill, and Chiang sent Japan the Potsdam Declaration. (Stalin wasn't included because Russia hadn't yet declared war on Japan.) The clause about the throne had been deleted. The terms were unconditional surrender. "The alternative for Japan," warned the declaration, "is prompt and utter destruction." The atomic bomb wasn't mentioned.

With no assurance that the throne would survive, Japan's leaders couldn't agree to surrender. On August 6 the first bomb obliterated Hiroshima, killing at least seventy thousand people. Japan's hard-liners still refused to submit. On August 9 the second bomb demolished Nagasaki, killing at least forty thousand. The emperor finally insisted on surrender. The next day, the Japanese government agreed to the Potsdam Declaration—on condition that the emperor remain.

Secretary of State Byrnes and an assistant began writing the American response. They didn't consult Under Secretary Grew, but this time he wasn't as easy to ignore. Grew opened the door between his office and Byrnes's. "Mr. Secretary," he said, "if you are working on the Japanese note I believe I and some others could be helpful." Byrnes unenthusiastically invited him and Dooman in. Grew never documented their contributions, but the American reply didn't insist on abolishing the throne. Instead it placed the emperor under the authority of the Supreme Commander of the Allied Powers. That was vague enough to allow Japan's leaders to accept the terms of surrender.

In a national radio broadcast on August 15, 1945, most Japanese heard the reedy voice of their emperor for the first time. Hirohito announced Japan's surrender, though he never uttered that word. He also repeated some of the old self-justifications and self-delusions. "Indeed," he said, "we declared war on America and Britain out of our sincere desire to ensure Japan's self-preservation and the stabilization of East Asia, it being far from our thought either to infringe upon the sovereignty of other nations or to embark upon territorial aggrandizement."

On the day the emperor spoke, Grew submitted his letter of resignation. Byrnes asked him to stay on and return to Japan as political advisor to General Douglas MacArthur, commander of the occupation of Japan, but Grew declined. He and Alice "didn't want to face our old friends in Japan as a conqueror." Grew was also getting sidelined again in the department by colleagues who disliked his views about Japan and his adamant warnings about Soviet Russia and communist China. After serving his country for forty-one years, it was time to step aside. He was sixty-five.

Admiral Yamamoto Isoroku, architect of the Pearl Harbor attack and commander in chief of the Japanese fleet, died on April 18, 1943, after American code breakers intercepted his flight plans and US fighter pilots shot down his plane over the Solomon Islands.

Matsuoka Yosuke died of tuberculosis in 1946 while in prison awaiting trial as a war criminal.

Hiranuma Kiichiro was sentenced to life in prison as a war criminal but was paroled in 1952 and died that year.

Togo Shigenori was sentenced to twenty years as a war criminal and died in prison in July 1950.

Admiral Nagano Osami died in prison in January 1947 while awaiting trial as a war criminal.

General Sugiyama Hajime committed suicide by shooting himself in the chest ten days after Japan surrendered.

Prince Konoye Fumimaro committed suicide in December 1945 by swallowing potassium cyanide rather than reporting to prison as a war criminal. His grandson, Hosokawa Morihiro, served as prime minister from 1993 to 1994.

General Tojo Hideki shot himself in the chest in September 1945 as American soldiers arrived at his home to arrest him, but he survived. He was convicted of war crimes and hanged in December 1948.

Marquis Kido Koichi was sentenced to life imprisonment as a war criminal but was released in 1955. He died in Tokyo in 1977 of cirrhosis of the liver.

Emperor Hirohito retained his throne but was forced to renounce his claim of divinity and was stripped of all power. To some controversy, he wasn't tried as a war criminal. He died in January 1989 and was succeeded by his son Akihito, who was succeeded in 2019 by his own son and Hirohito's grandson, Naruhito.

Baron Harada Kumao died in Tokyo in February 1946.

Admiral Nomura Kichisaburo was elected to Japan's Diet in 1954 and served there until his death in 1964.

Count Kabayama Aisuke died in Tokyo in 1953, a year after working with Grew and the Rockefeller Foundation to establish the International House of Japan, which continues to foster cultural exchange and international understanding.

In November 1945 the congressional committee investigating the attack on Pearl Harbor summoned Grew for extensive testimony. The hearings were deeply partisan, with Republicans eager to find Democratic scapegoats. Senator Homer Ferguson interrogated Grew about a rumor that he had given Hull a final report from Tokyo. Grew couldn't recollect any such report. Ferguson pressed him. "I did not submit, I did not file any report, any written report," said Grew. Ferguson didn't let up, but Grew had eluded bigger sharks. He eventually recovered a vague memory of making notes for an oral report for Hull. Ferguson pounced, demanding those notes. Oh, said Grew, I destroyed them—everything pertinent was already in the record.

The investigators also tried to pin down Grew on when he knew war was inevitable. His answer was always the same: never. During his entire stay in Tokyo, he said, "I was doing everything in my power to prevent a war between the United States and Japan, up to the very end. . . . That is the only position that I think any diplomatic representative should take."

Grew used the Japanese royalties from *Ten Years in Japan*, which sold 75,000 copies there in a year and a half, to start the Grew Foundation in Japan, with Count Kabayama in charge. One of the founding officers was Admiral Nomura. The organization, now the Grew Bancroft Foundation, grants scholarships to Japanese students for study in American liberal arts colleges.

In retirement Grew split his time between his homes in Washington, DC, and New England. He wrote his two-volume memoir, *Turbulent Era*, published in 1952, and donated his extensive papers to Harvard. He played lots of golf and reveled in the company of his daughters and grandchildren. Alice died in 1959. Grew followed on May 25, 1965, two days shy of eighty-five. He never returned to Japan.

Acknowledgments

Erik Larson's *In the Garden of Beasts* centers on the American ambassador to Germany as Nazism began infecting that country. The book made me wonder: Who was our man in Tokyo?

Anyone who writes about Joseph Grew is indebted to Waldo Heinrichs, whose biography of him—*American Ambassador: Joseph C. Grew and the Development of the United States Diplomatic Tradition*—is approaching sixty years old but remains the most thorough and insightful account of Grew's full diplomatic life.

The staff at Harvard's Houghton Library, which holds the Grew Papers, were unfailingly helpful during my weeks there. I also benefited from librarians and holdings at Yale, Trinity College, Columbia University, Central Connecticut State University, and the Franklin D. Roosevelt Presidential Library and Museum, among other institutions. At the Library of Congress, Erin Sidwell and Eiichi Ito went beyond duty to track down an obscure photograph in a Japanese newspaper.

A generous grant from the NEH's Public Scholars Program, which supports nonfiction books about noteworthy subjects for a general audience, allowed me to keep working on the project full-time. My thanks to Clyde Milner and Brandon Kendhammer for letters of recommendation.

Lilla Lyon, Joseph Grew's granddaughter, graciously answered questions by phone and email. She also loaned me a rare book about life in the Tokyo embassy during Grew's tenure, and shared a home video of a 1939 family reunion that gave me glimpses of Grew in motion.

I was lucky with editors. Alex Littlefield recognized the book's promise and offered an advance that made it possible. He also extended my deadline twice without worsening my guilt, and he responded quickly to questions. My exacting and astute line editor, Ivy Givens, made suggestions and asked clarifying questions that demonstrated how well she understood the book she was helping to improve. Ivy, too, always had time for questions. Copy editor Margaret Wimberger's fine mesh caught some errors; any that got through are mine. I couldn't be happier with Mark Robinson's ominous cover design. Photographer Robert Benson did his best to refute the adage about silk purses and sows' ears. I'm indebted to my agent, Deborah Grosvenor, for guiding me into Alex's hands and for fruitful conversations during the long process of transforming an idea into a book.

As I began writing, I was inspired by the quiet bravery and devotion to truth, patriotism, and diplomacy displayed by some Foreign Service officers and foreign affairs specialists in the first impeachment hearings against Donald Trump: William Taylor, Marie Yovanovich, Fiona Hill, George Kent, David Holmes, Alexander Vindman, and Jennifer Williams.

I wrote much of this book during the isolating worst of Covid, which blocked most of the social outlets that help offset the solitude of writing. Family and friends became even more precious. I was especially grateful for my rejuvenating sons, Ben and Alex, and for the indispensable Friday night cocktail dinners with the Bensons. Confinement also would have been far more bleak without the joyful tomfoolery of our dog Whiskey.

My wife, Jude, somehow maintained her cheerful spirits and bolstered mine while enduring another book, a pandemic, and terrifying surgery. I'm so thankful that she brightens every day.

Notes

Abbreviations

Some primary sources are abbreviated as follows:

GP = Joseph Clark Grew Papers, Houghton Library, Harvard.

Diary = Joseph Clark Grew Papers, Houghton Library, Harvard, Diary, by year.

Clippings = Joseph Clark Grew Papers, Houghton Library, Harvard, Clippings, by year.

Letters = Joseph Clark Grew Papers, Houghton Library, Harvard, Letters, by year.

SH = *Saionji-Harada Memoirs.*

TE = Grew, *Turbulent Era.*

TY = Grew, *Ten Years in Japan.*

FRUS = US Department of State, *Foreign Relations of the United States Diplomatic Papers, The Far East,* with date and volume number.

FRUS, Japan = US Department of State, *Papers Relating to the Foreign Relations of the United States, Japan, 1931–1941,* 2 volumes, with volume number and date.

PHA = United States Congress, *Hearings Before the Joint Committee on the Investigation of the Pearl Harbor Attack.*

Prologue

1 *piece of driftwood:* TY, 535.

1 *suspected spies:* Among many sources, TY, 533–34; Tolischus, *Tokyo Record,* 335–52; and Argall, *Life with the Enemy,* 155, 247–48.

2 *cover in 1934:* Time, November 12, 1934; and John Hersey, *Life,* July 15, 1940.

2 *"up to the end":* TY, x.

3 *"national hara-kiri":* Grew to Hull, November 3, FRUS, Japan, 1941, vol. 2, 704.

3 *"for all time":* TY, 470.

3 *All endorsed:* Fearey, "My Year," 117–18.

3 *thirteen-page cover letter:* Dated August 14, 1942, and bylined aboard the MS *Gripsholm,*

which picked up the detainees in Portuguese East Africa and took them to New York. GP, Official Dispatch no. 6018.

4 *"America the Beautiful":* Argall, *Life with the Enemy*, 285.

4 *gray flannel suit:* Undated, Clippings, 1942.

4 *"to describe in words":* Grinberg, Paramount, Pathe Newsreels, Clip no. 502795685, Collection: Sherman Grinberg Film Library.

4 *black limousine:* Fearey, "My Year," 127–29.

4 *"About twenty-five minutes later":* Fearey, "My Year," 127–29.

5 *"come to tell us?":* TE, 1330.

5 *"are eliminated":* This and "not sent," GP, Official Dispatch no. 6018.

Chapter 1: The Mission Begins

7 *Prime Minister Inukai Tsuyoshi:* See Byas, *Government by Assassination*, 22–26.

7 *saw a headline:* TY, 4.

8 *Japanese press:* See Kakegawa Tomiko, "The Press and Public Opinion in Japan, 1931–1941," in Borg and Okamoto, *Pearl Harbor as History*, 533–49.

9 *"most adventurous of all":* TY, 3.

9 *"a poor fourth!":* Diary, August 1–19, 1934.

9 *"walking a treadmill":* Letter to Dewitt Wallace, June 12, Letters I–Z, 1937.

9 *Kipling and Stevenson:* TE, 6.

10 *across the East:* All references to Grew's trip to the Far East from his *Sport and Travel in the Far East*, especially 40–52, 241–45.

10 *desperate compromise:* TE, 7. Tours, telegram, ibid., 7–11.

11 *"damned to all eternity":* Diary, October 30, 1932.

11 *"Accept unconditionally":* TE, 10.

12 *"shoot a tiger":* TE, 13.

12 *imperial Japan:* Details about imperial summons and ceremony, TY, 14–17.

14 *Tributes to the emperor:* Details taken from Diary, April 29, 1933; Fleisher, *Volcanic Isle*, 20; Morris, 52–53; and Ruth Benedict, *The Chrysanthemum and the Sword: Patterns of Japanese Culture* (Boston: Houghton Mifflin, 1946), 151, among other places.

14 *Meiji Constitution:* Lu, *From the Marco Polo Bridge*, 8–10.

Chapter 2: Settling In

17 *"cruel infliction":* TY, 19.

18 *Ishii Kikujiro:* Diary, June 21, 1932.

19 *"each country to the other":* Grew's speech to the America-Japan Society appears in TY, 22–27.

19 *"jacking up":* TY, 11; and Diary, June 21, 1932.

19 *"routine motions":* Diary, June 21, 1932.

20 *"stirred up":* Diary, June 21, 1932.

20 *best-informed member:* Diary, November 14, 1933.

20 *capital of Kyoto:* TY, 18.

20   *Police Board:* TY, 27.

20   *Japanese policemen:* Diary, July 14, 1932.

20   *"without their approval":* TY, 14.

21   *July 4 celebration:* TY, 28–29.

22   *ordered liquor:* Liquori Buton, Letters K–Z, 1932; reimbursement, Letters A–J, 1932; Berry
     Brothers, Letters A–J, 1932; Fortnum and Mason, Letters A–J, 1932. Grew also imported
     lots of tobacco. He and Alice were heavy cigarette smokers with stained teeth. In 1936, for
     instance, Grew ordered three thousand cigarettes in March and another three thousand in
     June. He also had standing monthly orders for one pound of pipe mixture from a tobacco-
     nist in Boston and two boxes of cigars from Havana.

22   *"informative contacts":* TY, 31.

Chapter 3: Temblors

23   *heat and humidity:* Diary, July 9, 13, and 26, 1932.

23   *earthquake:* Diary, June 10 and July 2, 1932.

23   *Kabuki and Noh:* TY, 20–22.

24   *"like a giant up here":* To Anita English, August 18, Letters A–J, 1932.

24   *Secretary of State Stimson:* TY, 38.

24   *dire memo:* August 13, in Diary before entry for August 27, 1932.

25   *English breakfast:* Mentioned in Hotta, *Japan 1941,* 87.

25   *kimonos with fedoras:* For examples, see photography of Kuwabara Kineo in *Tokyo Shitamachi
     1930* (*Downtown Tokyo 1930*) (Tokyo: Kawade Shobo, 2006).

25   *several sizes too big:* Morris, *Traveller from Tokyo,* 31.

27   *Prince Chichibu Yasuhito:* SH, August 18, 1932, 419.

27   *telegrammed Stimson:* September 3, FRUS, Japan, 1932, vol. 1, 102; and TY, 39–41.

Chapter 4: A Rash of Espionage

29   *National City Bank affair:* "Gendarme's Fear Led to Tokyo Spy Furor," *New York Times,*
     September 12, Clippings, 1932.

29   *"ludicrous if it were not":* TY, 41–43.

30   *a rash of others:* "Spy Scare," *Japan Chronicle,* September 13, Clippings, 1932; rumors, *Los
     Angeles Times,* September, Clippings, 1932.

31   *"Saving face":* October 8, 1932, TY, 66.

31   *"earn our salary":* Diary, November 30, 1932.

31   *"double hell on the liver":* Diary, March 31, 1940.

31   *On those evenings:* Grew had an account at the Old Corner Book Store in Boston. His orders
     while in Japan ranged from eight books in 1937 to sixty-four in 1933. He was also a member
     of the bookstore's Crime Club and automatically received books not included in these totals.
     Letters, Old Corner Book Store, 1933–41.

31   *allowed him to pay:* Diary, February 11, 1933.

31   *"delicious celery":* December 3, Letters K–Z, 1932.

32   *never invited any Japanese:* Diary, October 14, 1932.

32   *electric lights:* TY, 50–51.

32   *partial deafness:* Diary, May 30, 1934.

32   *birthday lunch:* Diary, November 3, 1932.

32   *garden party:* Diary, November 8, 1932.

33   *"potential capabilities":* Diary, November 9, 1932.

33   *"Dear Frank":* November 12 and December 5, Letters K–Z, 1932.

33   *off to Washington:* Diary, November 11, 1932.

34   *honor of him:* Special supplement, warning to Inukai, in Storry, *Double Patriots,* 108–9, 121.

34   *wrote to Stimson:* December 3, Letters K–Z, 1932.

34   *"cold bath":* SH, mid-September 1932, 430–31.

34   *long speech:* Matsuoka's speech, *Japan Times,* December 7, Clippings, 1932.

35   *"Fushun massacre":* Diary, December 13, 1932. See also Rana Mitter, *The Manchurian Myth: Nationalism, Resistance, and Collaboration in Modern China* (Berkeley: University of California Press, 2000), 112–14. Mitter found Hunter's report in a Chinese archive. See also "Atrocity Museum in China Is Built Around Mass Grave," *New York Times,* November 2, 1975: "Little illuminated signs among the skeletons point out such things as: 'Mother holding baby,' 'Pregnant woman,' 'Baby wrapped in charred cloth' and 'Sabre wound in skull.'"

35   *Madrigal Club:* Diary, December 20, 1932.

36   *geisha dinner:* Diary, December 23, 1932.

Chapter 5: A Year of Small Fires

39   *called Shanhaiguan:* See FRUS, 1933, vol. 3, chap. 1, January 1–January 31, and chap. 2, February 1–March 19. Also Judgment of the International Military Tribunal for the Far East, Part B, chap. 5, sec. 1, 617–18, which notes, "Thousands of peaceful citizens were slaughtered."

39   *"choosing between the two":* Diary, January 27–February 10, 1933.

40   *astonishing tours:* SH, January 2–13, 1932, 494–502.

41   *"true course":* SH, undated, 489.

41   *fall of 1932:* Takahashi, Araki, and the budget, all from SH, November 15, 1932, 489–90; October 26, 1932, 456–57; November 1, 1932, 465; November 7, 1932, 470; and November 20, 1932, 477.

41   *army opposed it:* SH, January 13, 1933, 503–4.

42   *"the pitfalls":* SH, January 21, 1933, 505.

42   *were mixed:* SH, February 1 and 5, 1933, 517 and 521.

42   *"old and worn":* Diary, February 11, 1933.

42   *"unpleasant atmosphere":* SH, February 15, 1933, 537.

42   *Saito visited Saionji:* SH, February 15, 1933, 537.

43   *news to Stimson:* February 20, FRUS, Japan, 1933, vol. 1.

43   *"Manchuria belongs to us":* Details taken from Stewart Brown, "Japan Stuns World, Withdraws from League," United Press, February 24, 1933.

43   *"one* fait accompli *after another":* February 20, 1933, TY, 75.

43   *"peace machinery":* Diary, February 23, 1933, 78–79.

Chapter 6: Keeping His Shirt On

45 *letter of congratulation:* Diary, January 13–26, 1933, Miscellaneous.

46 *"'Oh Chwist' again":* Francis Perkins, oral history interview by Dean Albertson, 1955, part 8, 30, Columbia Center for Oral History, Columbia University.

46 *"do my utmost":* TY, 3.

46 *"State Department":* Hull, *Memoirs*, vol. 1, 270.

47 *thirty-second birthday:* Diary, April 29, 1933.

47 *"more propitious":* Diary, April 3, 1933.

47 *"national hero":* Diary, April 28, 1933.

47 *Saint Luke's Hospital:* Diary, May 10, 1933.

47 *incidents and rumors:* April 21, FRUS, 1933, vol. 3.

48 *"shirt on":* Diary, May 10, 1933.

48 *five-page letter:* May 11, Letters A–L, 1933.

48 *caused a stir:* Responses of Hull and Hornbeck in Franklin D. Roosevelt Papers, Papers as President: The President's Secretary's File (PSF), 1933–1945, Box 42, 18, and 19, Franklin D. Roosevelt Presidential Library, Hyde Park, NY.

49 *"cut-and-dried representations":* May 8, Letters A–L, 1933.

Chapter 7: Lovers and Patriots

51 *outbreak of suicides:* Diary, May 10–24, 1933, Miscellaneous Notes. See also Stuart D. B. Picken, "Militarism and Suicide in Japan: Meiji to Showa," June 16, 2016, *Think*, https://think.iafor.org/militarism-meiji-to-showa/.

51 *to Kurihama:* Diary, June 1, 1933.

52 *flew to news agencies:* Fleisher noted, "It is still a common sight to see a newspaper reporter leaving his office with a basket of carrier pigeons." In Fleisher, *Volcanic Isle*, 247.

52 *USS* Houston: Events, Diary, June 2–9, 1933.

52 *freshly paid sailors:* "Japan Entertains US Sailors," *New York Sun*, June 3, Clippings, 1933.

52 *Kojunsha Club:* Invitation, Diary, June 20, 1933.

52 *In his speech:* Diary, June 25–30, Miscellaneous Notes.

53 *"any of the stuffiness":* Cecil Lyon, *The Lyon's Share* (New York: Vantage Press, 1973), 92.

53 *"Can you blame me?":* TY, 94.

53 *"your situation?":* Cecil Lyon, interview by John Bovey, 1988, in "Excerpts from the Japan Country Reader," unpaginated, https://www.adst.org/Readers/Japan.pdf.

53 *"To have given three daughters":* TY, 95.

53 *five hundred dollars:* Letter to his brother Randolph, August 19, Letters A–L, 1933.

54 *"Easy days, these":* Diary, July 13, 1933.

54 *more information:* SH, July 11 and 13, 1933, 640, 642. Also *Time*, July 31, in Clippings 1933; and Storry, *Double Patriots*, 128–33.

54 *"threat of assassination":* Diary, July 18, 1933.

54 *Hollywood movies there:* Diary, July 15 and 16, 1933, 21–25.

55 *"fine care-free life":* August 20, Letters A–L, 1933.

55   *"no great developments":* Diary, July 25–September 5, 1933.

55   *minister of justice:* SH, August 29, 1933, 681.

55   *repeated as facts:* SH, August 25, 1933, 673–75.

55   *"patriotic crimes":* "Castle Named in Hearing of Japan Cadets," *Honolulu Star-Bulletin*, August 28, Clippings, 1933.

55   *Hundreds of thousands of people:* For public reactions to the trial see Byas, *Government by Assassination*, 23–58; Maxon, *Japanese Foreign Policy*, 90–92; Storry, *Double Patriots*, 108–10; Asahi, *Media, Propaganda, and Politics*, 55–57; and articles from August to October in Clippings, 1933.

56   *closing argument:* SH, September 11, 1933, 688–89.

56   *press campaign:* SH, September 25 and 26, 1933, 699 and 701.

56   *"the intelligent public":* SH, September 20, 1933, 697.

56   *a brainstorm:* SH, 1933, 713–15.

Chapter 8: Bison and Nazis

57   *Elsie's wedding:* TY, 104–6; and several articles in October in Clippings, 1933.

57   *Prince and Princess Chichibu:* Letters M–Z, 1933 (under Maeda).

57   *gold lacquer jewelry box:* This and royal gifts, Diary, October 13, 1933.

57   *young farmers:* Storry, *Double Patriots*, 134–35.

58   *Buffalo Week:* "Three Bison Arrive from America and Are Taken to Ueno," *Japan Advertiser*, December 5, Clippings, 1933.

58   *Kenkokukai:* Diary, December 5, 1933.

59   *continued to balk:* Diary, November 30, 1933.

59   *cabinet meeting on December 5:* SH, 755–56.

59   *"voice of resentment":* SH, December 8 and 10, 1933, 757–60.

59   *joint statement on December 10:* SH, December 10, 1933, 757–60.

60   *crown prince:* Diary, December 23, 1933.

60   *Harada visited the palace:* SH, December 23, 1933, 768–70.

60   *naming celebration:* Diary, December 29, 1933; and Fleisher, *Volcanic Isle*, 14–15.

60   *grant amnesty:* SH, December 29, 1933, and January 3 and 16, 1934, 769–70, 773, 780; and "Japanese Amnesty," Reuters, February 10, 1934.

61   *"Horrible threat!":* TY, 109–10; and Diary, December 28, 1933.

Chapter 9: A Deceptive Calm

63   *Suetsugu Nobumasa:* Diary, January 16, 1933.

64   *war and the navy:* "Tokyo Critic of US Rebuked by Hirota," *New York Times*, January 26, 1934.

64   *"whiter and whiter":* Diary, March 22, 1934.

64   *"consult the Department":* Diary, April 9, 1934. The art exhibit opened at the Boston Museum of Fine Arts in September 1936.

65   *dispatch to Hull:* April 6, FRUS, 1934, vol. 3.

65   *thirty-eight-page memo:* April 14, 1934, Franklin D. Roosevelt Papers, Papers as President:

The President's Secretary's File (PSF), 1933–1945, Box 42, 63–101, Franklin D. Roosevelt Presidential Library, Hyde Park, NY.

66   *explanations and revisions:* Several versions, *New York Herald Tribune,* April 19, 1934; and *London Times,* April 24 and April 30, 1934. See also Akira Iriye, "The Role of the United States Embassy In Tokyo," In Borg and Okamoto, *Pearl Harbor as History,* 108–113; and Heinrichs, *American Ambassador,* 199–202.

66   *bright side:* Diary, April 23, 1934.

66   *"for the statement":* Diary, April 28, 1934.

66   *"deep-rooted antithesis":* Letter to Prentiss B. Gilbert, May 17, 1934, TY, 135–39.

67   *"notorious course":* Hull, *Memoirs,* vol. 1, 279.

68   *J. Pierrepont Moffat:* November 24, Letters K–Z, 1934.

Chapter 10: A Cabinet Falls

69   *American Revue Troupe:* Diary, March 1 and 28, April 5 and 13, 1934.

69   *Tokyo Club:* Good description in Argall, *Life with the Enemy,* 181–85.

70   *too nude:* Young, *Behind the Rising Sun,* 228–29.

70   *secret meeting:* Saito's proposal to Hull, May 16, FRUS, Japan, 1934, vol. 1.

70   *"tremendous import":* May 16, FRUS, 1934, vol. 3.

71   *"a sort of underwriting":* Hull, *Memoirs,* vol. 1, 278.

71   *short memo:* June 15, FRUS, 1934, vol. 3.

71   *dispatch written by William Phillips:* June 18, FRUS, Japan, 1934, vol. 1.

71   *a letter to Phillips:* June 13, Letters K–Z, 1934.

72   *diplomatic dinner:* Diary, July 2, 1934.

72   *"Watch Admiral Okada":* Diary, July 4, 1934.

72   *"as an oracle":* Diary, July 4, 1934.

72   *information from Count Kabayama:* Diary, June 29, 1934.

72   *how it happened:* All references and quotations about the selection of the new prime minister, SH, July 2–9, 1934, 920–39.

73   *cabinet more sympathetic:* Diary, July 6, 1934.

73   *dinner dance:* Diary, July 6, 1934. Lispenard Crocker, wife of the embassy's second secretary, Edward S. Crocker, wrote about this evening: "At half past eleven most of the party went into the swimming pool which had been lighted very prettily for the occasion. As it was too much trouble to get back into a stiff collar and heavy foreign clothes after the swim, the Ambassador put on a complete Japanese costume, sandals and all. He looked perfectly superb and then we had our waltz with his kimono sleeves flying about and my lovely blue-green and yellow print gown whirling about me." In Green, *Foreign Service Marriage,* 377.

73   *Grew drove:* Diary, July 14, 1934.

Chapter 11: A Swashbuckling Temper

75   *immensely popular:* See Morris, *Traveller from Tokyo,* 72–73.

75   *"accurately":* Diary, August 17 and 29, 1934, and Clippings, 1934.

75   *Japanese never yelled:* Randau and Zugsmith, *Setting Sun of Japan,* 74.

75   *paper streamers:* Diary, September 20, 1934.

76   *a typhoon:* Diary, September 10 and 21, 1934.

76   *to be reduced:* All references to budget conflicts are from SH, 1934: September 25, 1021; October 3, 1026–27; October 31, 1045–47; November 2, 1053–55; November 10, 1058; November 20, 1064–66; November 22, 1067–69; November 26–27, 1069–70; November 30–December 9, 1077–86.

77   *telegram to Hull:* August 20: FRUS, 1934, vol. 3.

77   *Two weeks later:* October 31 and December 27, FRUS, 1934, vol. 3.

77   *statements about Manchukuo:* November 6 and November 24, FRUS, 1934, vol. 3.

78   *"to lower American prestige":* December 27, FRUS, 1934, vol. 3.

78   *"steeped in it":* Diary, November 30, 1934.

78   *"so parsimonious":* Letter to Lilla Grew Moffat, December 29, Letters K–Z, 1934.

78   *"Banzai Babe!":* "Japan: Tokyo Team," *Time,* November 12, 1934.

78   *"They're nice little":* Japan News-Week, March 2, 1935.

78   *with thirteen homers:* Nicholas Dawidoff, *The Catcher Was a Spy: The Mysterious Life of Moe Berg* (New York: Vintage, 1995), 91.

78   *played golf with Ruth:* Diary, November 2, 4, 5, 6, and 16, 1934.

79   *a kimono:* Dawidoff, *Catcher Was a Spy,* 90–95.

79   *assassination plots:* SH, October 8 and November 28, 1934, 1030 and 1074–75; and TY, 148.

79   *naval tonnage:* Diary, February 1, 1934.

80   *seventeen-page memo:* Sent by pouch December 27, 1934, but not received until the following year: January 16, FRUS, 1935, vol. 3. Also in TY, 145–52, and seventeen pages in Diary, Appendix to last section of 1934.

Chapter 12: Phobias

83   *dented fender:* Speeding delivery truck and observations about Japanese drivers, Diary, January 13; March 17–April 1, 1935; and April 14, 1936. See also Young, *Behind the Rising Sun,* 5, 7, 17, 87; and Tolischus, *Tokyo Record,* 6.

84   *Japanese perspective:* Diary, January 9, 1934.

84   *long analysis:* February 6, FRUS, 1935, vol. 3.

85   *Paranoia still thrived:* "Japan Still Holds American as Spy," *New York Times,* May 3, Clippings, 1935; and Diary, May 2 and 7, 1935.

85   *Australian woman:* Diary, May 2, 1935.

85   *An American actress:* Young, *Behind the Rising Sun,* 206.

85   *Trappist monks:* Young, *Behind the Rising Sun,* 206.

85   *Mark A. Pierce:* Diary, May 2 and 26, 1935; Young, *Behind the Rising Sun,* 203–10; and "Seizure as Spy Related," *Los Angeles Times,* May 31, Clippings, 1935.

87   *Salt River Valley:* See Jack August, "The Anti-Japanese Crusade in Arizona's Salt River Valley: 1934–35," *Journal of the Southwest* 1, no. 2 (Summer 1979): 113–36; Eric Walz, "The Issei Community in Maricopa County: Development and Persistence in the Valley of the Sun, 1900–1940," *Journal of Arizona History* 38 (Spring 1997): 1–22; and "Silence Preferred on Anti-Alien Bills," *Japanese Advertiser,* March 2, Clippings, 1935.

88   *skull flag:* Diary, February 21, March 1, and March 2, 1935.

88   *Japanese descent:* Copy of Japanese American's letter sent by Grew to Hornbeck, April 13, Letters A–J, 1935.

89   *"American-born Japanese":* Diary, February 12, 1935.

Chapter 13: A Purge, an Organ, Another Assassination

91   *"too nationalistic":* Diary, January 30, 1935.

91   *American Garden Club:* Diary, May 13 and 15, 1935.

91   *Mr. and Mrs. America:* Diary, May 29 and June 20, 1935.

91   *American movies:* Diary, January 25 and February 12, 1935.

92   *Radio broadcasts:* Diary, February 24 and May 14, 1935.

92   *"hours on the links":* Diary, November 28, 1934.

92   *bad air and damp:* Health issues, Diary, April 15 and 17, May 12 and 21, 1935.

92   *Count Kabayama:* Diary, July 5, 1935.

92   *were all worried:* SH, June 8, 1935, 1242.

92   *Okada also blamed:* SH, June 13, 1935, 1245.

92   *Harada questioned:* SH, June 13, 1935, 1245.

93   *goals of Okada, Hayashi:* SH, July 14, 1935, 1270.

93   *Minobe Tatsukichi:* For the Minobe affair, Byas, *Government by Assassination,* is helpful, 270–75.

94   *The minister of justice told:* SH, June 4, 1237.

94   *Saionji told Harada:* SH, June 20, 1935, 1252–53.

94   *any message:* Diary, July 18, 1935; and TY, 159–60.

95   *Aizawa found Nagata:* For a detailed account of the murder and trial, see Byas, *Government by Assassination,* 95–118; Harada's account, SH, 1288–92; report that Masaki encouraged Aizawa, ibid., 1302; attacks on Hayashi and resignation, ibid., August 28–September 4, 1935, 1300–4.

95   *into killing Nagata:* SH, August 28–September 4, 1935, 1302.

95   *campaign against the war minister:* SH, August 28–September 4, 1935, 1300–4.

95   *He did so:* SH, August 28–September 4, 1935, 1300–4.

96   *"to chase out the Genro":* SH, September 26, 1935, 1325.

96   *"promotion of Hiranuma":* SH, October 1 and 2, 1935, 1329.

96   *the Kwantung Army in North China:* SH in 1935.

96   *an autonomous government:* SH, October 28, 1333–34.

96   *"Army is merely bluffing":* SH, December 12, 1382–83.

96   *reinvigorated Grew:* TY, 160.

97   *Alice's health worried him:* Letter to William Phillips, August 21, Letters K–Z, 1935.

97   *"Of course this deafness":* Letter to Dr. Le Mèe, October 6, Letters K–Z, 1935.

97   *first airplane flight:* Diary, October 14, 1935.

97   *J. P. Morgan Jr.:* Diary, October 16, 1935.

97   *Thomas Lamont:* According to Ron Chernow, Lamont wrote the press release that the Japanese government used to justify the invasion of Manchuria. See *The House of Morgan: An American Banking Dynasty and the Rise of Modern Finance* (New York: Grove Press, 2010), 338–40.

97   *The Grews reached Italy:* Diary, November 12, 1935.

97   *"a few good waltzes":* Diary, December 12, 1935.

97   *"A grand voyage"*: Diary, December 16, 1935.

98   *America-Japan Society:* Text of America-Japan speech, Diary, December 17–31, 1935, Appendices.

98   *Japan's side of the picture:* Memo to Hull, December 24, FRUS, 1935, vol. 3.

98   *liquor order:* To Adet, Moss & Co., December 17, Letters A–J, 1935.

98   *army officers:* Storry, *Double Patriots*, 180–81.

Chapter 14: Insurrection

99   *trial of Aizawa:* Byas, *Government by Assassination,* 99–118.

99   *snow on Tokyo*: Diary, February 4, 5, 6, and 9, 1936.

100 *Grews were hosting:* Diary, February 27, 1936.

100 *and drop his cigar:* Diary, May 16 and 18, 1933.

100 *"several prominent men"*: February 26, FRUS, 1936, vol. 4.

100 *before dawn:* Principal eyewitness sources for the February 26 incident: Grew's Diary, TY, and Clippings, 1936; Byas, *Government by Assassination*, 119–28, and "Land of the Rising Sun," 295–300; Fleisher, *Volcanic Isle*, 69–98; Green, *Foreign Service Marriage*, 418–21; Young, *Behind the Rising Sun*, 161–68; and Harada, SH, 1423–32. See also Shillony, *Revolt in Japan*; and Storry, *Double Patriots*.

102 *"killing those responsible"*: Quoted by Byas, *Government by Assassination*, 124.

102 *"harrowing experience"*: TY, 171–72.

103 *No forceful measures:* February 27, FRUS, 1936, vol. 4.

103 *Hirohito was angry:* SH, 1427.

103 *thousands of leaflets:* Quoted in Fleisher, *Volcanic Isle*, 94; Byas, *Government by Assassination*; and Storry, *Double Patriots*, among others, using slightly different translations.

104 *124 were charged:* Numbers about rebels and sentences taken from Shillony, *Revolt in Japan*, 198–208.

104 *against the military:* February 29, FRUS, 1936, vol. 4.

Chapter 15: A Lull

105 *telegram arrived:* Diary, April 1, 1936.

105 *"perfect day"*: Diary, March 8, 1936.

105 *Barbara Wertheim:* "Japan: A Clinical Note," *Foreign Affairs*, April 1936, reprinted in Tuchman's *Practicing History: Selected Essays* (New York: Ballantine, 1982), 93–97.

106 *"In real bewilderment"*: Diary, April 14, 1936.

106 *emperor asked Saionji:* SH, March 3, 1936, 1432–34.

107 *three directives:* SH, 1442.

107 *"running amuck"*: Diary, March 18, 1936.

108 *"even stronger"*: Auer, *From Marco Polo Bridge*, 71.

108 *new plots:* SH, March 26, 1936, 1463–64.

108 *"possible but probable"*: Letter to Hornbeck, May 2, Letters A–J, 1936.

108 *excluding Japanese:* Diary, April 26, 1936.

108 *"inside his lapel"*: Diary, March 20, 1936.

108 *now have Romania:* TY, 185.

108 *"We are gratified":* Diary, April 3, 1936.

108 *Two nights later:* Diary, April 5, 1936.

109 *"depressed and thoughtful":* Diary, April 26, 1936.

109 *"my dreams":* Diary, April 21, 1936.

109 *William Phillips:* May 5, Letters K–Z, 1936.

109 *"two schools of thought":* Grew to Hull, April 30, FRUS, 1936, vol. 4.

109 *confidential memo:* Dated August 22, 1936, but found in Diary, November 27–December 13, 1936, Appendices.

110 *Russia and Manchukuo:* Diary, March 30, 1936; and letter to Hornbeck, May 23, Letters A–J, 1936.

110 *blatantly and rampantly:* Diary, May 6, 20, and 21, 1936; and Grew to Hull, May 6, FRUS, 1936, vol. 4.

110 *Terauchi told Foreign Minister Arita:* SH, April 25, 1936, 1486–87.

110 *similar worries:* SH, June 26, 1936, 1536–37.

Chapter 16: A Pact

111 *Harada often checked:* SH, 1936: July 2, 1542; July 8, 1545; July 27, 1553; July 31, 1559–60; and September 3, 1594.

111 *obstacles to progress:* SH, early August 1936, 1564–65.

111 *Saionji spoke to Harada:* And Harada's subsequent conversations at the palace, SH, August 3–7, 1936, 1565–67.

111 *guarantee conflict:* SH, September 2, 1610–11.

112 *"stupid men":* SH, September 5, 1611.

112 *tercentenary celebration:* Diary, September 12–18; and Clark A. Elliott, "Harvard University in 1936: The Scientific Dimension," *Osiris* 14 (1999): 153–75.

112 *"Alice seems better":* Diary, September 19–24, 1936.

112 *"exceedingly vague":* Diary, October 20–23, 1936.

112 *"a bully talk":* Diary, October 20–23, 1936.

112 *repeated requests:* Diary, July 10, 1936. The State Department's cheapness constantly irked Grew. For example, a service in Japan translated Japanese newspaper articles into English, a crucial source of information to the embassy, but the department refused to pay for it, so Grew shelled out ten dollars a month himself. See Diary, April 24, 1936.

113 *most important post:* Letter from Grew to William Castle, March 1, Letters A–H, 1937.

113 *"greatest landslide":* Diary, November 2–4, 1936.

113 *"ready for anything":* TY, 189.

113 *military budget:* SH, August 18, 1936, 1576; and Diary, long memo before January 1–15, 1937.

113 *"one damn thing after another":* Diary, November 28, 1936.

114 *"stand to gain nothing":* SH, November 22, 1936, 1636.

114 *Nazis infiltrated:* Fleisher, *Volcanic Isle,* 190; and Donald M. McKale, "The Nazi Party in the Far East, 1931–45," *Journal of Contemporary History* 12, no. 2 (April 1977): 291–311.

114 *Japanese first name:* McKale, 302.

114 *state of savages:* Diary, September 6, 1940; and Hotta, *Japan 1941,* 103.

114 *Suiyuan Province:* Multiple dispatches from consulates and US embassy in China, June 5, July 31, August 10, October 9, November 13 and 20, and December 6, FRUS, 1936, vol. 4.

115 *"to check them":* SH, December 4, 1936.

Chapter 17: *Kokutai*

117 *the next premier:* The process is detailed in SH, January 23–29, 1937, 1691–99.

117 *Several hundred reporters:* Young, *Behind the Rising Sun,* 180–83.

118 *The commander told Ugaki:* Young, *Behind the Rising Sun,* 183; and Byas, *Government by Assassination,* 139.

118 *banned Japan's newspapers:* Grew to Hull, January 29, FRUS, 1937, vol. 4.

119 *"risk of his life":* SH, 1695.

119 *"an experienced man":* SH, February 9, 1937, 1709.

119 *"military man":* SH, February 16, 1937, 1718.

119 *like Saionji, knew better:* TY, March 19, 1937, 206–7.

119 *Japanese expansion:* TY, March 19, 1937, 206–7.

120 *"volcano here":* TY, March 19, 1937, 207.

120 *those principles:* For helpful descriptions of *kokutai,* see Byas, *Government by Assassination,* 255–56, 277–84; Storry, *Double Patriots,* 5; and William Theodore de Bary, Carol Gluck, and Arthur L. Tiedemann, eds., *Sources of Japanese Tradition: 1600 to 2000,* 2nd ed., vol. 2 (New York: Columbia University Press, 2005), 968. All quotations from *Kokutai no hongi* are from the excerpts in de Bary, Gluck, and Tiedemann, *Sources of Japanese Tradition,* 968–72.

121 *feeling poorly:* Diary, March 4, March 9, April 20, and June 21, 1937.

121 *caviar soirees:* Diary, April 16, 1937.

121 *"inside out for her":* Diary, April 13, 1937.

121 *great crowds:* Saeki Chizuru, "Helen Keller's Civil Diplomacy in Japan in 1937 and 1948," *Japan Review* 27 (2014): 201–22.

122 *jades and vases:* Diary, April 16, 1937.

122 *"visualize her":* Diary, April 16, 1937.

122 *serious misunderstanding:* Grew to Keller, April 16, Letters I–Z, 1937.

122 *"unpleasant experience":* Dooman interview.

123 *citing his health:* SH, May 3, 1764.

123 *"I won't do it":* SH, 1774–75.

123 *Konoye again refused:* SH, May 30, 1937, 1784. Subsequent details about the formation of the Konoye cabinet, 1784–89.

124 *accost citizens:* SH, May 30, 1937, 1794.

124 *new government:* SH, June 6, 1937, 1794.

124 *"what is their reason?":* SH, June 7, 1937, 1799.

124 *the hotheads:* SH, June 24–31, 1937, 1810–17.

Chapter 18: Quagmire

125 *vowing to fight:* Peck to Hull, July 12, 10:00 A.M., FRUS, 1937, vol. 3.

125 *"almost independent region":* Peck to Hull, July 12, 6:00 P.M., FRUS, 1937, vol. 3.

125 *"pathetic decision":* SH, July 12, 1937, 1820.

125 *with indigestion:* SH, July 13, 1937, 1822.

126 *couldn't even get reports:* SH, July 15, 1937, 1825.

126 *"unimaginable crisis":* SH, July 15, 1937, 1825.

126 *widening the conflict:* SH, July 14, 1937, 1825.

126 *"clamoring boisterously":* SH, July 14, 1937, 1824.

126 *the navy minister:* SH, July 24, 1937, 1841.

126 *sowing doubt:* SH, July 21, 1937, 1838.

126 *mighty Imperial Army:* Diary, July 29, 1937; and Hugh Byas, "Tokyo Sees Hope of Averting War," *New York Times*, July 29, 1937.

127 *"Chinese people":* Byas, "Tokyo Sees Hope."

127 *official news agency:* Byas, "Tokyo Sees Hope."

127 *$30 million war appropriation:* Associated Press, bylined Tokyo, July 28, 1937, printed in *New York Times*, July 29, 1937, in Clippings, 1937.

127 *military bustle:* Diary, July 31, 1937.

127 *"Facts are elusive":* Diary, July 27, 1937. See also July 28.

128 *national flags:* Diary, August 21, 1937.

128 *ice-cold gimlets:* Diary, August 7, 1937.

128 *he met Hirota:* September 1, 1937, GP, Conversations, 1937–38; and Diary, same date.

129 *Hirota told the Diet:* September 5, FRUS, Japan, 1937, vol. 1, 364–67.

130 *"no time for pussyfooting":* Diary, September 20, 1937.

130 *rejected the claim:* Wilfrid Fleisher, "Japan Note Rejects U.S. Protest; Bombings at Nanking to Continue," *New York Herald Tribune*, September 30, 1937.

130 *"son was conscripted":* Argall, *Life with the Enemy*, 116.

131 *Edward Crocker:* Green, *Foreign Service Marriage*, 439.

131 *Crocker's wife, Lispenard:* Green, *Foreign Service Marriage*, 442.

131 *banned them:* Diary, preface to September 8–25, 1937.

131 *"young one":* Argall, *Life with the Enemy*, 116.

131 *cotton sashes:* Green, *Foreign Service Marriage*, 442.

131 *"series of victories":* Diary, Preface to September 8–25, 1937.

132 *"interests of the state":* See Kakegawa Tomiko, "The Press and Public Opinion in Japan, 1931–1941," in Borg and Okamoto, *Pearl Harbor as History*, 533–49. For pressures on foreign correspondents in Japan, see "US Press Coverage of Japan, 1931–1941," also in Borg and Okamoto, 511–32.

132 *newspapers from Shanghai:* Diary, Preface to September 8–25, 1937.

Chapter 19: Bombing, Regrets, Bombing, Regrets

133 *a final draft:* Details of Grew's work habits taken from several sources, including Emmerson, *Japanese Thread*, 94; Dooman interview, 62–63; and Fearey, "My Year," 110, 117.

133 *in his diary:* Diary, August 27, 1937.

134 *receive this well:* Hull to Grew, September 2, FRUS, 1937, vol. 3.

134 *"divergence of views":* Diary, September 3, 1937.

134 *confidential letter:* September 15, FRUS, 1937, vol. 3; and Letters A–H, 1937. Also October 2, FRUS, 1937, vol. 3.

134 *"entire mission in Japan":* Emmerson and Holland, *Rising Sun,* 50.

135 *"quick and violent":* Hull, *Memoirs,* vol. 1, 545.

135 *another foreign war:* Clippings, October 1937.

135 *"dulcet to the ears":* Hull, *Memoirs,* vol. 1, 546.

135 *called a meeting:* Diary, October 7, 1937.

135 *"tumbling about my ears":* Diary, October 7, 1937.

135 *his exasperation:* Diary, Preface to September 26–October 10, 1937.

135 *"thunderbolts are unwise":* November 2, Letters A–H, 1937.

136 *as soon as possible:* SH, November 15 and 16, 1937, 1932–35.

136 *"do as they please":* SH, November 11, 1937, 1927.

136 *Konoye was pitiable:* SH, November 11, 1937, 1927.

137 *exchanges with Hull:* November 16, 18, 19, and 23, FRUS, 1937, vol. 3. See also Heinrich, *American Ambassador,* 250–54; and Akira Iriye, "The Role of the United States Embassy in Tokyo," in Borg and Okamoto, *Pearl Harbor as History,* 118.

137 *army officers:* SH, December 8, 1937, 1962–64.

138 *"no longer bear it":* And reactions of Harada and Kido, SH, December 12, 1937, 1970–71.

138 *the white race:* See Grew to Hull, January 21, FRUS, 1938, vol. 4.

138 *"Fascist tendencies":* SH, December 25, 1937, 1983. See also Tachibana Takashi, *Tokyo University and the War* (ScholarWorks@UMass Amherst, 2017), 119–21, https://scholarworks .umass.edu/cgi/viewcontent.cgi?article=1000&context=history_oapubs.

138 *emperor was alarmed:* SH, 1984.

138 *with a cold:* SH, 1985.

138 *citizens in Shanghai:* Diary, October 25, 1937.

138 *Shanghai bombing accidental:* Diary, October 26, 1937.

139 *"further bombing":* Diary, November 27, 1937.

Chapter 20: The *Panay* Incident

141 *"black day indeed":* Diary, December 13, 1937.

141 *Hirota at 11:30:* GP, Conversations, December 13, 1937.

141 *Japanese foreign minister:* Diary, December 13, 1937. See also GP, Conversations, December 13, 1937, 3:00 P.M.

142 *considering options:* For a thorough discussion, see Douglas Peifer, "Presidential Crisis Decision Making Following the Sinking of the *Panay,*" *International Journal of Naval History* (November 5, 2018), unpaginated, http://www.ijnhonline.org/2018/11/05/presidential-crisis -decision-making-following-the-sinking-of-the-panay/.

142 *more belligerent:* See *The Secret Diary of Harold L. Ickes,* vol. 2: *The Inside Struggle, 1936–1939* (New York: Da Capo Press, 1974), 274–76.

142 *note from Hirota:* December 14, FRUS, Japan, 1937, vol. 1, 524–26.

142 *"floorboards of our car":* Diary, December 14, 1937.

143 *"insane that night":* Argall, *Life with the Enemy,* 117.

143 *"to do everything":* Grew to Hull, December 14, FRUS, Japan, 1937, vol. 1, 526.

143 *astonished embassy staffer:* Fleisher, *Volcanic Isle,* 204; and TY, 234.

143 *"two Japans"*: TY, 236.

143 *wired Grew on December 16:* FRUS, Japan, 1937, vol. 1, 524–26.

144 *"visibly upset"*: December 17, FRUS, Japan, 1937, vol. 1, 528–29.

144 *designed to anger Americans:* Diary, December 17, 1937.

144 *newsreel of the attack:* Universal Pictures, *Norman Alley's Bombing of the USS Panay*, available at https://archive.org/details/1937-12-12_Bombing_of_USS_Panay and https://www.youtube.com/watch?v=CsFSoYKtroo. See also the photoessay in *Life*, January 10, 1938, 11–17.

144 *"Rot!"*: Diary, December 20, 1937.

145 *Japan's official response:* Grew to Hull, December 24, FRUS, Japan, 1937, vol. 1, 549–50.

145 *"Things happen unexpectedly"*: Diary, December 24, 1937.

145 *United States Navy arrived:* Yarnell to Swanson, two telegrams, December 23, FRUS, Japan, 1937, vol. 1, 542–47.

145 *Hirota's note:* December 25, FRUS, Japan, 1937, vol. 1, 551–52.

145 *eyes were brimming:* TY, 239–40.

145 *"eminently happy day"*: TY, 239.

146 *nod toward Grew:* The Japanese knew better. Hatoyama Ichiro, leader of the Seiyukai Party and Grew's sometime golf partner, was visiting America as the *Panay* crisis unfolded. He said, "But for the painstaking efforts of Mr. Grew, the American Ambassador in Tokyo, the affair would not have been brought to such a speedy and amicable settlement. This is not my own view; it is the unanimous opinion of the officials of the Japanese Embassy in Washington and Consulates there." *Japan Chronicle*, February 3, 1938, Clippings.

146 *had to pack fast and go:* TY, 243.

146 *20,000 Chinese females:* Judgment of the International Military Tribunal for the Far East, chap. 8, 1012.

146 *weapons of their own:* For a fascinating and thorough account of this contest, see Suping Lu, *The 1937–1938 Nanjing Atrocities* (Singapore: Springer, 2019), 529–63. See also Byas, *Japanese Enemy*, 62–63.

146 *"answer for everything"*: TY, 243.

147 *Japan's consul general:* In TY Grew calls him "my informant," but his diary identifies him as Consul General Okazaki from Shanghai.

147 *"cases of rape"*: TY, 243–44.

Chapter 21: Strenuous Stasis

149 *swollen knee:* Diary, "Health, Weather, Sport," in January, February 1938.

149 *fourteen days that month:* Diary, "Social Life."

149 *"nearing 58"*: Diary, "Health, Weather, Sport," February 1938.

149 *eighty-one holes:* Diary, September 9–11, 1938.

149 *Konoye announced:* For the negotiations between Japan and Chiang, see Lu, *From the Marco Polo Bridge*, 23–28.

150 *long-term war:* About Konoye's decision to end diplomacy for total war, Heinrichs writes, "Of all the gross miscalculations of that tragic half-year this was the worst." *American Ambassador*, 274.

150   *international image:* SH, 1999–2001.

150   *millions of deaths:* Estimates of casualties in the Sino-Japanese war vary. Japan: military casualties between 2.5 million and 5 million, with 500,000 to 700,000 dead. China: military casualties between 4 million and 10 million, with about 2 million dead. Chinese civilians: 10 million to 20 million dead, 80 million to 100 million refugees. Numbers aggregated from *New World Encyclopedia*; *Pacific War Encyclopedia*; Wikipedia, "Second Sino-Japanese War," https://en.wikipedia.org/wiki/Second_Sino-Japanese_War; and Rana Mitter, *China's War with Japan, 1937–45: The Struggle for Survival* (London: Penguin, 2014).

150   *a note:* FRUS, Japan, 1938, vol. 1, 580–81.

151   *suspect intellectuals:* SH, February 8 and 15, 1938, 2017–18 and 2035.

151   *enemies of the state:* Young, *Behind the Rising Sun*, 238–39.

151   *Suetsugu did nothing:* SH, February 17, 1938, 2034.

152   *weak and indecisive:* Mentions just in May 1938: SH, May 9, 2108; SH, May 10, 2109; SH, May 11, 2113–14; Diary, May 18; SH, May 24, 2130.

152   *"hold the reins":* SH, April 1, 1938, 2067–68.

152   *"troubled us so much":* SH, April 23, 1938, 2095.

152   *"difficult thing":* SH, March 29, 1938, 2067.

152   *military attaché:* Storry, *Double Patriots*, 224–25.

152   *"They are worried":* SH, February 16, 1938, 2026–29.

153   *above the emperor's health:* SH, May 10, 1938, 2110–11.

153   *Harada arranged it:* SH, February 16, 1938, 2032.

153   *chancery's clock:* Diary, May 23 and June 6, 1938.

153   *rainy season:* Diary, June 30, 1938.

153   *ripped up trees:* Diary, August 31 and September 2, 1938.

153   *Chiang Kai-shek:* See Lu, *From the Marco Polo Bridge*, 34–35.

153   *"fire-eater":* Diary, Summary of May 1938.

153   *meeting with Ugaki:* Grew's dispatch about the meeting: July 4, FRUS, Japan, 1938, 1, 605–11.

154   *"I had to jack him":* July 4, FRUS, Japan, 1938, vol. 1, 611–19.

154   *civilian casualties:* Diary, following the Conversation with Ugaki, July 4, 1938.

155   *in July:* Diary, July 18, 21, 30, 1938.

155   *"major wars":* Diary, Summary of July 1938. For complaints about the renovations, see also July 19 and Miscellaneous Notes for July.

155   *about a skirmish:* July 25 and 26, FRUS, 1938, vol. 3.

155   *audience with the emperor:* SH, July 21, 1938, 2189–90.

156   *attack as self-defense:* See Hata Ikuhiko, "The Japanese-Soviet Confrontation, 1935–1939," in Morley, *Deterrent Diplomacy*, 129–78; Lu, *From the Marco Polo Bridge*, 38–39; and Harada's account, SH, 2196–206.

156   *secure peace there:* SH, September 6 and 8, 1938, 2243–44 and 2247–49.

Chapter 22: Appeasement

157   *dithered about it:* SH, August 21, 1938, 2228–29.

157   *"extremely ominous":* SH, August 22, 1938, 2229.

157   *Konoye's villa:* SH, August 28, 1938, 2232–33.

158   *Tomita Kenji:* SH, August 28 and 29, 1938, 2232–33, 2235.

158   *"comfort women":* Yoshiaki Yoshimi, *Comfort Women* (New York: Columbia University Press, 2001), 63.

158   *"for the nation and for society":* SH, August 29, 1938, 2233–34.

158   *"very disagreeable":* SH, August 29, 1938, 2233–34, 2236, and September 4, 1938, 2241.

158   *Yonai Mitsumasa and Vice Minister Yamamoto:* SH, September 4, 1938, 2237.

159   *"five feet high":* Diary, Summary of August 1938. See also Diary, August Conversations, Horinouchi, August 1938; Clippings, "Machine-Gunning of Downed Plane Denied by Kawai," *Japan Times,* August 29, 1938; and "Japan Rejects US Protest in Attack on Plane," *New York Herald Tribune,* September 1, 1938.

159   *complained to Harada:* SH, September 23, 1938, 2265.

159   *moving rightward:* SH, September 27, 1938, 2267.

159   *he told Harada:* SH, September 27, 1938, 2267.

159   *suffer invasion:* TY, September 30, 1938, 252.

160   *"utterly insane":* Diary, Summary of September 1938.

160   *assassination plot:* See Storry, *Double Patriots,* 236–37; SH, September 30, 1938, 2278–79; and Lu, *From the Marco Polo Bridge,* 39.

160   *agreed to stay:* SH, September 29, 1938, 2273–77.

160   *Hitler and Mussolini:* Details from Ernest O. Hauser, "Japan Still Looks to America," *New York Times,* July 3, 1938, in Clippings, 1938.

161   *offensive to Germany:* Fleisher, *Volcanic Isle,* 295–96.

161   *Grew didn't hear:* Diary, October 8, 1938.

161   *pact went dormant:* see Lu, *From the Marco Polo Bridge,* 45–46.

Chapter 23: A New Order

163   *Japan's highest official:* TY, 263–70; Diary, October Conversations, Konoye, October 3, 1938; and October 3, FRUS, Japan, 1938, vol. 1, 782–85.

163   *specific remedies:* October 6, FRUS, Japan, 1938, vol. 1, 785–90.

164   *"little children":* Argall, *Life with the Enemy,* 50.

164   *Mount Fuji:* Diary, October 26, 1938, and October Conversations, Sawada, same date.

164   *Lutheran Brethren mission:* Johnson to Hull, October 27, FRUS, 1938, vol. 4; and Gauss to Hull, November 3, FRUS, 1938, vol. 4.

165   *"truth is sickening":* Diary, Summary of October 1938; also in TY, 266.

165   *"American-Japanese relations":* Diary, October 29, 1938.

165   *about the evening:* SH, October 29, 1938, 2324; and SH, October 31, 1938, 2325.

165   *"vigorous terms":* Diary, October Conversations, October 31, 1938.

165   *"steadily occurring":* Diary, October 31 and November 18, 1938.

166   *addressed the nation:* November 3, FRUS, Japan, 1938, vol. 1, 478–81.

166   *old friends:* TY, 255–56.

166   *Japan's reply:* FRUS, Japan, 1938, vol. 1, 797–800.

167   *Eugene Dooman:* For Dooman's account, see December 9, FRUS, Japan, 1938, vol. 1, 801–06.

167   *Chiang's government:* For how this loan happened, see Utley, *Going to War,* 44–49.

167   *foreign correspondents:* Diary, Summary of December 1938.

167 *statement about China:* December 22, FRUS, Japan, 1938, vol. 1, 482–83.

168 *note to Arita:* December 22, FRUS, Japan, 1938, vol. 1, 630–31.

168 *December 26:* December 26, FRUS, Japan, 1938, vol. 1, 631–32 and 818–20. Account in Diary, December Conversations, December 26, 1938.

168 *that very day:* December 28, FRUS, Japan, 1938, vol. 1, 633–41.

169 *State Department's response:* December 30, FRUS, Japan, 1938, vol. 1, 820–26.

Chapter 24: Maneuvers from All Directions

171 *he would quit:* SH, January 5, 1939, 2411.

172 *"for the worse":* Hull, *Memoirs*, vol. 1, 627.

172 *"Jewish blood":* Green, *Foreign Service Marriage*, 475.

172 *territorial ambitions in China:* Memorandum of Conversation, February 17, 1939, and FRUS, Japan, 1939, vol. 1, 830–31.

172 *"means precisely nothing":* Diary, February 17, 1939.

173 *"peace of the world":* Diary, March 22, 1939.

173 *British ambassador:* Diary, February 20, 1939.

173 *"losing ground":* Diary, February Conversations, Iwanaga, February 21, 1939.

173 *"anxiety on that score":* Diary, April 16, 1939.

173 *pulled Dooman aside:* TY, April 19, 1939, 280–81; and Grew to Hull, April 20, FRUS, 1939, vol. 3.

174 *a long summary:* May 8, FRUS, 1939, vol. 3.

174 *assured Grew:* Diary, May 9, 1939; and Grew to Hull, May 10, FRUS, 1939, vol. 3.

174 *would be welcome:* Examples from Clippings, 1939: "Ambassador Grew is highly respected by all classes of Japanese," *Yomiuri Shimbun*, May 6; "Mr. Grew has resided in Japan now for some years and his knowledge of the country is indeed profound," *Hochi*, May 13.

174 *secret place:* SH, May 18, 1939, 2532–33.

175 *"all kinds of maneuvers":* SH, March 23, 24, and 28, 1939, 2480–81 and 2484.

175 *Ribbentrop asked Oshima:* For a description of the machinations about the German proposal, see Lu, *From the Marco Polo Bridge*, 49–54.

175 *retract this pledge:* SH, April 7, 1939, 2488–90.

175 *War Minister Itagaki:* SH, April 12, 1939, 2495.

175 *"we understood the Army":* And following passage, SH, April 20, 1939, 2499–2501.

176 *wouldn't budge:* SH, May 7, 1939, 2516.

176 *study the issue further:* SH, May 9, 1939, 2523–24.

176 *"quite severely":* SH, May 10, 1939, 2521–22.

176 *"will of the Emperor":* SH, May 23, 1939, 2536–37.

176 *"rumors were rampant":* SH, 2537.

177 *"agents of the rightists":* SH, May 25 and 27, 1939, 2538–40.

177 *"diplomatically nor politically":* SH, May 11, 1939, 2525.

Chapter 25: Abrogation

179 *a shopkeeper's:* Details about this evening were taken from the full account in Dooman's letter to Hull, June 7, 1939, Franklin D. Roosevelt Papers, President's Secretary's File, Box 43, Japan,

1939–40, 26–46, Franklin D. Roosevelt Presidential Library, Hyde Park, NY; Dooman to Hull, May 23, FRUS, 1939, vol. 3; and Dooman interview, 73–77.

181   *long memo:* June 7, FRUS, 1939, vol. 3.

181   *Hull's answer:* Dated July 7 but received in late July, FRUS, Japan, 1939, vol. 2, 5–8.

182   *he should say:* FRUS, 1939, vol. 3.

182   *Sumner Welles replied:* August 1, FRUS, 1939, vol. 3.

182   *Dooman wired Hull again:* Dooman to Hull, August 3, FRUS, 1939, vol. 3.

182   *in his Memoirs:* Vol. 1, 631.

182   *"not pursued":* TE, vol. 2, 1294.

183   *US protests:* July 17, FRUS, Japan, 1939, vol. 1, 662–64.

183   *"everything else is impossible":* SH, July 6, 1939, 2573.

183   *"as dumb as you":* SH, July 6, 1939, 2573.

183   *"brains that are bad":* SH, August 16, 1939, 2612–14.

183   *"difficult as at present":* SH, July 24, 1939, 2589.

184   *Gallup poll: New York Times,* June 16, 1939.

185   *"no enlightenment":* Hull, *Memoirs,* vol. 1, 638.

Chapter 26: Gallons of Vinegar

187   *forces at Nomonhan:* For a thorough look at Japanese-Soviet border conflicts, see Hata Ikuhiko, "The Japanese-Soviet Confrontation, 1935–1939," with an introductory essay by Alvin D. Coox, in Morley, *Deterrent Diplomacy,* 121–78.

187   *"like a dream":* SH, August 22, 1939, 2616.

187   *"encirclement":* For a thorough discussion of German-Japanese relations at this time, see Hosoya, "Tripartite Pact," 191–257.

187   *"beyond me":* SH, August 24, 1939, 2619.

188   *through his nose:* SH, September 2, 1939, 2628.

188   *several imperial commands:* Lu, *From the Marco Polo Bridge,* 59–60. See also SH, 2624–26; and Hosoya, "Tripartite Pact," 194.

189   *246 letters:* He counted them up later. Diary, October 26, 1939.

189   *"intercept her fleet":* Diary, June 13, 1939, in Leave of Absence section.

189   *"out of China":* Diary, September 12, 1939, in Leave of Absence section.

189   *all social strata:* Listed in his "Horse's Mouth" speech, FRUS, Japan, 1939, vol. 2, 23.

189   *off-the-record talk:* Text can be found in Diary, appended to Leave of Absence section, 1939.

Chapter 27: The Horse's Mouth

191   *"keen to get going":* Diary, October 10, 1939.

191   *"a ticklish business":* Diary, October 13 and 15, 1939.

192   *that misjudgment:* "The Background of a Historic Address," TY, 294–97.

192   *introduction of Grew:* Reprinted in Diary, October 19, 1939.

192   *"horse's mouth":* For the full text, see FRUS, Japan, 1939, vol. 2, 19–29. TY contains an excerpt, 289–94.

193   *walked out:* Grew to Hull, October 19, FRUS, 1939, vol. 3.

193 *"rocked"*: For these and other reactions mentioned in this chapter, see Clippings, October–November 1939.

193 *Hugh Byas:* Diary, October 21, 1939.

193 *Japanese press:* In addition to the clippings referred to above, see Kakegawa Tomiko, "The Press and Public Opinion in Japan, 1931–1941," in Borg and Okamoto, *Pearl Harbor as History*, 547.

194 *Kabayama told Grew:* Diary, October 26, 1939.

194 *"keep it rolling":* Diary, Summary of October 1939.

194 *"allowances must be made": Japanese Advertiser*, October 31, 1939, in Clippings.

194 *new reality:* Hallett Abend, "Army's Hand Seen in Tokyo Reversal on Talk with US," *New York Times*, November 1, 1939, Clippings.

194 *November 4:* Diary, November Conversations, November 4, 1939.

195 *Nomura told Harada:* SH, November 5, 1939, 2681.

195 *excuses and rationales:* Diary, November 6, 1939.

195 *"doesn't understand":* Diary, November 15, 1939.

195 *wrote to Roosevelt:* Franklin D. Roosevelt Papers, President's Secretary's File, Box 43, Japan, 1939–40, 99–103, Franklin Delano Roosevelt Presidential Library, Hyde Park, NY.

195 *analysis of the situation:* December 1, FRUS, 1939, vol. 3.

197 *December 4:* Grew to Hull, December 4, FRUS, Japan, 1939, vol. 2, 40–43.

197 *"fringe of the problem":* Hull to Grew, December 8, FRUS, Japan, 1939, vol. 2, 46–48; Hull to Grew, December 18, 190–92.

198 *echoed the first:* Grew sent several telegrams to Hull on December 18, all in FRUS, 1939, vol. 3; Hull's response to Grew about the treaty, December 18, FRUS, Japan, 1939, vol. 2, 190–92.

198 *Japanese newspapers:* For coverage by the Japanese press, see Clippings, December 16–22, 1939, and Grew's summaries of press coverage in Diary, December 19 and 20, 1939.

199 *sway him:* FRUS, 1939, vol. 3.

199 *naïve appeasement:* Memo to Hull, December 19, 1939, cited and quoted by Hosoya Chihiro, "Miscalculations in Deterrent Policy: US–Japanese Relations, 1938–1941," in Conroy and Wray, *Pearl Harbor Reexamined*, 55–56. Hornbeck also attacked Grew's long analysis of December 1, 1939: see Emmerson, *Rising Sun*, 82–84.

199 *"screws on the Japanese": Henry Morgenthau Diary (China)*, vol. 1 (Washington, DC: Government Printing Office, 1965), 75.

199 *December 20 he wrote:* FRUS, Japan, 1939, vol. 2, 193–94.

199 *Japanese government's sincerity:* Hull, *Memoirs*, vol. 1, 727–28. See also Jonathan G. Utley, "Cordell Hull and the Diplomacy of Inflexibility," in Conroy and Wray, *Pearl Harbor Reexamined*, 77–78.

199 *deliver Hull's response:* FRUS, 1939, vol. 3, and Diary, both December 22, 1939.

200 *"present cabinet":* Quoted by Hosoya, "Tripartite Pact," 200–1.

Chapter 28: Fire-Eaters on All Sides

201 *"the Emperor":* Kenneth J. Ruoff, *Imperial Japan at Its Zenith: The Wartime Celebration of the Empire's 2,600th Anniversary* (Ithaca, NY: Cornell University Press, 2010), 57.

202   *burning incense:* See Fleisher, *Volcanic Isle,* 156–60; and Havens, *Valley of Darkness,* 19–20, 33.

203   *"Extravagance is the enemy":* Quoted by Havens, 15. Details about scarcities and rationing were taken from many contemporary sources in addition to Havens, including Grew's Diary; Argall, *Life with the Enemy;* Young, *Behind the Rising Sun;* Emmerson, *Japanese Thread;* Fleisher, *Volcanic Isle,* Morris, *Traveller from Tokyo;* and news stories in Clippings, 1940.

203   *"all directions":* Morris, *Traveller from Tokyo,* 92.

204   *for being pro-Western:* SH, January 7, 1940, 2727–28. See also Maxson, *Japanese Foreign Policy,* 140.

204   *"I hadn't noticed any, yet":* Diary, January 26, 1940.

204   *"running away":* SH, January 11, 1940, 2733.

204   *wrote to Roosevelt:* January 16, Letters K–Z, 1940.

205   *"both sides of the fence":* To George D. Andrews, January 16, Letters A–J, 1940.

205   *Grew's paraphrase:* Grew to Hull, January 5, FRUS, 1940.

205   *In a sharp reply:* January 31, Letters A–J, 1940.

Chapter 29: A Golden Opportunity

207   *Saito Takao:* For a thorough look at Saito and the aftermath, see Earl H. Kinmonth, "The Mouse That Roared: Saito Takao, Conservative Critic of Japan's 'Holy War' in China," *Journal of Japanese Studies* 25, no. 2 (Summer 1999): 331–60. See also Lu, *From the Marco Polo Bridge,* 70–71. For a contemporary account, see Newman, *Goodbye Japan,* 169–70. Grew's account: Diary, Summary of February 1940.

208   *"obsequious diplomacy":* "Tokyo Bid to US on Trade Assailed," *New York Times,* February 7, 1940, in story picked up from Associated Press, Clippings.

208   *cleared the room:* "Japanese Deputies in Riot Against Arita," Associated Press, March 19, 1940, Clippings.

208   *Germany and Italy:* "Japan Sees Injury to Anti-Red Pact," *New York Times,* February 9; and "Japan is 'Certain' on European War," Associated Press, March 22, 1940, Clippings.

208   *W. Cameron Forbes:* February 19, Letters A–J, 1940.

209   *Harada heard:* SH, 1940: February 2, 2755; March 13, 2776; March 16, 2777, 2780; March 21, 2782–83; March 24, 2788; March 25, 2789–90; and March 29, 2792.

209   *"relationship of mutuality":* "Japan Declares It Is 'Protector' of East Asia," Wilfrid Fleisher, *New York Herald Tribune,* April 16, 1940, Clippings.

209   *managed to be outraged:* For example, quotations from *Nichi Nichi* and *Hochi* in "Japan Finds Hull in Accord on Indies," *New York Times,* April 19, 1940, Clippings.

210   *"blood boil":* Diary, April 23, 1940.

210   *"stupid blustering":* Hugh Byas, "Japanese Jingoes Stupid, Says Arita," *New York Times,* May 3, 1940, Clippings.

210   *"would be nil":* See Tsunoda, "Navy's Role," 246.

211   *"Germany and Italy":* "Japanese Army Says Nation Has 'Golden Chance,'" *New York Herald Tribune,* June 30, 1940, in Clippings.

211   *better relations:* See, for instance, Grew to Hull, June 3 and 4, FRUS, 1940, vol. 4.

211   *smacking of appeasement:* See his memo to Hull, May 24, FRUS, 1940, vol. 4.

211   *told Grew to resume:* Hull to Grew, June 3 and 12, FRUS, 1940, vol. 4.

211   *June 10:* Grew's memo about the meeting is in FRUS, Japan, 1940, vol. 2, 67–78.

212 *postponed a decision:* See Hata Ikuhiko, "The Army's Move into Northern Indochina," in Morley, *Fateful Choice*, 155–208.

212 *Arita now doubted:* June 24, FRUS, Japan, 1940, vol. 2, 88–89.

212 *staked out his:* FRUS, Japan, 1940, vol. 2, 89–92.

213 *virtual monopoly:* Grew to Hull, July 1, FRUS, 1940, vol. 4.

213 *"harmoniously around Japan":* Hugh Byas, "Japan Demands Vast Sphere in East Asia and South Seas," *New York Times*, June 29, 1940. Grew sent the text of Arita's speech to Hull: FRUS, Japan, 1940, vol. 2, 92–94.

214 *one headline:* "Threat to Europeans Seen," quoted in *New York Times*, June 29, 1940.

214 *"European oppression":* *New York Times*, June 29, 1940, in story picked up from United Press.

214 *foreign policy statement:* SH, June 29, 1940, 2860–61.

214 *"golden opportunity":* Among many clippings, see *New York Herald Tribune*, June 30, 1940, and *New York Times*, July 3, 1940, in Clippings.

214 *"taxes the imagination":* Diary, Summary of June 1940.

215 *"part of them":* Diary, June 11, 1940.

215 *"the other Japan":* Heading for Grew's account of the funeral in TY, 319.

Chapter 30: Hell-Bent Toward the Axis

217 *"like strong wine":* Diary, Summary of July 1940, and July 11, 1940.

217 *kill list:* SH, July 4, 1940, 2869.

217 *the conspiracy:* Fleisher, *Volcanic Isle*, 100.

218 *"Changing World Situation":* See Hosoya, "Tripartite Pact," 208–11; and also Tsunoda, "Navy's Role," 247–49. Tsunoda says the "Outline" became the basis for the army's policies and had "a fatal influence upon subsequent events."

218 *Japanese Americans in Hawaii:* See Greg Robinson, *By Order of the President: FDR and the Internment of Japanese Americans* (Cambridge: Harvard University Press, 2001), 77.

218 *"one of the most important":* Diary, July 11, 1940, and memorandum to Hull about the meeting, FRUS, Japan, 1940, vol. 2, 94–100.

219 *Grew wrote to Hull:* July 11, FRUS, 1940, vol. 4.

220 *"answering this inquiry":* SH, July 17, 1940, 2880–81.

220 *"hell-bent towards the Axis":* Diary, Summary of July 1940. Excerpts in TY, 324–25.

220 *a typhoon:* Diary, Summary of July 1940.

220 *"speaks for itself":* Diary, Summary of July 1940. He repeated his frustrations about the United States government's rigidity in the Summary of September 1940.

221 *Hull's appeasement:* See James C. Thomson Jr., "The Role of the State Department," in Borg and Okamoto, *Pearl Harbor as History*, 100–2; and Utley, *Going to War*, 97–100.

221 *"We shall see":* Letters A–J, 1940.

Chapter 31: The Matsuoka Hurricane

223 *hidden Dictaphones:* Argall, *Life with the Enemy*, 249.

223 *"secret protection":* For Young's account of his arrest and trial, see his *Behind the Rising Sun*, 284–320. See also Diary, February 21 and 24, 1940.

223 *hatred of the Western media:* Details taken from Clippings, 1940: *New York Herald Tribune,* July 20 and 23; *New York Times,* July 20; United Press, August 5; and Associated Press, August 19.

223 *James Cox:* Details taken from Clippings, 1940: Associated Press, July 27 and 29; United Press, July 30; *New York Times,* August 15. Also Fleisher, *Volcanic Isle,* 307–10; Diary, July 31, 1940; and Ernest R. May, "US Press Coverage of Japan, 1931–1941," in Borg and Okamoto, *Pearl Harbor as History,* 526.

224 *Censorship of the press:* Details taken from Fleisher, *Volcanic Isle,* 244–89; Young, *Behind the Rising Sun,* 135–39; and Havens, *Valley of Darkness,* 22.

224 *newspaper staffers' wastebaskets:* Fleisher, *Volcanic Isle,* 291.

225 *thick pillow:* Diary, Summary of February 1940 and July 31, 1940, among many references to Japanese surveillance and spying.

225 *"precaution against espionage":* Associated Press, July 30, 1940, in Clippings.

225 *Salvation Army:* Quotation from the Adelaide *Advertiser,* August 7, 1940. See also Newman, *Goodbye Japan,* 227–28.

226 *Western missionaries:* See *New York Times,* August 24, 1940, in Clippings.

226 *Rotary Club chapters:* See *New York Times,* August 9, and Associated Press, August 15, in Clippings, 1940; and Young, *Behind the Rising Sun,* 245–46.

226 *bow tie:* Fleisher, *Volcanic Isle,* 304.

226 *"dynamite pills":* Young, *Behind the Rising Sun,* 16–17.

226 *Karuizawa:* Fleisher, *Volcanic Isle,* 304–6.

227 *great changes: New York Herald Tribune,* July 21, 1940, in Clippings.

227 *In their first meeting:* Diary, July 26, 1940.

227 *"basket of fishhooks":* Hull, *Memoirs,* vol. 1, 902.

227 *"through with toadying": New York Times,* August 1, 1940, in Clippings.

228 *small town:* Details about Matsuoka's biography were taken from many sources, primarily Lu, *Agony of Choice;* Frederick Moore, *With Japan's Leaders: An Intimate Record of Fourteen Years as Counsellor to the Japanese Government, Ending December 7, 1941* (New York: Charles Scribner's Sons, 1941); and Fleisher, *Volcanic Isle,* 48–54.

228 *"fall into paradoxes":* SH, February 7, 1932, 249.

228 *might be dangerous:* SH, June 13, 1940, 2849.

229 *"troublesome fellow":* SH, August 8 and October 30, 1940, 2907 and 2991.

229 *insane:* SH, October 8, 1940, 2962.

229 *"ball of fire": New York Times,* August 22, 1940, in Clippings.

Chapter 32: Green Light

231 *"'green light' telegram":* Diary, Summary of September 1940; also in TY, 334. The telegram itself: September 12, FRUS, 1940, vol. 4.

232 *stirred up:* Diary, Summary of November 1940; and TE, 1229–33.

233 *"would finish us":* Quotations and details taken from Tsunoda, "Navy's Role," 256–60.

233 *navy ministers:* Tsunoda, "Navy's Role," 275.

233 *"liaison conference":* Liaison conferences brought together the government and the military to discuss important issues. The government was represented by the prime minister, foreign

minister, ministers of war and the navy, and usually the finance minister and director of the planning board. The Supreme Command was represented by, among others, the chiefs and vice chiefs of the army and navy. When a liaison conference reached a decision about a vital issue, an imperial conference was held to seek the emperor's sanction. The same representatives attended, plus the president of the Privy Council and the emperor.

234 *distressing their emperor:* Details taken from SH, September 20, 1940, 2946–48; and Hosoya, "Tripartite Pact," 243.

234 *imperial conference:* Details taken from Ike, *Japan's Decision,* 5–13. Ike's invaluable book translates detailed notes taken during liaison and imperial conferences in 1940 and 1941.

235 *Matsuoka's written reply:* In Grew memorandum to Hull, FRUS, Japan, 1940, vol. 2, 293–94.

236 *return to normal:* Grew to Hull, 295–96.

236 *thirty single-spaced pages:* Grew to Hull, FRUS, Japan, 1940, vol. 1, 697–98.

237 *"in the past":* Diary, September 30, 1940.

237 *was angry:* SH, September 20, 1940, 2946 and 2950–52, and October 20, 1940, 2977–80.

237 *"diplomatic blunder":* SH, October 26, 1940, 2989. After Saionji's death, Harada stopped keeping his diary.

237 *"it is inevitable":* SH, October 14, 1940, 2968–69.

238 *"go to war":* New York Times, October 5, 1940, in Clippings.

238 *"challenge to America":* Quoted in Lu, *Agony of Choice,* 215. See also *New York Times*, October 4, 1940, in Clippings.

238 *"forcible intrusion":* Diary, October 5, 1940.

238 *join the Axis:* United Press, October 7, 1940, in Clippings.

238 *"obstruct our order":* United Press, October 13, 1940, in Clippings.

238 *"profound shock":* Diary, October 11, 1940.

239 *do something about them:* FRUS, Japan, 1940, vol. 1, 883–84.

239 *Japanese press:* See clippings from *Asahi, Nichi Nichi, Hochi, Yomiuri,* and *Miyako* in early November 1940, Clippings.

239 *commercial airliners:* Grew to Matsuoka, November 8 and 14, FRUS, Japan, 1940, vol. 1, 700–2, 703.

239 *home for tea:* Grew to Hull, November 11, FRUS, 1940, vol. 4; same date, FRUS, Japan, 1940, vol. 1, 702–3; and TY, 350–51.

Chapter 33: A Grim and Cruel Year

241 *sunny and crisp:* Details taken from Diary, November 10 and 11, 1940; *New York Times,* November 10, 1940; and Kenneth J. Ruoff, *Imperial Japan at Its Zenith: The Wartime Celebration of the Empire's 2,600th Anniversary* (Ithaca, NY: Cornell University Press, 2010), 15–17.

242 *weren't quite dead:* United Press and *New York Times,* November 12, 1940, in Clippings.

242 *"Tripartite Alliance":* Quoted by Tsunoda, "Navy's Role," 15. See also SH, 1940: August 31, 2926–27; October 7, 2965–66; and October 23, 2985–86.

242 *wide latitude:* SH, November 18, 1940, 3006–7.

242 *Joseph Newman: Goodbye Japan,* 274–77.

243 *"policy of appeasement":* Diary, Summary of December 1940. Also in TY, dated January 1, 1941, 358.

243 *eleven issues:* Memorandum, Grew to Hull, and Matsuoka's oral statements, December 17, FRUS, Japan, 1940, vol. 1, 895–900, and vol. 2, 299; and Grew to Hull, December 17, FRUS, 1940, vol. 4.

245 *"both barrels":* Diary, December 19, 1940.

245 *The event:* Details about the luncheon come from Diary; Argall, *Life with the Enemy,* 211–12; Newman, *Goodbye Japan,* 277–78; and news stories dated December 19–20 in Clippings, 1940, as well as excerpts sent by State Department and recorded in Diary, January 10, 1941. For the full text of Matsuoka's speech, see *Japan Times Weekly,* January 1941, in Clippings.

246 *desire for peace:* For the text of Grew's remarks, see Diary, December 1940, Appendices. In TY Grew dates his luncheon remarks as January 18, 1941, but that's inaccurate. He attended a different farewell luncheon for Nomura that day at which he didn't speak: TY, 366, and Diary, January 18, 1941.

246 *all over the United States:* Details about press coverage in America and Japan taken from mid-December stories in Clippings, 1940.

246 *letter to Roosevelt:* Complete texts of Grew's letter and Roosevelt's response on January 21, 1941, in TE, 1255–60; texts with some deletions, TY, 359–63.

247 *fireside chat:* Diary, December 30, 1940.

248 *"grim and cruel year":* Diary, Summary of December; also in TY, dated January 1, 1941, 357.

Chapter 34: Darkening

249 *Barbers' Association:* "Japan Curtails Liberties in Conforming to Axis," *Christian Science Monitor,* October 1940, undated, Clippings. Hair oils mentioned by Morris, *Traveller from Tokyo,* 45; curls by Newman, *Goodbye Japan,* 256.

249 *dragonflies:* "Japan Curtails Liberties."

250 *"gendarmes are busy":* Diary, Summary of August 1940.

250 *"Forbidden is Compulsory":* Diary, Calls and Callers, October 24, 1940.

250 *"insincere skiers":* Quoted by Grew, Diary, February 28, 1940.

250 *played through it all:* For example, see Diary, Summary of August 1940, and September 22, 1940.

250 *"indeed critical!":* Diary, February 22, 1941; and TY, 373.

250 *"bridge of sighs":* Diary, February 6, 1941.

251 *became slang:* See Randau and Zugsmith, *Setting Sun of Japan,* 16.

251 GOOD NEWS!: Quoted by Grew, Diary, May 17, 1941.

251 *dominate the world:* "Japanese Irked by Privation of 'New Life,'" *Christian Science Monitor,* November 1940, undated, Clippings.

252 *black market produce:* See, for instance, Newman, *Goodbye Japan,* 215–16; and "Hoarding and Racketeering Blamed," Associated Press, March 14, 1941, in Clippings.

252 *"shady business":* New York Times, June 2, 1941, in Clippings.

252 *Tokyo reeked:* Hotta, *Japan 1941,* 168.

252 *get ugly:* Diary, February 28, 1941; and TY, 374–75.

252 *shoved out of line:* Diary, January 25, 1941; and TY, 367–68.

253 *"hope and treasure":* Abend, *Japan Unmasked,* 258. See also Tolischus, *Tokyo Record,* 257–58; Newman, *Goodbye Japan,* 237–39; and Hotta, *Japan 1941,* 212.

253 *to Manchukuo to marry:* See "Japan Lacks Labor Supply in Manchuria," Associated Press, December, undated, Clippings, 1941; and Randau and Zugsmith, *Setting Sun of Japan*, 22–23.

253 *"racial heterogeneity":* Diary, March 31, 1941.

253 *bodies into the military:* See Morris, *Traveller from Tokyo*, 50–55; and Newman, *Goodbye Japan*.

254 *Principles and Science:* "Foreign Language Students to Be Watched Against Entanglement in Espionage Nets," *Japan Times and Advertiser*, February 6, 1941.

254 *treatment of dissidents:* Diary, May 1941.

255 *lost patriots:* Randau and Zugsmith, *Setting Sun of Japan*, 13.

255 *Japan's imperial destiny:* "Japan to Conduct Emergency Talks," *New York Times*, January 8, 1941.

255 *"captured alive":* Translation by Hotta, *Japan 1941*, 93.

255 *heroic death:* Ruth Benedict, *The Chrysanthemum and the Sword: Patterns of Japanese Culture* (Boston: Houghton Mifflin, 1946), 36–37.

Chapter 35: A Rumor of Pearl

257 *"talk around town":* Diary, January 27, 1941. Grew's telegram to Hull same day, FRUS, 1941, vol 4.

257 *Japanese admiral:* Fearey, *My Year*, 108.

257 *reported it:* See also Grew's testimony about the rumor in PHA, part 29, 2145–46. For Third Secretary Max Schmidt's account, see his interview with Thomas F. Conlon for the Foreign Affairs Oral History Project of the Association for Diplomatic Studies and Training, February 26, 1993. Shortly after Pearl Harbor, Schmidt changed his name, probably to shed its Germanic roots, and became Max Bishop.

258 *"crammed with them":* Diary, February 21, 1941.

258 *more of the same:* Summaries of coverage in "Vernaculars Score Roosevelt Speech," unidentified newspaper, January, undated, in Clippings, 1941.

258 *"all who wish it":* Hull, *Memoirs*, vol. 2, 983.

259 *principally by Hornbeck:* Dooman interview, 63–64.

259 *"application was refused":* Dooman interview, 65.

259 *"behind the scenes":* Diary, January 23, 1941.

260 Failure of a Mission: Diary, January 1941, Miscellaneous Notes.

260 *"nibbling policy":* FRUS, 1941, vol. 5.

260 *"relationship with our country":* Quoted in "The Dutch Challenge to Japan," editorial, *New York Herald Tribune*, February, undated, in Clippings, 1941.

260 *Japan's demands:* For a partial list, see Consul General at Batavia to Hull, January 21, FRUS, 1941, vol. 5. For a summary of the negotiations through May 1941, see Lu, *From the Marco Polo Bridge*, 149–53.

260 *"White Peril":* Grew, quoting press coverage, Diary, February 6, 1941.

260 *Admiral Yamamoto:* See Tsunoda, "Navy's Role," 279, 284–85.

261 *Ohashi Chuichi:* Dooman's memo, FRUS, Japan, 1941, vol. 2, 138–43. Grew sent two dispatches about the conversation, on February 14 and February 26, both in FRUS, 1941, vol 4.

262 *credentials to Roosevelt:* Hull's memorandum about the visit: FRUS, Japan, 1941, vol. 2, 387–89.

262 *"one in a hundred":* Hull, *Memoirs*, vol. 2, 985.

262 *laid out his views:* See Hosoyo Chihiro, "The Role of Japan's Foreign Ministry and Its Embassy in Washington, 1940–41," in Borg and Okamoto, *Pearl Harbor as History,* 149–50.

263 *"bachelor establishment":* Emmerson, *Japanese Thread,* 96.

Chapter 36: Negotiations

265 *"I will not fail":* Emmerson, *Japanese Thread,* 39–41.

265 *"military moves":* Quoted from the Japanese newspaper *Asahi,* "Matsuoka Said to Have Threatened London with 'Counter-Measures,'" United Press, February 21, 1941.

266 *misquoted again:* "Oceania . . . Foreign Minister Believes White Race 'Must Cede' Vast South Pacific Area," United Press, February 25, 1941, in Clippings; Diary, March 2, 1941; and Tolischus, *Tokyo Record,* 52–54.

266 BY FORCE!: Details taken from Tolischus, 71–72; "Ousting of Whites from Asia Admitted to Be Japan's Aim," *Christian Science Monitor,* March–April, undated, Clippings 1941; and Argall, *Life with the Enemy,* 215.

266 *wasn't going well:* Diary and TY, 373–74.

267 *issue ultimatums:* "Japan Sets Terms," *New York Times,* February 28, 1941; and Tolischus, *Tokyo Record,* 52.

267 *roar of banzais:* Details taken from "Matsuoka Leaves Tokyo for Berlin," *New York Times,* March 13, 1941; and Tolischus, *Tokyo Record,* 57.

267 *amateur diplomats:* The definitive study of this group is Butow's *John Doe Associates.* For the talks between Hull and Nomura, see also Tsunoda, "Navy's Role," 20–105; and Hosoya Chihiro, "The Role of Japan's Foreign Ministry and its Embassy in Washington, 1940–41," in Borg and Okamoto, *Pearl Harbor as History,* 149–64.

268 *"repercussions in all directions":* April 5, FRUS, 1941, vol. 4. See also February 5, March 1, April 8, April 11, and April 18.

269 *into his puppets:* Details about Matsuoka's trip taken from Hosoya Chihiro, "The Japanese-Soviet Neutrality Pact," in Morley, *Fateful Choice,* 64–85; Lu, *From the Marco Polo Bridge,* 132–40; Newman, *Goodbye Japan,* 298–300; Diary, entries in March and April 1941, especially March 27 and 28, April 22, and Summary of March; Hotta, *Japan 1941,* 58–59, 65–67; and contemporary newspaper stories in March and April from Clippings, 1941.

269 *"outtalk Matsuoka":* Diary, April 10, 1941.

270 *"would trust me":* Steinhardt to Hull, March 24, FRUS, 1941, vol. 4.

271 *Sir Stafford Cripps:* Grew's account of this episode, with Churchill's questions, in Diary, April 22, 1941.

271 *Not possible, said Steinhardt:* Steinhardt's memos to Hull about it, April 12 and 13, FRUS, 1941, vol. 4.

271 *blather about* hakko ichiu: For Matsuoka's answer to Churchill, shared with Grew by Craigie, see Diary, April 24, 1941.

272 *neutrality pact:* Nonaggression and neutrality pacts differ slightly. The former includes a promise not to attack the pact's other signatories, while the latter includes a promise to stay neutral if one of the signatories is attacked by a third power.

272 *"drink anything":* "Victor's Welcome Given to Matsuoka," *New York Times,* April 22, 1941. Tolischus repeated his original story in *Tokyo Record,* 107.

272　*"frolicsome":* Steinhardt to Hull, April 16, FRUS, 1941, vol. 4.

272　*a genius:* Diary, April 22, 1940.

Chapter 37: Bad Drafts

275　*he was drunk:* Diary, May 2, 1941.

275　*"back to Tokyo":* Konoye, "Memoirs," 3987.

276　*"strange character":* "Emperor Showa's Monologue" (circa April 23, 1946), 336, Appendix U in Auer, *From Marco Polo Bridge.*

276　*liaison conference:* Details from Ike, *Japan's Decision,* 19–24; and Konoye, "Memoirs," 3987.

277　*"dangerous thoughts":* Details taken from Tsunoda, "Navy's Role," 73–74; "Matsuoka Visions Axis 'Millennium,'" *New York Times,* April 26, 1941; and "Japan Censors Matsuoka, Bans Copies of Talk," *New York Herald Tribune,* June 18, 1941.

277　*belligerence and deceit:* FRUS, 1941, vol. 4.

278　*"practical results":* Quoted by Tsunoda, "Navy's Role," 92.

278　*"expressed their disagreement":* Details from Ike, *Japan's Decision,* 24–27.

278　*"entire Draft Understanding":* Quoted by Tsunoda, "Navy's Role," 82.

280　*"high-handed representations":* Konoye, "Memoirs," 3991.

Chapter 38: Too Much Matsuoka

281　*"unprecedented exchanges":* Diary, May 14. His dispatch to Hull about the conversation and Matsuoka's letter: FRUS, Japan, 1941, vol. 2, 145–48.

282　*"far-reaching implications":* Grew to Hull, May 15, FRUS, 1941, vol. 4.

282　*Matsuoka replied:* Grew to Hull, May 17, FRUS, 1941, vol. 4.

282　*"dangerous thing":* Diary, May 14, 1941.

282　*smoking pipes:* Grew to Hull, May 19, FRUS, 1941, vol. 4.

283　*"degenerate Yankeedom":* Not included in Grew's memo to Hull but found in his Diary's account.

283　*needed from there:* Details taken from Ike, *Japan's Decision,* 36–43.

283　*opposed an agreement:* Konoye, "Memoirs," 3991.

284　*In confidential rush cables:* Konoye, "Memoirs," 3991.

284　*"prayerful thought":* Diary, May 25, 1941, though Grew wrote and sent the telegram on May 27: see FRUS, 1941, vol. 4.

284　*"no doubt":* Grew to Hull, FRUS, 1941, vol. 4.

285　*untrustworthiness:* See memos to Hull on May 5, May 15, May 23, May 24, May 26, and June 10, in FRUS, 1941, vol. 4.

285　*self-righteousness:* See Tsunoda Jun's summary of Hornbeck's attitudes, "Navy's Role," 93–95.

286　*"changed situation":* Quoted, Grew to Hull, May 31, FRUS, 1941, vol. 4. For reactions in the Japanese press, see Diary, June, Japanese Press.

286　*Matsuoka's new book:* New York Times, June 5, 1941; Tolischus, *Tokyo Record,* 135; and Lu, *Agony of Choice,* 275.

286　*Liaison conferences:* Ike, *Japan's Decision,* 47–53.

287　*American mission:* Diary, June 6, 1941.

287 *private residence:* Diary, June 16, 1941.

287 *incident was banned:* See account in Newman, *Goodbye Japan*, 151–54.

287 *conference on June 16:* Ike, *Japan's Decision*, 53–56.

288 *"not impossible":* June 19, FRUS, 1941, vol. 4; and TY, 393–94.

Chapter 39: A Betrayal and a Purge

290 *"greatly astonished":* Konoye, "Memoirs," 3993.

290 *"a new orientation":* Diary, June 23, 1941; and TY, 395.

290 *"justice and humanity?":* Quoted by Hotta, *Japan 1941*, 110.

290 *a barometer:* Memorandum of a Conversation, June 22, FRUS, Japan, 1941, vol. 2, 493.

291 *"summer of 1941":* Quoted by Lu, *From the Marco Polo Bridge*, 175.

291 *out of the war:* Grew to Hull, July 2, FRUS, 1941, vol. 4.

291 *Japanese blather:* "Japanese Premier Seeks Our Amity," United Press, June 29, 1941, in Clippings; and Ballantine to Hull, June 30, FRUS, 1941, vol. 4.

291 *"shed blood":* Ike, *Japan's Decision*, 60. All following details from the liaison conferences of June 25, 26, 27, 28, 30, and July 1 are from ibid., 56–77.

292 *"Changing Situation":* Provisions of the policy found in Ike, *Japan's Decision*, 78–79.

292 *"no room at all":* "Diary of Admiral Kichisaburo Nomura, June–December, 1941," in Goldstein and Dillon, *Pacific War Papers*, 147. His request to return to Japan, 151.

292 *"His Majesty the Emperor":* Details from Tolischus, *Tokyo Record*, 147–48.

293 *it shocked them:* Ike, *Japan's Decision*, 93–103.

294 *"great annoyance":* Konoye, "Memoirs," 3997.

Chapter 40: The Freeze

295 *Hull and Under Secretary Sumner Welles:* July 17, 18, and 19, FRUS, 1941, vol. 4.

295 *angry note:* FRUS, 1941, vol. 4. Also Diary, same date.

295 *a conciliatory response:* July 11, FRUS, 1941, vol. 4.

296 *Vichy government:* See Nagaoka Shinjiro, "The Drive into Southern Indochina and Thailand," in Morley, *Fateful Choice*, 209–40.

296 *"done to stop it":* Quoted in Hotta, *Japan 1941*, 152.

296 *might be severed:* "Diary of Admiral Kichisaburo Nomura, June–December, 1941," in Goldstein and Dillon, *Pacific War Papers*, 155.

296 *"telegram from Nomura is":* Tsunoda, "Navy's Role," 163.

296 *military occupation:* See Konoye, "Memoirs," 3997.

296 *summoned Nomura and Welles:* See Memorandum by Welles, July 24, FRUS, Japan, 1941, vol. 2, 527–30.

297 *asked Grew to call:* Memorandum by Grew, July 26, FRUS, Japan, 1941, vol. 2, 532–34; and TY, 409–10.

297 *"sound and sensible":* Diary, Summary of March 1941.

298 *buried it:* Hotta, *Japan 1941*, 146.

298 *too late:* Memorandum by Grew, July 27, FRUS, Japan, 1941, vol. 2, 534–37.

298 *"utmost stupidity":* TY, 413–14.

298 *stop any oil:* Utley, *Going to War*, 153–57.

298 *"eventual war":* Diary, Summary of July 1941.

299 *American response:* August 8, FRUS, Japan, 1941, vol. 2, 552–53.

299 *"use of force":* "Diary of Admiral Kichisaburo Nomura, June–December, 1941," in Goldstein and Dillon, *Pacific War Papers*, 163.

300 *"thrust upon us":* Hull, *Memoirs*, vol. 2, 1015.

Chapter 41: The Crossroads of Peace and War

301 *in Honolulu:* For details about Konoye's plan and the US reaction from Japan's perspective, see Konoye, "Memoirs," from which his quotations are taken, 3999–4003.

302 *retaliation for the freeze:* See memorandums by Hull and Grew, August 13 and 15, FRUS, Japan, 1941, vol. 1, 907–10 and 911–13, respectively.

302 *bulletproof vest:* Diary, July 5 and 8, 1941; and Tolischus, *Tokyo Record*, 147, 224–25.

303 *two statements:* FRUS, Japan, 1941, vol. 2, 556–59.

303 *"crossroads of peace and war":* Quoted in Lu, *From the Marco Polo Bridge*, 195.

303 *meeting at 4:00 P.M.:* Details taken from Diary, August 18, 1941, and the three dispatches Grew sent that day: FRUS, 1941, vol. 4; FRUS, Japan, 1941, vol. 2, 560–64 and 565. Parts of these are reprinted in TY, 416–21. See also Memorandum by Dooman, FRUS, Japan, 1941, vol. 2, 559–60.

305 *from a Japanese perspective:* Grew to Hull, August 19, FRUS, 1941, vol. 4.

306 *"hazardous futility":* Memorandum, August 15, FRUS, 1941, vol. 4.

306 *seven more pages:* August 21, FRUS, 1941, vol. 4.

306 *sneered at Grew's description:* August 27, FRUS, 1941, vol. 4.

306 *memos by Hornbeck:* August 30 and September 5, FRUS, 1941, vol. 4. See also his memo dated September 2, which makes the same points.

306 *several dispatches from Grew:* August 27, two on August 29, and August 30, FRUS, 1941, vol. 4; and August 29, FRUS, Japan, 1941, vol. 2, 579–82.

Chapter 42: Rough Winds and Waves

309 *White House:* See Hull's memorandum, FRUS, Japan, 1941, vol. 2, 588–89; "Diary of Admiral Kichisaburo Nomura, June–December, 1941," in Goldstein and Dillon, *Pacific War Papers*, 176–77; and Konoye, "Memoirs," 4002.

310 *resolve all issues:* This theory is suggested by Ike in *Japan's Decision*, 130; Tsunoda, "Navy's Role," 178–79; and Hotta, *Japan 1941*, 171.

310 *"would be useless":* In Memorandum and Comment from Grew, September 4, FRUS, Japan, 1941, vol. 2, 593–95.

310 *"some risk must be run":* Memorandum and Comment, September 5, FRUS, Japan, 1941, vol. 2, 600–3.

310 *the emperor:* Details from Konoye, "Memoirs," 4004–05; Ike, *Japan's Decision*, 133–34; and Hotta, *Japan 1941*, 172–75.

311 *imperial conference:* Details about the conference come principally from Ike, *Japan's Decision*,

133–63, and Tsunoda, "Navy's Role," 175–79, which quotes archival documents from Japan's National Defense Agency.

312   *winds and waves:* This translation by Hotta, in *Japan 1941*, 176.

313   *secret dinner:* Details taken primarily from Grew to Hull, September 6, FRUS, Japan, 1941, vol. 2, 604 6 (reprinted in TY, 423 28); Konoye, "Memoirs," 4005–6; and Dooman, Occupation of Japan Project, Columbia Center for Oral History, Columbia University, 1962, 93–99.

315   *"possibility of acceptance":* This and following quotations, Hull, *Memoirs*, vol. 2, 1028–30.

Chapter 43: Tense Silence

317   *"attempt at repartee":* Diary, October 19, 1941, repeated in TY, 459.

317   *telegram to Hull:* FRUS, 1941, vol. 4.

318   *radio address:* "Japan Informs Third Powers It Will Push On," *New York Herald Tribune*, September 19, 1941, in Clippings.

318   *friend and president:* September 22, FRUS, 1941, vol. 4.

319   *generic reply:* FRUS, 1941, vol. 4.

319   *"world intrigue":* "Germany Envoy Urges Japanese to Join in War," *New York Herald Tribune*, September 28, 1941, in Clippings.

319   *asked Grew to call:* September 27, FRUS, Japan, 1941, vol. 2, 641–45.

320   *actions as preconditions:* Hull, *Memoirs*, vol. 2, 1033.

320   *one hundred to one:* Hull, *Memoirs*, vol. 2, 1033.

321   *longest telegrams ever:* September 29, FRUS, Japan, 1941, vol. 2, 645–50; and TY, 436–42. See also Diary, Summary of September 1941.

321   *breathing room:* The British, too, made this argument to Hull, which Grew heard about and attempted to refute in a dispatch on September 30, FRUS, 1941, vol. 4.

322   *"the ripples":* Diary, Summary of September 1941.

Chapter 44: Kabuki

323   *Navy Minister Oikawa:* Details taken from Tsunoda Jun, who cites Japan's Justice Ministry Archives, "Navy's Role," 210.

323   *Yamamoto:* Details taken from Fujiwara Akira, citing documents from Japan's Military Office, "The Road to Pearl Harbor," in Conroy and Wray, *Pearl Harbor Reexamined*, 153. For a slightly different translation, see Tsunoda, "Navy's Role," 286–87.

324   *harshness with harshness:* For the oral statement and memo about the conversation, see FRUS, Japan, 1941, vol. 2, 655–61.

324   *kill the summit:* After the war Ballantine said, "Mr. Hull was the one that dissuaded him [Roosevelt] from going." Dooman, Occupation of Japan Project, 208.

324   *"about-face in its policies":* Quoted by Tsunoda, "Navy's Role," 211.

324   *conference on October 4:* Ike, *Japan's Decision*, 179–81.

325   *high-level meetings:* Many following details about this interval come from excellent reportage by Tsunoda, "Navy's Role," 209–18, and Hotta, *Japan 1941*, 194–202.

325   *"Kiyomizu Temple":* This well-known remark appears in Konoye's autobiography, *My Struggle for Peace,* and has been variously translated. The "Memoirs" used in the war crimes trial translates it, "Sometimes it is necessary for a man to risk his life in one leap," 4013.

325   *a ministers' meeting:* Details taken from Tsunoda, "Navy's Role," 221–26, and Hotta, *Japan 1941,* 202–4.

327   *strain of a war:* Details taken from Konoye, "Memoirs," 4009–10, 4013; Tsunoda, "Navy's Role," 226–31; and Hotta, *Japan 1941,* 208–11.

Chapter 45: A Deadline for Diplomacy

331   *still applied:* Tsunoda, "Navy's Role," 243–45.

331   *"piece of ice":* Dooman interview, 71.

331   *with the United States:* Details about Togo's background and first days from Togo Shigenori, *The Cause of Japan* (New York: Simon & Schuster, 1956), 46–60; and Kase Toshikazu, *Journey to the Missouri* (New Haven, CT: Yale University Press, 1950), 56. Kase, Togo's secretary, dedicated his book to Grew, "in appreciation of our old friendship."

332   *"dead horse":* "Diary of Admiral Kichisaburo Nomura," in Goldstein and Dillon, *Pacific War Papers,* 194.

332   *Tojo began:* Details taken from Ike, *Japan's Decision,* 185–87, and Togo, *Cause of Japan,* 123–24. For transcriptions of the liaison conferences during this week and useful discussions of them, see Ike, *Japan's Decision,* 187–207; Tsunoda, "Navy's Role," 255–64; and Hotta, *Japan 1941,* 219–29.

332   *"diplomatic activity":* Togo, *Cause of Japan,* 124.

332   *"clever strategy":* Ike, *Japan's Decision,* 191–92.

332   *On October 30:* Ike, *Japan's Decision,* 196–99.

333   *"Japanese history":* Appended to the Diary entry for October 17, 1941.

333   *two excited dispatches:* Memorandum, October 25, FRUS, Japan, 1941, vol. 2, 697–98; and October 26, FRUS, 1941, vol. 4. The dispatches don't name Kabayama, referring only to "a wholly reliable source," but the call sheet in the Diary makes clear that the source was Kabayama.

334   *"around the corner":* Diary, October 21, 1941.

334   *what didn't exist:* Tsunoda, "Navy's Role," 256–58. Details about the November 1 conference are taken primarily from Ike, *Japan's Decision,* 199–207; Tsunoda, "Navy's Role," 255–64; Hotta, *Japan 1941,* 230–38; and Togo, *Cause of Japan,* 141–42.

336   *rainbow was fading:* Kabayama's visit: FRUS, Japan, 1941, vol. 2, 700–1. Grew's analysis, 701–4. The quotations from this latter dispatch are from Grew's first-person version, in Diary, Summary of November 1941, instead of the State Department's third-person paraphrase.

337   *usual snark:* Memorandum, November 5, FRUS, 1941, vol. 4.

337   *"weakness or anxiety":* Memorandum, October 15, FRUS, 1941, vol. 4.

Chapter 46: Offerings

339   *loud knocking:* Details about Kurusu's appointment and preparations are taken from his memoir, Saburo, *Desperate Diplomat,* 50–59; Togo, *Cause of Japan,* 150–52; Diary, November 4, 1941; TE, vol. 2, 1378; and Grew's testimony about Kurusu in PHA, part 2, 601.

340 *victimhood for Japan:* Transcription of the meeting in Ike, *Japan's Decision,* 208–39.

341 *"hope for now":* Diary, November 5, 1941.

341 *"at any time":* Hull, *Memoirs,* vol. 2, 1056–58.

341 *Plan A:* Hull, *Memoirs,* vol. 2, 1058–59.

341 *"shortest possible time":* FRUS, Japan, 1941, vol. 2, 719–22.

341 *Hull's Washington apartment:* For the Memorandum, Oral Statement, and Commercial Plan, see FRUS, Japan, 1941, vol. 2, 731–37.

341 *This treaty, noted Hull:* Hull, *Memoirs,* vol. 2, 1061.

342 *"he was deceitful":* Hull, *Memoirs,* vol. 2, 1062.

342 *"no last word between friends":* "Diary of Admiral Kichisaburo Nomura," in Goldstein and Dillon, *Pacific War Papers,* 203.

342 *diplomatic rut:* For Hull's account of the meeting, see Hull, *Memoirs,* vol. 2, 1064–67. The memorandum about the meeting: FRUS, Japan, 1941, vol. 2, 744–50.

342 *Hull's apartment:* November 19, FRUS, Japan, 1941, vol. 2, 751–53.

343 *aid to China:* Ike, *Japan's Decision,* 251.

343 *"an ultimatum":* Hull, *Memoirs,* vol. 2, 1068. Memorandum about the meeting, FRUS, Japan, 1941, vol. 2, 753–56. In his memoir Togo called Hull's description of Plan B as an ultimatum "absurd." *Cause of Japan,* 149. See also the dismantling of Hull's description by Schroeder, *Axis Alliance,* 77–81.

343 *commercial attaché:* FRUS, 1941, vol. 4.

343 *similar dispatch:* FRUS, Japan, 1941, vol. 2, 743–44.

Chapter 47: Decision for War

345 *put the odds:* Hull, *Memoirs,* vol. 2, 1072–74.

346 *"automatically going to happen":* Hull, *Memoirs,* vol. 2, 1074.

346 *"almost unreal":* Hull, *Memoirs,* vol. 2, 1074–76.

346 *read and grumble:* For Hull's account of these interactions on November 24 and 25, see *Memoirs,* vol. 2, 1076–79.

347 *the next morning at nine thirty:* PHA, part 3, 1095.

347 *the next day:* PHA, part 3, 1080.

347 *"govern your action":* Lu, *From the Marco Polo Bridge,* 229.

348 *broadcast to the nation:* Tolischus, *Tokyo Record,* 304.

348 *heading for Indochina:* PHA, part 11, 5434.

348 *Roosevelt agreed:* Hull, *Memoirs,* vol. 2, 1081–82.

348 *Hull Note:* For the Memorandum about the meeting, Hull's Oral Statement, and the proposal, see FRUS, Japan, 1941, vol. 2, 764–70.

348 *As Hull later said:* PHA, part 11, 5392. In his *Memoirs* Hull denied that the note was an ultimatum: vol. 2, 1084.

349 *"broken the whole matter off":* PHA, part 11, 5434–35.

349 *Oval Office:* Details taken from Hull's Memorandum, FRUS, Japan, 1941, vol. 2, 770–72; and Saburo, *Desperate Diplomat,* 98–100.

349 *"a new order":* November 27, 1941, "Diary of Admiral Kichisaburo Nomura," in Goldstein and Dillon, *Pacific War Papers,* 210.

350   *"Certain Probabilities":* FRUS, 1941, vol. 4.

350   *"despair which overpowered me":* Togo, *Cause of Japan*, 188.

350   *at four o'clock:* Details taken from Ike, *Japan's Decision*, 260–62.

350   *"the zero hour is":* In his memoir Togo says that when he and Tojo were in prison after the war, Tojo told him he didn't learn until the war crimes trial that the Japanese fleet had hidden in the Kurils on November 10 and left for Hawaii on November 26. "The high command did not divulge its secrets even to the full general who was Premier and Minister of War," wrote Togo. "It is easy to conceive how other ministers were treated." *Cause of Japan*, 115–17.

351   *from the inside:* References to November 29 and 30 and December 1, 1941, from Diary and TY, 482–85, and from Dooman interview, 60. In TY Grew protects Kabayama's identity. Dooman, speaking in 1962, misremembers the date as December 5.

351   *all secret papers:* PHA, part 12, 215. The State Department instructed Grew on December 5 to destroy all confidential files and codebooks, but the message was transmitted first to Beijing via naval radio, evidently to save money. Grew never received it. See ibid., 743–44.

351   *Smoke and paper ash:* Steve Twomey, *Countdown to Pearl Harbor: The Twelve Days to the Attack* (New York: Simon & Schuster, 2016), 191.

351   *Dowager Princess Kaya:* Diary and TY, 485.

Chapter 48: Infamy

353   *triple-priority telegram to Grew:* Details taken from TY, 486–89.

354   *Ten minutes later:* "Extracts from the Diary of Marquis Koichi Kido," in Goldstein and Dillon, *Pacific War Papers*, 134.

354   *dismissed it as irrelevant:* Togo, *Cause of Japan*, 220–23.

355   *"veritable inferno":* Diary, December 8, 1941.

356   *fourteen parts:* PHA, part 12, 238, then fourteen-part message, 239–45.

356   *"This means war":* PHA, part 10, 4660–64.

356   *"finally been lost":* PHA, part 12, 245, 248.

356   *Roosevelt called Hull:* Details from Hull's account in his *Memoirs*, vol. 2, 1095–97; "Diary of Admiral Kichisaburo Nomura," in Goldstein and Dillon, *Pacific War Papers*, 213; and Kurusu's memoir, *Desperate Diplomat*, 122–23.

357   *new reality:* Details about the internment taken from Diary; TY, 498–532; and Fearey, *My Year*.

359   *Grew saw Nomura:* Details from Kurusu, *Desperate Diplomat*, 141; and Fearey (who was walking with Grew), *My Year*, 125.

359   *never have happened:* Saburo, *Desperate Diplomat*, 143–44.

Chapter 49: Back Home

361   *first year home:* Details from Heinrichs, *American Ambassador*, 362–64. For the speeches, see GP, Speeches, 1942–45.

361   *100,000 copies:* Nakamura, *Japanese Monarchy*, 9.

361   *popular misconceptions:* TE, vol. 2, 1380; and Grew, *Report from Tokyo*.

361   *"brought on this war":* Grew, *Report from Tokyo*, 9–10.

361   *dual portrayal:* December 29, 1943. Text: "War and Post-War Problems in the Far East," *Department of State Bulletin* 10 (January–June 1944): 8–20. For responses to the speech, see Heinrichs, *American Ambassador,* 365–66, and Nakamura, *Japanese Monarchy,* 22–34.

362   *bestseller list:* Heinrichs, *American Ambassador,* 368–69.

363   *seventy thousand people.* Estimates of those killed at Hiroshima and Nagasaki vary widely— for Hiroshima from 70,000 to 140,000, for Nagasaki from 40,000 to 70,000. See Alex Wellerstein, "Counting the Dead at Hiroshima and Nagasaki," *Bulletin of the Atomic Scientists,* August 4, 2020, https://thebulletin.org/2020/08/counting-the-dead-at-hiroshima-and -nagasaki/.

363   *"could be helpful":* Quoted in Heinrichs, *American Ambassador,* 378.

364   *for the first time:* The text is widely available, sometimes called the Jewel Voice Broadcast. Many Japanese didn't accept responsibility for the war, and some still don't, seeing Japan as the victim. In October 1978 fourteen Japanese who had been convicted as Class A war criminals, including Tojo and Matsuoka, were enshrined as "Showa martyrs" in the Yasukuni Shrine. Nationalists remain influential in Japanese politics. For an enlightening discussion, see Ian Buruma, *The Wages of Guilt: Memories of War in Germany and Japan* (Farrar Straus & Giroux, 1994).

364   *"as a conqueror":* Letter to Elizabeth Sturgis Lyon, reprinted in TE, 1522.

365   *extensive testimony:* PHA, part 2, 560–603 and 615–770. For Ferguson, see 697–99.

365   *"to the very end":* PHA, part 2, 617.

366   *75,000 copies:* Japan Wikipedia: https://ja.wikipedia.org/wiki/%E3%82%B0%E3%83%AB %E3%83%BC%E3%83%BB%E3%83%90%E3%83%B3%E3%82%AF%E3%83%AD%E3%83% 95%E3%83%88%E5%9F%BA%E9%87%91.

Selected Bibliography

Abend, Hallett. *Japan Unmasked.* New York: Ives Washburn, 1941.

Argall, Phyllis. *My Life with the Enemy.* New York: Macmillan, 1944.

Asahi Shimbun. *Media, Propaganda, and Politics in Twentieth Century Japan.* London: Bloomsbury, 2015.

Auer, James E., ed. *From Marco Polo Bridge to Pearl Harbor: Who Was Responsible?* Tokyo: Yomiuri Shimbun, 2006.

Barnhart, Michael A. *Japan Prepares for Total War: The Search for Economic Security, 1919–1941.* Ithaca, NY: Cornell University Press, 1987.

Borg, Dorothy, and Shumpei Okamoto, eds. *Pearl Harbor as History: Japanese-American Relations, 1931–1941.* New York: Columbia University Press, 1973.

Burns, Richard Dean, and Edward M. Bennett, eds. *Diplomats in Crisis: United States-Chinese-Japanese Relations, 1919–1941.* Santa Barbara, CA: ABC-CLIO, 1974.

Butow, Robert J. C. *The John Doe Associates: Backdoor Diplomacy for Peace, 1941.* Stanford, CA: Stanford University Press, 1974.

Byas, Hugh. *Government by Assassination.* New York: Knopf, 1942.

———. *The Japanese Enemy, His Power and His Vulnerability.* New York: Knopf, 1942.

———. "Land of the Rising Sun." In *We Saw It Happen: The News Behind the News That's Fit to Print.* Edited by Hanson Baldwin and Shepard Stone. New York: Simon & Schuster, 1938.

Columbia Center for Oral History. "Occupation of Japan Project: Oral History, 1960–2003." New York: Columbia University, 1970.

Conroy, Hilary, and Harry Wray, eds. *Pearl Harbor Reexamined: Prologue to the Pacific War.* Honolulu: University of Hawaii Press, 1990.

Craigie, Robert. *Behind the Japanese Mask: A British Ambassador in Japan, 1937–1942.* London: Kegan Paul, 2004. First published 1946.

Dooman, Eugene H. Interview by Beate Gordon. May 1962. Occupation of Japan Project, Columbia Center for Oral History. New York: Columbia University, 1962.

Dower, John W. *War Without Mercy: Race and Power in the Pacific War.* New York: Pantheon, 1986.

Emmerson, John K. *The Japanese Thread: A Life in the Foreign Service.* New York: Holt, Rinehart and Winston, 1978.

————, and Harrison M. Holland. *The Eagle and the Rising Sun: America and Japan in the Twentieth Century.* New York: Addison-Wesley, 1988.

Farago, Ladislas. *The Broken Seal: The Story of "Operation Magic" and the Pearl Harbor Disaster.* New York: Random House, 1967.

Fearey, Robert A. "My Year with Ambassador Joseph C. Grew, 1941–1942: A Personal Account." *Journal of American-East Asian Relations* 1, no. 1 (Spring 1992): 99–136.

Feis, Herbert. *The Road to Pearl Harbor: The Coming of the War Between the United States and Japan.* Princeton, NJ: Princeton University Press, 1950.

Fleisher, Wilfrid. *Volcanic Isle.* Garden City, NY: Doubleday, Doran and Company, 1941.

Goldstein, Donald M., and Katherine V. Dillon, eds. *The Pacific War Papers: Japanese Documents of World War II.* Washington, DC: Potomac Books, 2004.

Green, Lispenard, ed. *A Foreign Service Marriage.* Washington, DC: privately printed, 1985.

Grew, Joseph C. Joseph Clark Grew Papers (MS Am 1687–1687.9). Houghton Library, Harvard University.

————. *Report from Tokyo: A Message to the American People.* New York: Simon & Schuster, 1942.

————. *Sport and Travel in the Far East.* Boston: Houghton Mifflin, 1910.

————. *Ten Years in Japan: A Contemporary Record Drawn from the Diaries and Private and Official Papers of Joseph C. Grew, United States Ambassador to Japan, 1932–1942.* New York: Simon & Schuster, 1944.

————. *Turbulent Era: A Diplomatic Record of Forty Years, 1904–1945.* Two volumes. Edited by Walter Johnson. Boston: Houghton Mifflin, 1952.

Harada Kumao. *The Saionji-Harada Memoirs, 1931–1940.* Washington, DC: University Publications of America, 1978.

Havens, Thomas R. H. *Valley of Darkness: The Japanese People and World War Two.* New York: W. W. Norton, 1978.

Heinrichs, Waldo H. *American Ambassador: Joseph C. Grew and the Development of the United States Diplomatic Tradition.* Boston: Little, Brown, 1966.

————. *Threshold of War: Franklin D. Roosevelt and American Entry into World War II.* New York: Oxford University Press, 1988.

Hornbeck, Stanley K. "Principles of American Policy in Relation to the Far East." Washington, DC: Government Printing Office, 1934.

————. *The United States and the Far East: Certain Fundamentals of Policy.* Boston: World Peace Foundation, 1942.

Hosoya Chihiro. "The Tripartite Pact, 1939–1940." In *Deterrent Diplomacy: Japan, Germany, and the USSR, 1935–1940.* Edited by James William Morley. New York: Columbia University Press, 1976.

Hotta, Eri. *Japan 1941: Countdown to Infamy.* New York: Knopf, 2013.

Hull, Cordell. *Memoirs,* 2 vols. New York: Macmillan, 1948.

Iguchi Takeo. *Demystifying Pearl Harbor: A New Perspective from Japan.* Tokyo: International House of Japan, 2010.

Ike Nobutaka, ed. *Japan's Decision for War: Records of the 1941 Policy Conferences.* Stanford: Stanford University Press, 1967.

Iriye Akira. *The Origins of the Second World War in Asia and the Pacific.* London: Longman, 1996.

————, ed. *Pearl Harbor and the Coming of the Pacific War: A Brief History with Documents and Essays.* Boston: Bedford/St. Martin's, 1999.

Kase Toshikazu. *Journey to the Missouri.* New Haven: Yale University Press, 1950.

Kato Matsuo. *The Lost War: A Japanese Reporter's Inside Story.* New York: Knopf, 1946.

Kido Koichi. *The Diary of Marquis Kido, 1931–45.* Frederick, MD: University Publications of America, 1984.

Kimura Masato and Tosh Minohara, eds. *Tumultuous Decade: Empire, Society and Diplomacy in 1930s Japan.* Toronto: University of Toronto Press, 2013.

Konoye Fumimaro. "Memoirs of Prince Konoye." PHA, part 20.

Lu, David J. *Agony of Choice: Matsuoka Yosuke and the Rise and Fall of the Japanese Empire, 1880–1946.* Lanham, MD: Lexington Books, 2002.

———. *From the Marco Polo Bridge to Pearl Harbor: Japan's Entry into World War II.* Washington, DC: Public Affairs Press, 1961.

Maxon, Yale Candee. *Control of Japanese Foreign Policy: A Study of Civil Military Rivalry, 1930–1945.* Westport, CT: Greenpoint Press, 1973. Reprint of 1957 edition.

Mayers, David. *FDR's Ambassadors and the Diplomacy of Crisis: From the Rise of Hitler to the End of World War II.* Cambridge: Cambridge University Press, 2012.

Mitchell, Richard H. *Thought Control in Prewar Japan.* Ithaca, NY: Cornell University Press, 1976.

Morley, James William, ed. The following titles are volumes in the series Japan's Road to the Pacific War:

———. *Deterrent Diplomacy: Japan, Germany, and the USSR, 1935–1940.* New York: Columbia University Press, 1976.

———. *The Fateful Choice: Japan's Advance into Southeast Asia, 1939–1941.* New York: Columbia University Press, 1980.

———. *The Final Confrontation: Japan's Negotiations with the United States, 1941.* New York: Columbia University Press, 1992.

Morris, John. *Traveller from Tokyo.* London: Cresset Press, 1943.

Nakamura Masanori. *The Japanese Monarchy: Ambassador Joseph Grew and the Making of the "Symbol Emperor System," 1931–1991.* Armonk, NY: M. E. Sharpe, 1992.

Newman, Joseph. *Goodbye Japan.* New York: L. B. Fischer, 1942.

Oka Yoshitake. *Konoe Fumimaro: A Political Biography.* Tokyo: University of Tokyo Press, 1972. Translated by Shumpei Okamoto and Patricia Murray, 1983.

Paper, Lew. *In the Cauldron: Terror, Tension, and the American Ambassador's Struggle to Avoid Pearl Harbor.* Washington, DC: Regnery History, 2019.

Randau, Carl, and Leane Zugsmith. *The Setting Sun of Japan.* New York: Random House, 1942.

Roosevelt, Franklin D. Papers, Franklin D. Roosevelt Presidential Library, Hyde Park, NY.

Saburo Kurusu. *The Desperate Diplomat: Saburo Kurusu's Memoir of the Weeks Before Pearl Harbor.* Edited by J. Barry Clifford and Masako R. Okura. Columbia: University of Missouri Press, 2016.

Schroeder, Paul W. *The Axis Alliance and Japanese-American Relations, 1941.* Ithaca, NY: Cornell University Press, 1958.

Shillony, Ben-Ami. *Revolt in Japan: The Young Officers and the February 26, 1936 Incident.* Princeton, NJ: Princeton University Press, 1973.

Storry, Richard. *The Double Patriots: A Study of Japanese Nationalism.* London: Chatto and Windus, 1957.

Togo Shigenori. *The Cause of Japan.* New York: Simon & Schuster, 1956.

Tohmatsu Haruo and H. P. Willmott. *A Gathering Darkness: The Coming of War to the Far East and the Pacific, 1921–1942*. Lanham, MD: Rowman & Littlefield, 2004.

Toland, John. *The Rising Sun: The Decline and Fall of the Japanese Empire, 1936–1945*. New York: Random House, 1970.

Tolischus, Otto D. *Tokyo Record*. New York: Reynal & Hitchcock, 1943.

Tsunoda Jun. "The Navy's Role in the Southern Strategy." In *The Fateful Choice: Japan's Advance into Southeast Asia, 1939–1941*. Edited by James William Morley. New York: Columbia University Press, 1980.

United States Congress. *Hearings Before the Joint Committee on the Investigation of the Pearl Harbor Attack*. Washington, DC: United States Government Printing Office, 1946.

United States Department of State. *Foreign Relations of the United States, Diplomatic Papers, the Far East, 1931–41*. Washington, DC: 1946–1963.

———. *Foreign Relations of the United States, Japan, 1931–1941*, 2 vols. Washington, DC: 1943.

Utley, Jonathan G. *Going to War with Japan, 1937–1941*. Knoxville: University of Tennessee Press, 1985.

Weil, Martin. *A Pretty Good Club: The Founding Fathers of the US Foreign Service*. New York: W. W. Norton, 1978.

Wohlstetter, Roberta. *Pearl Harbor: Warning and Decision*. Stanford, CA: Stanford University Press, 1962.

Yoshida Shigeru. *The Yoshida Memoirs: The Story of Japan in Crisis*. Boston: Houghton Mifflin, 1962.

Young, James R. *Behind the Rising Sun*. New York: Doubleday, Doran, 1941.

Index

About the Author

Steve Kemper is the author of *A Splendid Savage: The Restless Life of Frederick Russell Burnham*; *A Labyrinth of Kingdoms: 10,000 Miles through Islamic Africa*; and *Code Name Ginger: The Story Behind Segway and Dean Kamen's Quest to Invent a New World*. He lives in Connecticut.